Edition?

If you are wondering why you should buy this new edition of *Imaginative Writing*, here are 9 good reasons!

1. **New introductory chapter.** Chapter 1: An Invitation to the Writer will introduce the basic skills needed for your creative writing course, including reading like a writer, journaling, and participating in writer's workshops.
2. **New selections.** Over a quarter of the selections are new to this edition and feature contemporary favorites from all genres, such as David Sedaris, David Foster Wallace, Roger Bonair-Agard, and Alan Bennett.
3. **Refined poetry chapter.** A revised poetry chapter features an updated discussion of the differences between formal and free verse, expanded coverage of the role of sound in poetry, and a refined approach to the poetic line—all with new exercises to help you practice poetic technique.
4. **A broader approach to creative nonfiction.** A revised chapter and new selections move beyond the personal essay and the memoir to explore the possibilities of form.
5. **New coverage of the ten-minute play.** This new edition provides ample coverage of writing a ten-minute play—an achievable goal for the single-semester creative writing course.
6. **Revision in action.** Three new revision narratives have been added to Chapter 7: Development and Revision. They include early drafts, author reflections on writing process, and the published version, allowing you to trace the development of published pieces from several successful writers.
7. **New warm-ups.** Almost every chapter features a new visually arresting warm-up exercise chosen to jumpstart your imagination.
8. **New exercises.** New and refined "Try This," "Working Toward a Draft," and "Accomplishing a Draft" exercises appear throughout the text.
9. **New Appendix.** Appendix B: Line Editing provides illustrations of common line editing symbols and an opportunity for practice.

PEARSON

ADVANCE PRAISE FOR

IMAGINATIVE WRITING

THE ELEMENTS OF CRAFT

THIRD EDITION

I find Burroway's writing to be accessible and lucid without oversimplifying or "talking down" to students. Her frequent use of examples will keep students engaged while also illuminating concepts which may be new to them.

—Brent Newsom,
Texas Tech University

Imaginative Writing offers a thoughtful exploration of techniques, as well as select readings from established and emerging writers.

—Colleen J. McElroy,
University of Washington

I think the book is actually well written with students in mind. The prose emphasizes a lot of what Burroway discusses in the book. It's student and teacher friendly.

—Gerry LaFemina,
Frostburg Center for Creative Writing

I find the readings to be very engaging. I cannot say enough times how impressed I am with the thoughtfulness that went into the selection of these pieces. There are outstanding authors in this text, some of whom are usually included in creative writing texts but also some who are often neglected.

—Ethan Joella,
Albright College

Burroway's writing is lucid, charming, confident and convincing. Students find her explanations to be clear, and her use of examples are strongly linked to the explanations, offering further clarity.

—Jill Allen,
Florida Gulf Coast University

about the author

Photo: Karen Lucchini

JANET BURROWAY is the author of plays, poetry, essays, children's books, and eight novels including *The Buzzards, Raw Silk* (runner up for the National Book Award), *Opening Nights, Cutting Stone,* and *Bridge of Sand.* Her publications include a collection of personal essays, *Embalming Mom*, in addition to a volume of poetry, *Material Goods*, and two children's books in verse, *The Truck on the Track* and *The Giant Jam Sandwich.* Her most recent plays, *Medea with Child* (The Reva Shiner Award), *Sweepstakes, Division of Property* (Arts & Letters Award), and *Parts of Speech*, have received readings and productions in New York, London, San Francisco, Hollywood, Chicago, and various regional theaters. Her textbook *Writing Fiction*, now in its eighth edition, is the most widely used creative writing text in the United States. She is Robert O. Lawton Distinguished Professor Emerita at the Florida State University in Tallahassee.

PENGUIN ACADEMICS

IMAGINATIVE WRITING

THE ELEMENTS OF CRAFT

THIRD EDITION

Janet Burroway
Florida State University

Longman

Boston Columbus Indianapolis New York San Francisco Upper Saddle River
Amsterdam Cape Town Dubai London Madrid Milan Munich Paris Montreal Toronto
Delhi Mexico City Sao Paulo Sydney Hong Kong Seoul Singapore Taipei Tokyo

For Neal, Eleanor, Holly, and Thyra—who inherit the language.

Senior Acquisitions Editor: Vivian Garcia
Associate Development Editor: Erin Reilly
Senior Supplements Editor: Donna Campion
Executive Marketing Manager: Joyce Nilsen
Production Coordinator: Scarlett Lindsay
Project Coordination and Text Design: Elm Street Publishing Services
Electronic Page Makeup: Integra Software Services Pvt. Ltd.
Senior Cover Design Manager: Nancy Danahy
Cover Image: Paul Klee, *The Flora of the Heath*, 1925, 142, watercolor on paper on cardboard, 24.1 x 31.7 cm, Staatliche Graphische Sammlung, München. © 2009 Artists Rights Society (ARS), New York / VG Bild-Kunst, Bonn
Photo Researcher: Ilene Bellovin
Senior Manufacturing Buyer: Roy L. Pickering, Jr.
Printer and Binder: RR Donnelley & Sons Company / Crawfordsville
Cover Printer: Lehigh-Phoenix Color Corporation / Hagerstown

For permission to use copyrighted material, grateful acknowledgment is made to the copyright holders on pp. 383–386, which are hereby made part of this copyright page.

Library of Congress Cataloging-in-Publication Data
Burroway, Janet.
Imaginative writing : the elements of craft / Janet Burroway.
p. cm.
Includes index.
ISBN 978-0-205-75035-1
1. English language—Rhetoric. 2. Creative writing (Higher education) 3. College readers.
I. Title.

PE1408.B8843 2009
808'.042—dc22 2009031202

For more information about the Penguin Academics series, please contact us by mail at Pearson Education, attn: Marketing Department, 51 Madison Avenue, 29th Floor, New York, NY 10010, or visit us online at www.pearsonhighered.com/english.

1 2 3 4 5 6 7 8 9 10—DOC—13 12 11 10

Longman
is an imprint of

PEARSON

www.pearsonhighered.com

ISBN-13: 978-0-205-75035-1
ISBN-10: 0-205-75035-4

contents

preface

In the third edition of *Imaginative Writing* I have tried to refine and focus several features of the book without fundamentally changing its purpose, which is to provide a workable and energizing multigenre text for basic creative writing courses.

New to the Third Edition

- **New introductory chapter.** In response to reviewer requests, the student preface "Invitation to the Writer" has been expanded into a full chapter. This new chapter introduces students to important skills such as reading like a writer, journaling, and participating in the writer's workshop. The chapter also features an assortment of sample journal pages from established writers including former poet laureate Billy Collins and novelist-memoirist Ayelet Waldeman.
- **New selections.** Over a quarter of the selections in each genre are new to this edition and feature contemporary favorites including fiction writers such as David Foster Wallace, Naguib Mahfouz, and Tobias Wolff; poets such as Ted Kooser, Donald Hall, and Roger Bonair-Agard; playwrights such as Alan Bennett, Don Nigro, and Alice O'Neill; and creative nonfiction writers such as David Sedaris, Stuart Dybek, and Studs Terkel.
- **Refined poetry chapter.** A thoroughly revised poetry chapter features an updated discussion of the differences between formal and free verse, expanded coverage of the role of sound in poetry, and a refined approach to the poetic line. The chapter also features six new "Try This" exercises and a new Accomplishing the Draft exercise. The text features over thirty poems—a dozen of which are new to this edition—selected for their vividness, variety, and illustration of poetic techniques.
- **A broader approach to creative nonfiction.** As the creative nonfiction genre moves beyond the personal essay and the memoir, so does *Imaginative Writing*. A broadened discussion in Chapter 8: Creative Nonfiction, and new selections such as Wisenberg's "Margot's Diary," a meditative recreation of a document that does not exist and Terkel's "Jack Culberg, 79," an oral history entirely in the recorded words of its subject, explore the possibilities of form.
- **New coverage of the ten-minute play.** A new section on the ten-minute play outlines the development of this relatively new and newly popular phenomenon. Plays throughout the anthology exemplify the possibilities of the form.

- **New revision narratives.** Three new revision narratives have been added to Chapter 7: Development and Revision so that students can trace the development of published pieces.
- **New appendix.** The new Appendix B provides a list of common editing symbols, an example of line editing, and a "Try This" exercise that will help students put this new skill into practice.
- **New warm-ups.** Almost every chapter features a new visually arresting warm-up exercise. The new images and accompanying exercises have been chosen to captivate and inspire today's writer.
- **New exercises.** New and refined "Try This," "Working Toward a Draft," and "Accomplishing a Draft" exercises appear throughout the text.

The core organizing principle of *Imaginative Writing* remains the same, which is that students in a multigenre course can benefit from playing with various writing techniques before they settle into a particular form. Much, if not most, of the advice given to students is relevant to any sort of writing and to most of the genres: The need for significant detail, for example, applies equally to narrative scene, poetic line, and theatrical dialogue; voice is a concept that applies to a character, a narrator, a memoir, a lyric persona, and so forth. My expectation is that by discussing techniques and offering exercises that let students experiment with those techniques *before* they commit to a formal project will make the instruction less threatening and encourage a sense of adventure. Beginning this way will also make it possible to illustrate the extent to which *all* writing is imaginative (as well as autobiographical) and that different genres share similar sources and build on similar skills.

I have taken fiction and poetry as givens in a multigenre course. I have personally been convinced of drama's usefulness in developing a writer's facility (with characterization, dialogue, plot, pace, symbol). I have also wanted to acknowledge the growing popularity of creative nonfiction, the continuity of imaginative writing with the essay form students have inevitably studied, and the fact that emerging writers may find it easiest to begin with the material of their own lives.

The book is organized so that, roughly, the first five weeks of a semester will cover five areas of imaginative technique (image, voice, character, setting, and story), the sixth the processes of development and revision, with two weeks each devoted to creative nonfiction, fiction, poetry, and drama.

Each chapter begins with a graphic or photographic image accompanied by a "Warm-up" prompt, which may be assigned in class or as a journal entry or replaced by one of the instructor's invention.

Each of the technique chapters proceeds with a discussion of that technique, including illustrations from more than one genre (some invented and some taken from established writers); "Try This" exercises linked to particular aspects of the topic; then complete selections in the various genres. Like the "Warm-up" features, the "Try This" exercises can be used as in-class practice, assigned for journal entries, or left for the students to choose from. I think it's important, at least sometimes, to discuss resulting pieces in class, in order to get students used to a nonjudgmental discussion of roughs and written play. (This neutral way of workshopping is described at the end of the first chapter, "Invitation to the Writer.") Further comments and exercises among the selections at the end of each chapter link the readings to the techniques discussed and suggest *briefly*—there are no questions aimed at literary interpretation—how to read the selections for what can be taken away from them and made part of a repertoire of skills. But, of course, all the selections illustrate many things, and they can be assigned in any order or quantity that suits the individual instructor. The third edition, at the request of several reviewers, also contains development ideas at the end of each technique chapter, to aid those teachers who encourage students to be thinking toward a finished piece.

Chapter 7, "Development and Revision," suggests ways to use the material generated in the first five weeks toward the writing of finished pieces, and here too the workshop may prove a positive help to the writer through exploration rather than praise and critique. The "Try This" exercises in this chapter can be used in class or out, and if it feels right, students can be encouraged to exchange journal pieces and try developing and revising passages not their own. This chapter is followed by some examples, with discussion, of aspects of the rewriting process.

I've envisioned that for each of the final four chapters, dealing with creative nonfiction, fiction, poetry, and drama, one week will be spent discussing the genre and roughing out a draft, a second workshopping and working at revision. (Instructors will know what is comfortable and doable for their classes; my inclination would be to assign a short story and an essay of about 1,500 words each, three poems, and one ten-minute play.) Each of these final chapters outlines what is unique and defining about each of the genres in order to suggest ways of exploiting the particular nature of that genre and to help the students use what they have learned in the first six weeks. The chapters close with a sample format for the featured genre.

The exercises in these chapters are designed to promote development of some aspect of the genre under discussion or to aid revision in terms of focus, cutting, attention to language, originality, and so forth. At this point, the critical component of the workshop becomes relevant; students will no doubt be ready to talk about not only what sort of thing this piece of work *is* but whether and where it "works."

The order of presentation is always problematic in a writing text—everything really needs to be said at once—and many instructors will find that they would have chosen a different sequence for the techniques or the genres or both, so I'll say a little about my rationale. When I laid out the plan for the text *Writing Fiction* many years ago, I had, out of my classroom experience, a strong sense that students focusing on that form needed a sense of its structure and to face the question: What is a story? But for the more playful and process-oriented course for which *Imaginative Writing* is intended, it seems to me that the core need and the first skill is the one represented by the irreplaceable maxim: *Show; don't tell.* Again and again, I have seen an *aha!* moment in the classroom when a student suddenly grasps the principle of addressing the senses, a technique so simple and yet so elusive. It is also often revelatory that diction and point of view direct meaning, and I have addressed this issue second. From image and voice to character is a logical progression; then to the outside world of setting, and only then to a consideration of what it means to tell a story, whether in memoir, poetic, fictional, or dramatic form.

I put development and revision together, in the middle of the book, in the hope of suggesting that these are ongoing parts of the same process, rather than representing a beginning and an end.

When I came to ordering the genres, I reasoned that creative nonfiction offers beginning writers the easiest segue from the material of their own lives and from the essay writing they find most familiar. From the personal essay or memoir to fiction may prove a short imaginative step. Poetry leads them then to focus on density and the effects of language. Finally, drama in many ways asks that they distance themselves farthest from autobiography, that they externalize everything verbally or visually.

There is nothing sacred about this order, and I have tried to balance the chapters between self-containment and linkage, so that an instructor who prefers another sequence may shop around in the text and shape his or her course to fit. In practice, I think it may be most difficult to alter the sequence of the five techniques chapters, and no problem at all to switch—or omit—any of the genres.

Appendix A, "A Basic Prosody," offers more information about, and practice in, poetic form. Appendix B, "Line Editing," offers illustrations of common line editing symbols and an opportunity for practice. A glossary of the terms covered in the text follows the appendixes.

Also available with *Imaginative Writing* is a supplement containing a revised version of the collaborative exercises that appeared as an appendix in the first edition. These have been recast for ease of use, and represent a *bricolage* of suggestions for in-class play. Some involve writing, but most are taken from theater, art, dance, meditation, and physical therapy. Some instructors will be eager to try them; others may recoil from them as disruptively boisterous or dreamily New Age. But if I have any proselytizing to do, it is at this pulpit. I say to my students, and also to teachers considering the supplement: *Don't worry about it, go with it, give it a shot.* Students are often resistant to getting out of their chairs, embarrassed to pick up a felt-tip, reluctant to make a nonverbal sound. Yet simple stretching and breathing can break down the rigidity of the classroom. Repeated improvisations such as the "word-at-a-time story" sometimes become the cohesive social force in a writing class. Mask making sometimes begins with the groans of the artistically challenged and leads to breakthrough on character. Mirroring can teach more about narrative than a lecture on conflict or connection. I have over several years become convinced of the useful energy generated by each one of these exercises, and I've tried to indicate the purpose of each one. In the meantime, however, they are separately presented in a supplement to take or leave.

It often seems pretty well impossible to teach a course across the genres—a semester to do everything, as if you were asked to teach "Intro to Human Nature" or "The History of Work" in sixteen weeks. My hope is that this book will make it feel a little more possible. What *Imaginative Writing* is *not,* however, is comprehensive. It tries to cover the basics in a way that is sound but brief, overwhelming to neither the student nor the personality and methods of the instructor. I will be interested to hear from anyone who teaches from the book how well I have succeeded in this, and how I might improve the book in future editions (jburroway@fsu.edu).

Meanwhile, I am grateful to numbers of people, especially my colleagues at Florida State, Northwestern, and Chicago Dramatists; and always to my students and former students. Many of the readings, ideas, and exercises in this book are here thanks to their talent, invention, and spirited help. Creative writing exercises tend to be, like scientific information in a more generous time, freely offered, freely shared, and passed from hand to hand. I know that I have cadged, cobbled, and adapted my "Try This" exercises from Marta Mihalyi, Maria Irene Fornes, Aimee Beal, Margaret Rozga, Sarah Ruhl, Paula Vogel, Cheril Dumesnil, Laura-Gray Street, Mary Ann Lando, Gerald Shapiro, Matt Zambito, and Michael Kardos, many of them from the pedagogy panels of the Associated Writing Programs. Other ideas will have come to me third-hand, or I will have forgotten where I read or heard them; to those unacknowledged, equal thanks and apologies.

I have relied on the incisiveness and generosity of my reviewers: Jill Allen, Florida Gulf Coast University; Lawrence William Coates, Bowling Green State University; Aaron DiFranco, Napa Valley College; Brady Earnhart, University of Mary Washington; Ethan Joella, Albright College; Gerry LaFemina, Frostburg State University; Colleen J. McElroy, University of Washington; Brent Newsom, Texas Tech University; Joy Rothke, Gotham Writer's School NYC; and on the insight and cheer of my editors, Erin Reilly, Vivian Garcia, and Sarah Burkhart, to all of whom great thanks. My husband, Peter Ruppert, brings light to life and lit.

Janet Burroway

CHAPTER 1

Invitation to the Writer

I just realize that we start out in these very awkward ways, and we do look a little stupid as we draft, and that's all right... You have to be willing to go into the chaos and bring back the beauties.
Tess Gallagher

WARM-UP
Regard the art on the cover of this book. Relax, focus, take in the colors and the composition. Then freewrite a page of anything it suggests to you, reminds you of, or makes you feel. You don't need to make sense or sentences, nor stick to the subject. Just let it flow. Put the page away for a week. Take it out and see: Is there anything here you might use? Any idea worth more thought? Any phrase or image to pursue?

You . . .

You started learning to write—at the latest—as soon as you were born. You learned within hours to recognize an "audience," and within a few days that expressing yourself would elicit a response. Your basic desires created the fundamental form of story—I want, *I want*, I WANT!—with its end in gratification (comedy) or denial (tragedy). Within a year you had begun to understand the structure of sentences and to learn rules of immense subtlety and complexity, so that for no precisely understood reason you would always say "little red wagon" rather than "red little wagon." You responded to rhythm and rhyme (*One, two. Buckle my shoe.*). You matched images and explained their meanings (*This is a giraffe. Dog is hungry.*). You invented metaphors (*My toes are soldiers.*). By the time you could speak you were putting together personal essays about what you had done and what had happened to you and forecasting fantasies of your future exploits. By the time you started school, you had (mostly thanks to television) watched more drama than the nobility of the Renaissance, and you understood a good deal about how a character is developed, how a joke is structured, how a narrative expectation is met, and how dramatic exposition, recognition, and reversal are achieved. You understood the unspoken rules of specific traditions—that Bugs Bunny may change costume but the Road Runner may not, that the lovers will marry, that the villain must die.

You are, in fact, a literary sophisticate. You have every right to write.

This needs saying emphatically and often, because writing is one of those things—like public speaking, flying, and garden snakes—that often calls up unnecessary panic. Such fear is both normal (a high percentage of people feel it) and irrational (statistically, the chances of disaster are pretty low). It is true that some speakers do humiliate themselves, some planes do crash, some snakes are poisonous. Nevertheless, people do learn to speak, fly, and garden. And people learn to shrug at their dread and write.

. . . and writing . . .

All writing is imaginative. The translation of experience or thought into words is of itself an imaginative process. Although there is certainly such a thing as truth in writing, and we can spot falsity when we encounter it in print, these qualities are hard to define, hard to describe, and do not always depend on factual accuracy or inaccuracy. Often what is *most* original, that is, imaginative, is precisely what "rings true."

Aristotle said that when you change the form of a thing you change its purpose. For example, the purpose of an algebra class is to teach algebra. But if you take a photo of the class, the purpose of the photo *cannot* be to teach algebra. The picture would probably serve the purpose of commemorating the class and the people in it. On the other hand, if you wrote a short story about that class, its purpose might be (not to teach algebra or to commemorate the class, but) to reveal something about the emotional undertow, the conflict in or between students, the hidden relationships in that apparently staid atmosphere.

It's impossible to tell *the truth, the whole truth, and nothing but the truth* in words, because words are of a different form than experience, and their choice is determined by the vast array of cultural and personal influences. Writers learn very quickly that a written incident is not necessarily credible because it "really happened," and that convincing writing is in the writing and not in the facts. When you write about an experience, you put it in a new form and therefore furnish it with a new purpose. Part of the hard work and the pleasure of writing is discovering what that purpose is. You will never exactly "catch" an experience you have lived, but you may both discover and reveal new insights in the recasting of that experience.

All writing is autobiographical as well as invented. Just as it's impossible to write the whole and literal truth about any experience, so it's also impossible to invent without drawing on your own experience, which has furnished your brain. Your view of yourself, the place you live, the people you know, the institutions you live with, your view of nature and God or the gods will inform not only your dreams and daydreams, what you say, wear, think, and do, but also everything you write. What you write will inevitably reveal to a certain extent both what you think the world is like and what you think it *should* be like.

Between the two impossibilities—of perfectly capturing your experience in words and of avoiding it altogether—lies the territory that we call "creative." Begin by writing whatever comes to you, recording your observations, trying out your ideas, indulging your fantasies. *Then* figure out what you want to make of it, what its purpose is, and what it means. Then work toward making it "work"—that is, toward making it meaningful for the reader who is your partner in the imaginative act.

. . . and reading . . .

At the same time, you yourself need to become a reader of a writerly sort, reading greedily, not just for entertainment but also focusing on the craft, the choices, and techniques of the author; "reading the greats," in novelist Alan Cheuse's words, "in that peculiar way that writers read, attentive to the peculiarities of the language...soaking up numerous narrative strategies and studying various approaches to that cave in the deep woods where the human heart hibernates."

When you study a piece of writing as a student of literature, you focus on understanding what is there on the page and how the parts fit together, in order to tease out the story's significance. Reading as a writer involves all that but it is more concentrated, more active, and more selfish. It involves asking not only *What does this mean?* but also *How does it work? Why has the author made this choice of imagery, voice, atmosphere? What techniques of language, pacing, character, contribute to this effect?* As a writerly reader you pay close attention to the rhythm and flow of the language, to the way word choice influences an effect, to voice and point of view as means of building narrative—in Francine Prose's words, "not only who was speaking but who was being spoken to, where the listener and speaker were, and when and why the event—that is, the telling of the story—was occurring." This kind of reading becomes in itself an imaginative act as you put yourself in the position of the author to intuit the reason for her choices. Then the question naturally occurs: Can I *use* this effect, try these rhythms, create this sort of atmosphere? It is only one step further to imitation of such strategies, and to using imitation as way of developing your own skills.

Reader/writers sometimes become impatient with this process. "How do you know the author didn't just want to do it that way?" The answer is: You don't. But everything on the page is there because the writer chose that it should be there, and the effectiveness of the piece depends on those choices. The British critic F. R. Leavis used to observe that a poem is not a frog. In order to understand the way a frog works you must kill it, then splay out the various respiratory, digestive, muscular systems, and so forth. But when you "take apart" a piece of literature to discover how it is made, and then put it back together by reading it again, it is more alive than before. It will resonate with all you have learned, and you as a writer will know a little better how to reproduce such vitality.

. . . and this book . . .

My creative writing workshop exchanged a few classes with a group of student choreographers. The first time we came into the dance theater, we writers sat politely down in our seats with our notebooks on our laps. The choreographer-dancers did stretches on the carpet, headstands on the steps; some sat backward on the chairs; one folded herself down into a seat like a teabag in a teacup. When they started to dance they were given a set of instructions: *Group A is rolling through, up and under; Group B is blue Tuesday; Group C is weather comes from the west.* The choreographers began to invent movement; each made up a "line" of dance. They repeated and altered it. They bumped into each other, laughed, repeated, rearranged, and danced it through. They did it again. They adjusted. They repeated. They danced it through. Nobody was embarrassed and nobody gave up. They tried it again. One of the young writers turned to me with a face of luminous discovery. "We don't *play* enough," she said.

That's the truth. Writing is such a solitary occupation, and we are so used to moiling at it until it's either perfect or *due*, that our first communal experience of our writing also tends to be awful judgment. Even alone, we internalize the criticism we anticipate and become harsh critics of ourselves. "The progress of any writer," said the great poet Ted Hughes, "is marked by those moments when he manages to outwit his own police system."

Imaginative Writing assumes that you will play before you work—dance before performing, doodle before fiddling with, fantasize before forming, *anything goes* before *finish something.* This is not an unusual idea among writers and teachers of writing. ("Indulge yourself in your first drafts," says novelist Jonathan Lethem, "and write against yourself in revisions.") But it is easier to preach than to practice.

Nevertheless, most of the techniques that writers use are relevant to most forms of imaginative writing and can be learned by playing around in any form. So the first six chapters of this book talk about some techniques that are useful in any sort of writing or relevant to more than one genre, and suggest ways to play with those techniques. The purpose of these chapters is to free the imagination. The seventh chapter talks about ways to develop and revise your experiments into a finished piece. The last four chapters discuss what is particular to each of four genres, and how you can mold some of what you have written toward each of them.

Note: The word "genre," can be confusing because it has two distinct but overlapping meanings when applied to writing. In the first definition it refers to the different kinds or forms of literature—nonfiction, poetry, fiction, drama, and so forth—and that is the way it is used throughout this book. In its second meaning, "genre" refers to certain traditions within fiction, as a *western, detective story, spy story, romance, science fiction, horror,* and so forth. These fiction genres are often discouraged in creative writing courses because they rely on set narrative elements that have less to do with good writing than with the expectations of particular fans.

The romance, for example, must have a plucky heroine, a handsome hero with a secret past, a dark lady, a mansion, a forest, and usually a flight through the woods in scanty clothing. Many instructors feel that whereas learning the techniques of good writing may help you write good genre fiction, learning the particular traditions of a given fictional genre will not necessarily help you write well or honestly in the tradition called "mainstream" or "literary."

The tendency of recent literature is in any case to move further away from rigid categories, toward a loosening or crossing of genre (in the sense of literary form). Many writers are eager to experiment with pieces that blur the distinction between two genres or even follow two genre patterns at once. So "short short" stories may have elements of poetry or essay; the "prose poem" may be seen as a lyric or a story. An essay might be structured with a refrain. So Adam Thorpe ends the novel *Ulverton* in the form of a film script; columnist Maureen Dowd frequently writes a political essay in the form of a fantasy play; Michael Chabon and others write detective or science fiction with literary ambition and intent—"genre fiction" pressing at the bounds of "the fiction genre" with results that have been called "slipstream" or "interstitial" fiction.

So there is a lot of "do this" in the following pages, but a good deal more of "try this." The overriding idea of the book is *play*—serious, strenuous, dedicated, demanding, exhilarating, enthusiastic, repeated, perfected play. It is the kind of play that makes you a superior swimmer or singer, a first-rank guitar, pool, polo, piano, or chess player. As with any sport or musical skill, a writer's power grows by the practice of the moves and the mastering of the instrument.

Insofar as writing is a skill, it can only be learned by doing. Insofar as writing is "inspired," it may pour out of you obsessively, feverishly, without your seeming to have to make any effort or even without your seeming to have any responsibility for it. When that happens, it feels wonderful, as any writer will tell you. Yet over and over again, writers attest to the fact that the inspiration only comes with, and as a result of, the doing.

. . . and your journal . . .

While you use this book you will be writing one—a journal that should be, first of all, a physical object with which you feel comfortable. Some writers keep notes in a shoebox or under the bed, but your journal probably needs to be light enough to carry around easily, sturdy enough to stand up to serious play, large enough to operate as a capacious holdall for your thoughts. Think of it as a handbag, a backpack, a trunk, a cupboard, an attic, a warehouse of your mind. Everything can go into it: stuff you like and what you paid too much for, what Aunt Lou gave you and the thing you found in the road, this out-of-date whatsit and that high-tech ware. You never know what you're going to need; absolutely anything may prove useful later on.

TRY THIS 1.1

In other words, write any sort of thing in your journal, and write various kinds of things:

- An observation
- An overheard conversation
- Lists
- Longings
- Your response to a piece of music
- A rough draft of a letter
- Names for characters
- Quotations from what you are reading
- The piece of your mind you'd like to give so-and-so
- An idea for a story
- A memory
- A dream
- A few lines of a poem
- A fantasy conversation
- Titles of things you are never going to write
- Something else

Your journal is totally forgiving; it is 100 percent rough draft; it passes no judgments.

Throughout *Imaginative Writing* there will be prompts, trigger lines, and ideas for playing in your journal. Here are a few general suggestions:

- **Freewrite.** Gertrude Stein called this "automatic writing." Either on a regular schedule or at frequent intervals, sit down and write without any plan whatsoever of what you are going to write. Write anything that comes into your head. It doesn't matter what it is *at all.* This is the equivalent of volleying at tennis or improvisation at the piano; it puts you in touch with the instrument and limbers the verbal muscles.
- **Focused freewrite.** Pick a topic and focus on it. Write for five or ten minutes saying anything at all about it—*anything at all*—in any order.
- **Brainstorm.** Start with the question *What if...?* Finish the question and then free-associate around it, absolutely anything that pops into your head—ideas, situations, connections, solutions, and images, no matter how bizarre. This is a problem-solving technique that can also generate energy for imaginative writing. If you need an idea, or if your character is facing a decision, or if you don't know what your setting looks like—whatever the problem, whatever idea might be struggling to surface—brainstorm it and let your mind run free.
- **Using the world.** A journal is not a diary. Your journal may include your own feelings and problems, but training yourself to observe the outside world will help develop the skills of an imaginative writer. Make a daily habit of

recording something you experienced or noticed. It may be an overheard remark, an unexpected sight, a person who caught your attention, even a news item or something you learned in a class. Knowing that you are going to write every day will give you a habit of listening and seeing with writing in mind. A writer is a kind of benevolent cannibal who eats the world—or at least, you'll experience the world with an eye and ear toward what use you can make of it.

Make a habit, rather than a chore, of writing in your journal. If you skip a day, it's not the end of the world, but it may well be that, as with a physical workout, you have to coax or cajole yourself into writing regularly before you get to the point when you look forward to that part of your life, can't wait for it, can't do without it. You will know some of the patterns that help you create a habit. Write first thing in the morning? At the same hour every day? After a shower? With a cup of coffee? Before you fall asleep? Use your self-discipline to make yourself sit down and write, but once you get there, tell your inner critic to hush, give yourself permission to write whatever you please, and *play*.

TRY THIS 1.2

Here is a list of lists:

- Things on which I am an expert
- Things I have lost
- Signs of winter
- What is inside my body
- Things people have said to me
- What to take on the journey
- Things I have forgotten
- Things to make lists of

Pick any one of these items to generate a list in your journal.
Pick a single word from your list and write a paragraph about it. Is this the germ of a memoir or a story?
Write a single line about each item on the list. Is this the start of a poem?

JOURNAL EXCERPTS

What follows is a series of snippets, generously offered from the journals of well-established writers, to indicate what a variety of entries a journal might contain. Some of these may be the germ of a story, novel, essay, poem, or play; some may never find their way into a published piece. Some are observations, some are fantasy, some are lists, names, an image, an action, a quotation. Some may suggest a kind of writing you wouldn't think to include in your own journal. Try it.

FROM THE JOURNAL OF: Ayelet Waldman

Old graveyard:
Delia Floyd
Mehitabel Witham
Joshua Horton
Seth Hewins
Sally Prince Holt
Jonah Fisher
Mehitabel Faulkner
Hepziabah Faulkner "I am ready"

Old man in walker—freckled pate, zipper cardigan, and black shoes two sizes too large. You could fit two fingers between his heel and the back of the shoe. They're obviously worn, but not at all worn out. He must have bought them years ago, before his body began to shrink. Even his feet are smaller than they were.

FROM THE JOURNAL OF: Billy Collins

"People think there is no preparation to write poetry. Not like painting, or music. So in my kingdom, you would have to learn to play the trumpet before you would be allowed to write a poem."

Kafka: "The meaning of life is that it will end."

In America, we cannot seem to get enough of what we don't need.

The mind needs to get used to something better than television.

as in music there are "rests" in poetry—obviously at the end of lines and stanzas but anywhere else the poet has sufficient control of cadence to give the reader no option but to pause.

"motives for writing: to continue to speak after you are dead and (from daniel menaker) to win the love of strangers."

celery salt is an insult to the bloody mary

FROM THE JOURNAL OF: Cris Mazza (as a college-student, 19 years old)

But right then another arm-lock on my neck. The back of my chair was between us (I sitting, he standing), but I felt those shoulders over my own.
"I need to beat you up once a day for my only meanness—it's the only time all day I have physical communication with someone." Ha Ha.
"Me too."
That was the real laugh, I mean, he really laughed. I don't know why. But he said we need each other.

Beauty too
intense to
be that of

a child,
too honest
to be that
of an adult

sprawled out
like a rag doll
someone had
thrown up
there.

not a crime—
a reality

I knew how she felt, the way my entrails were fluttering, the way I danced around inside when a slow-moving, slow-talking narrow-eyed man tried it with ME.

Yes, I overheard something. I wasn't listening though. I was thinking about something else. When his eyes hit, wham—like that—then I was part of it all right. I knew it. I had to help carry the AV equipment back for that reason.

FROM THE JOURNAL OF: Patricia Henley

"carry me" = take me

"levee hollers"—is/was this a common term? Did someone's mama and daddy meet at a levee holler?

Axe Jesus. A bumper sticker.

Jimmy's grandpa has a jar of coins buried somewhere and a roomful of Elvis memorabilia. Or maybe it's just music memorabilia.

Lucky was sent to live with Quakers at a boarding school in Pennsylvania when the schools were closed due to de-segregation. Arrangements had been made. She was seven years old. She had a suitcase from the goodwill and a cardboard box of books. She drank whole milk straight from the cow. Her own mother, when she saw her, seemed less and less like where she came from.

FROM THE JOURNAL OF: Philip Graham

There was no anger in her silence, like my father's; rather, fear. And couldn't fear be soothed into something else?

Those drawings were how she talked to me, a sign language caught on paper, shadings of her secret self I could spend my life translating.

I'd somehow engineered a strange reversal of personalities.

John Hawkes's novel *Sweet Willam:* the grotesque rendered even more vivid by the elegance of Hawkes's prose.

(continued)

the name of a malaria drug, Halfan

He'd twist himself into a little knot, try to coil himself so tight he'd finally feel something besides this damned airy floating. But he was never able to squeeze himself into pain; not even a tiny twinge: not even a hint of the lightest touch.

Most of the dead floated, traveling with the help of their own invisible wind. Only those newly arrived kept walking, an echo of the life they'd so recently lived... No blindness at all but a world alive with scent and touch, antennae exchanging encyclopedic caresses. It was all he'd ever hoped to accomplish in his lifetime: the afterlife was a virtual reality, beyond any technological breakthrough. There was nowhere he couldn't enter, no person's secrets he couldn't uncover.

Those ants pushing and pulling away the smallest pieces of her cracker. But it was *hers*, and she cried out, but the ants ignored her. She cried out again, now in angry frustration, and began to crawl after them. Her mother scooped her up at her wails, but no soothing could quiet her. She had no words yet to explain to her mother, and the ants escaped.

Following invisible designs inside herself, a picture she drew that I'd never see.

I wanted to bring her back, to have her arrive from wherever she was inside herself and see me at the table, across from her, waiting patiently.

the choppy, swaying gait of goats

He'd always believed that humans were some clever sort of larvae, firing off constructs—Stonehenge to the World Trade Center, knife to computer—that were bits of brain. And it was all leading to an artificial intelligence—that wasn't artificial at all, being a product of brain—that would finally leave the larval stage behind and yet be its apotheosis, its crowning, transcendent glory.

TRY THIS 1.3

Take a notebook with you to any public place and make a list of the proper names you find there (a graveyard, a candy store, a restaurant, a street, a theater...). Write a paragraph of anything at all that these names, or one of them, suggests to you.

TRY THIS 1.4

Find five quotations you admire for some reason or other. Quote them in your journal. Write a sentence or two after each specifying what has attracted you to this particular combination of words.

TRY THIS 1.5

Listen, alone and intently, to a piece of music you care about. After listening for five or fifteen minutes, write anything the music suggests to you. If it has lyrics, don't use the words of the song, but the images in your own brain, the words that paint your feeling. Don't try to make sense, or even sentences; let the music dictate your words.

A word about your workshop . . .

Many of us think of the primary function of a writing workshop as being to criticize, in order to improve, whatever piece of writing is before us. This is, again, absolutely natural, not only because of the way the writing workshop has evolved over the years but because nothing is more natural than to judge art. We do it all the time and we do it out of a valid impulse. If you tell me you've just seen a movie, I don't ask the plot; I ask: *How was it?* Art *sets out to* affect us emotionally and intellectually, and whether it has achieved this is of the first interest. The poet and critic John Ciardi said of literature that "it is never only about ideas, but about the experience of ideas," and the first thing we want to know is, naturally, "how was the experience?"

But if the first thing you and your workshop expect is a writer at *play,* and if in order to play you banish your inner critic and give yourself permission to experiment, doodle, and dance, it doesn't make a lot of sense to subject that play to immediate assessment. In any case it's likely that the fragments produced by the exercises in the early chapters of this book will be read aloud rather than reproduced and read in advance. I'm going to suggest that for most of the time this book is being used, you avoid the phrases, *I like, I don't like, This works, This doesn't work*—and all their equivalents. It may be harder to forgo praise than blame, but praise should be a controlled substance too. Instead, discipline yourself to explore whatever is in front of you. Not *What I like,* but *What this piece is like.* Interrogate it, suggest its context, explore its nature and its possibilities:

- *What is the conflict in this situation?*
- *This reminds me of...*
- *It's like...*
- *I think this character wants...*
- *What if...?*
- *The rhythm is...*
- *Could this be expanded to...?*
- *The atmosphere seems...* and so forth.

This kind of descriptive, inquisitive, and neutral discussion of writing is *hard.* It will pay off in the freedom that each writer feels to write and in the flexibility of critical response you're developing in the workshop. In the later part of the course, when everyone is writing in a particular form and revision is the legitimate focus of the work, there will be a time to discuss not only *what this piece is trying to do* but also where and whether it succeeds. At that point, critique will help. This later critical function of the workshop is discussed further in Chapter 7, "Development and Revision." Meanwhile keep in mind that even when you arrive at the point that criticism is relevant and helpful, there are a few basic protocols for the workshop that should always be observed:

- It is the obligation of each reader to prepare in advance, focusing on what succeeds in the piece, and where and why, then noting judiciously where improvement is needed, and why.
- The piece is under discussion. The author is not. Make sure your comments relate to the nature of the writing and not (even by implication) to the character of the writer. Separate the writer from the voice or character.
- Continue to interrogate the piece: *What kind is it? What does it suggest? What is its apparent aim?*
- The goal of the workshop is to make *this* piece the best that it can be. There's no place for dismissal or disregard. On the contrary, the workshop is there to identify and foster the promise in every story, essay, poem, or drama.
- As the writer, your obligation is to listen attentively, take everything in, and keep your natural defensiveness in check. Your workshop leader may (or may not) offer you a chance to speak. But this is the least important part of the workshop process for *you*. The most important part comes later, when you get back to work. Then (and only then) you will begin to sort out what's most useful.

TRY THIS 1.6

Make use of these prompts or trigger lines for easy freewrites. Pick one of them—quickly; don't think about it too much—write it down and keep writing. Anything at all. Whatever the prompt suggests. Keep going. A little bit more.

- This journal is...
- My mother used to have...
- There was something about the way he...
- The house we lived in...
- In this dream I was...
- She got out of the car...
- The first thing I want in the morning...

More to Read

Bernays, Anne, and Pamela Painter. *What If...?* New York: Longman, 2003. Print.

Friedman, Bonnie. *Writing Past Dark*. New York: HarperCollins, 1993. Print.

Prose, Francine. *Reading Like a Writer: A Guide for People Who Love Books and for Those Who Want to Write Them*. New York: HarperCollins, 2007. Print.

CHAPTER 2

Image

- *Image and Imagination*
- *Concrete, Significant Details*
- *Figures of Speech*

When I talk about pictures in my mind I am talking, quite specifically, about images that shimmer round the edges . . . You just lie low and let them develop.
Joan Didion

G. Baden/Corbis

WARM-UP
Describe this scene using each of the five senses at least once. Supply the color. Let us see the sea. What sounds do we hear? What smell predominates? What is the texture of the sand or surfboard or water? What does the youth taste? Do your choices create a mood, a judgment, an emotion?

Image and Imagination

There is a simple trick at the heart of imaginative writing.

If I say, "Not everything that appears to be valuable is actually valuable," you will understand me in a general kind of way, but you won't think I've said anything very interesting (and you might feel a little preached at). Whereas if I say, "All that glistens is not gold," you literally "see" what I "mean."

The trick is that if you write in words that evoke the senses, if your language is full of things that can be seen, heard, smelled, tasted, and touched, you create a world your reader can enter.

Mary Karr begins *The Liars Club* this way:

> My sharpest memory is of a single instant surrounded by dark. I was seven, and our family doctor knelt before me where I sat on a mattress on the bare floor. He wore a yellow golf shirt unbuttoned so that sprouts of hair showed in a V shape on his chest. I had never seen him in anything but a white starched shirt and a gray tie. The change unnerved me. He was pulling at the hem of my favorite nightgown—a pattern of Texas bluebonnets bunched into nosegays tied with a ribbon against a field of nappy white cotton. I had tucked my knees under it to make a tent. He could easily have yanked the thing over my head with one motion, but something made him gentle. "Show me the marks," he said....

We do not know the situation here, but the details—the dark, the mattress, bare floor, the sprouts of hair where a gray tie should be, the knees tucked under the gown, the doctor's gentle voice—draw us immediately into the situation and make us hungry to know just what this child has suffered. We are "hooked."

It's no accident that the words *image* and *imagination* have the same root (Latin *imago,* a picture or portrayal), because what all imaginative writing has in common is that it calls up pictures in the mind. Any sort of writing—reports, treatises, theories, instructions—may be enlivened by examples. But the kinds of writing we group under the heading *imaginative*—poetry, song lyrics, play scripts, film scripts, personal essays, memoirs, stories, novels—exist fundamentally as re-presentations. They portray people, places, and objects, as if physically present. Any particular piece of imaginative writing may or may not be "imaginary" in the sense of being made up; it may or may not have its origins in "real" people or what "really" happened. What all such pieces invariably have in common is that the writing calls up sense impressions in the mind—readers *see, hear, smell, taste,* and *feel* the scene by responding through their imaginations.

Novelist Robert Olen Butler points out that *all* art objects are sensuous and are produced by a process that is sensuous rather than logical. Artists in other media than literature are clear about the nature of their process, because they work with material that is fundamentally of the senses. The musician deals in sound, the painter in color and composition, the sculptor in texture, the dancer in bodily movement. But because as writers we deal in a medium of words, which are abstract symbols, we may find it harder to set logic and argument aside. Writing as an art begins when we surrender ourselves to the world of images.

An image is a word or series of words that evokes one or more of the five senses. *An image appeals to the senses.* This is the foundation of imaginative writing. If you can "grok" that fact (a useful word that means to understand in the gut as well as the head), you are on your way to being a writer.

Here is a thought that does not contain an image:

It is best to consider consequences before proceeding.

Here is an image that contains the same thought:

Look before you leap.

A thought without an image:

It's important to reassure your offspring of your affection.

An image that contains the thought:

Have you hugged your child today?

A thought without an image:

The situation is being manipulated by peripheral interests.

An image that contains the thought:

Wag the dog.

A thought without an image:

I will do everything in my power to overturn this unjust verdict.

An image that contains the thought:

I will fall like an ocean on that court! (Arthur Miller, *The Crucible*)

A thought without an image:

The verses I am writing have no vitality; they are unattractive and stale.

An image that contains the thought:

They are not pigs, they are not even fish, / Though they have a piggy and a fishy air—(Sylvia Plath, "Stillborn")

Notice that every case of flat writing above is full of abstractions (*actually, affection, power, vitality, before*), generalizations (*everything, all, consequences, verses*), and judgments (*valuable, important, best, unjust, no vitality, unattractive, stale*). When these are replaced with nouns that call up a sense image (*gold, child, dog, ocean, court, pigs, fish*) and with verbs that represent actions we can visualize (*glisten, look, leap, hug, wag, fall*), the writing comes alive. At the same time, the ideas, generalizations, and judgments are *also* present in the images.

Notice too that Miller's image "fall like an ocean" has weight and texture; Plath's image of poems that have a "fishy air" suggests not just the sight of a fish but its smell. All of the five senses go into the making of imagery, and a writer working at full stretch will make use of them all.

It's not that abstractions, generalizations, and judgments are useless or bad writing in themselves; on the contrary, they are important to all human communication.

- *Abstractions* are the names of ideas or concepts, which cannot in themselves be experienced directly through one or more of our senses, such as *intelligence, criticism, love, anger.*
- *Generalizations* can only be vaguely visualized because they include too many of a given group: *something, creatures, kitchen equipment.*
- *Judgments* tell us what to think about something instead of showing it: *beautiful, insidious, suspiciously.*

Human beings are able to communicate largely because they are capable of these kinds of conceptual thinking.

But it is sense impressions that make writing vivid, and there is a physiological reason for this. Information taken in through the five senses is processed in the *limbic system* of the brain, which generates sensuous responses in the body: heart rate, blood/oxygen flow, muscle reaction, and so forth. Emotional response consists of these physiological reactions, and so in order to have an effect on your reader's emotions, you must literally get into the limbic system, which you can only do through the senses. Now, the images of a film strike the eye directly, as *images,* just as the sounds of music strike the ear directly as sound, the smells of perfume or food strike the nose directly, and so forth. But the images of written literature (including sound, smell, taste, feel) strike the eye as little symbols on the page, which must be translated by the brain into the sound that these symbols represent, which must then be translated into the sense that our language signifies by that particular sound. It's a complicated process that demands a lot of a reader, who will thank you for making it worthwhile.

And it is a dynamic process, to which readers actively bring their own memories and experience. Words not only *denote,* or literally refer to their meaning, but *connote,* suggest or imply through layers of connection in our experience and culture. Often using the imagery of one sense will suggest the other senses as well, and will resonate with ideas, qualities, and emotions that are not stated. Strong images tend to demand active verbs that make for energy in the prose or the poetic line.

Here is a single sentence from Margaret Atwood's *Cat's Eye,* in which the heroine describes the zoology building where her father worked when she was a child.

> The cellar smells strongly of mouse droppings, a smell which wafts upward through the whole building, getting fainter as you go up, mingling with the smell of green Dustbane used to clean the floors, and with the other smells, the floor polish and furniture wax and formaldehyde and snakes.

We are ostensibly given only a series of smells from a child's point of view, but as those smells rise we experience traveling upward through the building, also seeing the floors, the furniture, the snakes. The "rising" smells also help build the suggestion of the sinister, from *mouse* to *Dustbane* to *formaldehyde* to *snakes*. There is an echo of fear implied in "getting fainter as you go up," which seems to apply to courage as well as smells.

Notice also how the passage bristles with active verbs. These smells don't just lie there, they *waft, get fainter, mingle*; you *go*; the Dustbane is *used to clean*. This is important. Active verbs are images too. "Look before you leap" contains no visible objects, but we can see the actions. Passive verbs, linking verbs, all forms of the verb *to be*, invite flat, generalized writing, whereas active verbs jump-start the mind.

TRY THIS 2.1

Open a textbook, a how-to book, a form letter, something not intended to be a work of the imagination. Identify words that represent abstractions, generalizations, and/or judgments. Make a list of at least ten of these. Pick two or three of them and invent an image that suggests each word. Let your imagination loose—this is a sense impression, not a definition! Examples:

Capitalism
Dotted line across Nevada
Rollerblade straight:
Sign here.

Shame
Okra in the gumbo.
One cross-section surfaces:
Perfect flower,
Pool of slime.

Or this succinct example from Barbara Drake:

Hunger
How terrible—this little blob of jelly has a mouth.

Concrete, Significant Details

> The greatest writers are effective largely because they deal in particulars and report the details that matter.
>
> *William H. Strunk*

Writers are frequently advised: *show, don't tell.* What this means is that it is crucial to address the senses. Vivid writing contains **concrete, significant details.**

- *Concrete* means that there is an image, something that can be seen, heard, smelled, tasted, or touched.

- *Significant* means that the specific image also suggests an abstraction, generalization, or judgment.
- *Detail* means that there is a degree of focus and specificity.

The notion of *detail* is important to the image because it moves away from the generalized and toward the particular. For example, *creature* is a generalized notion, hard to see except in the vaguest way. *Animal* is still vague; *four-legged animal* is a little more specific; *domestic animal* a little more; *dog* narrows the field; *mixed-breed Shepherd* we can see; *old Sammy asleep on the red rug, his haunches twitching in his dream* brings the dog into sharp focus in our minds. At the same time this last sentence resonates with the ideas of age and uneasy sleep. If it said *his teeth bared and gnashing in his dream,* we'd also guess that old Sam has a capacity for meanness. Notice how the narrowing specificity of the noun invites active verbs.

TRY THIS 2.2

Begin with the largest general category you can think of—minerals, food, structures—think big. Then narrow the category step by step, becoming more specific until you have a single detailed image. Try it again with the same large category but narrow in another direction. Can you, *without naming a quality,* make your image suggest an idea or direct our attitude toward the thing you describe?

If specificity as well as concreteness is crucial to vivid writing, so too is the significance carried in those concrete details; the ideas or qualities that they suggest; the way they reveal character, attract or warn us; the way they lead us to think and feel. A list of physical details without such hints will not move us: *The lawn is green; there are four trees; there is a white picket fence about three feet high and a flagstone walk leading up to the white door.* We want to have our intellects and emotions also directed toward the *meaning* of the details.

A survey of any bookshelf will turn up dozens of examples of this principle. Here, for instance, is a scene from Anne Tyler's *Accidental Tourist.* The protagonist's wife has left him and he is having trouble sleeping.

> The dog, sighing, roused himself and dropped off the bed to pad downstairs behind him. The floorboards were cool underfoot, the kitchen linoleum cooler still; there was a glow from the refrigerator as Macon poured himself a glass of milk. He went to the living room and turned on the TV. Generally some black-and-white movie was running—men in suits and felt hats, women with padded shoulders. He didn't try to follow the plot. He took small, steady sips of milk, feeling the calcium traveling to his bones. Hadn't he read that calcium cures insomnia? He absently stroked the cat, who had somehow crept into his lap. It was much too hot to have a cat in his lap, especially this one—a loose-strung, gray tweed female who seemed made of some unusually dense substance. And the dog, most often, would be lying on top of his feet. "It's just you and me, old buddies," Macon would tell them. The cat made a comma of sweat across his bare thighs.

In this passage, Tyler makes continual reference to the senses, letting us feel the floor, the cat, and the heat; see the glow of the refrigerator and the TV; taste the milk and the "calcium traveling to his bones"; hear the dog sigh and the man talking to the animals. The writing is alive because we do in fact live through our sense perceptions, and Tyler takes us past words and through thought to let us perceive the scene in this way.

At the same time, a number of ideas not stated reverberate off the images. We are aware of generalizations the author does not need to make because we will make them ourselves. Tyler could have had her character "tell" us: *The house felt eerie. I was desperately lonely and neither the television nor the animals were really company. I thought if I did something sensible and steady it would help, but I just felt trapped. When I tried to be cheerful it got worse.* This version would be very flat, and none of it is necessary. The eeriness is inherent in the light of the refrigerator and TV; the loneliness in the sigh, the sips, and the absent stroking of the cat. The sense of entrapment is in the cat on his thighs and the dog on his feet. The emotion of the paragraph begins with a sigh and ends in sweat. Notice how deftly Tyler tells us—"men in suits and felt hats, women with padded shoulders"—that at this late hour, all there is on TV is film noir, which adds a connotation of further eeriness, seediness, and despair.

John Gardner in *The Art of Fiction* speaks of concrete details as "proofs," which establish in the reader such firm confidence that the author is an authority, that we will believe whatever she or he tells us. An author who is vague and opinionated, on the other hand, makes us uneasy and suspicious. And this applies to characters as well—a fact you can exploit. Any character—whether in a memoir, a fiction, poetry, or drama—who speaks in generalizations and judgments will undermine our trust.

> It is odd but I must tell you that I have never felt so self-assured, so splendid, so brilliant.... Apparently, it is necessary to find someone completely inferior to appreciate one's own excellence. To be a prince in name is nothing. To be a prince in essence—it's heaven, it's pure joy.
>
> *"Ivona, Princess of Burgundia," Witold Gombrowicz*

We don't have to know anything about this character or the play he comes from to know that we mistrust his judgment.

This book has begun by insisting on imagery because it is so central to literature and also because many beginning writers try to make their, or their characters', emotions felt by merely naming them, and so fail to let us experience those emotions. Here is a passage from a young writer, which fails through lack of appeal to the senses.

> Debbie was a very stubborn and completely independent person and was always doing things her way despite her parents' efforts to get her to conform. Her father was an executive in a dress manufacturing company and was able to afford his family all the luxuries and comforts of life. But Debbie was completely indifferent to her family's affluence.

This passage contains a number of judgments we might or might not share with the author, and she has not convinced us that we do. What constitutes stubbornness? Independence? Indifference? Affluence? Further, since the judgments are supported by generalizations, we have no sense of the individuality of the characters, which alone would bring them to life on the page. What things was she always doing? What efforts did her parents make to get her to conform? What sort of executive is the father? What dress manufacturing company? What luxuries and comforts?

> Debbie would wear a tank top to a tea party if she pleased, with fluorescent earrings and ankle-strap sandals.
>
> "Oh, sweetheart," Mrs. Chiddister would stand in the doorway wringing her hands. "It's not *nice*."
>
> "Not who?" Debbie would say, and add a fringed belt.
>
> Mr. Chiddister was Artistic Director of the Boston branch of Cardin, and had a high respect for what he called "elegant textures," which ranged from handwoven tweed to gold filigree, and which he willingly offered his daughter. Debbie preferred her laminated bangles.

We have not passed a final judgment on the merits of these characters, but we know a good deal more about them, and we have drawn certain interim conclusions that are our own and have not been forced on us by the author. Debbie is independent of her parents' values, rather careless of their feelings, energetic, a little trashy. Mrs. Chiddister is quite ineffectual. Mr. Chiddister is a snob, though maybe Debbie's taste is so bad we'll end up on his side.

But maybe that isn't at all what the author had in mind. The point is that we weren't allowed to know what the author did have in mind. Perhaps it was more like this version.

> One day Debbie brought home a copy of *Ulysses*. Mrs. Strum called it "filth" and threw it across the sunporch. Debbie knelt on the parquet and retrieved her bookmark, which she replaced. "No, it's not," she said.
>
> "You're not so old I can't take a strap to you!" Mr. Strum reminded her.
>
> Mr. Strum was controlling stockholder of Readywear Conglomerates, and was proud of treating his family, not only on his salary, but also on his expense account. The summer before he had taken them to Belgium, where they toured the American Cemetery and the torture chambers of Ghent Castle. Entirely ungrateful, Debbie had spent the rest of the trip curled up in the hotel with a shabby copy of some poems.

Now we have a much clearer understanding of *stubbornness, independence, indifference,* and *affluence,* both their natures and the value we are to place on them. This time our judgment is heavily weighted in Debbie's favor—partly because people who read books have a sentimental sympathy with other people who read books—but also because we hear hysteria in "filth" and "take a strap to you," whereas Debbie's resistance is quiet and strong. Mr. Strum's attitude toward his expense account suggests that he's corrupt, and his choice of "luxuries" is morbid. The passage does contain two overt judgments, the first being that Debbie was "entirely ungrateful." Notice that by the time we get to this, we're aware that the judgment is Mr. Strum's and that Debbie has little enough to be grateful for. We understand not only what the author says but also that she means the opposite of what she says, and we feel doubly clever to get it; that is the pleasure of irony. Likewise, the judgment that the book of poems is "shabby" shows Mr. Strum's crass materialism toward what we know to be the finer things.

TRY THIS 2.3
Pick a vivid passage of fiction or creative nonfiction and *spoil it* by replacing specific details with generalizations and judgments. Exchange with a person who has similarly spoiled a favorite passage. Create a new and different passage by replacing the generalizations and judgments with your own choice of sensory details. Compare the results.

TRY THIS 2.4
Write down a bumper sticker you like. (It's a good idea to exchange with someone else so you are working with one you don't actually remember.) Describe the car (van, truck, SUV) this bumper sticker is stuck on—make, model, year, color, condition. Open the door. Describe the smells and textures. Name three objects you find. Name a fourth object you're surprised to find there. Look up. Here comes the owner. Who, walking how, wearing what, carrying what, with what facial expression? The owner says something. What?

Figures of Speech

> A metaphor goes out and comes back; it is a fetching motion of the imagination.
>
> *Tony Hoagland*

English is a language unusually rich in *tropes* or **figures of speech**—that is, expressions not meant to be taken literally, but as standing for something related in some way (the word *trope* comes from a Greek word meaning *to twist* or *turn*). Tropes almost invariably involve an image. The number and variety of common figures of speech make English difficult to learn as a foreign language, but also makes it fertile ground for creative writing. (Notice that *fertile ground* here is a trope, specifically a metaphor in which the language is compared to soil.)

There are many different kinds of figures of speech, but the five major tropes are usually considered to be:

- **Metonymy,** in which one thing is represented by another thing associated with it, as in *all the crowns of Europe* (where *crowns* stands for *kings*)
- **Synecdoche,** in which a part stands for the whole, as in *all hands on deck* (where *hands* stands for *men*)

- **Personification,** in which human characteristics are bestowed on anything nonhuman, as in *the breathing city* or *the gentle breeze*
- **Metaphor,** a comparison as in *the woman is a rose*
- **Simile,** a comparison as in *the woman is like a rose*

Though these are five of the most frequently used figures of speech in English, you may be familiar with others, such as **hyperbole,** which is extreme exaggeration, and **oxymoron,** which links two contradictory words. And who hasn't enjoyed groaning at a **pun?** In medieval and Renaissance rhetoric, dozens of such tropes were identified, classified, and debated, and skill in using these "ornaments" much admired.

The rhetorical debate has lost its urgency, but the use of figurative language in literature retains its force, slightly turning or twisting the reader's perspective to offer a new or unusual view of the familiar. When Todd McEwen in the memoir of his sister, "A Very Young Dancer," says that her suitor, "Jay, suddenly tired of Moira's perpetual mystery, announced, *The wallet is closed*"—he (and Jay) are using a metonymy in which the wallet stands for love and indulgence. If a fictional narrator observes, "Rub two guilts together and they burst into blame," she is personifying the abstractions *guilt* and *blame* with ironic reference to the notion of rubbing sticks together. If a poems begins:

I keep stepping on the ugly nap
Of all our local comings and disappearings...

The "nap" is a synecdoche for the more obvious word *carpet,* and moves our focus inward, toward a detail or close-up. It is said of filmmaking that "every close-up is synecdoche," meaning that when, for example, we see a close-up of a hand, we assume that it stands for the whole person. If we see that hand go limp, it may be metonymy suggesting that person's death.

Of all the possible figures of speech to be used by the poet, the playwright, the essayist, and the story writer, metaphor and simile are the most common and the most crucial. A *metaphor* assumes or states a comparison, without acknowledging that it is a comparison: *my electric muscles shock the crowd; her hair is seaweed and she is the sea.* The metaphor may come in the form of an adjective: *they have a piggy and a fishy air.* Or it may come as a verb: *the bees shouldering the grass.*

A simile makes a comparison between two things using the words *like* or *as: his teeth rattled like dice in a box; my head is light as a balloon; I will fall like an ocean on that court!*

Both metaphor and simile compare things that are both alike and different, and it is in the tension between this likeness and difference that their literary power lies.

From earliest infancy, our brains are busy registering likeness and difference. This is a major way we learn, about both behavior and what things mean. A smile on Mother's face expresses and promises pleasure, so a smile on a different face also reassures us. If we fall and are told to "be careful," then "be careful" will suggest alarm when we reach for the glass of milk. We compare an experience in the past to a current problem in order to predict the future. The habit of comparison is so natural that our language is full of metaphor and simile we use without knowing we are doing so. *Don't split a gut. Let's go for all the marbles. It doesn't compute. That went belly up. He lays it on with a trowel. I'm fed to the teeth. Read my lips.* Many popular metaphors, like these, are reused until they become *clichés*, comparisons that have lost their freshness.

Metaphor is central to imaginative writing because it offers a particularly exact and resonant kind of concrete detail. When we speak of "the eyes of a potato," or "the eye of the needle," we mean simply that the leaf bud and the thread hole *look like eyes.* We don't mean to suggest that the potato or the needle can see. The comparisons do not suggest any essential or abstract quality to do with sight.

But in literature both metaphor and simile have developed so that the resonance of comparison is precisely in the essential or abstract quality that the two objects share. When a writer speaks of "the eyes of the houses" or "the windows of the soul," the comparison of eyes to windows does contain the idea of transmitting vision between the inner and the outer. When Shakespeare's Jacques claims that "all the world's a stage," the significance lies not in the physical similarity of the world to a stage (he isn't backtracking in history to claim the world is flat), but in the essential qualities that such similarity implies: the pretense of the actors, the briefness of the play, the parts that men and women must inevitably play from babyhood to old age.

A metaphor presents us with a comparison that also conveys an abstraction or a judgment. A good metaphor resonates with the essential, and this is the writer's principle of choice. So Peter Hoeg, in *Smilla's Sense of Snow,* speaks of rain showers that "slap me in the face with a wet towel." Well, rain showers can patter gently on your face, or dribble down your neck, or bring May flowers. But the rain showers that Hoeg is talking about have a vicious nature that lies in the metaphor: They hit hard, they sting, and they seem to hurt on purpose.

Hoeg's metaphor contains a complex of meanings; yet it is *brief.* Because a metaphor condenses so many connotations into the tension between the images, it tends to be not only concrete but concise. So although you might in one context choose to say, "He was so angry that I thought he was going to hit me," if you sense that the moment wants the special intensity of metaphor, you could also pack that meaning into: "His face was a fist."

A metaphor is a particular and particularly imaginative kind of significant detail, comparing two sensible images and letting the abstraction remain unvoiced between them. But even if part of the comparison is an abstraction, that part will be made vivid by the "thingness" of the comparison. Robert Frost's famous "Fire and Ice" develops a simple but striking metaphor in which the objects are compared to the qualities themselves:

Some say the world will end in fire,
Some say in ice.
From what I've tasted of desire
I hold with those who favor fire.
But if it had to perish twice,
I think I know enough of hate
To say that for destruction ice
Is also great
And would suffice.

TRY THIS 2.5

Write this poem: The first line consists of an abstraction, plus a verb, plus a place. The second line describes attire. The third line summarizes an action. Let it flow; don't worry too much about making sense.

Examples (by Carissa Neff)

Beauty creeps out the window
Wearing nothing but taut bare skin.
Leaving a trail of wrinkles behind her.

Hunger yells in the hallway,
Draped in cymbals;
He stomps and shouts, "Hear me now!"

The major danger of metaphor is **cliché.** Those "windows of the soul," those "eyes like pools" are so familiar that they no longer hold any interest, whereas a fresh metaphor surprises us with the unlikeness of the two things compared while at the same time convincing us of the aptness or truth of the likeness. A clichéd metaphor fails to surprise us and so fails to illuminate. Sometimes as a writer you will find yourself with a gift of fresh comparison, and sometimes the first image that comes to mind will be tired and stale. All writers experience this, and the good ones learn to overcome it. The first thing to do is to make yourself alert to clichés in your own writing and the world around you, and then to labor (which may mean to dream) your way toward those images that illuminate the everyday and make the familiar strange.

TRY THIS 2.6

Quickly list as many clichéd metaphors as you can think of: *the path of life, eyes like pools, crazy as a bedbug, nose to the grindstone,* and so forth. Then switch half a dozen of the comparisons: *eyes like bedbugs, nose to the path, the grindstone of life.* Some of these might be fresh and apt! In any case, the exercise will help you become aware of clichés and so help you avoid them.

My own long relationship with cliché is a paradox, for I find that my language is least fresh when I am most determined to write well. If I sit rigid with good intentions, my inner critic takes up residence on my shoulder, sneering *that's silly, that's far-fetched, what a crock, nobody'll believe that!*—with the result that I fall back on usual phrases. But if I knock her off her perch and let myself try anything that comes to mind, *some* of it will be silly, some far-fetched, and among the verbal rubble there is almost bound to be a salvageable building block, a serviceable cooking pot, a precious stone.

More to Read

Rico, Gabriele Lusser. *Writing the Natural Way*. Los Angeles: J. P. Tarcher, Inc., 1983. Print.

READINGS

The readings that follow employ imagery and metaphor in a wide variety of ways. For example, Annie Dillard's "*from* Heaven and Earth in Jest," a short essay from her book *Pilgrim at Tinker Creek,* represents a single sharp observation of nature, dense with metaphor. David Sedaris's "What I Learned" satirizes higher education by substituting bizarre details for the familiar and expected ones.

Read each selection once, fast, for content and pleasure; then a second time consciously aware of images and metaphors. What effect do they have on you? How? What technique might you imitate, absorb, try, steal?

Among the readings you'll find some triggers for play in your journal. These are not connected to the readings in any direct or literal way, but may suggest peripheral ways to practice some shape, subject, or skill the writers display. At the end of this and further chapters you will find suggestions for developing your ideas toward a draft of a finished piece.

CREATIVE NONFICTION

ANNIE DILLARD

from Heaven and Earth in Jest

A couple of summers ago I was walking along the edge of the island to see what I could see in the water, and mainly to scare frogs. Frogs have an inelegant way of taking off from invisible positions on the bank just ahead of your feet, in dire panic, emitting a froggy "Yike!" and splashing into the water. Incredibly, this amused me, and, incredibly, it amuses me still. As I walked along the grassy edge of the island, I got better and better at seeing frogs both in and out of the water. I learned to recognize, slowing down, the difference in texture of the light reflected from mudbank, water, grass, or frog. Frogs were flying all around me. At the end of the island I noticed a small green frog. He was exactly half in and half out of the water, looking like a schematic diagram of an amphibian, and he didn't jump.

He didn't jump; I crept closer. At last I knelt on the island's winter-killed grass, lost, dumb-struck, staring at the frog in the creek just four feet away. He was a very small frog with wide, dull eyes. And just as I looked at him, he slowly crumpled and began to sag. The spirit vanished from his eyes as if snuffed. His skin emptied and drooped; his very skull seemed to collapse and settle like a kicked tent. He was shrinking before my eyes like a deflating football. I watched the taut, glistening skin on his shoulders ruck and rumple and fall. Soon, part of his skin, formless as a pricked balloon, lay in floating folds like bright scum on top of the water: it was a monstrous and terrifying thing. I gaped bewildered, appalled. An oval shadow hung in the water behind the drained frog; then the shadow glided away. The frog skin bag started to sink.

I had read about the giant water bug, but never seen one. "Giant water bug" is really the name of the creature, which is an enormous, heavy-bodied brown beetle. It eats insects, tadpoles, fish, and frogs. Its grasping forelegs are mighty and hooked inward. It seizes a victim with these legs, hugs it tight, and paralyzes it with enzymes injected during a vicious bite. That one bite is the only bite it ever takes. Through the puncture shoot the poisons that dissolve the victim's muscles and bones and organs—all but the skin—and through it the giant water bug sucks out the victim's body, reduced to a juice. This event is quite common in warm fresh water. The frog I saw was being sucked by a giant water bug. I had been kneeling on the island grass; when the unrecognizable flap of frog skin settled on the creek bottom, swaying, I stood up and brushed the knees of my pants. I couldn't catch my breath.

DAVID SEDARIS

What I Learned

It's been interesting to walk around campus this afternoon, as when *I* went to Princeton things were completely different. This chapel, for instance—I remember when it was just a clearing, cordoned off with sharp sticks. Prayer was compulsory back then, and you couldn't just fake it by moving your lips; you had to know the words, and really mean them. I'm dating myself, but this was before Jesus Christ. We worshipped a God named Sashatiba, who had five eyes, including one right here, on the Adam's apple. None of us ever met him, but word had it that he might appear at any moment, so we were always at the ready. *Whatever you do, don't look at his neck,* I used to tell myself.

It's funny now, but I thought about it a lot. Some people thought about it a little too much, and it really affected their academic performance. Again, I date myself, but back then we were on a pass-fail system. If you passed, you got to live, and if you failed you were burned alive on a pyre that's now the Transgender Studies Building. Following the first grading period, the air was so thick with smoke you could barely find your way across campus. There were those who said that it smelled like meat, no different from a barbecue, but I could tell the difference. I mean, really. Since when do you grill hair? Or those ugly, chunky shoes we all used to wear?

It kept you on your toes, though, I'll say that much. If I'd been burned alive because of bad grades, my parents would have killed me, especially my father, who meant well but was just a little too gung ho for my taste. He had the whole outfit: Princeton breastplate, Princeton nightcap; he even got the velvet cape with the tiger head hanging like a rucksack from between the shoulder blades. In those days, the mascot was a sabretooth, so you can imagine how silly it looked, and how painful it was to sit down. Then, there was his wagon, completely covered with decals and bumper stickers: "I hold my horses for Ivy League schools," "My son was accepted at the best university in the United States and all I got was a bill for a hundred and sixty-eight thousand dollars." On and on, which was just so... *wrong.*

One of the things they did back then was start you off with a modesty seminar, an eight-hour session that all the freshmen had to sit through. It might be different today, but in my time it took the form of a role-playing exercise, my classmates and I pretending to be graduates, and the teacher assuming the part of an average citizen: the soldier, the bloodletter, the whore with a heart of gold.

"Tell me, young man. Did you attend a university of higher learning?"

To anyone holding a tool or a weapon, we were trained to respond, "What? Me go to college?" If, on the other hand, the character held a degree, you were allowed to say, "Sort of," or, sometimes, "I think so."

"So where do you sort of think you went?"

And it was the next bit that you had to get just right. Inflection was everything, and it took the foreign students forever to master it.

"Where do you sort of think you went?"

And we'd say, "Umm, Princeton?"—as if it were an oral exam, and we weren't quite sure that this was the correct answer.

"Princeton, my goodness," the teacher would say. "That must have been quite something!"

You had to let him get it out, but once he started in on how brilliant and committed you must be it was time to hold up your hands, saying, "Oh, it isn't that hard to get into."

Then he'd say, "Really? But I heard—"

"Wrong," you'd tell him. "You heard wrong. It's not that great of a school."

This was the way it had to be done—you had to play it down, which wasn't easy when your dad was out there, reading your acceptance letter into a bullhorn.

I needed to temper my dad's enthusiasm a bit, and so I announced that I would be majoring in patricide. The Princeton program was very strong back then, the best in the country, but it wasn't the sort of thing your father could get too worked up about. Or, at least, most fathers wouldn't. Mine was over the moon. "Killed by a Princeton graduate!" he said. "And my own son, no less."

My mom was actually jealous. "So what's wrong with matricide?" she asked. "What, I'm not good enough to murder?"

They started bickering, so in order to make peace I promised to consider a double major.

"And how much more is that going to cost us?" they said.

20 Those last few months at home were pretty tough, but then I started my freshman year, and got caught up in the life of the mind. My idol-worship class was the best, but my dad didn't get it. "What the hell does that have to do with patricide?" he asked.

And I said, "Umm. *Everything*?"

He didn't understand that it's all connected, that one subject leads to another and forms a kind of chain that raises its head and nods like a cobra when you're sucking on a bong after three days of no sleep. On acid it's even wilder, and appears to eat things. But, not having gone to college, my dad had no concept of a well-rounded liberal-arts education. He thought that all my classes should be murder-related, with no lunch breaks or anything. Fortunately, it doesn't work that way.

In truth, I had no idea what I wanted to study, so for the first few years I took everything that came my way. I enjoyed pillaging and astrology, but the thing that ultimately stuck was comparative literature. There wasn't much of it to compare back then, no more than a handful of epic poems and one novel about a lady detective, but that's part of what I liked about it. The field was new, and full of possibilities, but try telling that to my parents.

"You mean you *won't* be killing us?" my mother said. "But I told everyone you were going for that double major."

25 Dad followed his "I'm so disappointed" speech with a lecture on career opportunities. "You're going to study literature and get a job doing *what*?" he said. "*Literaturizing*?"

We spent my entire vacation arguing; then, just before I went back to school, my father approached me in my bedroom. "Promise me you'll keep an open mind," he said. And, as he left, he slipped an engraved dagger into my book bag.

I had many fine teachers during my years at Princeton, but the one I think of most often was my fortune-telling professor—a complete hag with wild gray hair, warts the size of new potatoes, the whole nine yards. She taught us to forecast the weather up to two weeks in advance, but ask her for anything weightier and you were likely to be disappointed.

The alchemy majors wanted to know how much money they'd be making after graduation. "Just give us an approximate figure," they'd say, and the professor would shake her head and cover her crystal ball with a little cozy given to her by one of her previous classes. When it came to our futures, she drew the line, no matter how hard we begged—and, I mean, we really tried. I was as let down as the next guy, but in retrospect, I can see that she acted in our best interests. Look at yourself on the day that you graduated from college, then look at yourself today. I did that recently, and it was, like, "What the hell happened?"

The answer, of course, is life. What the hag chose not to foretell—and what we, in our certainty, could not have fathomed—is that stuff comes up. Weird doors open. People fall into things. Maybe the engineering whiz will wind up brewing cider, not because he has to but because he finds it challenging. Who knows? Maybe the athlete will bring peace to all nations, or the class moron will go on to become the President of the United States—though that's more likely to happen at Harvard or Yale, schools that will pretty much let in anybody.

There were those who left Princeton and soared like arrows into the bosoms of power and finance, but I was not one of them. My path was a winding one, with plenty of obstacles along the way. When school was finished, I went back home, an Ivy League graduate with four years' worth of dirty laundry and his whole life ahead of him. "What are you going to do now?" my parents asked.

And I said, "Well, I was thinking of washing some of these underpants."

That took six months. Then I moved on to the shirts.

"Now what?" my parents asked.

And, when I told them I didn't know, they lost what little patience they had left. "What kind of a community-college answer is that?" my mother said. "You went to the best school there is—how can you not know something?"

And I said, "I don't know."

In time, my father stopped wearing his Princeton gear. My mother stopped talking about my "potential," and she and my dad got themselves a brown-and-white puppy. In terms of intelligence, it was just average, but they couldn't see that at all. "Aren't you just the smartest dog in the world?" they'd ask, and the puppy would shake their hands just like I used to do.

My first alumni weekend cheered me up a bit. It was nice to know that I wasn't the only unemployed graduate in the world, but the warm feeling evaporated when I got back home and saw that my parents had given the dog my bedroom. In place of the Princeton pennant they'd bought for my first birthday was a banner reading, "Westminster or bust."

I could see which way the wind was blowing, and so I left, and moved to the city, where a former classmate, a philosophy major, got me a job on his ragpicking crew. When the industry moved overseas—this the doing of *another* former classmate—I stayed put, and eventually found work skinning hides for a ratcatcher, a thin, serious man with the longest beard I had ever seen.

At night, I read and reread the handful of books I'd taken with me when I left home, and eventually, out of boredom as much as anything else, I started to write myself. It wasn't much, at first: character sketches, accounts of my day, parodies of articles in the alumni newsletter. Then, in time, I became more ambitious, and began crafting little stories about my family. I read one of them out loud to the ratcatcher, who'd never laughed at anything but roared at the description of my mother and her puppy. "My mom was just the same," he said. "I graduated from Brown, and two weeks later she was raising falcons on my top bunk!" The story about my dad defecating in his neighbor's well pleased my boss so much that he asked for a copy, and sent it to his own father.

This gave me the confidence to continue, and in time I completed an entire book, which was subsequently published. I presented a first edition to my parents, who started with the story about our neighbor's well, and then got up to close the drapes. Fifty pages later, they were boarding up the door and looking for ways to disguise themselves. Other people had loved my writing, but these two didn't get it at all. "What's wrong?" I asked.

My father adjusted his makeshift turban, and sketched a mustache on my mother's upper lip. "What's wrong?" he said. "I'll tell you what's wrong: you're killing us."

"But I thought that's what you wanted?"

"We did," my mother wept, "but not this way."

It hadn't occurred to me until that moment, but I seemed to have come full circle. What started as a dodge had inadvertently become my life's work, an irony I never could have appreciated had my extraordinary parents not put me through Princeton.

TRY THIS 2.7

Write, quickly, a couple of pages about something banal that you've done in the past few days. Then replace at least fifteen nouns with other nouns that are in some way extreme, or inappropriate to the subject at hand. Any usable ideas in there?

FICTION

NADINE GORDIMER

The Diamond Mine

Love during wartime

I'll call her Tilla. You may call her by another name. You might think you knew her. You might have been the one. It's not by some simple colloquial habit that we "call" someone instead of naming: call him up.

It is during the war, your war, the forties, that has sunk as far away into the century as the grandfathers' 1914. He is blond, stocky in khaki, attractively near-sighted, so that the eyes, which are actually having difficulty with focus, seem to be concentrating attentively on her. This impression is emphasized by his lashes, blond and curly as his hair. He is completely different from the men she knows in the life of films—the only men she knows, apart from her father—and whom she expected to come along one day not too far off, Robert Taylor or even the foreigner, Charles Boyer. He is different because—at last—he is real. She is sixteen. He is no foreigner, no materialization of projection from Hollywood. He's the son of friends of her maternal grandmother, detailed to a military training camp in the province where the girl and her parents live. Some people even take in strangers from the camp for the respite of weekend leave; with a young daughter in the house, this family would not go so far as to risk that, but when the man of the family is beyond call-up age an easy way to fulfill patriotic duty is to offer hospitality to a man vouched for by connections. He's almost to be thought of as an elective grandson of the old lady. In war these strangers, remember, are Our Boys.

When he comes on Friday night and stays until Sunday his presence makes a nice change for the three, mother, father, and daughter, who live a quiet life, not given to socializing. That presence is a pleasant element in the closeness between parents and daughter: he is old enough to be an adult like them and, only eight years ahead of her, young enough to be her contemporary. The mother cooks a substantial lunch on the Sundays he's there; you can imagine what the food must be like in a military camp. The father suggests a game of golf—welcome to borrow clubs—but it turns out the soldier doesn't play. What's his game, then? He likes to fish. But his hospitality is four hundred miles from the sea; the soldier laughs along in manly recognition that there must be a game. The daughter: for her, she could never tell anyone, his weekend presence is a pervasion that fills the house, displaces all its familiar odors of home, is fresh and pungent—he's here. It's the emanation of khaki washed with strong soap and fixed—as in perfume the essence of flowers is fixed by alcohol—by the pressure of a hot iron.

The parents are reluctant cinema-goers, so it is thoughtful of this visiting friend of the family to invite the daughter of the house to choose a film she'd like to see on a Saturday night. She has no driving license yet (seventeen was the qualifying age in those days) and the father does not offer his car to the soldier. So the pair walk down the road from streetlight to streetlight, under the trees, all that autumn, to the small town's center, where only the cinema and the pub in the hotel are awake. She is aware of window dummies, in the closed shops that her mother's friends patronize, observing her as she walks past with a man. If she is invited to a party given by a school friend, she must be home strictly by eleven, usually fetched by her father. But now she is with a responsible friend, a family connection, not among unknown youths on the loose; if the film is a nine-o'clock showing, the pair are not home before midnight, and the lights are already extinguished in the parents' bedroom. It is then that, schoolgirlish, knowing nothing else to offer, she makes cocoa in the kitchen, and it is then that he tells her about fishing. The kitchen is locked up for the night, the windows are closed, and it is amazing how strong that presence of a man can be, that stiff-clean clothing warmed—not a scent, not a breath but, as he moves his arms graphically in description of playing a catch, it comes from the inner crease of his bare elbows, where the sun on Maneuvers hasn't got at the secret fold, from that center of being, the pliant hollow that vibrates between his collarbones as he speaks, the breastplate rosy down to where a few brownish-blond hairs disappear into the open neck of the khaki shirt. He will never turn dark, his skin retains the sun, glows. Him.

5 Tilla has never gone fishing. Her father doesn't fish. Four hundred miles from the sea, the boys at school kick and throw balls around—they know about, talk about football and cricket. The father knows about, talks about golf. Fishing. It opens the sea before her, the salt wind gets in her narrowed eyes, conveying to her whole nights passed alone on the rocks. He walks from headland to headland on down-wet sand, the tide is out—sometimes in midsentence there's a check, half smile, half breath, because he's thinking of something this child couldn't know. This is his incantation; it shuts out the parade-ground march toward killing and blinds the sights that the gun trains on sawdust-stuffed figures on which he is being drilled to see the face of the enemy, to whom he himself is the enemy, with guts (he pulls the intricately perfect innards out of the fish he's caught, a fisherman's simple skill) in place of sawdust. The sleeping parents are right: he will not touch her innocence of what this century claims, commands from him.

As they walk home where she used to race her bicycle up and down under the trees, the clothing on their arms—the khaki sleeve, the sweater her mother has handed her as a condition of permission to be out in the chill night air—brushes by proximity, not intention. The strap of her sandal slips, and as she pauses to right it, hopping on one leg, he steadies her by the forearm and then they walk on hand in hand. He's taking care of her. The next weekend, they kiss in one of the tree-dark intervals between streetlights. Boys have kissed her; it happened only to her mouth. The next Saturday, her arms went around him, his around her, her face approached, was pressed, breathed in, and breathed against the hollow of neck where the pendulum of heartbeat can be felt, the living place above the breastplate from which the incense of his presence had come. She was there.

In the kitchen there was no talk. The cocoa rose to the top of the pot, made ready. All the sources of warmth that her palms had extended to, everywhere in the house, as a domestic animal senses the warmth of a fire to approach, were in this body against hers, in the current of arms, the contact of chest, belly muscles, the deep strange heat from between his thighs. But he took care of her. Gently loosened her while she was discovering that a man has breasts, too, even if made of muscle, and that to press her own against them was an urgent exchange, walking on the wet sands with the fisherman.

The next weekend leave—but the next weekend leave is cancelled. Instead there's a call from the public phone at the canteen bar. The mother happened to answer and there were expressions of bright and encouraging regret that the daughter tried to piece into what they were responding to. The family was at supper. The father's mouth bunched stoically: Marching orders. Embarkation. The mother nodded round the table, confirming. She—the one I call Tilla—stood up, appalled at the strength to strike the receiver from her mother and the inability of a good girl to do so. Then her mother was saying, but of course we'll take a drive out on Sunday, say goodbye and Godspeed. Grandma'd never forgive me if she thought...Now, can you tell me how to get there, beyond Pretoria, I know...I didn't catch it, what mine? And after the turnoff at the main road? Oh, don't bother, I suppose we can ask at a petrol station if we get lost, everyone must know where that camp is. Is there something we can bring you, anything you'll need...

It seems they're to make an outing of it. Out of her stun: that essence, ironed khaki and soap, has been swept from the house, from the kitchen, by something that's got nothing to do with a fisherman, except that he is a man and, as her father has stated—embarkation—men go to war. Her mother makes picnic preparations: Do you think a chicken or pickled ox tongue, hard-boiled eggs... Don't know where one can sit to eat in a military camp, there must be somewhere for visitors. Her father selects from his stack of travel brochures a map of the local area to place on the shelf below the windshield. Petrol is rationed, but he has been frugal with coupons; there are enough to provide a full tank. Because of this, plans for the picnic are abandoned—no picnic—her mother thinks, Wouldn't it be a nice gesture to take the soldier out for a restaurant lunch in the nearest city? There won't be many such luxuries for the young man on his way to war in the North African desert.

10 They have never shown her the mine, the diamond mine, although ever since she was a small child they have taken her to places of interest as part of her education. They must have talked about it—her father is a mining-company official himself, but his exploitation is gold, not precious stones—or more likely it has been cited in a general-knowledge text at school: some famous diamond was dug up there.

The camp is on part of the vast mine property, commandeered by the Defense Force. Over the veld there are tents to the horizon, roped and staked, dun as the scuffed and dried grass and the earth scoured by boots—boots tramping everywhere, khaki everywhere, the wearers replicating one another, him. Where will they find him? He did give a tent number. The numbers don't seem to be consecutive. Her father is called to a halt by a replica with a gun, slow-spoken and polite. The car follows given directions retained differently by the mother and the father; the car turns, backs up, take it slowly for heaven's sake.

She is the one: There. There he is.

Of course, when you find him you see that there is no one like him, no bewilderment. They are all laughing in the conventions of greeting, but his eyes have their concentrated attention for her. It is his greeting of the intervals between streetlights, and of the kitchen. This weekend that ends weekends seems also to be the first of winter; it's suddenly cold, wind bellies and whips at that tent where he must have slept, remote, between weekends. It's the weather for hot food, shelter. At the restaurant, he chooses curry and rice for this last meal. He sprinkles grated coconut and she catches his eye and he smiles for her as he adds dollops of chutney. The smile is that of a greedy boy caught out and is also as if it were a hand squeezed under the table. No wine—the father has to drive, and young men oughtn't to be encouraged to drink, enough of that in the Army—but there is ice cream with canned peaches, coffee served, and peppermints with the compliments of the management.

It was too warm in the restaurant. Outside, high-altitude winds carry the breath of what must be early snow on the mountains, far away, unseen, as this drive back to the camp carries the breath of war, far away, unseen, where all the replicas in khaki are going to be shipped. No heating in the family car of those days, the soldier has only his thin, well-pressed khaki and the daughter, of course, like all young girls, has taken no precaution against a change in the weather—she is wearing a skimpy flounced cotton dress (secretly chosen, although he, being older, and a disciple of the sea's mysteries, probably won't even notice) that she was wearing the first time they walked to the cinema. The mother, concealing, she believes, irritation at the fecklessness of the young—next thing she'll have bronchitis and miss school—fortunately keeps a rug handy and insists that the passengers in the back seat put it over their knees.

15 It was easy to chat in the preoccupations of food along with the budgerigar chitter of other patrons in the restaurant. In the car, headed back for that final place, the camp, the outing is over. The father feels an obligation: at least, he can tell something about the diamond mine that's of interest, and soon they'll actually be passing the site of operations again, though you can't see much from the road.

The rug is like the pelt of some dusty pet animal settled over them. The warmth of the meal inside them is bringing it to life, a life they share, one body. It's pleasant to put their hands beneath it; the hands, his right, her left, find one another.

...You know what a diamond is, of course, although you look at it as something pretty a woman wears on her finger, hmm? Well, actually it consists of pure carbon crystallized...

He doesn't like to be interrupted, so there's no need to make any response, even if you still hear him. The right hand and the left hand become so tightly clasped that the pad of muscle at the base of each thumb is flattened against the bone and interlaced fingers are jammed down between the joints. It isn't a clasp against imminent parting, it's got nothing to do with any future, it belongs in the urgent purity of this present.

...The crystallization in regular octahedrons, that's to say eight-sided, and in allied forms and the cut and polished ones you see in jewelry more or less follow...

20 The hands lay together, simply happened, on the skirt over her left thigh, because that is where she had slipped her hand beneath the woolly comfort of the

rug. Now he slowly released, first fingers, then palms—at once awareness signalled between them, that the rug was their tender accomplice, it must not be seen to be stirred by something—he released himself from her and for one bereft moment she thought he had left her behind, his eight-year advantage prevailed against such fusion of palms as it had done, so gently (oh, but why), when they were in the dark between trees, when they were in the kitchen.

...colorless or they may be tinted occasionally yellow, pink, even black...

The hand had not emerged from the rug. She followed as if her eyes were closed or she were in the dark; it went as if it were playing—looking for a place to tickle, as children do to make one another wriggle and laugh—where her skirt ended at her knee, going under her knee without displacing the skirt and touching the tendons and the hollow there. She didn't want to laugh (what would her father make of such a response to his knowledgeable commentary), so she glided her hand to his and put it back with hers where it had been before.

...one of the biggest diamonds in the world after the Koh-i-noor's hundred and nine carats, but that was found in India...

The hand, his hand, pressed fingers into her thigh through the cotton flounce, as if testing to see what was real about her, and stopped, and then out of the hesitation went down and, under the rug, up under the gauze of skirt, moved over her flesh. She did not look at him and he did not look at her.

...and there are industrial gems you can cut glass with, make bits for certain drills, the hardest substance known...

At the taut lip of her panties he hesitated again, no hurry, all something she was learning, he was teaching, the anticipation in his fingertips, he stroked along one of the veins in there in the delicate membranelike skin that is at the crevice between leg and body (like the skin that the sun on Maneuvers couldn't reach in the crook of his elbow), just before the hair begins. And then he went in under the elastic edge and his hand was soft on soft hair, his fingers like eyes attentive to her.

...Look at this veld—nothing suggests one of the greatest ever, anywhere, down there, down in what we call Blue Earth, the diamondiferous core...

She has no clear idea of where his hand is now, what she feels is that they are kissing, they are in each other's mouths although they cannot look at one another.

Are you asleep back there? The mother is remarking her own boredom with the mine. He is eight years older, able to speak: Just listening. His finger explores deep down in the dark, the hidden entrance to some sort of cave with its slippery walls and smooth stalagmite. She's found, he's found her.

The car is passing the mine processing plant.

...product of the death and decay of forests millennia ago, just as coal is, but down there the ultimate alchemy, you might say...

Those others, the parents, they have no way of knowing. It has happened, it is happening under the old woolly rug that was all they could provide for her. She is free of them. Found, and they don't know where she is.

At the camp, the father shakes the soldier's hand longer than in the usual grip. The mother for a moment looks as if she might give him a peck on the cheek, Godspeed, but it is not her way to be familiar.

Aren't you going to say goodbye? She's not a child, good heavens, a mother shouldn't have to remind of manners.

He's standing outside one of the tents with his hands hanging open at his sides as the car is driven away, and his attention is upon her until, with his furry narrowed sight, he'll cease to be able to make her out, while she can still see him, see him until he is made one with all the others in khaki, replicated, crossing and crowding, in preparation to embark.

If he had been killed in that war they would have heard through the grandmother's connections.

Is it still you, somewhere, old.

TRY THIS 2.8

Write a paragraph about a thrilling or anguishing incident from your childhood or adolescence. Evoke the emotion you felt in images of all five senses how the scene (perhaps including your own body) looked to you, sounded, felt, smelled, tasted. Allow yourself whatever personification, metaphor, or simile occurs to you, no matter how extreme.

POEMS

ROGER BONAIR-AGARD

American History looks for light—a prayer for the survival of Barack Obama

...Float like a butterfly, sting like a bee
the hands can't touch what the eyes can't see...
Muhammed Ali

(i) *the bullet speaks of purpose*

Trajectory is everything
the difference between a kiss off
the ribcage or the blessed blood
of a ripe organ   The brain
protests the most   neurons
firing over and around the holy
landing   trying to make sense
of it   the wailing and the vivid

snapshots   metal tendrils reaching
trying to block out the light

(ii) *Malcolm pulls Obama's coat*

there is no doubt
in my mind they will come for you
dozens at a time
miniature fighter planes built
for such an idealism as yours
They are amazing fish
fanning their steel gills
like razors   their fins peeling back
formations neat and orderly as a school
barreling toward the abdomen
heart   spleen   kidney anywhere
there is light

(iii) *Obama plays the dozens*

I'm so fast I'll be gone by trigger time
I'm so bad I beat Hillary by 30
I'm so slick not even Bill could sink me
I'm so badass my name is Barack
I'm so chameleon my name is Hussein
I'm so pretty your Mama canvassed for me
I'm so pretty your Mama voted for me
I'm so pretty your Mama is my Mama
I'm so good I shook up the world
I'm so fast I dodged a circus of bullets
I'm so fast I take off the switch and be in bed
        before the light comes off

(iv) *the bullet takes the bait*

Neither disease nor plane crash
not knife or hurricane or freak accident
is as dramatic as me
See the body begin the decompose
in an instant See the body
become particular See
the body become tendrils
of impressionist thought See how
marvellous my entrances
how devastating my exit wounds
I save my best work for the stage.

(v) *Bruce Lee knows from bullets*

See this fist
this quick a capella kick
kung fu   sho nuff
what   see this
sidestep   Tae Kwon Don't
you never think steel is hard
as bone   -   Barack   I legacy you
Me   -   every dragon flow
strict mantis pose
struck to cobra swift release

Don't you never think
steel is hard as home
See this river flow   bones
see how bullets bury
what they can't kill
See how i live
ecstatic   -   fly jumpsuit
dramatic   -   Barack   I legacy you
Me   -   like i loaned Muhammed
the butterfly and the bee   we stay
vested   -   historically protected B
We battle terrific   Fuck Chuck Norris
me and Jim Kelly's got your hood
and your dome   Don't you never
think steel be hard like stone

BILLY COLLINS

Snow Day

Today we woke up to a revolution of snow,
its white flag waving over everything,
the landscape vanished,
not a single mouse to punctuate the blankness,
and beyond these windows

the government buildings smothered,
schools and libraries buried, the post office lost
under the noiseless drift,
the paths of trains softly blocked,
the world fallen under this falling.

In a while, I will put on some boots

and step out like someone walking in water,
and the dog will porpoise through the drifts,
and I will shake a laden branch
sending a cold shower down on us both.

But for now I am a willing prisoner in this house,
a sympathizer with the anarchic cause of snow.
I will make a pot of tea
and listen to the plastic radio on the counter,
as glad as anyone to hear the news

that the Kiddie Corner School is closed,
the Ding-Dong School, closed,
the All Aboard Children's School, closed,
the Hi-Ho Nursery School, closed,
along with—some will be delighted to hear—

the Toadstool School, the Little School,
Little Sparrows Nursery School,
Little Stars Pre-School, Peas-and-Carrots Day School
the Tom Thumb Child Center, all closed,
and—clap your hands—the Peanuts Play School.

So this is where the children hide all day,
these are the nests where they letter and draw,
where they put on their bright miniature jackets,
all darting and climbing and sliding,
all but the few girls whispering by the fence.

And now I am listening hard
in the grandiose silence of the snow,
trying to hear what those three girls are plotting,
what riot is afoot,
which small queen is about to be brought down.

YUSEF KOMUNYAKAA

Facing It

My black face fades,
hiding inside the black granite.
I said I wouldn't,
dammit: No tears.
I'm stone. I'm flesh.
My clouded reflection eyes me
like a bird of prey, the profile of night
slanted against morning. I turn

this way—the stone lets me go.
I turn that way—I'm inside
the Vietnam Veterans Memorial
again, depending on the light
to make a difference.
I go down the 58,022 names,
half-expecting to find
my own in letters like smoke.
I touch the name Andrew Johnson;
I see the booby trap's white flash.
Names shimmer on a woman's blouse
but when she walks away
the names stay on the wall.
Brushstrokes flash, a red bird's
wings cutting across my stare.
The sky. A plane in the sky.
A white vet's image floats
closer to me, then his pale eyes
look through mine. I'm a window.
He's lost his right arm
inside the stone. In the black mirror
a woman's trying to erase names:
No, she's brushing a boy's hair.

TRY THIS 2.9

Write a paragraph or a poem exploring your relationship with an animal or a machine. Describe the animal or machine using at least three of the senses.

Or:

Write a poem or paragraph about a relationship between surface and depth—in an eye, a mirror, water, metal ...

DRAMA

DON NIGRO

Come into the Garden, Maud

Characters

JOHN: twenty-seven
PHOEBE: twenty-one
JILL: twenty-four

Setting: Stage right, a chair with a small wooden table on which are a lamp and telephone in John's house. Stage left, the same, with a phone book, in Phoebe's house. The rest of the stage is in darkness.

Playwright's Note: Late one night in Malvern, in 1993, the phone rang, and it was a slightly inebriated man who announced, with no preamble whatsoever, "Your cat's in my garden." It took me a long time to convince him that he had the wrong number, as he was, in fact, as I was finally able to establish, attempting to reach a relative of mine with the same last name whose cat kept relieving himself in this man's garden. We finally straightened it out, but for some reason the incident stayed with me. There was something rather unsettling about the ability of a total stranger to make a noise in my kitchen in the middle of the night and thrust one unexpectedly into a violent disagreement about the nature of reality—that is, whether or not there was a cat, or a garden, and if it was my cat, and if my cat was indeed in his garden. It seemed to me to be a rather profound question, somehow. The title is from Tennyson's long poem, Maud, *part of which I set to music for James Joyce to sing in* Lucia Mad.

■ ■ ■

Phoebe turns on the light by her telephone. She wears a rather fetching nightie. She sits, looks up a number in the book, dials. John's telephone rings. After a bit, John appears, wearing only pajama bottoms, turns on his lamp, and picks up the phone.

JOHN: Hello?
PHOEBE: Your cat's in my garden.
JOHN: What?
PHOEBE: Your cat's in my garden.
JOHN: I think you've got the wrong number.
PHOEBE: No I don't.
JOHN: Yes you do.
PHOEBE: Is this the Murphy residence?
JOHN: Yes.
PHOEBE: Your cat's in my garden.
JOHN: Who are you trying to reach?
PHOEBE: Murphy.
JOHN: Well, there's about a hundred Murphys in the phone book. You've just got the wrong one.
PHOEBE: I don't think so.
JOHN: I'm afraid you do. Good-bye.

(He hangs up, turns off the light, and goes, as Phoebe redials. John's phone rings. He returns, turns on the light, picks up the phone.)

Hello?

PHOEBE: Your cat's in my garden.
JOHN: My cat is not in your garden.

PHOEBE: Yes she is. I can see her out my window.

JOHN: Maybe you can see a cat out your window, but it's not mine, because I don't have a cat.

PHOEBE: Yes you do.

JOHN: No I don't.

PHOEBE: I know you have a cat, because it's in my garden.

JOHN: Look, it's four o'clock in the morning, and you have the wrong number, so would you please stop calling me?

PHOEBE: Your cat is in my garden. Don't you care?

JOHN: NO, I DONT CARE, BECAUSE I DON'T HAVE ANY GODDAMNED CAT. I HATE CATS, AND I HATE YOU, SO STOP BOTHERING ME.

(He slams down the phone, turns off the light, goes. Phoebe redials. John's phone rings. He returns, turns on the light, and picks up the phone.)

WHAT?

PHOEBE: That was very rude. Why would you hate me? What did I ever do to you?

JOHN: You keep calling me at four o'clock in the morning.

PHOEBE: Only because your cat's in my garden.

JOHN: MY CAT IS NOT IN YOUR GARDEN.

PHOEBE: I think you're in a serious state of denial.

JOHN: WILL YOU PLEASE JUST LEAVE ME ALONE?

PHOEBE: (*Starting to cry.*) Well, I'm sorry. I was just worried about your cat. You don't have to yell at me.

(*She cries.*)

JOHN: Don't cry. I didn't mean to yell at you. I'm really tired, and you've just called me three times in the middle of the night to tell me my cat's in your garden.

PHOEBE: So you admit it.

JOHN: No, I don't admit it.

PHOEBE: You just said your cat was in my garden.

JOHN: No, I just—what number were you calling?

PHOEBE: Well, yours, of course.

JOHN: Which Murphy were you calling?

PHOEBE: I was calling you.

JOHN: What's my name?

PHOEBE: You mean you don't know?

JOHN: Yes, I know.

PHOEBE: Then what are you asking me for?

JOHN: Looks, Miss—

PHOEBE: Phoebe.

JOHN: Phoebe. That's a lovely name, Phoebe.

PHOEBE: Thank you.

JOHN: The problem is, I don't know anybody named Phoebe.

PHOEBE: You know me.

JOHN: No, I don't know you.

PHOEBE: Yes you do. Your cat's in my garden.

(*Pause.*)

JOHN: What is my cat doing in your garden, Phoebe?

PHOEBE: Wait a minute. Let me look. (*She peers downstage through an invisible window.*) It's really dark out there. When I first called, she was having sexual intercourse. Well, I presume that's what it was. There was certainly a hell of a lot of screaming going on. Cats are a lot like people, don't you think? You really might want to consider getting her fixed.

JILL: (*Entering, wearing the tops of John's pajamas.*) Who are you talking to?

JOHN: Nobody.

PHOEBE: What?

JILL: It must be somebody.

JOHN: It's just some girl who says my cat's in her garden.

PHOEBE: Who's that? Mrs. Murphy?

JOHN: No, it's not.

PHOEBE: You're not cheating on Mrs. Murphy, are you?

JOHN: There is no Mrs. Murphy.

JILL: Johnny, who is that?

JOHN: It's Phoebe.

JILL: Phoebe who?

JOHN: I don't know.

PHOEBE: So you're sleeping with a woman you're not married to? Is that it?

JOHN: Yes, Phoebe, that's it, that is exactly it, I am sleeping with a woman I'm not married to. I hope that doesn't shock you too much.

PHOEBE: I just hope Mrs. Murphy doesn't find out.

JILL: You told me you weren't seeing anybody.

JOHN: I'm not seeing anybody.

PHOEBE: Then who is that woman?

JOHN: I wasn't talking to you, Phoebe. I was talking to Jill.

JILL: I want to know who this Phoebe is, and I want to know right now.

JOHN: It's a wrong number.

JILL: Then how do you know her name?

JOHN: We were just talking.

JILL: Why are you talking to a wrong number?

JOHN: Because she won't shut up.

JILL: Why don't you just hang up the phone?

JOHN: Because she keeps calling back.

JILL: Why would a wrong number keep calling back?

JOHN: She says my cat's in her garden.

JILL: You don't have a cat.

JOHN: I know that.

JILL: I'm going home.

JOHN: No, wait, wait, Jill, I swear it's the truth. Wait. Phoebe, will you tell Jill why you called, please?

PHOEBE: OK.

JOHN: Talk to her.

JILL: I don't want to talk to her.

JOHN: Talk to her. What have you got to lose?

JILL: (*Hesitating, then taking the phone.*) Hello?

PHOEBE: Hi, Jill.

JILL: Who is this?

PHOEBE: This is Phoebe. Listen, Jill, does Mrs. Murphy know you're there?

JILL: John told me he wasn't married.

JOHN: I'm not married. (*Taking the phone.*) Phoebe, just tell her about the cat, all right?

JILL: I don't sleep with married men.

PHOEBE: I don't blame you, Jill.

JOHN: PHOEBE, WILL YOU JUST TELL HER ABOUT THE DAMNED CAT?

PHOEBE: All right, all right. Boy, men get so hysterical when their cats run away, don't they, Jill?

JILL: Phoebe, I'm a little confused here.

PHOEBE: Men confuse me, too. I'd much rather have a cat, but I'm allergic.

JILL: So am I.

PHOEBE: Really? Then how can you sleep with John? Don't you sneeze while you're doing it?

JILL: There's no cat here.

PHOEBE: I know. She's in my garden. And she seems to be growing.

JILL: So John gives you the cat when a woman sleeps over, is that how it works?

PHOEBE: You mean he threw the cat out when he knew you were coming? Boy, is Mrs. Murphy gonna be pissed.

JILL: He says there is no Mrs. Murphy.

PHOEBE: Then who is that tall woman in the straw hat I see watering his flowers all the time?

JILL: John, you son of a bitch, you ARE married.

JOHN: (*Taking the phone.*) Phoebe, what the hell have you been telling her?

JILL: That does it. I'm putting my clothes on and getting out of here. Goodbye, Phoebe.

(*Jill slams down the phone and stomps off.*)

JOHN: Jill. Wait a minute. I can explain this. Well, some of it.

(*He goes after her. Phoebe redials. The phone rings. John returns after a bit, weary, and picks up the phone.*)

Hello, Phoebe. How are you?

PHOEBE: Is Jill all right? I think we got disconnected.

JOHN: Jill has locked herself in the bathroom with her clothes and turned on the shower.

PHOEBE: Gee, I hope she's not going to cut her throat or something.

JOHN: Sounds like a serious option to me, at this point.

PHOEBE: Well, you shouldn't be cheating on your wife like that.

JOHN: I'M NOT MARRIED.

PHOEBE: Then you shouldn't be cheating on that woman in the straw hat.

JOHN: Phoebe, I am not the person you think I am.

PHOEBE: Wait. There's something happening in the garden.

JOHN: What? My cat is eating your watermelons?

PHOEBE: Maybe that's not your cat after all.

JOHN: Oh, no, it's my cat, Phoebe. My cat loves watermelons.

PHOEBE: But this seems to be a lot bigger than a cat. This is a very large object moving in my garden.

JOHN: Maybe it's a bear.

PHOEBE: It could be a bear. I don't know. It seems—

JOHN: What? It's doing the tango, isn't it, Phoebe?

PHOEBE: No, but it seems to have—noticed me. John, there's this big, dark thing in my garden, and it's looking at this window. This is kind of scary. It's so dark out there, I can't see it real clearly, but it seems to be coming toward the house.

JOHN: Phoebe, are you on drugs?

PHOEBE: No, just valium, but it doesn't work on me. This is really spooky. This is pretty alarming. John, could you come over here?

JOHN: I don't know where you live, Phoebe.

PHOEBE: Yes you do. I live right next door.

JOHN: Nobody lives next door to me, Phoebe. There's woods on one side and an empty house on the other.

PHOEBE: It's not empty. It's my house.

JOHN: It isn't your house. Nobody lives there.

PHOEBE: John, this thing is up against the window. It's trying to look in the window at me. You've got to help me.

JOHN: Take it easy, Phoebe. Just tell me your address.

PHOEBE: It's right next to your address. John, it's banging against the window. It wants in my house.

JOHN: Just tell me your last name and I'll look your address up in the phone book.

PHOEBE: You know my last name.

(*Sound of glass shattering.*)

Oh, my God. It broke the glass. John, get over here right now. I mean it. Right now.

(*Blackout on Phoebe. Sound of the dial tone.*)

JOHN: Phoebe? Hello? Did you hang up? I'm talking to a dial tone here. (*John hangs up. Pause.*) Weird. Very weird. (*He waits. The phone rings. He picks it up.*) Hello? Phoebe? Hello? (*Silence from the other end.*) Phoebe? Talk to me. Hello? Is anybody there?

(*The light fades on him and goes out.*)

END OF PLAY

TRY THIS 2.10

Write two pages of dialogue between two people, one on a cell phone, the other on a land line. They disagree about an object, animal, place, or person. Develop the disagreement using concrete significant details. We should learn where each of them is.

WORKING TOWARD A DRAFT

Take any passage you have written and underline the abstractions, especially the names of qualities and judgments. Replace each of these with its opposite. In some instances this will make nonsense. In some it may provide an insight. Do any of the changes suggest a way of enriching your idea? Pursue the possibility in a few paragraphs of focused freewrite (see page 6).

Look over the exercises you have done and the passages in your journal, and pick one that interests you. Draw a grid with six boxes across and ten down. Then, with that passage in mind, write at random in a scattering of the boxes:

Five nouns
Five verbs
Four adjectives
Three adverbs
Four exclamations

Now fill in the boxes in such a way as to connect the words into sentences. Again, some may be nonsense. Some may be, or suggest, poetry. Do any give you insight into the piece you were thinking about?

CHAPTER 3

Voice

- *Your Voice*
- *Persona*
- *Irony*
- *Character Voice*
- *Point of View*

Finding your own voice as a writer is in some ways like the tricky business of becoming an adult . . . you try on other people's personalities for size and you fall in love.

A. Alvarez

"Queen of the Scottish Faeries" Illustration by Rutu Modan 2007

WARM-UP

Write a speech balloon for each of these characters. Then write a paragraph in the voice of each. Try for subject matter, attitude, word choice, word order, and rhythm such that each paragraph comes recognizably from this character and none of the others.

YOU PICK UP THE PHONE AND SOMEONE SAYS, "HELLO. You're home, are you?" and with just these five words you know, although you haven't heard from him for ten years, that Uncle Ed is calling. You turn on the radio and hear "...because the American people..." and before the familiar phrase is out you know exactly which politician is giving a speech. How do you recognize these voices? How is it possible to be so certain with so little information?

Of course, when you literally *hear* a voice, you have many subtle aural clues—accent, volume, tone, timbre, pitch, rhythm—to help you identify it. As a writer you have only the words, their choice and arrangement, with which to create a unique voice. Yet writers' voices are recognizable, too. They too create patterns that approximate all the qualities named above. As a reader you fall in love with particular poetic or narrative voices and as a writer you may "try on" or imitate those voices as part of the process of finding your own.

Diction (which is a combination of **vocabulary,** the words chosen, and **syntax,** the order in which they are used) can impart particularity to a poem or prose just as tone and pitch and timbre make up a particular voice. Diction will convey not only the facts but what we are to make of them, not only the situation but its emotional coloration, not only the identity but also the attitude of the person who speaks to us from the page. Joan Didion expresses this phenomenon in terms of "grammar," in the essay "Why I Write":

> All I know about grammar...is its infinite power. To shift the structure of a sentence alters the meaning of that sentence, as definitely and inflexibly as the position of a camera alters the meaning of the object photographed. Many people know about camera angles now, but not so many people know about sentences. The arrangement of the words matters, and the arrangement you want can be found in the picture in your mind.

Beyond imitation, if as a writer you pay attention to the image in your mind, and if you develop the flexibility of vocabulary and syntax that allows you to be true to that image, you will be on your way to a voice that is recognizably your own.

Your Voice

> We can only talk about ourselves in the language we have available. If that language is rich, it illuminates us. But if it is narrow or restricted, it represses and conceals us.
>
> *Jaan Whitehead*

An author's voice has a quality developed over time, involving recurrent word choice, syntax, imagery, idiom, rhythm, and range. It comes about by a mostly automatic process, the result of practice and the growing confidence that practice brings. Don't worry about "finding your voice." Worry about saying things as clearly, precisely, and vividly as you can. Make your language as rich, flexible, and varied as you can make it. In other words: seek *to voice,* and *your voice* will follow.

The language that comes naturally to you is the fine and proper foundation of your voice. Nothing rings more false than a writer who puts on the airs of critical jargon or medieval fantasy or high culture, without having a convincing command of that language. On the other hand, training your awareness of language, stretching both the quantity and the flexibility of your vocabulary, playing at different human voices, can all expand your range.

It can't hurt to go about adding to your vocabulary in even a self-improvement sort of way—buy a word-a-day calendar, subscribe to "Wordsmith" or "Merriam Webster's Word of the Day" online, read "On Language" in the Sunday magazine of the *New York Times.* Buy a really good dictionary. Dissect the diction of the authors you read, and if you don't know a word, look it up. Every writer I know owns a *Roget's Thesaurus,* a blessed aid to locating—not a fancier word to say what you mean! (that *chicken* is not, really, a *chanticleer*)—but the word with that exact shade of meaning you almost have in mind (it might well be a *broiler* or a *bantam* or a *Rhode Island Red*).

Alert yourself to language as it is used around you. Listen to people talking, note the flavor of different idioms, record bits of conversation, wander around in the dictionary, push the words around on the page. When you get to the point of revising your manuscript, pay attention to the small unease this or that word occasions in you and focus on how it might please you better.

Begin by knowing, and exploring, the fact that you already have a number of different voices. You speak differently in class from the way you speak (even to the same people) at a party or a bar. You have one diction for your diary and another for your history paper. You use one style of vocabulary and syntax to console a friend and another to ditch a date.

You also have a different vocabulary for shades of meaning, so that according to the circumstances you might describe someone as *stuck-up, snobbish, arrogant, haughty,* or *imperious.* There is no such thing as an exact synonym. Each word would be appropriate to a description of a different person, a different mood or tone, a different medium, even a different speaker.

TRY THIS 3.1

Stuck-up, snobbish, arrogant, haughty, imperious. Pick three of these words and produce an image in words of a person who fits each of them. To what extent does "the picture dictate the arrangement" of the words?

Then:

Pick one of the following words and list as many synonyms for it as you can. Pick three of the synonyms and produce an image in words that expresses each. How do the images differ?

awesome
shabby
weird
far
smart
red

Persona

> And so there exists a definite sense of a *person*, a perfectly *knowable* person, behind the poem.
>
> *Mary Oliver*

A **persona** is a mask adopted by the author, which may be a public manifestation of the author's self, or a distorted or partial version of that self, or a fictional, historical, or mythological character. The concept of a persona allows us to acknowledge that, just as no written account can tell the whole truth about an event, so no "I" of a poem, essay, or story is exactly the same as the person who writes. When you write "as yourself" in your own voice—in a personal essay or a lyric poem, for example—there is nevertheless a certain distance between the person you are as you go about living your daily life and the *persona* in which you write. The version of yourself that you choose to reveal is part of your meaning. No matter how earnest your attempt to tell "exactly what happened," "the author" is always a partial or slightly idealized you, writing from a frame of mind more focused and consistent—and probably more virtuous—than any person ever possessed. Even if you are confessing terrible sins, you write as one-who-confesses, which is a particular, and admirable, version of your composite total self.

When you speak in your "own" voice, that voice may be relatively intimate and confiding—one that, though artful, we trust to be as honest with us as possible, as in this memoir-poem of Anne Sexton's, "Young."

> A thousand doors ago
> when I was a lonely kid
> in a big house with four
> garages and it was summer
> as long as I could remember
> I lay on the lawn at night,
> clover wrinkling under me,
> the wise stars bedding over me,
> my mother's window a funnel
> of yellow heat running out,
> my father's window, half shut,
> an eye where sleepers pass
> and the boards of the house
> were smooth and white as wax
> and probably a million leaves
> sailed on their strange stalks
> as the crickets ticked together
> and I, in my brand new body,
> which was not a woman's yet,
> told the stars my questions
> and thought God could really see
> the heat and the painted light,
> elbows, knees, dreams, goodnight.

Here one may feel how the words are "found in the picture" in the poet's mind, how for example the "thousand doors ago" or the "window a funnel of yellow heat running out" reach for an exactness of image, mood, and memory. But the diction might instead signal a more fanciful mask, like this one in which Anne Sexton plays on a conventional image of power and malevolence for her persona:

Her Kind

I have gone out, a possessed witch,
haunting the black air, braver at night;
dreaming evil, I have done my hitch
over the plain houses, light by light:
lonely thing, twelve-fingered, out of mind.
A woman like that is not a woman, quite.
I have been her kind....

Prose writers can exercise a similar range of personae. One way of looking at the author of a memoir or personal essay is that that writer is the main character or protagonist of a true story. Again, the persona may be confessional and direct:

> When my family packed up and moved from the backwoods of Tennessee to the backwoods of Ohio I was not quite six years old. Like most children at that age I was still a two-legged smudge. Hardly a thing about me was definite except my way of talking, and that soon landed me in trouble. The kids in Ohio took one listen to my Tennessee accent and decided I was a hick. They let me know their opinion by calling me not only hick but hillbilly, ridge runner, clodhopper, and hayseed.

"Coming from the Country," Scott Russell Sanders

But this is far from the only way you might choose to present your "self" as author. Any number of masks may be donned. Here is Dave Barry writing from the persona of Ignorant Literal-Minded Guy, a mask that has been enormously popular among American essayists since Mark Twain:

> ...obviously the real cause of the California electricity shortage is: college students. I base this statement on widespread observation of my son, who is a college student, and who personally consumes more electricity than Belgium. If my son is in a room, then every electrical device within 200 yards of that room—every light, computer, television, stereo, video game, microwave oven, etc.—will be running. My son doesn't even have to turn the devices on; they activate themselves spontaneously in response to his presence.

This comic persona depends partly on exaggeration and an inflated vocabulary, out of tone in relation to the content: *widespread observation, personally consumes, electrical device, spontaneously in response.* It also mocks scientific logic, "basing the statement" on a single case.

TRY THIS 3.2

Imagine (remember?) that you have borrowed ("borrowed"?) a car and been involved in a fender bender. Write an explanation for the police report. Write a **monologue** (a speech for one voice) explaining the accident to the friend (parent?) whose car you borrowed. Write a letter telling about it to a friend who thinks you are truly cool.

Irony

The great critic and teacher Lionel Trilling identified three sorts of **irony** available to the writer.

1. Verbal irony: the device by which we say one thing and mean another.
2. Dramatic irony: the mainly theatrical device by which the audience has crucial information that the characters do not.
3. Cosmic irony: our perception of the human condition, in which our efforts are thwarted, often by our best intentions.

The first of these, verbal irony, is a way of using voice. It is achieved by some sort of mismatch between the tone and the content and is capable of myriad effects: serious, comic, threatening, satirical, and so forth. Sarcasm is a crude manifestation of everyday irony: "I really do appreciate you emptying the cat box while I'm eating." The previous passage by Dave Berry is an example of irony as comedy, the tone suggesting scientific objectivity, the content a domestic complaint. A mismatch between tone and content can also set the scene, as in the understated opening to Michael Chabon's literary detective novel *The Yiddish Policemen's Union.*

> Nine months Landsman's been flopping at the hotel Zamenhof without any of his fellow residents managing to get themselves murdered. Now somebody has put a bullet in the brain of the occupant of 208. . . .

Or it can convey a political point, as in Jonathan Swift's famous "A Modest Proposal," in which he enthusiastically "solves" both the overpopulation and the food shortage in Ireland.

> I have been assured by a very knowing American of my acquaintance in London, that a young healthy child well nursed is at a year old a most delicious, nourishing, and wholesome food, whether stewed, roasted, baked, or boiled. . . .

Irony is often achieved by using formal or understated language for extreme events, but it can also be a way of characterizing through the voice of someone who makes verbal mountains of molehills. This is Doris from the monologue *A Cream Cracker Under the Settee* by Alan Bennett:

> Couple came round last week. Braying on the door. They weren't bona fide callers, they had a Bible. I didn't go. Only they opened the letter box and started shouting about Jesus. "Good news," they kept shouting.

"Good news." They left the gate open, never mind good news. They ought to get their priorities right. Shouting about Jesus and leaving gates open. It's hypocrisy is that.

TRY THIS 3.3

Pick a story from today's newspaper about an outrageous or terrible event. Write a paragraph about it in the tone of an official who considers it politically necessary, a Sunday school teacher explaining it as God's plan, or a social scientist analyzing it for current trends.

Then:

Write a paragraph about a trivial matter (dividing a cookie, breaking a fingernail, the coffee being too hot, or something similar) in a tone of outrage.

Character Voice

"I'll tell my state as though 'twere none of mine."

Robert Browning

In ways other than ironic, you may also speak in the persona of a character who is largely or totally unlike you. A **character**'s voice is a chosen mimicry and is one of the most rewarding devices of imaginative writing, a skill to pursue in order to develop rich characters both in their narratives and in their dialogue. Your voice will never be entirely absent from the voice of the characters you create, but the characters too can be distinct and recognizable.

The voice of a character requires, beyond invention, an imaginative leap into the mind and diction of another person. The best way to develop this capability is, first, to listen to other people speaking and to become aware of their speech patterns, vocabulary choice, habits of diction; and then to practice launching yourself into the voices you have heard. You already have a foundation for this skill through your knowledge of other writers' efforts. Here, for example, are some very brief examples, most of them familiar to you, of characters announcing their own identities. Notice how much they tell you about themselves, the worlds they inhabit, and their attitudes, in a very few words:

Call me Ishmael. (*Moby Dick,* Herman Melville)

My name is Bond—James Bond. (the series of Bond novels by Ian Fleming)

My name is Ozymandias, King of Kings.
Look on my works, ye mighty, and despair. (*Ozymandias,* Percy Bysshe Shelley)

Out of the ash
I rise with my red hair.
And I eat men like air. (*Lady Lazarus,* Sylvia Plath)

I am but mad north-northwest: when the wind is southerly, I know a hawk from a handsaw. (*Hamlet,* Shakespeare)

I am the resurrection, and the life: he that believeth in me, though he were dead, yet shall he live. (John 11:25)

I am a man more sinn'd against than sinning. (*King Lear,* Shakespeare)

If you really want to hear about it, the first thing you'll probably want to know is where I was born, and what my lousy childhood was like, and how my parents were occupied and all before they had me, and all that David Copperfield kind of crap....(*The Catcher in the Rye,* J. D. Salinger)

When I look back on my childhood, I wonder how I survived at all. It was, of course, a miserable childhood: the happy childhood is hardly worth your while. Worse than the ordinary miserable childhood is the miserable Irish childhood, and worse yet is the miserable Irish Catholic childhood. (*Angela's Ashes,* Frank McCourt)

TRY THIS 3.4
Write a short character sketch of someone in your family. Write a monologue in which that person tells you an anecdote from his or her childhood.

You could say, and be roughly accurate, that there is a hierarchy of distance between the author and the voice. The memoirist or personal essayist is most likely to be closest to the person writing; the lyric poet is somewhat more distanced by the artifice of the language; the fiction writer has a range of masks from "author" to characters; and the dramatist speaks only through the characters, theoretically never speaking in his/her own voice except in stage directions.

The voices that you as author create involve not just word choice but the fundamental human capacity for mimicry—which, however, can be deliberately cultivated by careful listening, trial, and error. A character's voice comes out of, and can convey, a historical period, a class, a set of circumstances, emotions, and the myriad quirks of typicality and eccentricity. Think of the differences in speech between a televangelist and a hip-hop groupie, or even a "master stylist" and the neighborhood barber. Voice, said Philip Roth, is "something that begins at around the back of the knees and reaches well above the head."

Great potential for contrast, irony, and conflict enters the writing when one voice is set off against another. Characters reveal themselves in conversation and confrontation not only in the ideas they consciously express but in the diction they use, the things that "just slip out," and the things they refuse or fail to say. The next chapter will look at dialogue, which can lead not only to character revelation but to the heart of story, which is discovery and decision.

TRY THIS 3.5

Go back to the character in your "bumper sticker" exercise on page 21. Find a few more details to describe that character. Then pick a trigger line from those below and use it to start a monologue in that character's voice. If you feel you are not catching the voice, never mind; keep going.

- I don't normally dress this way, but...
- I had a dream last night...
- I'll tell you what doesn't make any sense...
- I'm sorry, I didn't see you...
- What I need is some kind of work that...
- I remember when you could...

Point of View

> I am the narrator. I am just up in the sky telling the story. I just know everything. So pay no attention to me.
>
> *Josiah Sable, ten years old*

Closely allied to the concept of voice is **point of view.** We're used to using the phrase "point of view" as a synonym for "opinion," as in, "It's my point of view that young people watch too much television." But point of view as a literary technique is a complex and specific concept, dealing with vantage point and addressing the question: *Who* is standing *where* to watch the scene? The answer will involve the voice of the teller, the intended listener, and the distance or closeness of both the action and the diction. An author's view of the world, as it is and as it ought to be, will ultimately be revealed by manipulation of the point of view, but not vice versa—identifying the author's beliefs will not describe the point of view of the work.

Point of view is a slippery concept, but one over which you gradually gain control as you write. Apart from significant detail, there is no more important skill for a writer to grasp, for, as Carol Bly says in *The Passionate, Accurate Story,* these are the two skills that "divide master from apprentice." Once you have chosen a point of view, you have in effect made a "contract" with the reader, and it will be difficult to break the contract gracefully. If you have restricted yourself to the mind of Sally Anne for five pages, as she longingly watches Chuck and his R&B band, you will violate the contract by suddenly dipping into Chuck's mind to let us know what he thinks of groupies. We are likely to feel misused—and likely to cancel the contract altogether if you suddenly give us an omniscient lecture on the failings of the young.

The first point of view decision that you as a writer must make is the **person** in which you speak: *first person* (I walked out into the rain), *second person* (You walked out into the rain), or *third person* (She walked out into the rain).

All of the examples of persona in this chapter so far are in the **first person:** *I was a lonely kid...I have gone out, a possessed witch...I was not quite six years old...I base this statement...Call me Ishmael,* and so forth. The first person is the point of view most frequent in memoir, personal essay, and lyric poetry. Characters in a play speak, of course, in the first person. It is also the voice of much fiction, in which case it will be the voice of the **central narrator,** the *I* writing *my* story as if it were memoir; or else of a **peripheral narrator,** someone on the edge of the action, but nevertheless our eyes and ears in the story and therefore the person with whom we identify and with whom we must be moved or changed if the story is to succeed.

Notice that when you are writing in the first person voice of a fictional or dramatic character, the whole range of intimacy and distance is also possible in the diction. Bohumil Hrabel's young railway employee in the novel *Closely Observed Trains* tells his own story and takes us into his confidence as if he were writing a confessional memoir, in spite of the fact that he never existed:

> I always had the impression—and I still have and always shall have—that behind every window there was at the very least one pair of eyes watching me. If anyone spoke to me I blushed, because I felt uncomfortably aware that there was something about me that disturbed and upset everybody. Three months ago I slashed my wrists, and on the face of it I had no reason to do such a thing, but I did have a reason, and I knew what it was, and I was only afraid that everyone who looked at me was guessing at what that reason could be.

By contrast, in the play *Our Country's Good,* Timberlake Wertenberger's Judge Collins of eighteenth-century Australia uses the distanced diction of profound and self-satisfied authority:

> This land is under English law. The court found them guilty and sentenced them accordingly...I commend your endeavor to oppose the baneful influence of vice with the harmonizing acts of civilization, Governor, but I suspect your edifice will collapse without the mortar of fear.

The **second person** is being used whenever the pronoun "you" occurs, but this may simply mean, in dialogue, that one character is addressing another. Sometimes it indicates not the point of view of the story but a general truth, possibly one in a character's mind:

> Maureen was trying to write her weekly letter to Len. It was heavy going; you can't say much in a letter.

The Ice Age, *Margaret Drabble*

Or the pronoun "you" may represent the convention of the author addressing the reader:

> You might think it's a bit rare, having long-distance cross-country runners in Borstal...but you're wrong, and I'll tell you why.

The Loneliness of the Long Distance Runner, *Alan Sillitoe*

Often, as in this case, the "you" refers to the person who is assumed to read or receive the piece. The basic point of view is still first person, as it is in Sharon Olds's poem "Feared Drowned," of which these are the first two stanzas:

> Suddenly nobody knows where you are,
> your suit black as seaweed, your bearded
> head slick as a seal's.
>
> Somebody watches the kids. I walk down the
> edge of the water, clutching the towel
> like a widow's shawl around me...

This use of the second person, as someone to whom speech, a poem, or story is addressed, can enhance a sense of intimacy, even make us feel as readers/viewers that we are overhearing something private.

The **second person** is the basic point of view of a piece only when the "you" is a character—usually in fact the reader, whom the author *turns into* a character by assuming she knows just how "you" behave in the situation she invents. Here is an example from Lorrie Moore's story "How to Be a Writer":

> First, try to be something, anything, else. A movie star/astronaut. A movie star/missionary. The movie star/kindergarten teacher. President of the World. Fail miserably. It is best if you fail at an early age—say, fourteen. Early, critical disillusionment is necessary so that at fifteen you can write long haiku sequences about thwarted desire. It is a pond, a cherry blossom, a wind brushing against sparrow wing leaving for mountain. Count the syllables. Show it to your mom.

The second person as a basic point of view, in which "you" become the character, tends to be experimental and self-conscious, and may be set aside or saved for special effects.

TRY THIS 3.6

Write about a situation in which you were badly stressed. But write about it in the first person *from the point of view of someone else* who was present.

Or:

Write about it in the second person, keeping in mind that you're trying to make your reader identify and "become you."

The **third person** is frequently used in poetry and fiction, as well as being the basic voice of the nonfiction writer. This is the voice with the greatest range of effects, from total objectivity to great intimacy.

The third person voice in imaginative writing can be roughly divided into three techniques:

- The **omniscient** or godlike narrator, who may know anything past, present, or future and is free to tell us readers what to think or feel

- The **limited omniscient,** who may go into the mind of one or perhaps two characters and also observe from the outside
- The **objective,** who may know no more than a person observing the scene—the facts and whatever is present to the senses

The omniscient author was a frequent stance of nineteenth-century fiction, where the persona of "author" took on an all-knowing quality:

> Caroline Helstone was just eighteen years old; and at eighteen the true narrative of life has yet to be commenced. Before that time, we sit listening to a tale, a marvelous fiction; delightful sometimes, and sad sometimes; almost always unreal. . . . Hope, when she smiles on us, and promises happiness tomorrow, is implicitly believed;—Love, when he comes wandering like a lost angel to our door, is at once admitted, welcomed, embraced. . . . Alas, Experience! No other mentor has so wasted and frozen a face . . .

Shirley, *Charlotte Brontë*

This voice obviously involves a lot of "telling," and in order to avoid that outdated tone, in the twentieth century it became usual for "the author" to assume the more modest capability of the limited omniscient, able to go into one character's mind and emotions and also to tell us objectively what, if we were present, we would be able to perceive for ourselves, but not to leap from the mind of one character to another.

> By the time they were halfway through Harvard Yard, Tip was seriously questioning the wisdom of his own decision to leave the house at all. His leg had progressed far beyond aching. The pain in his sciatic nerve was sharp and somewhat electrical in nature. . . . He had, despite all better knowledge, dug the crutches into his brachial plexus and slowly crushed it, sending a radiation up his neck and into the back of his head that was like a persistent hammer slamming a reluctant nail.

Run, *Ann Patchett*

The perception in these two passages involves the vulnerability and inexperience of youth, but in the first the convention of "the author" holds all the answers, whereas in the second "the author" is an unvoiced presence. We experience Tip's pain and his self-questioning from the inside, while at the same time getting a quasiscientific explanation of the source of pain. Since Tip is a scientist, this factual information is appropriate to the character.

In the objective viewpoint, the author may choose a strictly journalistic stance, reporting only what may be seen, heard, smelled, tasted, touched, and objectively known. This is a favorite stance of Ernest Hemingway. In the story, "Hills Like White Elephants," Hemingway reports what is said and done by a quarreling couple, both without any direct revelation of the characters' thoughts and without comment.

> The American and the girl with him sat at a table in the shade, outside the building. It was very hot and the express from Barcelona would come in forty minutes. It stopped at this junction for two minutes and went on to Madrid.
>
> "What should we drink?" the girl asked. She had taken off her hat and put it on the table.
>
> "It's pretty hot," the man said.
>
> "Let's drink beer."
>
> "Dos cervezas," the man said into the curtain.
>
> "Big ones?" a woman asked from the doorway.
>
> "Yes. Two big ones."
>
> The woman brought two glasses of beer and two felt pads. She put the felt pads and the beer glasses on the table and looked at the man and the girl. The girl was looking off at the line of hills. They were white in the sun and the country was brown and dry.

The narrative remains clipped, austere, and external. What Hemingway gains by this pretense of objective reporting is that the reader is allowed to discover what is really happening through gestures, repetitions, and slips of the tongue, as in life.

TRY THIS 3.7

Take any passage you have written in the first person and recast it in the objective voice. Try to reveal the thoughts and feelings of the original through speech, gesture, action, and image.

Beyond the choice of person, point of view importantly involves the question of the **distance** between the author/reader and the characters. John Gardner in *The Art of Fiction* succinctly illustrates some of the possibilities of distance in the third person:

1. It was winter of the year 1853. A large man stepped out of a doorway.
2. Henry J. Warburton had never cared much for snowstorms.
3. Henry hated snowstorms.
4. God how he hated these damn snowstorms.
5. Snow. Under your collar, down inside our shoes, freezing and plugging up your miserable soul.

From the impersonality of *large man* through increasingly familiar designations (full name, first name, pronoun), to the identification implied in the second person (*your collar, your shoes, your soul*), these examples reduce the formality of the diction and therefore the psychic and psychological distance between the author-and-reader and the character.

The degree of distance will involve a series of questions, of which *who speaks?* is only the first. It will also involve *to whom?* (the reader? another character? the self?), *in what form?* (a story? a journal? a report? a daydream?), *at what distance?*

(an old man telling the story of his youth? a prisoner recounting his crime?), and *with what limitations?* (is the narrator a liar? a child? crazy?). The voice of the speaker, whether autobiographical, poetic persona, narrator, or character, always involves these issues. Because the author *inevitably wants to convince us to share the same perspective,* the answers will also help reveal her or his final opinion, judgment, attitude, or message.

In many ways, our language has been impoverished—by politics, ads, ignorance, and suspicion of eloquence. In the Renaissance it was socially valuable to be able to speak well; you could talk yourself into court or into bed. Whereas in America, and especially from the latter half of the twentieth century, we have tended to equate eloquence with arrogance at best and dishonesty at worst, preferring people who, like, you know, well, kinda couldn't exactly, like, say what they mean. Sort of. Whole concepts have disappeared via advertising from our fund of expression. We no longer have meaningful ways to say *the real thing,* or *the right choice,* or *new and improved,* or *makes you feel young again,* or *just do it.* The words *wonderful, great, grand, distinctive, elegant, exclusive, purity, pleasure, passion, mastery, mystery,* and *natural* have been co-opted and corrupted. If I say so much as, "Ask your doctor..." it's clear that I've got something to sell.

Paradoxically, this impoverishment allows the writer myriad ways to characterize. Though it may be difficult to write convincingly from the lofty perspective of all-knowing authority, a rich awareness of voice and voices, their particular idioms and diction, can give you a range of perspectives from which to write. You can make legitimate and revealing use of jargon, cliché, malapropisms (misused words), overstatement, and so forth, in the mouth of a character. Such language is a way of signaling distance between author and character, a distance that the reader understands and shares. A famous example is Amanda Wingfield of Tennessee Williams's *The Glass Menagerie,* who here berates her son:

> Oh, I can see the handwriting on the wall as plain as I see the nose in front of my face! It's terrifying! More and more you remind me of your father! He was out all hours without explanation—then *left!* And me with the bag to hold.

TRY THIS 3.8

Write a speech in which a character strings together a bunch of clichés or jargon phrases. Let the clichés characterize. However, be sure you have some sympathy for the character.

If you persevere in writing, "your voice" will inevitably take on a coloration that is entirely your own. At the same time, voice is a powerful force for exploring the inner lives of others. Story writer Grace Paley describes the process: "...what we write about is *what we don't know about what we know*...when you take this other voice—you're making a 'pull.' You're pulling towards another head. And that pull toward what you *don't* know...well, that's the story itself. The story is that stretching...that *act* of stretching."

More to Read

Oliver, Mary. *A Poetry Handbook.* New York: Harcourt Brace, 1994. Print.
Alvarez, A. *The Writer's Voice.* New York: W. W. Norton, 2005. Print.

READINGS

CREATIVE NONFICTION

ALICE WALKER

Beauty: When the Other Dancer Is the Self

It is a bright summer day in 1947. My father, a fat, funny man with beautiful eyes and a subversive wit, is trying to decide which of his eight children he will take with him to the county fair. My mother, of course, will not go. She is knocked out from getting most of us ready: I hold my neck stiff against the pressure of her knuckles as she hastily completes the braiding and then beribboning of my hair.

My father is the driver for the rich old white lady up the road. Her name is Miss Mey. She owns all the land for miles around, as well as the house in which we live. All I remember about her is that she once offered to pay my mother thirty-five cents for cleaning her house, raking up piles of her magnolia leaves, and washing her family's clothes, and that my mother—she of no money, eight children, and a chronic earache—refused it. But I do not think of this in 1947. I am two and a half years old. I want to go everywhere my daddy goes. I am excited at the prospect of riding in a car. Someone has told me fairs are fun. That there is room in the car for only three of us doesn't faze me at all. Whirling happily in my starchy frock, showing off my biscuit-polished patent-leather shoes and lavender socks, tossing my head in a way that makes my ribbons bounce, I stand, hands on hips, before my father. "Take me, Daddy," I say with assurance; "I'm the prettiest!"

Later, it does not surprise me to find myself in Miss Mey's shiny black car, sharing the back seat with the other lucky ones. Does not surprise me that

I thoroughly enjoy the fair. At home that night I tell the unlucky ones all I can remember about the merry-go-round, the man who eats live chickens, and the teddy bears, until they say: that's enough, baby Alice. Shut up now, and go to sleep.

It is Easter Sunday, 1950. I am dressed in a green, flocked, scalloped-hem dress (handmade by my adoring sister, Ruth) that has its own smooth satin petticoat and tiny hot-pink roses tucked into each scallop. My shoes, new T-strap patent leather, again highly biscuit-polished. I am six years old and have learned one of the longest Easter speeches to be heard that day, totally unlike the speech I said when I was two: "Easter lilies/pure and white/blossom in/the morning light." When I rise to give my speech I do so on a great wave of love and pride and expectation. People in the church stop rustling their new crinolines. They seem to hold their breath. I can tell they admire my dress, but it is my spirit, bordering on sassiness (womanishness), they secretly applaud.

5 "That girl's a little *mess*," they whisper to each other, pleased.

Naturally I say my speech without stammer or pause, unlike those who stutter, stammer, or, worst of all, forget. This is before the word "beautiful" exists in people's vocabulary, but "Oh, isn't she the *cutest* thing!" frequently floats my way. "And got so much sense!" they gratefully add...for which thoughtful addition I thank them to this day.

It was great fun being cute. But then, one day, it ended.

I am eight years old and a tomboy. I have a cowboy hat, cowboy boots, checkered shirt and pants, all red. My playmates are my brothers, two and four years older than I. Their colors are black and green, the only difference in the way we are dressed. On Saturday nights we all go to the picture show, even my mother; Westerns are her favorite kind of movie. Back home, "on the ranch," we pretend we are Tom Mix, Hopalong Cassidy, Lash LaRue (we've even named one of our dogs Lash LaRue); we chase each other for hours rustling cattle, being outlaws, delivering damsels from distress. Then my parents decide to buy my brothers guns. These are not "real" guns. They shoot "BBs," copper pellets my brothers say will kill birds. Because I am a girl, I do not get a gun. Instantly I am relegated to the position of Indian. Now there appears a great distance between us. They shoot and shoot at everything with their new guns. I try to keep up with my bow and arrows.

One day while I am standing on top of our makeshift garage—pieces of tin nailed across some poles—holding my bow and arrow and looking out toward the fields, I feel an incredible blow in my right eye. I look down just in time to see my brother lower his gun.

10 Both brothers rush to my side. My eye stings, and I cover it with my hand. "If you tell," they say, "we will get a whipping. You don't want that to happen, do you?" I do not. "Here is a piece of wire," says the older brother, picking it

up from the roof; "say you stepped on one end of it and the other flew up and hit you." The pain is beginning to start. "Yes," I say. "Yes, I will say that is what happened." If I do not say this is what happened, I know my brothers will find ways to make me wish I had. But now I will say anything that gets me to my mother.

Confronted by our parents we stick to the lie agreed upon. They place me on a bench on the porch and I close my left eye while they examine the right. There is a tree growing from underneath the porch that climbs past the railing to the roof. It is the last thing my right eye sees. I watch as its trunk, its branches, and then its leaves are blotted out by the rising blood.

I am in shock. First there is intense fever, which my father tries to break using lily leaves bound around my head. Then there are chills: my mother tries to get me to eat soup. Eventually, I do not know how, my parents learn what has happened. A week after the "accident" they take me to see a doctor. "Why did you wait so long to come?" he asks, looking into my eye and shaking his head. "Eyes are sympathetic," he says. "If one is blind, the other will likely become blind too."

This comment of the doctor's terrifies me. But it is really how I look that bothers me most. Where the BB pellet struck there is a glob of whitish scar tissue, a hideous cataract, on my eye. Now when I stare at people—a favorite pastime, up to now—they will stare back. Not at the "cute" little girl, but at her scar. For six years I do not stare at anyone, because I do not raise my head.

Years later, in the throes of a mid-life crisis, I ask my mother and sister whether I changed after the "accident." "No," they say, puzzled. "What do you mean?"

What do I mean? 15

I am eight, and, for the first time, doing poorly in school, where I have been something of a whiz since I was four. We have just moved to the place where the "accident" occurred. We do not know any of the people around us because this is a different county. The only time I see the friends I knew is when we go back to our old church. The new school is the former state penitentiary. It is a large stone building, cold and drafty, crammed to overflowing with boisterous, ill-disciplined children. On the third floor there is a huge circular imprint of some partition that has been torn out.

"What used to be here?" I ask a sullen girl next to me on our way past it to lunch.

"The electric chair," says she.

At night I have nightmares about the electric chair, and about all the people reputedly "fried" in it. I am afraid of the school, where all the students seem to be budding criminals.

"What's the matter with your eye?" they ask, critically. 20

When I don't answer (I cannot decide whether it was an "accident" or not), they shove me, insist on a fight.

My brother, the one who created the story about the wire, comes to my rescue. But then brags so much about "protecting" me, I become sick.

After months of torture at the school, my parents decide to send me back to our old community, to my old school. I live with my grandparents and the teacher they board. But there is no room for Phoebe, my cat. By the time my grandparents decide there *is* room, and I ask for my cat, she cannot be found. Miss Yarborough, the boarding teacher, takes me under her wing, and begins to teach me to play the piano. But soon she marries an African—a "prince," she says—and is whisked away to his continent.

At my old school there is at least one teacher who loves me. She is the teacher who "knew me before I was born" and bought my first baby clothes. It is she who makes life bearable. It is her presence that finally helps me turn on the one child at the school who continually calls me "one-eyed bitch." One day I simply grab him by his coat and beat him until I am satisfied. It is my teacher who tells me my mother is ill.

My mother is lying in bed in the middle of the day, something I have never seen. She is in too much pain to speak. She has an abscess in her ear. I stand looking down on her, knowing that if she dies, I cannot live. She is being treated with warm oils and hot bricks held against her cheek. Finally a doctor comes. But I must go back to my grandparents' house. The weeks pass but I am hardly aware of it. All I know is that my mother might die, my father is not so jolly, my brothers still have their guns, and I am the one sent away from home.

"You did not change," they say.

Did I imagine the anguish of never looking up?

I am twelve. When relatives come to visit I hide in my room. My cousin Brenda, just my age, whose father works in the post office and whose mother is a nurse, comes to find me. "Hello," she says. And then she asks, looking at my recent school picture, which I did not want taken, and on which the "glob," as I think of it, is clearly visible, "You still can't see out of that eye?"

"No," I say, and flop back on the bed over my book.

That night, as I do almost every night, I abuse my eye. I rant and rave at it, in front of the mirror. I plead with it to clear up before morning. I tell it I hate and despise it. I do not pray for sight. I pray for beauty.

"You did not change," they say.

I am fourteen and baby-sitting for my brother Bill, who lives in Boston. He is my favorite brother and there is a strong bond between us. Understanding my feelings of shame and ugliness he and his wife take me to a local hospital, where the "glob" is removed by a doctor named O. Henry. There is still a small bluish crater where the scar tissue was, but the ugly white stuff is gone. Almost immediately I become a different person from the girl who does not raise her head. Or so I think. Now that I've raised my head I win the boyfriend of my dreams. Now that I've raised my head I have plenty of friends. Now that I've raised my head classwork comes from my lips as faultlessly as Easter speeches did, and I leave high school as valedictorian, most popular student, and *queen*, hardly believing my luck. Ironically, the girl who was voted most beautiful in our class (and was) was later shot twice through the chest by a male companion, using a "real" gun, while she was pregnant. But that's another story in itself. Or is it?

"You did not change," they say.

It is now thirty years since the "accident." A beautiful journalist comes to visit and to interview me. She is going to write a cover story for her magazine that focuses on my latest book. "Decide how you want to look on the cover," she says. "Glamorous, or whatever."

Never mind "glamorous," it is the "whatever" that I hear. Suddenly all I can think of is whether I will get enough sleep the night before the photography session: if I don't, my eye will be tired and wander, as blind eyes will.

At night in bed with my lover I think up reasons why I should not appear on the cover of a magazine. "My meanest critics will say I've sold out," I say. "My family will now realize I write scandalous books."

"But what's the real reason you don't want to do this?" he asks.

"Because in all probability," I say in a rush, "my eye won't be straight."

"It will be straight enough," he says. Then, "Besides, I thought you'd made your peace with that."

And I suddenly remember that I have.

I remember:

I am talking to my brother Jimmy, asking if he remembers anything unusual about the day I was shot. He does not know I consider that day the last time my father, with his sweet home remedy of cool lily leaves, chose me, and that I suffered and raged inside because of this. "Well," he says, "all I remember is standing by the side of the highway with Daddy, trying to flag down a car. A white man stopped, but when Daddy said he needed somebody to take his little girl to the doctor, he drove off."

I remember:

I am in the desert for the first time. I fall totally in love with it. I am so overwhelmed by its beauty, I confront for the first time, consciously, the meaning of the doctor's words years ago: "Eyes are sympathetic. If one is blind, the other will likely become blind too." I realize I have dashed about the world madly, looking at this, looking at that, storing up images against the fading of the light. *But I might have missed seeing the desert!* The shock of that possibility—and gratitude for over twenty-five years of sight—sends me literally to my knees. Poem after poem comes—which is perhaps how poets pray.

On Sight

I am so thankful I have seen
The Desert
And the creatures in the desert
And the desert Itself.

The desert has its own moon
Which I have seen
With my own eye.
There is no flag on it.
Trees of the desert have arms
All of which are always up
That is because the moon is up
The sun is up
Also the sky
The stars
Clouds
None with flags.
If there *were* flags, I doubt
the trees would point.
Would you?

But mostly, I remember this:

I am twenty-seven, and my baby daughter is almost three. Since her birth I have worried about her discovery that her mother's eyes are different from other people's. Will she be embarrassed? I think. What will she say? Every day she watches a television program called "Big Blue Marble." It begins with a picture of the earth as it appears from the moon. It is bluish, a little battered-looking, but full of light, with whitish clouds swirling around it. Every time I see it I weep with love, as if it is a picture of Grandma's house. One day when I am putting Rebecca down for her nap, she suddenly focuses on my eye. Something inside me cringes, gets ready to try to protect myself. All children are cruel about physical differences, I know from experience, and that they don't always mean to be is another matter. I assume Rebecca will be the same.

But no-o-o-o. She studies my face intently as we stand, her inside and me outside her crib. She even holds my face maternally between her dimpled little hands. Then, looking every bit as serious and lawyerlike as her father, she says, as if it may just possibly have slipped my attention: "Mommy, there's a *world* in your eye." (As in, "Don't be alarmed, or do anything crazy.") And then, gently, but with great interest: "Mommy, where did you *get* that world in your eye?"

For the most part, the pain left then. (So what, if my brothers grew up to buy even more powerful pellet guns for their sons and to carry real guns themselves. So what, if a young "Morehouse man" once nearly fell off the steps of Trevor Arnett Library because he thought my eyes were blue.) Crying and laughing I ran to the bathroom, while Rebecca mumbled and sang herself off to sleep. Yes indeed, I realized, looking into the mirror. There *was* a world in my eye. And I saw that it was possible to love it: that in fact, for all it had taught me of shame and anger and inner vision, I *did* love it. Even to see it drifting out of orbit in boredom, or rolling up out of fatigue, not to mention floating back at attention in excitement (bearing witness, a friend has called it), deeply suitable to my personality, and even characteristic of me.

That night I dream I am dancing to Stevie Wonder's song "Always" (the name of the song is really "As," but I hear it as "Always"). As I dance, whirling and joyous, happier than I've ever been in my life, another bright-faced dancer joins me. We dance and kiss each other and hold each other through the night. The other dancer has obviously come through all right, as I have done. She is beautiful, whole and free. And she is also me. 50

TRY THIS 3.9

Everyone hates something about his or her body. Write a poem or a few paragraphs in the first person about what you hate about yours. What tone will you choose? Are you laughing at yourself, genuinely grieving, wry, angry, over it?

WARREN J. BOWE

Guns for Teachers

Finally the Republicans have found a meaningful way to support teachers. As both a teacher and a citizen, I spotted the win-win logic of Representative Frank Lasee's proposal immediately. Not only would schools be safer, but the billions added to Wisconsin's economy by a new school gun industry would be a great windfall for the state.

With more than 60,000 teachers in Wisconsin's public schools alone, such a law would help both mom-and-pop gun shops and the big retailers. Specialty products could include guns manufactured in school colors or engraved with school logos. Gun accessories will bring in additional revenue. I would need an everyday holster as well as one for such special occasions as parent-teacher conferences, concerts, athletic events, etc.

While this proposed legislation is way better than that supporting the shooting of feral cats, a few kinks would need to be worked out. For example, would the state taxpayers fund the law, or would teachers have to pay for the heat they pack? Would there be a special ammunition budget? Would we be given extra in-service time for range practice? Could we implement merit pay for those of us who are crack shots?

And, most important, how threatening would students need to be before we get to shoot them? In the interim, maybe we could just start hitting them again.

TRY THIS 3.10

Bowe's mini-essay belongs to the long tradition of **epistolary essays,** written in the form of a letter, in this case a letter to the editor. It is also in the tradition of "A Modest Proposal." Write a "modest proposal." Pick an issue you really care about and "solve" it with a solution drastically worse than the problem. If the problem is one covered in the news, you might send it as a letter to the editor.

CALVIN TRILLIN

Rock Threat Subsides

May 20, 1991

Parents who have been worried about their children being turned into mindless layabouts by rock-music lyrics will be relieved to hear that, according to the latest scientific studies, teenagers pay virtually no attention to the lyrics of rock songs. In other words, just what is turning these teenagers into mindless layabouts is still open to question.

I should also say, in the spirit of generational fairness, that there have been no studies so far to see what is turning so many parents into mindless layabouts. That is probably a much longer story.

According to an article I read in the *Washington Post,* one of the most thorough studies ever done on the impact of rock lyrics was recently completed by two psychologists from California State University at Fullerton, Jill Rosenbaum and Lorraine Prinsky. They found that most teenagers don't listen closely to the words of rock songs, don't catch a lot of what they do hear, and don't much care one way or the other. When the teenagers in the survey were asked why they listen to a rock song, "I want to listen to the words" finished dead last.

This information should change one of the standard discussions that parents and teenagers have about rock music—a discussion traditionally carried on in the family automobile at a time when the music blaring from a boom box in the back seat is loud enough to turn the windshield wipers on and off.

5 Parent (in a patient and mature tone): I can't imagine why you listen to that moronic garbage.

Teenager: Uhnnn.

Parent: It's just a lot of thugs making as much noise as they can.

Teenager: Nghh.

Parent: Half the time, you can't even make out the words to the song anyway.

10 Teenager: Actually, much more than half the time. But the latest study indicates that this makes no difference whatsoever in my enjoyment of this art form.

That's right. Teenagers don't care about the words. They listen to the lyrics of rock songs about as carefully as their parents listen to the lyrics of "The Star-Spangled Banner."

The California study found that the messages supposedly encoded in some rock songs—exhortations to become dope fiends and burn down cities and worship Satan and engage in hideous sexual excesses and leave the dinner table without being asked to be excused and that sort of thing—were lost on teenagers, even when the researchers furnished printouts of the lyrics for the teenagers to peruse. This is, of course, good news for parents and discouraging news for anybody who has put a lot of effort into trying to use rock lyrics to encourage teenagers to do wicked things.

Since teenagers don't listen carefully to the lyrics, they tend to form their opinion of what the song is about from the title. For instance, the Bruce Springsteen hit "Born in the USA" is described by the *Post* as having "in every verse explicit references to despair and disillusionment." But kids from fourth grade through college who were tested by researchers from the University of California at Los Angeles were mostly under the impression that "Born in the USA" was a patriotic song.

These results shouldn't surprise anybody. Most grownups don't get much past the title of anything, which is why title-writing is such an art. The military is particularly adept at titles. The invasion of Panama, for instance, was called Operation Just Cause. Think of what the public impression of that episode would have been if the Pentagon had chosen a name that would have been, in fact, much less subject to differences of opinion: Operation Tiny Country. Think of how the public view of the war in the Persian Gulf might have differed if our military effort to drive Iraqis from Kuwait had been called not Operation Desert Storm but Operation Restore Despot.

The results of these rock-lyrics studies seem to indicate that putting warning 15
labels on rock records would only draw teenagers' attention to something they might otherwise ignore—sort of like marking the spines of innocent-looking novels, "Warning: This Book Has Some Good Parts."

The results also mean that concerned citizens would be wasting their time mounting a campaign to encourage songwriters to compose more uplifting lyrics. That's a shame. I was sort of looking forward to the forces of good coming up with a song that featured endless repetition of some lyric like "I wanna clean my room" or "I appreciate the great burden of responsibility my father carries and the sacrifices he's made on behalf of me and my siblings, and I have only the greatest respect for him." With the right tune, we now know, that might have made the charts, but nobody would have been listening anyway.

TRY THIS 3.11
Identify a "social problem" that you think is really no problem at all. Write two reassuring pages arguing your point. (Extra points for comedy.)

FICTION

THOMAS MCGUANE

Cowboy

The old fella makes me go into the house in my stocking feet. The old lady's in a big chair next to the window. In fact, the whole room is full of big chairs, but she's only in one of them—though, big as she is, she could fill up several. The old man says, "I found this one in the loose-horse pen at the sale yard."

She says, “What’s he supposed to be?”

He says, “Supposed to be a cowboy.”

“What’s he doin’ in the loose horses?”

I says, “I was lookin’ for one that would ride.”

“You was in the wrong pen, son,” the old man says. “Them’s canners. They’re goin’ to France in cardboard boxes.”

“Soon as they get a steel bolt in the head.” The big old gal laughs in her chair.

Now I’m sore. “There’s five in there broke to death. I rode ’em with nothin’ but binder twine.”

“It don’t make a shit,” the old man says. “Ever’ one of them is goin’ to France.”

The old lady don’t believe me. “How’d you get in them loose horses to ride?”

“I went in there at night.”

The old lady says, “You one crazy cowboy, go in there in the dark. Them broncs kick your teeth down your throat. I suppose you tried them bareback?”

“Naw, I drug the saddle I usually ride at the Rose Bowl Parade.”

“You got a horse for that?”

“I got Trigger. We unstuffed him.”

The old lady addresses the old man. “He’s got a mouth on him. This much we know.”

“Maybe he can tell us what good he is.”

I says, “I’m a cowboy.”

“You’re a outta-work cowboy.”

“It’s a dying way of life.”

“She’s about like me—she’s wondering if this ranch’s supposed to be some kinda welfare agency for cowboys.”

I’ve had enough. “You’re the dumb honyocker drove me out here.”

I think that’ll be the end of it, but the old lady says, “Don’t get huffy. You got the job. You against conversation or something?”

We get outside and the old sumbitch says, “You drawed lucky there, son. That last deal could’ve pissed her off.”

“It didn’t make me no nevermind if it did or didn’t.”

“She hadn’t been well. Used to she was sweet as pudding.”

“I’m sorry for that. We don’t have health, we don’t have nothin’.”

She must have been afflicted something terrible, because she was ugly morning, noon, and night for as long as she lasted—she’d pick a fight over nothing, and the old sumbitch got the worst of it. I felt sorry for him, little slack as he cut me.

Had a hundred seventy-five sweet-tempered horned Herefords and fifteen sleepy bulls. Shipped the calves all over for hybrid vigor, mostly to the South. Had some go clear to Florida. A Hereford that still had its horns was a walking miracle, and the old sumbitch had a smart little deal going. I soon learned to give him credit for such things, and the old lady barking commands offen the sofa weren't no slouch neither. Anybody else seen their books might've said they could be wintering in Phoenix.

They didn't have no bunkhouse, just a LeisureLife mobile home that had lost 30
its wheels about thirty years ago, and they had it positioned by the door of the barn so it'd be convenient for the hired man to stagger out at all hours and fight breech births and scours and any other disorder sent us by the cow gods. We had some doozies. One heifer got pregnant, and her calf was near as big as she was. Had to reach in with a saw and take it out in pieces. When we threw the head out on the ground, she turned to it and lowed like it was her baby. Everything a cow does is designed to turn it into meat as fast as possible so that somebody can eat it. It's a terrible life.

The old sumbitch and I got along good. We got through calving and got to see them pairs and bulls run out onto the new grass. Nothing like seeing all that meat feel a little temporary joy. Then we bladed out the corrals and watched them dry under the spring sun at long last. Only mishap was when the manure spreader threw a rock and knocked me senseless and I drove the rig into an irrigation ditch. The old sumbitch never said a word but chained up and pulled us out with his Ford.

We led his cavvy out of the hills afoot with two buckets of sweet feed. Had a little of everything, including a blue roan I fancied, but he said it was a Hancock and bucked like the National Finals in Las Vegas, kicking out behind and squalling, and was just a man-killer, "Stick to the bays," he said. "The West was won on a bay horse."

He picked out three bays, had a keg of shoes, all ones and oughts, and I shod them best I could, three geldings with nice manners, stood good to shoe. About all you could say about the others was they had four legs each, and a couple, all white-marked from saddle galls and years of hard work, looked like no more summers after this. They'd been rode many a long mile. We chased 'em back into the hills and the three shod ones whinnied and fretted. "Back to work," the old sumbitch says to them.

We shod three 'cause one was going to pack a ton of fencing supplies—barb wire, smooth wire, steel T-posts, old wore-out Sunflower fence stretchers that could barely grab on to the wire, and staples—and we was at it a good little while where the elk had knocked miles of it down, or the cedar finally give out and had to be replaced by steel. That was where I found out that the old sumbitch's last good time was in Korea, where the officers at the front would yell over the radio, "Come on up here and die!" Said the enemy was coming in waves. Tells me all this while the stretcher's pulling that wire squealing through the staples. The sumbitch was a tough old bastard. "They killed a pile of us and we killed a pile of them." *Squeak.*

We hauled the mineral horseback, too, in panniers—white salt and iodine 35
salt. He didn't have no use for blocks, so we hauled it in sacks and poured it into the troughs he had on all these bald hilltops where the wind would blow away

the flies. Most of his so-called troughs were truck tires nailed onto anything flat—plywood, old doors, and suchlike—but they worked good. A cow can put her tongue anywhere in a tire and get what she needs, and you can drag one of them flat things with your horse if you need to move it. Most places we salted had old buffalo wallers where them buffalo wallered. They done wallered their last—had to get out of the way for the cow and the man on the bay horse.

I'd been rustling my own grub in the LeisureLife for quite some time when the old lady said it was time for me to eat with the white folks. This was not necessarily a good thing. The old lady's knee replacements had begun to fail, and both me and the old sumbitch was half-afraid of her. She cooked as good as ever, but she was a bomb waiting to go off, standing bowlegged at the stove and talking ugly about how much she did for us. When she talked, the old sumbitch would move his mouth as though he was saying the same words, and we had to keep from giggling, which wasn't hard. For if the old lady caught us at that there'd a been hell to pay.

Both the old sumbitch and the old lady was heavy smokers, to where a oxygen bottle was in sight. So they joined a Smoke-Enders deal the Lutherans had, and this required them to put all their butts in a jar and wear the jar around their necks on a string. The old sumbitch liked this O.K. because he could just tap his ash right under his chin and not get it on the truck seat, but the more that thing filled up and hung around her neck the meaner the old lady got. She had no idea the old sumbitch was cheating and setting his jar on the woodpile when we was working outside. She was just more honest than him, and in the end she give up smoking and he smoked away, except he wasn't allowed to smoke in the house no more, nor buy ready-mades, 'cause the new tax made them too expensive and she wouldn't let him take it out of the cows, which come first. She said it was just a vice and if he was half the man she thought he was he'd give it up as a bad deal. "You could have a long and happy old age," she said, real sarcastic-like.

One day me and the old sumbitch is in the house hauling soot out of the fireplace, on account of they had a chimbley fire last winter. Over the mantel is a picture of a beautiful woman in a red dress with her hair piled on top of her head. The old sumbitch tells me that's the old lady before she joined the motorcycle gang.

"Oh?"

"Them motorcycle gangs," he says, "all they do is eat and work on their motorcycles. They taught her to smoke, too, but she's shut of that. Probably outlive us all."

"Looks to me she can live long as she wants."

"And if she ever wants to box you, tell her no. She'll knock you on your ass. I guarantee it. Throw you a damn haymaker, son."

I couldn't understand how he could be so casual-like about the old lady being in a motorcycle gang. When we was smoking in the LeisureLife, I asked him about it. That's when I found out that him and the old lady was brother and sister. I guess that explained it. If your sister wants to join a motorcycle gang, that's her business. He said she even had a tattoo—"Hounds from Hell," with a dog shooting flames out of his nostrils and riding a Harley.

That picture on the mantel kind of stayed in my mind, and I asked the old sumbitch if his sister'd ever had a boyfriend. Well, yes, quite a few, he told me, quite a damn few. "Our folks run them off. They was just after the land."

45 He was going all around the baler hitting the zerks with his grease gun. "I had a lady friend myself. She'd do anything. Cook. Gangbusters with a snorty horse, and not too damn hard on the eyes. Sis run her off. Said she was just after the land. If she was, I never could see it. Anyway, went on down the road long time ago."

Fall come around and when we brought the cavvy down two of them old-timers who'd worked so hard was lame. One was stifled, one was sweenied, and both had crippling quarter cracks. I thought they needed to be at the loose-horse sale, but the old sumbitch says, "No mounts of mine is gonna feed no Frenchman," and that was that. So we made a hole, led the old-timers to the edge, and shot them with a elk rifle. First one didn't know what hit him. Second one heard the shot and saw his buddy fall, and the old sumbitch had to chase him around to kill him. Then he sent me down the hole to get the halters back. Lifting those big heads was some chore.

I enjoyed eating in the big house that whole summer until the sister started giving me come-hither looks. They was fairly limited except those days when the old sumbitch was in town after supplies. Then she dialed it up and kind of brushed me every time she went past the table. There was always something special on the town days—a pie, maybe. I tried to think about the picture on the mantel, but it was impossible, even though I knew it might get me out of the LeisureLife once and for all. She was getting more and more wound up, while I was pretending to enjoy the food or going crazy over the pie. But she didn't buy it—called me a queer and sent me back to the trailer to make my own meals. By calling me a queer, she more or less admitted what she'd been up to, and I think that embarrassed her, because she covered up by roaring at everyone and everything, including the poor old sumbitch, who had no idea what had gone sideways while he was away. It was two years before she made another pie, and then it was once a year on my birthday. She made me five birthday pies in all—sand cherry, every one of them.

I broke the catch colt, which I didn't know was no colt, as he was the biggest snide in the cavvy. He was four, and it was time. I just got around him for a couple of days, then saddled him gently as I could. The offside stirrup scared him, and he looked over at it, but that was all it was to saddling. I must've had a burst of courage, 'cause next minute I was on him. That was O.K., too. I told the old sumbitch to open the corral gate, and we sailed away. The wind blew his tail up under him, and he thought about bucking but rejected the idea and that was about all they was to breaking Olly, for that was his name. Once I'd rode him two weeks, he was safe for the old sumbitch, who plumb loved this new horse and complimented me generously for the job I'd did.

We had three hard winters in a row, then lost so many calves to scours we changed our calving grounds. The old sumbitch just come out one day and looked at where he'd calved out for fifty years and said, "The ground's no good. We're movin." So we spent the summer building a new corral way off down the creek. When we's finished, he says, "I meant to do this when I got back from overseas and now it's finished and I'm practically done for, too. Whoever gets the place next will be glad his calves don't shit themselves into the next world like mine done."

50 Neither one of us had a back that was worth a damn, and the least we could do was get rid of the square baler and quit hefting them man-killing five-wire bales. We got a round baler and a DewEze machine that let us pick up a bale from the truck without laying a finger on it. We'd tell stories and smoke in the cab on those cold winter days and roll out a thousand pounds of hay while them old-time horned Herefords followed the truck. That's when I let him find out I'd done some time.

"I figured you musta been in the crowbar hotel."

"How's that?"

"Well, you're a pretty good hand. What's a pretty good hand doin' tryin' loose horses in the middle of the night at some Podunk sale yard? Folks hang on to a pretty good hand, and nobody was hangin' on to you. You want to tell me what you done?"

I'd been with the old sumbitch for three years and out of jail the same amount of time. I wasn't afraid to tell him what I done 'cause I had started to trust him, but I sure didn't want him telling nothing to his sister. I told him I rustled some yearlings, and he chuckled like he understood entirely. I had rustled some yearlings, all right, but that's not what I went up for.

55 The old man paid me in cash, or, rather, the old lady did, since she handled anything like that. They never paid into workmen's comp, and there was no reason to go to the records. They didn't even have my name right. You tell people around here your name is Shane, and they'll always believe you. The important thing is I was working my tail off for that old sumbitch, and he knew it. Nothing else mattered, even the fact that we'd come to like each other. After all, this was a goddamn ranch.

The old fella had several peculiarities to him, most of which I've forgotten. He was one of the few fellas I ever heard of who would actually jump up and down on his hat if he got mad enough. You can imagine what his hat looked like. One time he did it 'cause I let the swather get away from me on a hill and bent it all to hell. Another time a Mormon tried to run down his breeding program to get a better deal on some replacement heifers, and I'll be damned if the old sumbitch didn't throw that hat down and jump on it, right in front of the Mormon, causing the Mormon to get into his Buick and ease on down the road without another word. One time when we was driving ring shanks into corral poles I hit my thumb and tried jumping on my hat, but the old sumbitch gave me such an odd look I never tried it again.

The old lady died sitting down. I went in, and there she was, sitting down, and she was dead. After the first wave of grief, the old sumbitch and me fretted about rigor mortis and not being able to move her in that seated position. So we stretched her onto the couch and called the mortician and he called the coroner and for some reason the coroner called the ambulance, which caused the old sumbitch to state, "It don't do you no nevermind to tell nobody nothing." Course he was right.

Once the funeral was behind us, I moved out of the LeisureLife, partly for comfort and partly 'cause the old sumbitch falled apart after his sister passed, which I never would've suspected. Once she's gone, he says, he's all that's left of his family and he's alone in life, and about then he notices me and tells me to get my stuff out of the LeisureLife and move in with him.

We rode through the cattle pritnear ever' day year round, and he come to trust me enough to show how his breeding program went, with culls and breed-backs and outcrosses and replacements, and took me to bull sales and showed me what to expect in a bull and which ones were correct and which were sorry. One day we's looking at a pen of yearling bulls on this outfit near Luther and he can't make up his mind and he says he wished his sister was with him and he starts snuffling and says she had an eye on her wouldn't quit. So I stepped up and picked three bulls out of that pen, and he quit snuffling and said damn if I didn't have an eye on me, too. That was the beginning of our partnership.

One whole year I was the cook, and one whole year he was the cook, and back and forth like that, but never at the same time. Whoever was cook would change when the other fella got sick of his recipes, and ever once in a while a new recipe would come in the *AgriNews*, like that corn chowder with the sliced hot dogs. I even tried a pie one time, but it just made him lonesome for days gone by, so we forgot about desserts, which was probably good for our health, as most sweets call for gobbing in the white sugar.

The sister never let him have a dog 'cause she had a cat and she thought a dog would get the cat. It wasn't much of a cat, anyhow, but it lived a long time, outlived the old lady by several moons. After it passed on, we took it out to the burn barrel and the first thing the old sumbitch said was "We're gettin' a dog." It took him that long to realize that his sister was gone.

Tony was a Border collie we got as a pup from a couple in Miles City that raised them. You could cup your hands and hold Tony when we got him, but he grew up in one summer and went to work and we taught him "down," "here," "come by," "way to me," and "hold 'em," all in one year or less, 'cause Tony would just stay on his belly and study you with his eyes until he knew exactly what you wanted. Tony helped us gather, mother up pairs, and separate bulls, and he lived in the house for many a good year and kept us entertained with all his tricks. Finally, Tony grew old and died. We didn't take it so good, especially the old sumbitch, who said he couldn't foresee enough summers for another dog. Plus that was the year he couldn't get on a horse no more and he wasn't about to work no stock dog afoot. There was still plenty to do and most of it fell to me. After all, this was a goddamn ranch.

The time had come to tell him why I went to jail and what I did, which was rob that little store at Absarokee and shoot the proprietor, though he didn't die. I had no idea why I did such a thing—then or now. I led the crew on the prison ranch for a number of years and turned out many a good hand. They wasn't nearabout to let me loose until there was a replacement good as me who'd stay awhile. So I trained up a murderer from Columbia Falls, could rope, break horses, keep vaccine records, fence, and irrigate. Once the warden seen how good he was, they paroled me out and turned it all over to the new man, who was never getting out. The old sumbitch could give a shit less when I told him my story. I could've told him all this years before when he first hired me, for all he cared. He was a big believer in what he saw with his own eyes.

I don't think I ever had the touch with customers the old sumbitch had. They'd come from all over looking for horned Herefords and talking hybrid vigor, which I may or may not have believed. They'd ask what we had and I'd point to the corrals and say, "Go look for yourself." Some would insist on seeing the old sumbitch, and I'd tell them he was in bed, which was pritnear the only place you could find him now that he'd begun to fail. Then the state got wind of his condition and took him to town. I went to see him there right regular, but it just upset him. He couldn't figure out who I was and got frustrated 'cause he knew I was somebody he was supposed to know. And then he failed even worse. The doctors told me it was just better if I didn't come round.

The neighbors claimed I was personally responsible for the spread of spurge, Dalmatian toadflax, and knapweed. They got the authorities involved and it was pretty clear that I was the weed they had in mind. If they could get the court to appoint one of their relatives ranch custodian while the old sumbitch was in storage they'd get all that grass for free till he was in a pine box. The authorities came in all sizes and shapes, but when they were through they let me take one saddle horse, one saddle, the clothes on my back, my hat, and my slicker. I rode that horse clear to the sale yard, where they tried to put him in the loose horses 'cause of his age. I told them I was too set in my ways to start feeding Frenchmen and rode off toward Idaho. There's always an opening for a cowboy, even a old sumbitch like me if he can halfway make a hand.

The Book of Sand

. . . thy rope of sands . . .
George Herbert (1593–1623)

The line consists of an infinite number of points; the plane, of an infinite number of lines; the volume, of an infinite number of planes; the hypervolume, of an infinite number of volumes . . . No—this, *more geometrico*, is decidedly not the best way to begin my tale. To say that the story is true is by now a convention of every fantastic tale; mine, nevertheless, *is* true.

I live alone, in a fifth-floor apartment on Calle Belgrano. One evening a few months ago, I heard a knock at my door. I opened it, and a stranger stepped in. He was a tall man, with blurred, vague features, or perhaps my nearsightedness made me see him that way. Everything about him spoke of honest poverty: he was dressed in gray, and carried a gray valise. I immediately sensed that he was a foreigner. At first I thought he was old; then I noticed that I had been misled by his sparse hair, which was blond, almost white, like the Scandinavians'. In the course of our conversation, which I doubt lasted more than an hour, I learned that he hailed from the Orkneys.

I pointed the man to a chair. He took some time to begin talking. He gave off an air of melancholy, as I myself do now.

"I sell Bibles," he said at last.

"In this house," I replied, not without a somewhat stiff, pedantic note, "there 5
are several English Bibles, including the first one, Wyclif's. I also have Cipriano de Valera's, Luther's (which is, in literary terms, the worst of the lot), and a Latin copy of the Vulgate. As you see, it isn't exactly Bibles I might be needing."

After a brief silence he replied.

"It's not only Bibles I sell. I can show you a sacred book that might interest a man such as yourself. I came by it in northern India, in Bikaner."

He opened his valise and brought out the book. He laid it on the table. It was a clothbound octavo volume that had clearly passed through many hands. I examined it; the unusual heft of it surprised me. On the spine was printed *Holy Writ*, and then *Bombay*.

"Nineteenth century, I'd say," I observed.

"I don't know," was the reply. "Never did know." 10

I opened it at random. The characters were unfamiliar to me. The pages, which seemed worn and badly set, were printed in double columns, like a Bible. The text was cramped, and composed into versicles. At the upper corner of each page were Arabic numerals. I was struck by an odd fact: the even-numbered page would carry the number 40,514, let us say, while the odd-numbered page that followed it would be 999. I turned the page; the next page bore an eight-digit number. It also bore a small illustration, like those one sees in dictionaries: an anchor drawn in pen and ink, as though by the unskilled hand of a child.

It was at that point that the stranger spoke again.

"Look at it well. You will never see it again."

There was a threat in the words, but not in the voice.

I took note of the page, and then closed the book. Immediately I opened it again. In vain I searched for the figure of the anchor, page after page. To hide my discomfiture, I tried another tack.

"This is a version of Scripture in some Hindu language, isn't that right?"

"No," he replied.

Then he lowered his voice, as though entrusting me with a secret.

"I came across this book in a village on the plain, and I traded a few rupees and a Bible for it. The man who owned it didn't know how to read. I suspect he saw the Book of Books as an amulet. He was of the lowest caste; people could not so much as step on his shadow without being defiled. He told me his book was called the Book of Sand because neither sand nor this book has a beginning or an end."

He suggested I try to find the first page.

I took the cover in my left hand and opened the book, my thumb and forefinger almost touching. It was impossible: several pages always lay between the cover and my hand. It was as though they grew from the very book.

"Now try to find the end."

I failed there as well.

"This can't be," I stammered, my voice hardly recognizable as my own.

"It can't be, yet it *is*," The Bible peddler said, his voice little more than a whisper. "The number of pages in this book is literally infinite. No page is the first page; no page is the last. I don't know why they're numbered in this arbitrary way, but perhaps it's to give one to understand that the terms of an infinite series can be numbered any way whatever."

Then, as though thinking out loud, he went on.

"If space is infinite, we are anywhere, at any point in space. If time is infinite, we are at any point in time."

His musings irritated me.

"You," I said, "are a religious man, are you not?"

"Yes, I'm Presbyterian. My conscience is clear. I am certain I didn't cheat that native when I gave him the Lord's Word in exchange for his diabolic book."

I assured him he had nothing to reproach himself for, and asked whether he was just passing through the country. He replied that he planned to return to his own country within a few days. It was then that I learned he was a Scot, and that his home was in the Orkneys. I told him I had great personal fondness for Scotland because of my love for Stevenson and Hume.

"And Robbie Burns," he corrected.

As we talked I continued to explore the infinite book.

"Had you intended to offer this curious specimen to the British Museum, then?" I asked with feigned indifference.

"No," he replied, "I am offering it to you," and he mentioned a great sum of money.

I told him, with perfect honesty, that such an amount of money was not within my ability to pay. But my mind was working; in a few moments I had devised my plan.

"I propose a trade," I said. "You purchased the volume with a few rupees and the Holy Scripture; I will offer you the full sum of my pension, which I have just received, and Wyclif's black-letter Bible. It was left to me by my parents."

"A black-letter Wyclif!" he murmured.

I went to my bedroom and brought back the money and the book. With a bibliophile's zeal he turned the pages and studied the binding.

"Done," he said. 40

I was astonished that he did not haggle. Only later was I to realize that he had entered my house already determined to sell the book. He did not count the money, but merely put the bills into his pocket.

We chatted about India, the Orkneys, and the Norwegian jarls that had once ruled those islands. Night was falling when the man left. I have never seen him since, nor do I know his name.

I thought of putting the Book of Sand in the space left by the Wyclif, but I chose at last to hide it behind some imperfect volumes of the *Thousand and One Nights*.

I went to bed but could not sleep. At three or four in the morning I turned on the light. I took out the impossible book and turned its pages. On one, I saw an engraving of a mask. There was a number in the corner of the page—I don't remember now what it was—raised to the ninth power.

I showed no one my treasure. To the joy of possession was added the fear that it 45
would be stolen from me, and to that, the suspicion that it might not be truly infinite. Those two points of anxiety aggravated my already habitual misanthropy. I had but few friends left, and those, I stopped seeing. A prisoner of the Book, I hardly left my house. I examined the worn binding and the covers with a magnifying glass, and rejected the possibility of some artifice. I found that the small illustrations were spaced at two-thousand-page intervals. I began noting them down in an alphabetized notebook, which was very soon filled. They never repeated themselves. At night, during the rare intervals spared me by insomnia, I dreamed of the book.

Summer was drawing to a close, and I realized that the book was monstrous. It was cold consolation to think that I, who looked upon it with my eyes and fondled it with my ten flesh-and-bone fingers, was no less monstrous than the book. I felt it was a nightmare thing, an obscene thing, and that it defiled and corrupted reality.

I considered fire, but I feared that the burning of an infinite book might be similarly infinite, and suffocate the planet in smoke.

I remembered reading once that the best place to hide a leaf is in the forest. Before my retirement I had worked in the National Library, which contained nine hundred thousand books; I knew that to the right of the lobby a curving staircase descended into the shadows of the basement, where the maps and periodicals are kept. I took advantage of the librarians' distraction to hide the Book of Sand on one of the library's damp shelves; I tried not to notice how high up, or how far from the door.

I now feel a little better, but I refuse even to walk down the street the library's on.

TRY THIS 3.12
Pick an incident from your life. In one page, recount it in the language of either a cowboy or a cop. In another page, recount it in the voice of either a cultivated collector of books or a preacher.

POEMS

WILLIAM TROWBRIDGE

Kong Looks Back on His Tryout with the Bears

If it had worked out, I'd be on a train to Green Bay,
not crawling up this building with the air corps
on my ass. And if it weren't for love, I'd drop
this shrieking little bimbo sixty stories
and let them take me back to the exhibit,
let them teach me to rumba and do imitations.
They tried me on the offensive line, told me
to take out the right cornerback for Nagurski.
Eager to please, I wadded up the whole secondary,
then stomped the line, then the bench and locker room,
then the east end of town, to the river.
But they were not pleased: they said
I had to learn my position, become a team player.
The great father Bear himself said that,
so I tried hard to know the right numbers
and how the arrows slanted toward the little o's.
But the o's and the wet grass and the grunts
drowned out the count, and the tight little cheers
drew my arrow straight into the stands,
and the wives tasted like flowers and raw fish.
So I was put on waivers right after camp,
and here I am, panty sniffer, about to die a clown,
who once opened a hole you could drive Nebraska through.

TRY THIS 3.13

Write from the point of view of anything not human—an insect, an android, a potato, a belly button. Try to invent and develop a diction that represents the frame of reference of this thing. For instance, if you are writing from the point of view of a shoe, it is likely to have extensive knowledge of and opinions about flooring, but a limited concept of the sky or human heads.

SIÂN B. GRIFFITHS

Fistful

The dead can be very useful sometimes.
Clint Eastwood, *A Fistful of Dollars*

Sometimes, it's all about how you wear your poncho,
or the layering of dust on your boots.

or how you sit a bucking mule
while five men scoff from a high-barred gate.

Where words unhinge from speaking mouths,
it's useful to be the man with no name
or the dark-eyed woman, clamped in a locket that laments its own opening.

Engineer the corpses,
and the dead are only sleeping,
secrets ever-burning on their cold parched lips.

All the Winchesters, all the Remingtons,
all the six guns unholstered in this border town
are not enough to kill the dead;
their stories hide in the sheepskin vests
of the nameless living.

MATT BONDURANT

The Pathos of Charles Schulz

The clearest example the spelling-bee episode,
Charlie Brown traveling to "the big city"

with Snoopy on an empty bus,
a small child and beagle on public transit.

In the final round, to win the whole thing,
Charlie gets B-E-A-G-L-E.

Snoopy blinks twice, in his seat deep among children.
Charlie fumbles, sweats. He can't do it.

Riding the bus back with the moon in the window
the color and shape of a cashew nut,

the texture of a lemon slice, a wedge of pear,
shining in a pallid shaft on the two companions

as they travel over the river toward home.
Snoopy plays a mournful tune on his mouth-harp

as Charlie looks out the window.
Nobody says anything.

At home, Chuck goes into the pale light of the kitchen
and fixes himself a bowl of cold cereal,

his broad face quiet, his orange-on-a-stick-head bowed,
sitting at the kitchen table in the middle of the night,

spooning soggy flakes into his mouth.
Snoopy lies on top of his doghouse and stares up at the stars.

Woodstock flutters from the heavens
to rest on his distended puppy-belly.

This is no gift of resolve or insight,
no cartoonish god-machine,

no possibility, for any of us, to rid ourselves
of this one simple thing.

TRY THIS 3.14
Write a poem about a movie, a cartoon strip, or a pop song. As the persona of the poet, you will be making a different point than the film, strip, or song.

BARBARA HAMBY

Ode to American English

I was missing English one day, American, really,
    with its pill-popping Hungarian goulash of everything
from Anglo-Saxon to Zulu, because British English
    is not the same, if the paperback dictionary
I bought at Brentano's on the Avenue de l'Opéra
    is any indication, too cultured by half. Oh, the English
know their dahlias, but what about doowop, donuts,
    Dick Tracy, Tricky Dick? With their elegant Oxfordian

accents, how could they understand my yearning for the hotrod,
hotdog, hot flash vocabulary of the U. S. of A.,
the fragmented fandango of Dagwood's everyday flattening
of Mr. Beasley on the sidewalk, fetuses floating
on billboards, drive-by monster hip-hop stereos shaking
the windows of my dining room like a 7.5 earthquake,
Ebonics, Spanglish, "you know" used as comma and period,
the inability of 90% of the population to get the present perfect:
I have went, I have saw, I have tooken Jesus into my heart,
the battle cry of the Bible Belt, but no one uses
the King James anymore, only plain-speak versions,
in which Jesus, raising Lazarus from the dead, says,
"Dude, wake up," and the L-man bolts up like a B-movie
mummy. "Whoa, I was toasted." Yes, ma'am,
I miss the mongrel plentitude of American English, its fall-guy,
rat-terrier, dog-pound neologisms, the bomb of it all,
the rushing River Jordan backwoods mutability of it, the low-rider,
boom-box cruise of it, from New Joisey to Ha-wah-ya
with its sly dog, malasada-scarfing beach blanket lingo
to the ubiquitous Valley Girl's *like-like* stuttering,
shopaholic rant. I miss its quotidian beauty, its querulous
back-biting righteous indignation, its preening rotgut
flag-waving cowardice. *Suffering Succotash,* sputters
Sylvester the Cat, *sine die,* say the pork-bellied legislators
of the swamps and plains. I miss all those guys, their Tweety-bird
resilience, their Doris Day optimism, the candid unguent
of utter unhappiness on every channel, the midnight televangelist
euphoric stew, the junk mail, voice mail vernacular.
On every *boulevard* and *rue* I miss the Tarzan cry of Johnny
Weismueller, Johnny Cash, Johnny B. Goode,
and all the smart-talking, gum-snapping hard-girl dialogue,
finger-popping x-rated street talk, sports babble,
Cheetoes, Cheerios, chili dog diatribes. Yeah, I miss them all,
sitting here on my sidewalk throne sipping champagne
verses lined up like hearses, metaphors juking, nouns zipping
in my head like Corvettes on Dexedrine, French verbs
slitting my throat, yearning for James Dean to jump my curb.

TRY THIS 3.15

An **ode** is a serious, meditative lyric poem that treats a noble subject in a dignified manner. Write an ode to something hip, pop, trivial, or trashy that you really love.

JANE MARTIN

French Fries

An old woman in a straight-back chair holding a McDonald's cup. She is surrounded by several bundles of newspapers. She wears thick glasses that distort her eyes to the viewer.

ANNA MAE: If I had one wish in my life, why I'd like to live in McDonald's. Right there in the restaurant. 'Stead of in this old place. I'll come up to the brow of the hill, bowed down with my troubles, hurtin' under my load and I'll see that yellow horseshoe, sort of like part of a rainbow, and it gives my old spirit a lift. Lord, I can sit in a McDonald's all day. I've done it too. Walked the seven miles with the sun just on its way, and then sat on the curb till five minutes of seven. First one there and the last one to leave. Just like some ol' french fry they forgot.

I like the young people workin' there. Like a team of fine young horses when I was growin' up. All smilin'. Tell you what I really like though is the plastic. God gave us plastic so there wouldn't be no stains on his world. See, in the human world of the earth it all gets scratched, stained, tore up, faded down. Loses its shine. All of it does. In time. Well, God he gave us the idea of plastic so we'd know what the everlasting really was. See if there's plastic then there's surely eternity. It's God's hint.

You ever watch folks when they come on in the McDonald's? They always speed up, almost run the last few steps. You see if they don't. Old Dobbin with the barn in sight. They know it's safe in there and it ain't safe outside. Now it ain't safe outside and you know it.

I've seen a man healed by a Big Mac. I have. I was just sittin' there. Last summer it was. Oh, they don't never move you on. It's a sacred law in McDonald's, you can sit for a hundred years. Only place in this world. Anyway, a fella, maybe thirty-five, maybe forty, come on in there dressed real nice, real bright tie, bran' new baseball cap, nice white socks and he had him that disease. You know the one I mean, Cerebral Walrus they call it. Anyway, he had him a cock leg. His poor old body had it two speeds at the same time. Now he got him some coffee, with a lid on, and sat him down and Jimmy the tow-head cook knew him, see, and he brought over a Big Mac. Well, the sick fella ate maybe half of it and then he was just sittin', you know, suffering those tremors, when a couple of *ants* come right out of the burger. Now there ain't no ants in McDonald's no way. Lord sent those ants, and the sick fella he looked real sharp at the burger and a bunch *more* ants marched on out nice as you please and his head lolled right over and he pitched himself out of that chair and banged his head on the floor, loud. Thwack! Like a bowling ball dropping. Made you half sick to hear it. We jump up and run over but he was cold out. Well those servin' kids, so cute, they watered him, stuck a touch pepper up his nostril, slapped him right smart, and bang, up he got. Standin' an' blinkin'. 'Well, how are you?,' we say. An he looks us over, looks right in our eyes, and he say, 'I'm fine.' And he was. He was fine! Tipped his Cincinnati Reds baseball cap, big 'jus'-swallowed-the-canary' grin, paraded out of there clean, straight like a pole-bean poplar, walked him a plumb line without no trace of the 'walrus.' Got outside, jumped up, whooped, hollered, sang him the National Anthem, flagged down a Circle Line bus, an' rode off up Muhammad Ali Boulevard wavin' an' smilin' like the King of the Pharoahs. Healed by a Big Mac. I saw it.

McDonald's. You ever seen anybody die in a McDonald's? No sir. No way. Nobody ever has died in one. Shoot, they die in Burger Kings all the time. Kentucky Fried Chicken's got their own damn ambulances. Nooooooooo, you can't die in a McDonald's no matter how hard you try. It's the spices. Seals you safe in this life like it seals in the flavor. Yessssssss, yes!

I asked Jarrell could I live there. See they close up around ten, and there ain't a thing goin' on in 'em till seven a.m. I'd just sit in those nice swingy chairs and lean forward. Rest my head on those cool, cool, smooth tables, sing me a hymn and sleep like a baby. Jarrell, he said he'd write him a letter up the chain of command and see would they let me. Oh, I got my bid in. Peaceful and clean.

Sometimes I see it like the last of a movie. You know how they start the picture up real close and then back it off steady and far? Well, that's how I dream it. I'm living in McDonald's and it's real late at night and you see me up close, smiling, and then you see the whole McDonald's from the outside, lit up and friendly. And I get smaller and smaller, like they do, and then it's just a light in the darkness, like a star, and I'm in it. I'm part of that light, part of the whole sky, and it's all McDonald's, but part of something even bigger, something fixed and shiny... like plastic.

I know. I know. It's just a dream. Just a beacon in the storm. But you got to have a dream. It's our dreams make us what we are.

Blackout

TRY THIS 3.16

A prop is a kind of significant detail for the stage. The props in Jane Martin's *French Fries* are subordinated to the voice of the character, but with a little imagination you can see how the actress might make use of the cup, a hamburger, fries, the newspapers, and her glasses. Write a short monologue in which a character reveals himself/herself through voice, and also through relation to an object onstage.

WORKING TOWARD A DRAFT

Take a poem or fragment of a poem you have written and recast it in the second person. Who is the "you" to whom this poem might be addressed? How does using the second person alter the meaning?

Or:

Take a passage from your journal and rewrite it in the voice of Oscar Wilde, Pocahontas, Miss Manners, Donald Trump, Donald Duck, Hannah Montana, Jack Bauer, Annie Oakley, or The Godfather. Read it aloud to your group without telling them which of these possibilities you have chosen. Can they identify the voice? Does the exercise complicate or develop your ideas about the passage?

CHAPTER 4

Character

- *As Desire*
- *As Image*
- *As Voice*
- *As Action*
- *As Thought*
- *As Presented by the Author*
- *As Conflict*
- *Stock and Flat Characters*

I write because I want to have more than one life.
Anne Tyler

John Grant

WARM-UP

What does this woman want? Write about what she misses, covets, regrets, dreams of, longs for, deeply desires. What does she want for her daughter? How much of this will she be willing to tell the daughter? What will she admit to no one? Will the daughter share her desires?

NADIA SITS ACROSS FROM ME AT DINNER. SHE IS PETITE, dark-haired. She gestures delicately with her fork. She makes a political point to the famous, bald man beside me, who is sweating and drinking his fourth glass of wine. Nadia's voice is light, her phrases follow each other steadily. The famous man takes another piece of pie. He wipes his forehead with a knuckle, wipes the knuckle on his napkin, flaps the napkin toward Nadia as he replies to her question with a little explosion of sound. I miss some of what he says because his mouth is full of pie. I think: *She's smarter than he is, but he doesn't realize it because he's so impressed with his own fame; actually, underneath, he is terrified of being found out, and he's going to eat and drink himself to death trying to fill the void of his own ego.*

I hardly know these people! How did I come to such conclusions?!

Everything we know about other people we know through our five senses. The outer expresses the inner. Words, actions, and things, which can be seen and heard, express and reveal character and feeling that can be neither seen nor heard. Literature, of course, allows us a freedom that life does not, to be both inside and outside a character, to know thoughts as we can only know them in ourselves, while at the same time seeing the externals as we can for everyone *except* ourselves. In addition, literature can offer an authoritative voice to help us interpret and draw conclusions about the characters.

In nonfiction, fiction, poetry, and drama, there are essentially five possible methods of presenting a character to the reader:

Directly, through:

1. image (or "appearance")
2. voice (or "speech")
3. action
4. thought

Or **indirectly,** through:

5. "telling" or interpreting as an author

Each of these methods is discussed in this chapter, but I want to start with a necessity of all character—the phenomenon of desire—because in order to engage the attention and emotions of your reader you will need, even before you begin to write, to invent, intuit, or decide what each of your characters *wants.*

Character as Desire

> We yearn. We are the yearning creatures of this planet.... Yearning is always part of fictional character.
>
> *Robert Olen Butler*

The importance of desire in creating character can scarcely be overstated. Novelist Butler calls it *yearning,* to indicate its poignant and obsessive nature. Nor is such desire a small thing. Aristotle declared that the nature of a man's desire determined the nature of his morality: He who wants good is good;

he who wants evil is evil. (And it follows pretty well that he who wants the trivial is trivial, she who wants peace is peaceful, and so forth.)

Those of us who write are often excellent observers, and we can fall into the trap of creating fictional people who passively observe. Such passive characters lie flat on the page. The characters who stand up and make us care are so in love that they are willing to risk their reputations and their souls (Anna Karenina, for example); or so committed to a cause that they will devote their lives to it (Robin Hood, among many); or driven by a passion to know (like Faust) or to revenge (as in *Hamlet*), or to solve the mystery, climb the mountain, uncover the past, find out who they really are. Of course, the desire need not be as grand as these examples, and in modern literature the questing, conflicted nature of the desire is often and profoundly the point. But it is nevertheless so, that this quality of yearning or determination is what makes us catch our breath, hope for the best, fear the worst, and in short identify with what is, after all, a series of little squiggly lines on a page. "We know rationally," says William Logan, "that Prospero and Miranda never existed, much less Ariel or Caliban; that the real Caesar was not Shakespeare's Caesar; but we can be moved to tears by Ophelia's death, or Cordelia's. The bundles of words behave as if they had private psychologies."

You will have the makings of a character when you can fill out this sentence:

____(name)____ is a ____(adj.)____ ____-year-old ____(noun)____ who wants ________________.

It isn't so important to trace the motive back to some childhood experience or trauma as it is to explore the nature and reality of the character's desire. What is her deepest need, longing, hope, apart from food and air? What can't he live without?

In thinking about your character's desire, it's a good idea to think both generally and specifically, or about the deep desire and the immediate desire. In filling in the preceding sentence, you might think: *Jeremy Glazer is a belligerent 17-year-old basketball player who wants respect.* "Respect" in this case, an abstraction, represents what Jeremy deeply desires. As a writer you need to ask what, in the particular situation he finds himself in, would represent respect for Jeremy? Being placed on the starting team? Being included in the locker room banter? Or is it his father's acknowledgment that basketball matters as much as his grades? What a character wants deeply (and which can be expressed in an abstraction) will always have a particular manifestation in a particular situation and can be expressed in a way that leads to image and action.

TRY THIS 4.1

Choose a character you have thought and written about before. Fill out the sentence with blanks shown earlier. Then quickly jot down what makes your character:

- laugh
- flinch

(continued)

(Try This 4.1 continued)

- yell
- blush
- get a lump in the throat

Imagine your character in a situation that produces one of these emotions. What does he or she *want* in that situation? What is the deep, abstract desire? What, in this specific situation, does he or she want that would fulfill, at least temporarily, that desire?

Character as Image

> The first thing is to see the people every minute.... You have got to learn to paint with words.
>
> *Flannery O'Connor*

Sometimes a beginning writer skips the externals in order to try to take us directly to the abstract essence of a character. But if you let your reader get to know your characters through the sense details, as in life, these images will convey the essence in the way discussed in Chapter 1: How does this character laugh, what is he wearing, how does she move, what gesture does he make, what objects does he carry, what does she eat and drink, what is the tone of her voice, his laugh, the texture of his skin, the smell of her hair?

> Swollen feet
> tripping on vines in the heat,
> palms thick and green-knuckled,
> sweat drying on top of old sweat.
> She flicks her tongue over upper lip
> where the salt stings her cracked mouth.
>
> *"sus plumas el viento," Gloria Anzaldúa*

The first half dozen lines of this sharply realized miniature portrait convey much more than the images themselves. We already know the basic elements of this woman's life, her gender and status, her suffering. We know how poverty feels and tastes, the toll on the body of long overwork.

Especially in fiction and memoir, when a character is first introduced, it's important to let us experience that person through the senses (including sight), and it's often effective to emphasize a particular physical characteristic that can later remind us of the character as a whole. Here is an example from Ayelet Waldman's *Daughter's Keeper:*

> As a little girl she had been beautiful, rosy-cheeked and blond-ringleted. Today she wore baggy jeans and a ragged green sweatshirt that had been washed so often that its zipper arced in waves from her neck to her waist. Her best feature remained her hair, which hung, an unwashed mass of blond, brown, and red kinky curls, down to the middle of her back. She'd swept part of it off her face and clipped it back with a chipped tortoise-shell barrette.

Here a series of visible clues (*baggy, ragged, unwashed, chipped*) give us a sense of the young woman's attitudes and lifestyle, while the vivid picture of her hair ensures that the next time this character appears on the scene, the author need only mention the hair to evoke the character. But sometimes the images that evoke character are not direct images of that character at all, but of something in the surroundings.

> I often wonder who will be the last person to see me alive. If I had to bet, I'd bet on the delivery boy from the Chinese take-out. I order four nights out of seven. Whenever he comes I make a big production of finding my wallet. He stands in the doorway holding the greasy bag while I wonder if this is the night I'll finish off my spring roll, climb into bed, and have a heart attack in my sleep.

The History of Love, *Nicole Krauss*

Notice how, in this brief passage, the loneliness and longing of the old man are conveyed in the apparently mundane images of the Chinese take-out delivery, as well as in the clipped, almost throw-away rhythm of his voice.

Traditionally, the characters in a play may be minimally described (*Lisa, in her teens, scruffy; Ludovico, blind, a former spy*), for the very good reason that the people in the audience will have the live actor in front of them to offer a sense impression, heightened by costume, makeup, and lighting. But playwrights can and often do vividly signal in their stage directions the physical attributes, gestures, and clothes of their characters, and actors can and often do gratefully make use of this information to explore the character's inner life.

> Leaning on the solitary table, his head cupped in one hand as he pages through one of his comic books, is Sam. A black man in his mid-forties. He wears the white coat of a waiter.

"'Master Harold'...and the Boys," Athol Fugard

Or:

> ...Lou, the magician, enters. He is dressed in the traditional costume of Mr. Interlocutor: tuxedo, bow tie, top hat festooned with all kinds of whatnots that are obviously meant for good luck, he does a few catchy "soft shoe" steps & begins singing a traditional version of a black play song.

"spell #7," Ntozake Shange

TRY THIS 4.2

If people are characterized by the objects they choose, own, wear, and carry with them, they are also revealed in what they throw away. *Garbology* is the study of society or culture by examining and analyzing its refuse. Write a character sketch by describing the contents of your character's waste basket.

Character as Voice

As a writer you need to hear a character's voice in your head in order to bring him or her to life successfully. This involves moving beyond inventing or remembering the character to inhabiting his or her persona, a challenging task if your character is significantly different from the person you are. As a first step, it's always good practice to write a monologue in your character's voice. Thinking *from the point of view of that character* will help you to find the diction and the rhythm of his or her speech and thought. Keep going even if you feel you haven't "caught" the character, because sometimes the very fact of continuing will allow you to slip or sidle into the voice you seek.

TRY THIS 4.3

Write a quick sketch of a character you have already worked with—no more than two or three focused details. Then pick one of the trigger lines below and write a monologue in that character's voice. Keep going a little bit past the place you want to stop.

- It doesn't take much, does it, for...
- And what I said was true...
- I know right away I'm going to...
- I've become a different person since...
- I don't like anyone to watch me...
- You call that music?

Now look over the monologue and highlight a few phrases that seem to you to catch that character's voice. Pick one of these and use it to begin another short monologue.

One of the ways we understand people is by assessing, partly instinctively and partly through experience, what they express voluntarily and involuntarily. When someone chooses to wear baggy jeans as opposed to slim-fits, or a shaved head, a tuxedo, body piercing, a string of pearls—these are choices, largely conscious, that signal: *I am a member of this group.* Other "body language" will strike the viewer as involuntary (dishevelment, poor taste, blushing, slurring, staring, sweating, clumsiness) and so as a betrayal of characteristics that have not been chosen. In the same way speech may be consciously chosen both in its style (the rapper's patter, the lawyer's convolutions) and content (she tells him she's angry, but not that she's broke). On the whole, it is human nature to give the involuntary more credibility than the chosen. We say that *what he said was very generous, but he kept checking to see how it was going over.* His glances *belied* his words. In this case, we say that the words represent the *text,* and that what we read by other means is the *subtext.*

Speech belongs largely in the voluntary category, though like appearance it can (and does) betray us. Talking is an intentional attempt to express the inner as the outer. But when people talk in literature they convey much more than the information in their **dialogue.** They are also working for the author—to reveal themselves, advance the plot, fill in the past, control the pace, establish the tone, foreshadow the future, establish the mood. What busy talk!

> **NELL:** So just fill me in a bit more could you about what you've been doing.
>
> **SHONA:** What I've been doing. It's all down there.
>
> **NELL:** The bare facts are down here but I've got to present you to an employer.
>
> **SHONA:** I'm twenty-nine years old.
>
> **NELL:** So it says here.
>
> **SHONA:** We look young. Youngness runs in our family.
>
> **NELL:** So just describe your present job for me.
>
> **SHONA:** My present job at present. I have a car. I have a Porsche. I go up the M1 a lot. Burn up the M1 a lot. Straight up the M1 in the fast lane to where the clients are, Staffordshire, Yorkshire, I do a lot in Yorkshire. I'm selling electric things. Like dishwashers, washing machines, stainless steel tubs are a feature and the reliability of the program....

Top Girls, *Caryl Churchill*

Notice how the characters produce tension by contradicting each other (*Fill me in; it's all down there; but I've got to present you; I'm twenty-nine; so it says*). This is known as "no dialogue," in which characters are in many and various ways saying "no" to each other. They may be angry or polite, disagreeing, contradicting, qualifying, or frankly quarreling, but whatever the tone, they spark our interest because we want to find out what will happen in this overt or implied conflict.

Notice also how Shona's description of her job reveals the subtext. She falters between concrete imagery and flimsy generalization, contradicting in generalization what she tries to prove by making up convincing details. She is spinning lies without sufficient information or imagination, so it's no great surprise when Nell ends the exchange with, "Christ, what a waste of time...Not a word of this is true, is it?"

Dramatic dialogue is always **direct** as in this example, all the words spoken. In fiction, nonfiction, or poems, direct dialogue of this sort is lively and vivid, but sometimes the narrative needs to cover ground faster, and then dialogue may be **indirect** or **summarized.** Summarized dialogue, efficient but textureless, gives us a brief report:

> *Shona claimed she had sales experience, but Nell questioned both her age and her expertise.*

Indirect dialogue gives the flavor of the dialogue without quoting directly:

> *Nell wanted her to fill in the facts, so Shona repeated that she was twenty-nine, claimed that looking young ran in the family, and that she drove a Porsche up to*

Staffordshire to sell dishwashers and washing machines. But she couldn't seem to come up with the word "appliances."

There's a strong temptation to make dialogue eloquent (you are a writer, after all), and the result is usually that it becomes stilted. People are often *not* eloquent, precisely about what moves them most. Half the time we aren't really sure what we mean, and if we are, we don't want to say it, and if we do, we can't find the words, and if we can, the others aren't listening, and if they are, they don't understand.... In fact, the various failures to communicate can make the richest sort of dialogue, just as the most stunted language is sometimes the most revealing of character.

In this example from David Mitchell's *Black Swan Green*, thirteen-year-old Jason Taylor comes home from school. Notice how in this short space Mum's actions contradict her words, her "sarky" (sarcastic) tone conceals her secret, and Jason's thoughts contradict his responses. Notice also that we are never in doubt who's speaking, though there is only one "he said."

> Mum was at the dining room table...Dad's fireproof document box was out and open. Through the kitchen hatch I asked if she'd had a good day. "Not a good day, exactly." Mum didn't take her eyes off her calculator. "But it's certainly been a real revelation."
>
> "That's good," I said, doubting it. I got a couple of Digestives and a glass of Ribena. Julia's snaffled all the Jaffa Cakes 'cause she's at home all day revising for her A levels. Greedy moo. "What're you doing?"
>
> "Skateboarding."
>
> I should've just gone upstairs. "What's for dinner?"
>
> "Toad."
>
> One unsarky answer to one simple question, that's all I wanted. "Doesn't Dad usually do all the bank statements and stuff?"
>
> "Yes." Mum finally looked at me. "Isn't your lucky old father in for a pleasant surprise when he gets home..."

Debate and argument can make interesting dialogue if the matter itself is interesting, but in imaginative writing debate and argument are usually too static to be of interest, too simple and too single. Eudora Welty explained in an interview with the *Paris Review,* "Sometimes I needed to make a speech do four or five things at once—reveal what the character said but also what he thought he said, what he hid, what others were going to think he meant, and what they misunderstood—and so forth—all in this single speech....I used to laugh out loud sometimes when I wrote it."

If a character expresses in dialogue what he/she means, that character has done only one thing, whereas as a writer you are constantly trying to mean more than you say, to give several clues at once to the inner lives of your characters. If Jeannine says:

> I feel that civilization is encroaching on nature, and that the greed of the developers will diminish the value of all our lives—

—she has expressed an opinion, but little of her inner life is revealed: her emotions, her history, her particularities. This is the dialogue equivalent of the vague category images described in Chapter 2. But if she says:

> They should lock up that builder. He's massacred the neighborhood.
> I remember how the lilac and wisteria used to bloom, and then the
> peonies, and the daffodils. What fragrance in this room! But now.
> Smell the stink of that site next door. It just makes me sick.

—the same opinion is expressed, but her emotions—anger, nostalgia, and defeat—also are vividly revealed, and through particular detail.

TRY THIS 4.4

Write a "dialogue" between two characters, only one of whom can speak. The other is physically, emotionally, or otherwise prevented from saying what he/she wants to say. Write only the words of the one, only the appearance and actions of the other.

Character as Action

> By our actions we discover what we really believe and, simultaneously, reveal ourselves to others.
>
> *John Gardner*

I have said that a character is first of all someone who *wants*. Whatever the nature of that desire, it will lead the character toward action and therefore toward potential change. The action may be as large as a military charge or as small as removing a coffee cup, but it will signal or symbolize for the reader that a significant change has occurred. The characters who interest and move us are those who are capable of such change.

Playwright Sam Smiley observes that "Any significant discovery forces change in conditions, relationships, activity or all three." And, he says, "The quickest and best way to know someone is to see that person make a significant decision.... At the instant a character makes a choice, he changes from one state to another; his significant relationships alter; and usually he must follow a new line of action as a consequence."

If we grant that *discovery* and *decision* are the two agents of human change, characters will be *in action* when these are possible. Action as in *action-packed* is a crude but effective way of getting discovery and decision into a work:

> There's the bad guy! (discovery) Quick, I will load my revolver, hide behind this pillar, turn and shoot. (decision) But wait! There's his accomplice on the catwalk above me! (discovery) I will roll under this forklift to avoid his bullet! (decision)

The thriller, the cop show, the alien, and the spy are enormously popular (and money-making) genres because they simplify and exaggerate our experience of what action is. But of course most human discovery, decision, and change take place in the realm of work, love, relationship, and family, and it's important for the literary writer to recognize discovery and decision in these areas, where they are likely to be both complex and difficult.

One reason that debate and argument seem static is that characters holding forth with well thought-out positions seem unlikely to change, whereas dialogue that represents potential change *becomes* itself dramatic action. In dramatic dialogue, in ways large and small, characters are constantly making discoveries and decisions. Look again at the previous exchange between Nell and Shona. What does Nell discover about Shona? What does Shona decide to say to prove herself? Look at the exchange between Jason and his mum. What does Jason want? Discover? Decide? What discovery and decision of Mum's can you infer from the subtext?

Change may seem most obvious in literature with a strong story line, and of course discovery and decision will often involve a physical action: she opens the letter, he picks up the phone, she slams the door, he steps on the gas. But change also importantly occurs in the mind, and even in the gentlest piece of memoir or the slightest nature lyric, the persona is made aware of something that seems important, something that has not before been present to the mind, and now is, and so changes the entire mental landscape. Frequently (by no means always; still, frequently) in the tradition of memoir this mental change has to do with a new perspective on the complexity of life and human beings; frequently in lyric poetry it has to do with the ephemeral quality of beauty, and therefore an awareness of death.

The change from alive-to-dead is a major one, as is the change from in-danger-to-triumphant-hero. But discovery and decision are no less present in the subtle and profound exchanges of ordinary life.

Loveliest of trees, the cherry now
Is hung with snow along the bough
And stands about the woodland ride
Wearing white for Easter tide.

Now of my threescore years and ten
Twenty will not come again,
And take from seventy springs a score,
That only leaves me fifty more.

And since, to look at things in bloom,
Fifty years is little room,
About the woodland I will go
To see the cherry hung with snow.

"II" from A Shropshire Lad, *A. E. Housman*

In this very low-key poem (you can hear the stillness, the deliberate pace, in the rhythm), the poet makes two discoveries and a decision. The first discovery is of the snow on the trees; the second is of the brevity of life. The decision is simply to walk in the woods, but in following this "new line of action" he also "changes from one state to another," in that he acknowledges his mortality.

TRY THIS 4.5

Take a monologue you have already written and add actions, in the form of either narration or stage directions. Make the action contradict or qualify the speech. ("I'm not worried about it at all. These things don't throw me." [*She twists her hands.*]) and so forth. Remember that a good way to reveal characters' feelings is through their relationships to objects.

Character as Thought

Although discovery and decision necessarily *imply* thought, image, speech, and action are all external manifestations—things that we could observe. Imaginative writing has the power also to take us inside the minds of characters to show us what they are thinking. Again, different degrees of the revelation of thought are appropriate to different forms of literature:

- In a memoir or personal essay we count on the honest thoughts of the author but can't credibly see into the minds of other characters. (Even this quasi-rule is sometimes broken; Tom Wolfe in his techniques of "new journalism" frequently turns what his interviewees say into a kind of mental patter or stream of consciousness, as if these quotations were in fact their thoughts.)
- A character in a drama is necessarily speaking and therefore making his/her thoughts external, but there are a number of theatrical traditions to let us know that we are overhearing thoughts—as in soliloquy, aside, voice-over. Many characters in modern drama speak directly to the audience, and usually do so with an assumed honesty toward what is going on in their minds, whereas in dialogue with other characters they may lie, conceal, stumble, or become confused.
- Fiction usually (except in the case of the objective narrator) gives us the thoughts of at least the central character.
- A persona in poetry is usually sharing thoughts. Poetry also has the same freedom as fiction, to be presented from the point of view of a character—and this character may reveal what's on his or her mind.

Aristotle suggested a useful way of looking at thought in relation to desire. A persona or character begins with a certain desire, and therefore a certain specific goal in mind. Thought is the process by which she works backward to decide what to do in the immediate situation that presents itself. "Loveliest of Trees" is a condensed poetic demonstration of this process. *The chances are I will die at about seventy. I'm twenty now. That means I have fifty years left. That's not many years to look at these trees. I will look at them now.* My apologies to Housman for this rude paraphrase—but it does show not only Aristotle's understanding of the thought process, but also how crucial to the beauty of the poem is Housman's diction.

Thought, like dialogue, is also action when it presents us with the process of change. Since both discovery and decision take place in the mind, thought is material to every character and is in fact the locus of action and the dwelling place of desire. In the first lines of any poem, the first page of every story, the curtain rise of every drama, you can find a human consciousness yearning for whatever might occur in the last line, on the last page, in the last scene. The action proceeds because that consciousness makes a lightning-fast leap backward to the present moment, to decide what action can be taken now, at this moment, in this situation, to achieve that goal. At every new discovery, the mind repeats the process, ever changing in the service of a fixed desire.

TRY THIS 4.6

Pick a character. What is your character's deep desire? What is the situation that character is in now—where, doing what, in the company of whom? Make a list, inventing as you go, of the character's thought process, backward from the ultimate desire to the specific action (or inaction) that would lead eventually toward that desire.

Character as Presented by the Author

Appearance, speech, action, and thought are the direct methods of presenting character. The *indirect method* is **authorial interpretation**—"telling" us the character's background, motives, values, virtues, and the like. The advantages of the indirect method are enormous, for its use leaves you free to move in time and space; to know anything you choose to know whether the character knows it or not; and godlike, to tell us what we are to feel. The indirect method allows you to convey a great deal of information in a short time.

> The port town of Veracruz is a little purgatory between land and sea for the traveler, but the people who live there are very fond of themselves and the town they have helped to make... and they carry on their lives of alternate violence and lethargy with a pleasurable contempt for outside opinion....

Ship of Fools, *Katherine Anne Porter*

The disadvantage of this indirect method is that it bars us readers from sharing the immediacy and vividness of detail and the pleasure of judging for ourselves. In the summarized judgments of this passage, for example, we learn more about the attitude of the narrator than about the town. Nevertheless, the indirect method is very efficient when you want to cover the exposition quickly, as A.S. Byatt does in this passage from "Crocodile Tears."

The Nimmos spent their Sundays in those art galleries that had the common sense to open on that dead day.... They liked buying things, they liked simply looking, they were happily married and harmonious in their stares, on the whole. They engaged a patch of paint and abandoned it, usually simultaneously, they lingered in the same places, considering the same things. Some they remembered, some they forgot, some they carried away.

Thus in a few sentences of the first paragraph, Byatt tells us everything we need to know about the Nimmos' marriage—especially since Mr. Nimmo is going to die on the next page, and the story will concern itself with Mrs. Nimmo's flight from the scene. Notice that although this passage is full of analysis and interpretation, we are given some images to look at: "...harmonious in their stares... They engaged a patch of paint and abandoned it..." In an instance like this, authorial interpretation functions for pace and structure. But it is not a very useful mode to describe human change, which involves action and therefore calls for the immediacy of scene, and of the direct presentation of character.

TRY THIS 4.7

Write a paragraph of no more than a hundred words presenting a character through authorial interpretation. Cover at least five years in the character's life, four qualities he or she possesses, three important events, and two habitual actions.

Character as Conflict

The meaning of life must be conceived in terms of the specific meaning of a personal life in a given situation.

Victor Frankl

Rich characterization can be effectively (and quite consciously) achieved by producing a conflict between methods of presentation. A character can be directly revealed to us through *image, voice, action,* and *thought.* If you set one of these methods at odds with the others, then dramatic tension will be produced. Imagine, for example, a character who is impeccable and expensively dressed, who speaks eloquently, who acts decisively, and whose mind is revealed to us as full of order and determination. He is inevitably a flat character. But suppose that he is impeccable, eloquent, and decisive, and that his mind is a mess of wounds and panic. He is at once interesting.

Here is the opening passage of Saul Bellow's *Seize the Day,* in which appearance and action are blatantly at odds with thought. Notice that it is the tension between suppressed thought and what is expressed through appearance and action that produces the rich character conflict.

When it came to concealing his troubles, Tommy Wilhelm was not less capable than the next fellow. So at least he thought, and there was a certain amount of evidence to back him up. He had once been an actor—no, not quite, an extra—and he knew what acting should be. Also, he was smoking a cigar, and when a man is smoking a cigar, wearing a hat, he has an advantage: it is harder to find out how he feels. He came from the twenty-third floor down to the lobby on the mezzanine to collect his mail before breakfast, and he believed—he hoped—he looked passably well: doing all right.

Thought is most frequently at odds with one or more of the other three methods of direct presentation—reflecting the difficulty we have expressing ourselves openly or accurately—but this is by no means always the case. The author may be directly telling us what to think and contradicting herself by showing the character to be someone else entirely. A character may be successfully, calmly, even eloquently, expressing fine opinions while betraying himself by pulling at his ear, or herself by crushing her skirt. Captain Queeg of Herman Wouk's *The Caine Mutiny* is a memorable example of this, maniacally clicking the steel balls in his hand as he defends his disciplinary code. Often we are not privy to the thoughts of a character at all, so that the conflicts must be expressed in a contradiction between the external methods of direct presentation, appearance, speech, and action. Notice that the notion of "betraying oneself" is again important here. We're more likely to believe the evidence unintentionally given than deliberate expression.

TRY THIS 4.8

Write a short character sketch (it may be from life), focusing on how your character makes a living. Put your character in a working situation and let us know by a combination of direct and indirect methods what that work is; how well he/she does it; what it looks, sounds, smells like; and how the character feels about it. Contrast the methods.

TRY THIS 4.9

Write a stage direction for two people that conveys the emotional relationship between them. They may gesture, move, touch, and relate to objects or elements of the place; but there is no dialogue.

Stock and Flat Characters

I have insisted on the creation of character through an understanding of desire and through many methods of presentation. But it would be impractical and unnecessary to go through this process for every passerby on the fictional street, and boring to present such characters fully.

Flat characters are those defined by a single idea or quality. They may exist only to fulfill a function, and we need know little about them. It's true nevertheless that they can be brought to brief life in an image—notice that the take-out delivery boy in the passage from Nicole Krauss's *History of Love,* "stands in the doorway holding the greasy bag"—but neither the author nor the reader needs to stop to explore their psychology, or to give them the complexity that would make them *round.*

Stock characters or *caricatures* are related to flat characters in that they insistently present a single idea or quality. If you have aimed for a lifelike and complex character, and someone says you've created a stock character, that's not good. But some writers, especially in drama, effectively use stock characters as a way of satirizing human types. Eugene Ionesco takes the technique to its extreme in *The Bald Soprano:*

> MRS. SMITH: There, it's nine o'clock. We've drunk the soup, and eaten the fish and chips, and the English salad. The children have drunk English water. We've eaten well this evening. That's because we live in the suburbs of London and because our name is Smith.

TRY THIS 4.10

Go back to something you have written and find a character who appears only briefly or is named or referred to without appearing. Characterize that person with a single vivid image.

Or:

Pick two stock characters from the list below. Decide what one wants from the other. Caricature them by writing a dialogue between them.

Absent-minded professor
Drug pusher
Naïve girl
Rock or hip-hop wannabe
Rich widow
Evangelist

More to Read

Chiarella, Tom. *Writing Dialogue.* Cincinnati: Story Press, 1998. Print.
Minot, Stephen. *Three Genres.* Upper Saddle River, N.J.: Prentice Hall, 2002. Print.

READINGS

CREATIVE NONFICTION

STUART DYBEK

Thread

The year after I made my first Holy Communion, I joined the Knights of Christ, as did most of the boys in my fourth-grade class. We'd assemble before mass on Sunday mornings in the sunless concrete courtyard between the convent and the side entrance to the sacristy. The nuns' courtyard was private, off-limits, and being allowed to assemble there was a measure of the esteem in which the Knights were held.

Our uniforms consisted of the navy blue suits we'd been required to wear for our first Holy Communion, although several of the boys had already outgrown them over the summer. In our lapels we wore tiny bronze pins of a miniature chalice engraved with a cross, and across our suit coats we fit the broad satin sashes that Sister Mary Barbara, who coached the Knights, would distribute. She had sewn them herself. At our first meeting Sister Mary Barbara instructed us that just as in the days of King Arthur, the responsibility of the Knights was to set an example of Christian gentlemanliness. If ever called upon to do so, each Knight should be ready to make the ultimate sacrifice for his faith. She told us that she had chosen her name in honor of Saint Barbara, a martyr whose father had shut her up in a tower and, when she still refused to deny her Christian faith, killed her. I'd looked up the story of Saint Barbara in *The Lives of the Saints.* After her father had killed her—it didn't say how—he'd been struck by lightning, and so Saint Barbara had become the patron of fireworks and artillery, and the protectress against sudden death.

Our sashes came in varying shades of gold, some worn to a darker luster and a bit threadbare at the edges and others crisp and shining like newly minted coins. We wore them diagonally in the swashbuckling style of the Three Musketeers. It felt as if they should have supported the weight of silver swords ready at our sides.

Once outfitted, we marched out of the courtyard into the sunlight, around St. Roman Church, and through its open massive doors, pausing to dip our fingers in the marble font of holy water and cross ourselves as if saluting our Lord—the bloodied, lifesized Christ crowned with thorns and crucified in the vestibule. Then we continued down the center aisle to the front pews that were reserved for the Knights.

5 In the ranking order of the mass we weren't quite as elite as the altar boys, who got to dress in actual vestments like the priest, but being a Knight seemed an essential step up the staircase of sanctity. Next would be torchbearer, then altar boy, and beyond that, if one had a vocation, subdeacon, deacon, priest.

Though I couldn't have articulated it, I already understood that nothing was more fundamental to religion than hierarchies. I was sort of a child prodigy when it came to religion, in the way that some kids had a gift for math or were spelling whizzes. Not only did I always know the answer in catechism class, I could anticipate the question. I could quote Scripture and recite most any Bible story upon command. Although I couldn't find my way out of our parish, the map of the spiritual world was inscribed on my consciousness. I could enumerate the twelve choirs of angels. From among the multitude of saints, I could list the various patrons—not just the easy ones like Saint Nicholas, patron of children, or Saint Jude, patron of hopeless cases, but those whom most people didn't even know existed: Saint Brendan the Navigator, patron of sailors and whales; Saint Stanislaus Kostka, patron of broken bones; Saint Anthony of Padua, whose name, Anthony, I would take later when I was confirmed, patron of the poor; Saint Bonaventure of Potenza, patron of bowel disorders; Saint Fiacre, an Irish hermit, patron of cabdrivers; Saint Alban, patron of torture victims; Saint Dismas, the Good Thief who hung beside Christ, patron of death row inmates; Saint Mary Magdalen, patron of perfume.

I could describe their powers with the same accuracy that kids described the powers of superheroes—Batman and Robin, Green Lantern, the Flash—but I knew the difference between saints and comic book heroes: the saints were real.

I didn't doubt either their existence or their ability to intercede on behalf of the faithful with God. In the dimension of the spiritual world there was the miraculous and the mysterious, but never the impossible. At each mass, we would witness the miraculous in the transubstantiation of bread and wine into the body and blood of Christ. And when I encountered mysteries such as the mystery of the Trinity, I believed. Mystery made perfect sense to me.

My holy medal turning green around my neck, I practiced small rituals: wore a thumbed cross of ashes on my forehead on Ash Wednesday as a reminder of mortality, wore a scapular wool side against the skin of my chest as a reminder of Christ's suffering, and I offered up my own small suffering as I offered up the endless ejaculations I kept careful count of for the poor souls in Purgatory.

That was an era for ceremony, a time before what my aunt Zosha came to derisively refer to as Kumbaya Catholicism, when the mass was still in Latin and on Good Fridays weeping old women in babushkas would walk on their knees up the cold marble aisle to kiss the glass-encased sliver of the True Cross that the priest presented at the altar rail. After each kiss, he would wipe the glass with a special silk kerchief for sanitary purposes.

It was a time of cold war, when each Sunday mass ended with a prayer "for the conversion of Russia," a more severe time when eating meat on Friday, the day of Christ's crucifixion, could send a soul to Hell. Before receiving Communion, one was required to fast from the night before. To receive Communion without fasting was a mortal sin, and there could be no greater blasphemy than to take the body and blood of Christ into one's mouth with mortal sin on the soul. Sometimes at Sunday mass, women, weak from fasting, would faint at church.

Once mass began, the Knights would rise in unison and stand and kneel to the ebb and flow of the ceremony with a fierce attention that should have been accompanied by the rattling of our sabers and spurs against the marble. Our boyish, still unbroken voices were raised in prayer and hymn. At Communion time, it was the privilege of the Knights to be the first to file from the pews, leading the rest of the congregation to the Communion rail. There we would kneel in a long row of navy blue slashed with diagonals of gold, awaiting the priest. Often the priest was Father Fernando, the first Mexican priest at our parish. He'd served as a chaplain in the Marine Corps and lost an eye to shrapnel while administering the last rites to dying soliders in Korea, and he distributed the Eucharist to us as if reviewing the troops. Usually Father Fernando wore a brown glass eye, but he'd been shattering glass eyes lately—the rumor was he'd been going out drinking with Father Boguslaw—and when he'd break one he'd wear a pair of sunglasses with the lens over the good eye popped out.

Sometimes, approaching the Communion rail, I'd be struck by the sight of my fellow Knights already kneeling, by their frayed cuffs and the various shades of socks and worn soles. It never failed to move me to see my classmates from the perspective of their shoes.

One Sunday, sitting in the pew, watching flashes of spring lightning illuminate the robes of the angels on the stained glass windows, my mind began to drift. I studied my gold sash, upon which the tarnishing imprint of raindrops had dried into vague patterns—it had begun to rain just as we marched in off the street. There was a frayed edge to my sash, and I wrapped a loose thread around my finger and gently tugged. The fabric bunched and the thread continued to unwind until it seemed the entire sash might unravel. I pinched the thread and broke it off, then wound it back around my finger tightly enough to cut off my circulation. When my fingertip turned white, I unwound the thread from my finger and weighed it on my open hand, fitting it along the various lines on my palm. I opened my other palm and held my hands out to test if the balance between them was affected by the weight of the thread. It wasn't. I placed the thread on my tongue and let it rest there, where its weight was more discernible. I half expected a metallic taste of gold, but it tasted starchy, like any other thread. Against the pores of my tongue, I could feel it growing thicker with the saliva that was gathering in my mouth. I swallowed both the saliva and the thread.

15 Immediately after, when it was already too late, it occurred to me that I had broken my fast.

It would be a mortal sin for me to receive the host. Yet the primary duty of a Knight was to march to the Communion rail leading the congregation. Not only was the enormous humiliation I would feel if I remained seated while the others filed up to the altar more than I was willing to face, but in a sudden panic I worried that I'd be kicked out of the Knights, my ascent up the staircase of sanctity over almost before it had begun. I sat trying to figure a way out of the predicament I'd created, feeling increasingly anxious, a little sick, actually, as if the thread were winding around my stomach. I thought about how not a one of my classmates would have even realized that his fast had been broken by swallowing a thread, and since he wouldn't have realized it was a sin, then it wouldn't have been one. It didn't seem quite fair that my keener understanding made me more culpable. Perhaps a thread didn't count as food, I thought, but I knew I was grasping for excuses—it seemed a dubious distinction to risk one's soul upon. The choir was singing the *Agnus Dei;* Communion would be next. My suit coat felt pasted to my back by a clammy sweat as I thought up various plans at what seemed a feverish pace and rejected them just as feverishly. Maybe I could pretend to be even sicker than I was feeling and run from church with my hand over my mouth as if I were about to vomit; or I could pretend to faint. But not only did the notion of making up a lie in order not to receive Communion seem too devious, I didn't have the nerve to carry off a spectacle like that. To do so would probably be a mortal sin against the Eighth Commandment; I'd just be getting myself in deeper.

Then a detail mentioned in passing by Sister Aurelia back in third grade when we practiced for our first Holy Communion occurred to me. She'd told us that if, at the Communion rail, one should ever realize he had a mortal sin on his soul that he'd somehow forgotten about until that moment, then he was merely to clasp a hand in a *mea culpa* over his heart and bow his head, and the priest would understand and move on.

Communion time arrived, and on trembling legs I marched to the rail with the other Knights. How fervently I wished that I were simply going to receive Communion. I felt alone, separated from the others by my secret, and yet I became aware of an odd kind of excitement bordering on exhilaration at what I was about to do. Father Fernando wearing his one-eyed pair of dark glasses approached, an altar boy at his elbow, holding a paten to catch the host in case it should slip from the priest's hand. I could hear their soles on the carpet as they paused to deliver a host and moved to the next Knight. I could hear Father Fernando muttering the Latin prayer over and over as he deposited a host upon each awaiting tongue. *Corpus domini nostri Jesu Christi... May the body of our Lord, Jesus Christ, preserve your soul in everlasting life.*

So this is the aching flush of anticipation, I thought, that a penitent sinner would feel, a murderer, perhaps, or a thief, someone who had committed terrible crimes and found himself at the Communion rail.

Father Fernando paused before me, and I clapped a fist against my heart and 20
bowed my head. He stopped and squinted down at me through the missing lens of his dark glasses, trying to catch my eyes and having a hard time doing it with his single good eye. Finally he shrugged and moved on, wondering, I was sure, what grievous sin I had committed.

I never told him, nor anyone else. I had swallowed a thread. No one but God would ever be the wiser. It was my finest hour as a theologian. Only years later did I realize it would be that moment I'd think back to when I came to wonder how I'd lost my faith.

LOIS-ANN YAMANAKA

JohnJohn's World

So silent, I think.

■ ■ ■

He stands near the white gingers, pulls the blossoms petal by petal from their lush bouquets. He throws handfuls in the air like confetti caught in the trade winds. A quiet joy, my JohnJohn, surrounded for a moment by the intense fragrance of flowers, the white shower of ginger falling around him.

■ ■ ■

And I think, "He loves me. He loves me not."

And I know: He loves me. Forty-three times a day.

From some psychology journal, I know the human animal needs forty-three hugs a day to survive.

No one has ever held me in a full embrace forty-three times a day like JohnJohn does. Doesn't know that a hug should end when a hug should end. It's his autism, I think. What Bruno Bettelheim called a lack of social awareness and social relationships.

But something passes back and forth between us again and again. I feel it inside me like the surging of kinetic waves. Forty-three times a day.

■ ■ ■

It is another Saturday. JohnJohn holds my hand as we wait in line at the supermarket. He looks at all of the Mylar balloons bobbing in the air-conditioned draft at the checkout. Today he wants the balloons. All of them.

I know he might throw a fabulous autistic tantrum as soon as I say the word *no*. So I try not to panic. We need to cross "groceries" off our never-ending to-do list. I try to ignore him. I put the celery and cheese slices on the conveyor belt. Coffee, frozen chicken, cat food.

He lets go of my hand. "Ba-noon," he says, a whisper at first.

I acknowledge him with a nod for the language that I long for, my prayers since his diagnosis filled with begging God for JohnJohn's words.

A bag of apples and a dozen eggs glide away from us.

He steps away from me.

"JohnJohn—" I call him.

He tries to gather up the balloons tied to racks of the *Enquirer* and *Woman's Day*, pulls and yanks at the ribbons with tiny jingle bells on their ends. A Happy Birthday balloon gets away.

The entire supermarket goes silent.

Then JohnJohn screams.

Someone gasps. Women stare and pull their own children closer to them as I struggle to get screaming and crying, feet-kicking, back-arching JohnJohn out of the market. A security guard steps toward us. The clerk shakes his head at my abandoned shopping cart full of groceries, the spin of apples on a conveyor belt.

In JohnJohn's world, I can afford to buy him every balloon on every trip to the market. In JohnJohn's world, he takes all of the shiny balloons home to our yard full of white ginger blossoms and lets all of them go. Watches them spin their silver way in the trade winds, over treetops and rooftops, out of the valley. A moment of beauty, his silent freedom.

■ ■ ■

There was a speech pathologist who said to me, "I think the Department of Education is doing more than its share in providing services for John. My schedule is very full." She saw him for fifteen minutes on Mondays, Wednesdays, and Fridays. I was asking for Tuesdays and Thursdays. He was still preverbal.

I heard the whispering. "John is very low-functioning."

There was a special education teacher who slapped him across the face, dragged him across the floor, then put her knee on his back. "It was an unintentional block," the principal told me. "John hit her first."

I listened to their test results: "Cognitive understanding of language: 23 months. Emerging skills: 2 years, 9 months. Cognitive verbal expressive ability: 23 months. Emerging skills: 2 years, 8 months." He was ten years old.

There was a therapeutic aide from the Department of Health who read romance novels while JohnJohn ate his lunch alone. "John needs to use a napkin to wipe his face at lunch," she told me. "Do you let him use his hand at home?"

■ ■ ■

His silence screams from their memos:

> To: Principal
> Fr: Room 44
> Cc: VP and parents
> Re: John
>
> John bolted out of the classroom. He began to hit and bite as I led him to the assembly. I have scratches on my face and neck, and bruises and bite marks on my arms. John raged for one hour and thirty-eight minutes.

■ ■ ■

> To: Principal
> Fr: Room 44
> Cc: VP, SSC, and parents
> Re: John's *aggressive* behavior

John lunged at Max's face. We had a hard time pulling him off. We need an emergency IEP meeting. This is now a staff and student safety issue.

■ ■ ■

To: Principal
Fr: Room 44
Cc: VP, SSC, EA, TA, and parents
Re: John's escalating *violent* behavior

John picked up a chair and threw it at me. I evacuated the other children and staff to a safe area outside. Have his parents consulted their psychiatrist to possibly increase meds?

■ ■ ■

To: Principal
Fr: Room 44
Cc: VP, SSC, Occ. T, Phys. T, Sp. T, PPT, TA, EA, and parents
Re: John's *self-mutilation*

John tore off his shirt in the middle of the field. He gouged himself repeatedly. Do I need to fill out any paperwork to document what happened?

■ ■ ■

What would JohnJohn tell me if he could?
He would tell me how light attracts light.
How light also attracts darkness.
He would tell me about forgiveness.
And then he would tell me about love.

■ ■ ■

I cannot recall my mother or father, my sisters, or anyone else in my family saying the words *I love you* to me as a child. I was told that our actions speak louder than words. It was even biblical.

I would even venture to say that no one has *ever* really loved me. It's the stuff of years of therapy, hundreds of bad poems and angst-ridden stories, suicide letters documenting names and places, and one too many soulful karaoke ballads from the pit of my bleeding heart.

I have heard the words *I love you* but know that I never *truly* believed the words spoken to me by the hometown boy in the back seat of my mother's Corolla. A friend or two in a *Beaches* moment. This man, that man. This girl, that poet. Always a cheap bottle of merlot.

And then for the first time I heard the words *I love you.*

It was Christmas morning. JohnJohn stood over me. He was five. He was singing the ABC song, a song that we sang to him over and over, praying for language to sink in through repetition and rote.

That morning he sang a child's song to me. The moment lasted the sweetest forever. It was almost a dream, the song he sang with so much love for me.

A song that he never sang again.

"I love you, JohnJohn," I said as he crawled under the covers this cold morning.

He did not look at me, but I heard him, as I would hear him again and again many times a day for the weeks, months, and years to come: "Ai yav you."

Never withholding the words *I love you* from me as many times as I needed to hear them each and every day.

■ ■ ■

JohnJohn loved his educational aide Nohea. When he could no longer manage the day loaded with sensory input, she walked with him in a calm silence.

On one of their long walks, JohnJohn looked into a room full of second-graders. The teacher, not stopping her lesson, waved him in with a broad grin.

A jar with holes punched into its cover with a chrysalis inside.

A calendar.

"It will be a monarch butterfly in fourteen days," the teacher JohnJohn would call Mrs. O told the class.

JohnJohn visited her classroom every day after lunch.

Fourteen days later, a second-grade girl knocked on the door to JohnJohn's special ed classroom. She led JohnJohn and Nohea to the big field by the basketball courts.

Mrs. O's children formed a small circle around him. "The class voted," she said. "We want JohnJohn to release the butterfly." Mrs. O slowly opened the jar, then stepped toward JohnJohn.

Afraid, he backed away. Nohea placed her hands on his shoulders. "You can do it," she whispered in his ear. She took JohnJohn's hand and moved his finger toward the unfurling wings.

The butterfly stepped out of the jar and onto JohnJohn's trembling finger. It rested there, taking in the world, the sunlight, the trade winds, and JohnJohn's wide eyes as he lifted his hand to the sky for that ceremonious moment of first flight.

■ ■ ■

There are moments when I know that JohnJohn's inner world is without boundary.

When he was seven, he took the bag of yellow magnetic alphabet letters to the refrigerator as he had done many times before. But this time, one by one, I listened to the slow snap of plastic letters onto cold metal. I peered at him from behind the living room wall. JohnJohn had spelled out his first word.

U-N-I-V-E-R-S-A-L.

"Such a big and profound word, JohnJohn." I spoke with my mind, my heart, fluttering inside me. "Yes, you are *universal*. You are the moon and the stars, the oceans and the mountains, the planets and galaxies, a million constellations."

I remained still as he began to compose another word.

D-I-M-E-N-S-I-O-N-A-L.

"Yes, you are multi*dimensional*," I told him, "layers upon layers of depth and knowledge, all inside of you, my little JohnJohn."

I held him close to me when he was done, breathing in the sweet of his neck and hair. Hug number twenty-five.

We left his words there for years, the mold and dust of time on yellow plastic. It was a reminder of his message to all of us:

Universality, all of us here for a reason, the universality of the human experience no matter what our circumstance.

Dimensionality, all of us multifaceted beings of mind, body, soul, and light.

■ ■ ■

Daylight seeps through the shower trees, the flutter of rice sparrows in and out of shadows. A light rain slants in the northerly trade winds. White and yellow ginger blooms through late summer.

It is a silent world in the valley we call home.

JohnJohn loves the sky, the movement of the clouds down the Ko'olau Mountains, iridescent bubbles floating down from the top of his tree house, the butterflies that lift themselves from our purple crownflower tree.

His cousin Samantha looks down at JohnJohn from the top of the tree house. She puts the bubble wand back in the plastic bottle.

"Why is JohnJohn always covering his ears like that?" she asks me.

■ ■ ■

They would say.

Because he is.

> ***Autistic:***
> Hyperawareness to environmental input.
> Multisensory integration deficits.
> Augmented response to sound.
> Stereotyped motor behavior.
> Auditory overstimulation.
> Failure to habituate.
> Developmental delay.
> Hypersensitivity.

"Why?" she asks again.

I tell her because he is our JohnJohn, my JohnJohn:

He can hear the sound of the butterfly's wings.

TRY THIS 4.11
Describe in as accurate detail as you can any moment of humiliation or shame—either your own or one you observed. What did you learn from it?

FICTION

ALICE MUNRO

Prue

Prue used to live with Gordon. This was after Gordon had left his wife and before he went back to her—a year and four months in all. Some time later, he and his wife were divorced. After that came a period of indecision, of living together off and on; then the wife went away to New Zealand, most likely for good.

Prue did not go back to Vancouver Island, where Gordon had met her when she was working as a dining-room hostess in a resort hotel. She got a job in Toronto, working in a plant shop. She had many friends in Toronto by that time, most of them Gordon's friends and his wife's friends. They liked Prue and were ready to feel sorry for her, but she laughed them out of it. She is very likable. She has what eastern Canadians call an English accent, though she was born in Canada—in Duncan, on Vancouver Island. This accent helps her to say the most cynical things in a winning and lighthearted way. She presents her life in anecdotes, and though it is the point of most of her anecdotes that hopes are dashed, dreams ridiculed, things never turn out as expected, everything is altered in a bizarre way and there is no explanation ever, people always feel cheered up after listening to her; they say of her that it is a relief to meet somebody who doesn't take herself too seriously, who is so unintense, and civilized, and never makes any real demands or complaints.

The only thing she complains about readily is her name. Prue is a schoolgirl, she says, and Prudence is an old virgin; the parents who gave her that name must have been too shortsighted even to take account of puberty. What if she had grown a great bosom, she says, or developed a sultry look? Or was the name itself a guarantee that she wouldn't? In her late forties now, slight and fair, attending to customers with a dutiful vivacity, giving pleasure to dinner guests, she might not be far from what those parents had in mind: bright and thoughtful; a cheerful spectator. It is hard to grant her maturity, maternity, real troubles.

Her grownup children, the products of an early Vancouver Island marriage she calls a cosmic disaster, come to see her, and instead of wanting money, like other people's children, they bring presents, try to do her accounts, arrange to have her house insulated. She is delighted with their presents, listens to their advice, and, like a flighty daughter, neglects to answer their letters.

5 Her children hope she is not staying on in Toronto because of Gordon. Everybody hopes that. She would laugh at the idea. She gives parties and goes to parties; she goes out sometimes with other men. Her attitude toward sex is very comforting to those of her friends who get into terrible states of passion and jealousy, and feel cut loose from their moorings. She seems to regard sex as a wholesome, slightly silly indulgence, like dancing and nice dinners—something that shouldn't interfere with people's being kind and cheerful to each other.

Now that his wife is gone for good, Gordon comes to see Prue occasionally, and sometimes asks her out for dinner. They may not go to a restaurant; they may go to his house. Gordon is a good cook. When Prue or his wife lived with him he couldn't cook at all, but as soon as he put his mind to it he became—he says truthfully—better than either of them.

Recently he and Prue were having dinner at his house. He had made Chicken Kiev, and crème brûlée for dessert. Like most new, serious cooks, he talked about food.

Gordon is rich, by Prue's—and most people's—standards. He is a neurologist. His house is new, built on a hillside north of the city, where there used to be picturesque, unprofitable farms. Now there are one-of-a-kind, architect-designed, very expensive houses on half-acre lots. Prue, describing Gordon's house, will say, "Do you know there are four bathrooms? So that if four people want to have baths at the same time there's no problem. It seems a bit much, but it's very nice, really, and you'd never have to go through the hall."

Gordon's house has a raised dining area—a sort of platform, surrounded by a conversation pit, a music pit, and a bank of heavy greenery under sloping glass. You can't see the entrance area from the dining area, but there are no intervening walls, so that from one area you can hear something of what is going on in the other.

10 During dinner the doorbell rang. Gordon excused himself and went down the steps. Prue heard a female voice. The person it belonged to was still outside, so she could not hear the words. She heard Gordon's voice, pitched low, cautioning. The door didn't close—it seemed the person had not been invited in—but the voices went on, muted and angry. Suddenly there was a cry from Gordon, and he appeared halfway up the steps, waving his arms.

"The crème brûlée," he said. "Could you?" He ran back down as Prue got up and went into the kitchen to save the dessert. When she returned he was climbing the stairs more slowly, looking both agitated and tired.

"A friend," he said gloomily. "Was it all right?"

Prue realized he was speaking of the crème brûlée, and she said yes, it was perfect, she had got it just in time. He thanked her but did not cheer up. It seemed it was not the dessert he was troubled over but whatever had happened at the door. To take his mind off it, Prue started asking him professional questions about the plants.

"I don't know a thing about them," he said. "You know that."

"I thought you might have picked it up. Like the cooking."

"She takes care of them."

"Mrs. Carr?" said Prue, naming his housekeeper.

"Who did you think?"

Prue blushed. She hated to be thought suspicious.

"The problem is that I think I would like to marry you," said Gordon, with no noticeable lightening of his spirits. Gordon is a large man, with heavy features. He likes to wear thick clothing, bulky sweaters. His blue eyes are often bloodshot, and their expression indicates that there is a helpless, baffled soul squirming around inside this doughty fortress.

"What a problem," said Prue lightly, though she knew Gordon well enough to know that it was.

The doorbell rang again, rang twice, three times, before Gordon could get to it. This time there was a crash, as of something flung and landing hard. The door slammed and Gordon was immediately back in view. He staggered on the steps and held his hand to his head, meanwhile making a gesture with the other hand to signify that nothing serious had happened, Prue was to sit down.

"Bloody overnight bag," he said. "She threw it at me."

"Did it hit you?"

"Glancing."

"It made a hard sound for an overnight bag. Were there rocks in it?"

"Probably cans. Her deodorant and so forth."

"Oh."

Prue watched him pour himself a drink. "I'd like some coffee, if I might," she said. She went to the kitchen to put the water on, and Gordon followed her.

"I think I'm in love with this person," he said.

"Who is she?"

"You don't know her. She's quite young."

"Oh."

"But I do think I want to marry you, in a few years' time."

"After you get over being in love?"

"Yes."

"Well. I guess nobody knows what can happen in a few years' time."

When Prue tells about this, she says, "I think he was afraid I was going to laugh. He doesn't know why people laugh or throw their overnight bags at him, but he's noticed they do. He's such a proper person, really. The lovely dinner. Then she comes and throws her overnight bag. And it's quite reasonable to think of marrying me in a few years' time, when he gets over being in love. I think he first thought of telling me to sort of put my mind at rest."

She doesn't mention that the next morning she picked up one of Gordon's cufflinks from his dresser. The cufflinks are made of amber and he bought them in Russia, on the holiday he and wife took when they got back together again.

They look like squares of candy, golden, translucent, and this one warms quickly in her hand. She drops it into the pocket of her jacket. Taking one is not a real theft. It could be a reminder, an intimate prank, a piece of nonsense.

She is alone in Gordon's house; he has gone off early, as he always does. The housekeeper does not come till nine. Prue doesn't have to be at the shop until ten; she could make herself breakfast, stay and have coffee with the housekeeper, who is her friend from olden times. But once she has the cufflink in her pocket she doesn't linger. The house seems too bleak a place to spend an extra moment in. It was Prue, actually, who helped choose the building lot. But she's not responsible for approving the plans—the wife was back by that time.

When she gets home she puts the cufflink in an old tobacco tin. The children bought this tobacco tin in a junk shop years ago, and gave it to her for a present. She used to smoke, in those days, and the children were worried about her, so they gave her this tin full of toffees, jelly beans, and gumdrops, with a note saying, "Please get fat instead." That was for her birthday. Now the tin has in it several things besides the cufflink—all small things, not of great value but not worthless, either. A little enamelled dish, a sterling-silver spoon for salt, a crystal fish. These are not sentimental keepsakes. She never looks at them, and often forgets what she has there. They are not booty, they don't have ritualistic significance. She does not take something every time she goes to Gordon's house, or every time she stays over, or to mark what she might call memorable visits. She doesn't do it in a daze and she doesn't seem to be under a compulsion. She just takes something, every now and then, and puts it away in the dark of the old tobacco tin, and more or less forgets about it.

GABRIEL GARCÍA MÁRQUEZ

The Handsomest Drowned Man in the World

A Tale for Children, Translated by Gregory Rabassa

The first children who saw the dark and slinky bulge approaching through the sea let themselves think it was an empty ship. Then they saw it had no flags or masts and they thought it was a whale. But when it washed up on the beach, they removed the clumps of seaweed, the jellyfish tentacles, and the remains of fish and flotsam, and only then did they see that it was a drowned man.

They had been playing with him all afternoon, burying him in the sand and digging him up again, when someone chanced to see them and spread the alarm in the village. The men who carried him to the nearest house noticed that he weighed more than any dead man they had ever known, almost as much as a horse, and they said to each other that maybe he'd been floating too long and the water had got into his bones. When they laid him on the floor they said he'd been taller than all the other men because there was barely enough room for him in the house, but they thought that maybe the ability to keep on growing after death was part of the nature of certain drowned men. He had the smell of the sea about him and only his shape gave one to suppose that it was the corpse of a human being, because the skin was covered with a crust of mud and scales.

They did not even have to clean off his face to know that the dead man was a stranger. The village was made up of only twenty-odd wooden houses that had stone courtyards with no flowers and which were spread about on the end of a desertlike cape. There was so little land that mothers always went about with the fear that the wind would carry off their children and the few dead that the years had caused among them had to be thrown off the cliffs. But the sea was calm and bountiful and all the men fit into seven boats. So when they found the drowned man they simply had to look at one another to see that they were all there. That night they did not go out to work at sea. While the men went to find out if anyone was missing in neighboring villages, the women stayed behind to care for the drowned man. They took the mud off with grass swabs, they removed the underwater stones entangled in his hair, and they scraped the crust off with tools used for scaling fish. As they were doing that they noticed that the vegetation on him came from faraway oceans and deep water and that his clothes were in tatters, as if he had sailed through labyrinths of coral. They noticed too that he bore his death with pride, for he did not have the lonely look of other drowned men who came out of the sea or that haggard, needy look of men who drowned in rivers. But only when they finished cleaning him off did they become aware of the kind of man he was and it left them breathless. Not only was he the tallest, strongest, most virile, and best built man they had ever seen, but even though they were looking at him there was no room for him in their imagination.

They could not find a bed in the village large enough to lay him on nor was there a table solid enough to use for his wake. The tallest men's holiday pants would not fit him, nor the fattest ones' Sunday shirts, nor the shoes of the one with the biggest feet. Fascinated by his huge size and his beauty, the women then decided to make him some pants from a large piece of sail and a shirt from some bridal brabant linen so that he could continue through his death with dignity. As they sewed, sitting in a circle and gazing at the corpse between stitches, it seemed to them that the wind had never been so steady nor the sea so restless as on that night and they supposed that the change had something to do with the dead man. They thought that if that magnificent man had lived in the village, his house would have had the widest doors, the highest ceiling, and the strongest floor, his bedstead would have been made from a midship frame held together by iron bolts, and his wife would have been the happiest woman. They thought that he would have had so much authority that he could have drawn fish out of the sea simply by calling their names and that he would have put so much work into his land that springs would have burst forth from among the rocks so that he would have been able to plant flowers on the cliffs. They secretly compared him to their own men, thinking that for all their lives theirs were incapable of doing what he could do in one night, and they ended up dismissing them deep in their hearts as the weakest, meanest, and most useless creatures on earth. They were wandering through the maze of fantasy when the oldest woman, who as the oldest had looked upon the drowned man with more compassion than passion, sighed:

5 "He has the face of someone called Esteban."

It was true. Most of them had only to take another look at him to see that he could not have any other name. The more stubborn among them, who were the youngest, still lived for a few hours with the illusion that when they put his clothes on and he lay among the flowers in patent leather shoes his name might be Lautaro. But it was a vain illusion. There had not been enough canvas, the poorly cut and worse sewn pants were too tight, and the hidden strength of his heart popped the buttons on his shirt. After midnight the whistling of the wind died down and the sea fell into its Wednesday drowsiness. The silence put an end to any last doubts: he was Esteban. The women who had dressed him, who had combed his hair, had cut his nails and shaved him were unable to hold back a shudder of pity when they had to resign themselves to his being dragged along the ground. It was then that they understood how unhappy he must have been with that huge body since it bothered him even after death. They could see him in life, condemned to going through doors sideways, cracking his head on crossbeams, remaining on his feet during visits, not knowing what to do with his soft, pink, sea lion hands while the lady of the house looked for her most resistant chair and begged him, frightened to death, sit here, Esteban, please, and he, leaning against the wall, smiling, don't bother, ma'am, I'm fine where I am, his heels raw and his back roasted from having done the same thing so many times whenever he paid a visit, don't bother, ma'am, I'm fine where I am, just to avoid the embarrassment of breaking up the chair, and never knowing perhaps that the ones who said don't go, Esteban, at least wait till the coffee's ready, were the ones who later on would whisper the big boob finally left, how nice, the handsome fool has gone. That was what the women were thinking beside the body a little before dawn. Later, when they covered his face with a handkerchief so that the light would not bother him, he looked so forever dead, so defenseless, so much like their men that the first furrows of tears opened in their hearts. It was one of the younger ones who began the weeping. The others, coming to, went from sighs to wails, and the more they sobbed the more they felt like weeping, because the drowned man was becoming all the more Esteban for them, and so they wept so much, for he was the most destitute, most peaceful, and most obliging man on earth, poor Esteban. So when the men returned with the news that the drowned man was not from the neighboring villages either, the women felt an opening of jubilation in the midst of their tears.

"Praise the Lord," they sighed, "he's ours!"

The men thought the fuss was only womanish frivolity. Fatigued because of the difficult nighttime inquiries, all they wanted was to get rid of the bother of the newcomer once and for all before the sun grew strong on that arid, windless day. They improvised a litter with the remains of foremasts and gaffs, tying it together with rigging so that it would bear the weight of the body until they reached the cliffs. They wanted to tie the anchor from a cargo ship to him so that he would sink easily into the deepest waves, where fish are blind and divers die of nostalgia, and bad currents would not bring him back to shore, as had happened with other bodies. But the more they hurried, the more the women thought of ways to waste time. They walked about like startled hens, pecking with the sea charms on their breasts, some interfering on one side to put a scapular of the good wind on the drowned man, some on the other side to put a wrist compass on him, and after a great deal of *get away from there, woman, stay out of the way, look, you almost made me fall on top of the dead man,* the men began to feel mistrust in their livers and started grumbling about why so many main-alter decorations for a stranger, because no matter how many nails and holy water jars he had on him, the sharks would chew him all the same, but the women kept piling on their junk relics, running back and forth, stumbling, while they released in sighs what they did not in tears, so that the men finally exploded with *since when has there ever been such a fuss over a drifting corpse, a drowned nobody, a piece of cold Wednesday meat.* One of the women, mortified by so much lack of care, then removed the handkerchief from the dead man's face and the men were left breathless too.

He was Esteban. It was not necessary to repeat it for them to recognize him. If they had been told Sir Walter Raleigh, even they might have been impressed with his gringo accent, the macaw on his shoulder, his cannibal-killing blunderbuss, but there could be only one Esteban in the world and there he was, stretched out like a sperm whale, shoeless, wearing the pants of an undersized child, and with those stony nails that had to be cut with a knife. They only had to take the handkerchief off his face to see that he was ashamed, that it was not his fault that he was so big or so heavy or so handsome, and if he had known that this was going to happen, he would have looked for a more discreet place to drown in, seriously, I even would have tied the anchor off a galleon around my neck and staggered off a cliff like someone who doesn't like things in order not to be upsetting people now with this Wednesday dead body, as you people say, in order not to be bothering anyone with this filthy piece of cold meat that doesn't have anything to do with me. There was so much truth in his manner that even the most mistrustful men, the ones who felt the bitterness of endless nights at sea fearing that their women would tire of dreaming about them and begin to dream of drowned men, even they and others who were harder still shuddered in the marrow of their bones at Esteban's sincerity.

10 That was how they came to hold the most splendid funeral they could conceive of for an abandoned drowned man. Some women who had gone to get flowers in the neighboring villages returned with other women who could not believe what they had been told, and those women went back for more flowers when they saw the dead man, and they brought more and more until there were so many flowers and so many people that it was hard to walk about. At the final moment it pained them to return him to the waters as an orphan and they chose a father and mother from among the best people, and aunts and uncles and cousins, so that through him all the inhabitants of the village became kinsmen. Some sailors who heard weeping from a distance went off course and people heard of one who had himself tied to the mainmast, remembering ancient fables about sirens. While they fought for the privilege of carrying him on their shoulders along the steep escarpment by the cliffs, men and women became aware for the first time of the desolation of their streets, the dryness of their courtyards, the narrowness of their dreams as they faced the splendor and beauty of their drowned man. They let him go without an anchor so that he could come back if he wished and whenever he wished, and they all held their breath for the fraction of centuries the body took to fall into the abyss. They did not need to look at one another to realize that they were no longer all present, that they would never be. But they also knew that everything would be different from then on, that their houses would have wider doors, higher ceilings, and stronger floors so that Esteban's memory could go everywhere without bumping into beams and so that no one in the future would dare whisper the big boob finally died, too bad, the handsome fool has finally died, because they were going to paint their house fronts gay colors to make Esteban's memory eternal and they were going to break their backs digging for springs among the stones and planting flowers on the cliffs so that in future years at dawn the passengers on great liners would awaken, suffocated by the smell of gardens on the high seas, and the captain would have to come down from the bridge in his dress uniform, with his astrolabe, his pole star, and his row of war medals and, pointing to the promontory of roses on the horizon, he would say in fourteen languages, look there, where the wind is so peaceful now that it's gone to sleep beneath the beds, over there, where the sun's so bright that the sunflowers don't know which way to turn, yes, that's Esteban's village.

TRY THIS 4.12

Imagine an impossible event. Write a page about it in the calmest, most detailed and natural voice you can summon. Write about it as if you were describing a walk to the post office.

THEODORE ROETHKE

I Knew a Woman

I knew a woman, lovely in her bones,
When small birds sighed, she would sigh back at them;
Ah, when she moved, she moved more ways than one:
The shapes a bright container can contain!
Of her choice virtues only gods should speak,
Or English poets who grew up on Greek
(I'd have them sing in chorus, cheek to cheek).

How well her wishes went! She stroked my chin,
She taught me Turn, and Counter-turn, and Stand;
She taught me Touch, that undulant white skin;
I nibbled meekly from her proffered hand;
She was the sickle; I, poor I, the rake,
Coming behind her for her pretty sake
(But what prodigious mowing we did make).

Love likes a gander, and adores a goose:
Her full lips pursed, the errant note to seize;
She played it quick, she played it light and loose;
My eyes, they dazzled at her flowing knees;
Her several parts could keep a pure repose,
Or one hip quiver with a mobile nose
(She moved in circles, and those circles moved).

Let seed be grass, and grass turn into hay:
I'm martyr to a motion not my own;
What's freedom for? To know eternity.
I swear she cast a shadow white as stone.
But who would count eternity in days?
These old bones live to learn her wanton ways:
(I measure time by how a body sways).

CAROLE SIMMONS OLES

Stonecarver

for Father

Don't look at his hands now.
Stiff and swollen, small finger

curled in like a hermit:
needing someone to open the ketchup,
an hour to shave.
That hand held the mallet,
made the marble say
Cicero, Juno, and *laurel.*

Don't think of his eyes
behind thick lenses squinting
at headlines, his breath
drowning in stonedust and Camels,
his sparrow legs.

Think of the one who slid
3 floors down scaffolding ropes
every lunchtime,
who stood up to Donnelly the foreman
for more time to take care.

Keep him the man in the photo,
straight-backed on the park bench
in Washington, holding hands
with your mother.
Keep his hands holding
calipers, patterns, and pointer,
bringing the mallet down
fair on the chisel,
your father's hands sweeping off dust.

ALLEN GINSBERG

To Aunt Rose

Aunt Rose—now—might I see you
with your thin face and buck tooth smile and pain
            of rheumatism—and a long black heavy shoe
                for your bony left leg
        limping down the long hall in Newark on the running carpet
            past the black grand piano
                in the day room
                    where the parties were
and I sang Spanish loyalist songs
            in a high squeaky voice
                (hysterical) the committee listening
            while you limped around the room

collected the money—
Aunt Honey, Uncle Sam, a stranger with a cloth arm
in his pocket
and huge young bald head
of Abraham Lincoln Brigade

—your long sad face
your tears of sexual frustration
(what smothered sobs and bony hips
under the pillows of Osborne Terrace)
—the time I stood on the toilet seat naked
and you powdered my thighs with Calomine
against the poison ivy—my tender
and shamed first black curled hairs
what were you thinking in secret heart then
knowing me a man already—
and I an ignorant girl of family silence on the thin pedestal
of my legs in the bathroom—Museum of Newark.

Aunt Rose
Hitler is dead, Hitler is in Eternity; Hitler is with
Tamburlane and Emily Brontë
Though I see you walking still, a ghost on Osborne Terrace
down the long dark hall to the front door
limping a little with a pinched smile
in what must have been a silken
flower dress
welcoming my father, the Poet, on his visit to Newark
—see you arriving in the living room
dancing on your crippled leg
and clapping hands his book
had been accepted by Liveright

Hitler is dead and Liveright's gone out of business
The Attic of the Past and *Everlasting Minute* are out of print
Uncle Harry sold his last silk stocking
Claire quit interpretive dancing school
Buba sits a wrinkled monument in Old
Ladies Home blinking at new babies

last time I saw you was the hospital
pale skull protruding under ashen skin
blue veined unconscious girl
in an oxygen tent
the war in Spain has ended long ago
Aunt Rose

ELIZABETH JENNINGS

One Flesh

Lying apart now, each in a separate bed,
He with a book, keeping the light on late,
She like a girl dreaming of childhood,
All men elsewhere—it is as if they wait
Some new event: the book he holds unread,
Her eyes fixed on the shadows overhead,

Tossed up like flotsam from a former passion,
How cool they lie. They hardly ever touch,
Or if they do it is like a confession
Of having little feeling—or too much.
Chastity faces them, a destination
For which their whole lives were a preparation.

Strangely apart, yet strangely close together,
Silence between them like a thread to hold
And not wind in. And time itself's a feather
Touching them gently. Do they know they're old,
These two who are my father and my mother
Whose fire from which I came, has now grown cold?

TED KOOSER

Tattoo

What once was meant to be a statement—
a dripping dagger held in the fist
of a shuddering heart—is now just a bruise
on a bony old shoulder, the spot
where vanity once punched him hard
and the ache lingered on. He looks like
someone you had to reckon with,
strong as a stallion, fast and ornery,
but on this chilly morning, as he walks
between the tables at a yard sale
with the sleeves of his tight black T-shirt
rolled up to show us who he was,
he is only another old man, picking up
broken tools and putting them back,
his heart gone soft and blue with stories.

TRY THIS 4.13

Write a poem, a short essay, or a short-short story about the young person you can still see within an old person.

DRAMA

ALAN BENNETT

Bed Among the Lentils

Susan is a vicar's wife. She is thin and nervous and probably smokes. She sits on an upright chair in the kitchen. It is evening.

Geoffrey's bad enough but I'm glad I wasn't married to Jesus. The lesson this morning was the business in the Garden of Gethsemane when Jesus prays and the disciples keep falling asleep. He wakes them up and says, 'Could you not watch with me one hour'? It's my mother.

I overslept this morning, flung on a cardigan and got there just as everybody was standing up. It was Holy Communion so the militants were out in force, the sub-zero temperature in the side-chapel doubtless adding to the attraction.

Geoffrey kicks off by apologising for his failure to de-frost the church. (Subdued merriment.) Mr Medlicott has shingles, Geoffrey explains, and, as is well known, has consistently refused to initiate us lesser mortals into the mysteries of the boiler. (Helpless laughter.)

Mrs Belcher read the lesson. Mr Belcher took the plate round. 'Big day for you', I said to them afterwards.

The sermon was about sex. I didn't actually nod off, though I have heard it before. Marriage gives the OK to sex is the gist of it, but while it is far from being the be all and end all (you can say that again) sex is nevertheless the supreme joy of the married state and a symbol of the relationship between us and God. So, Geoffrey concludes, when we put our money in the plate it is a symbol of everything in our lives we are offering to God and that includes our sex. I could only find 10p.

Thinking about the sermon during the hymn I felt a pang of sympathy for the Deity, gifted with all this sex. No fun being made a present of the rare and desiccated conjunctions that take place between Geoffrey and me. Or the frightful collisions that presumably still occur between the Belchers. Not to mention whatever shame-faced fumblings go on between Miss Budd and Miss Bantock. 'It's all right if we offer it to God, Alice'. 'Well, if you say so, Pauline'.

Amazing scenes at the church door. Geoffrey had announced that after Easter the bishop would be paying us a visit so the fan club were running round in small circles, Miss Frobisher even going so far as to squeeze my elbow.

Meanwhile, Geoffrey stands there the wind billowing out his surplice and ruffling his hair, what 'Who's Who in the Diocese of Ripon' calls 'his schoolboy good looks'. I helped put away the books while he did his 'underneath this cassock I am but a man like anybody else' act. 'Such a live wire', said Mrs Belcher, 'really putting the parish on the map'. 'That's right', burbles Mrs Shrubsole, looking at me. 'We must cherish him'.

We came back and I cherished him with some chicken wings in a tuna fish sauce. He said, 'That went down well'. I said, 'The chicken wings'? He said, 'My sermon. I felt it hit the nail on the head'. He put his hand over mine, hoping, I suppose, that having hit one nail he might hit another, but I said I had to go round with the parish magazine. 'Good girl', he said. 'I can attack my paperwork instead'.

Roads busy. Sunday afternoon. Families having a run out. Wheeling the pram, walking the dog. Living. Almighty God unto whom all hearts be open, and from whom no secrets are hid, cleanse the thoughts of our hearts by the inspiration of thy holy spirit that we may perfectly love thee and worthily magnify thy glorious name and not spend our Sunday afternoons parked in a lay-by on the Ring Road wondering what happened to our life.

When I got back Geoffrey was just off to Evensong, was I going to come? When I said 'No' he said, 'Really? Then I'd better pretend you have a headache'.

Why? One of the unsolved mysteries of life, or the unsolved mysteries of my life, is why the vicar's wife is expected to go to church at all. A barrister's wife doesn't have to go to court, an actor's wife isn't at every performance, so why have I always got to be on parade? Not to mention the larger question of whether one believes in God in the first place. It's assumed that being the vicar's wife one does but the question has never actually come up, not with Geoffrey anyway. I can understand why, of course. To look at me, the hair, the flat chest, the wan smile, you'd think I was just cut out for God. And maybe I am. I'd just like to have been asked that's all. Not that it matters of course. So long as you can run a tight jumble sale you can believe in what you like.

It could be that Geoffrey doesn't believe in God either. I've always longed to ask him only God never seems to crop up. 'Geoffrey', I'd say. 'Yes, Susan'? 'Do you really believe in God? I mean, cards on tables, you don't honestly, do you? God's just a job like any other. You've got to bring home the bacon somehow'. But no. Not a word. The subject's never discussed.

After he'd gone I discovered we were out of sherry so I've just been round to the off-licence. The woman served me. Didn't smile. I can't think why. I spend enough.

Go to black.

Come up on Susan on the steps of the side-chapel, polishing a candlestick. Afternoon.

We were discussing the ordination of women. The bishop asked me what I thought. Should women take the services? So long as it doesn't have to be me, I wanted to say, they can be taken by a trained gorilla. 'Oh yes', Geoffrey chips in, 'Susan's all in favour. She's keener than I am, aren't you, darling'? 'More sprouts anybody'? I said.

On the young side for a bishop, but he's been a prominent sportsman at university so that would explain it. Boxing or rugby. Broken nose at some stage anyway. One of the 'Christianity is common sense' brigade. Hobby's bricklaying apparently and refers to me throughout as 'Mrs Vicar'. Wants beer with his lunch and Geoffrey says he'll join him so this leaves me with the wine. Geoffrey's all over him because the rumour is he's shopping round for a new Archdeacon. Asks Geoff how outgoing I am. Actually says that. 'How outgoing is Mrs Vicar'? Mr Vicar jumps in with a quick rundown of my accomplishments and an outline of my punishing schedule. On a typical day, apparently, I kick off by changing the wheel on the Fiesta, then hasten to the bedside of a dying pensioner, after which, having done the altar flowers and dispensed warmth and appreciation to sundry parishioners en route, I top off a thrill-packed morning by taking round Meals on Wheels…somehow—and this to me is the miracle', says Geoffrey—'somehow managing to rustle up a delicious lunch in the interim', the miracle somewhat belied by the flabby lasagna we are currently embarked on. 'The ladies', says the bishop. 'Where would we be without them'?

Disaster strikes as I'm doling out the tinned peaches: the jug into which I've decanted the Carnation milk gets knocked over, possibly by me. Geoffrey, for whom turning the other cheek is part of the job, claims it caught his elbow and his lordship takes the same line, insisting he gets doused in Carnation milk practically every day of his life. Still, when I get a dishcloth and sponge off his gaiters I catch him giving me a funny look. It's Mary Magdalen and the Nivea cream all over again. After lunch Geoffrey's supposed to be taking him on a tour of the parish but while we're having a cup of instant he claps his hand to his temple because he's suddenly remembered he's supposed to be in Keighley blessing a steam engine.

We're stacking the dishwasher and I ask Geoffrey how he thinks it's gone. Doesn't know. 'Fingers crossed', I say. 'I think there are more constructive things we could do than that', he says crisply, and goes off to mend his inner tube. I sit by the Aga for a bit and as I doze off it comes to me that by 'constructive things' he perhaps means prayer.

When I wake up there's a note from Geoffrey. 'Gone to talk to the Ladies Bright Hour. Go to bed'. I'm not sleepy and anyway we're running low on sherry so I drive into Leeds. I've stopped going round the corner now as I owe them a bit on the side and she's always so surly. There's a little Indian shop behind the Infirmary I've found. It's a newsagents basically but it sells drink and anything really, the way they do. Open last thing at night, Sundays included, my ideal. Ramesh he's called. Mr Ramesh I call him, though Ramesh may be his Christian name. Only not Christian of course. I've been once or twice now, only this time he sits me in the back place on a sack of something and talks. Little statuette of a god on the wall. A god. Not The God. Not the definite article. One of several thousand apparently. 'Safety in numbers', I said but he didn't understand. Looks a bit more fun than Jesus anyway. Shows me pictures of other gods, getting up to all sorts. I said, 'She looks a very busy lady. Is that yoga'? He said, 'Well, it helps'. He's quite athletic himself apparently, married, but his wife's only about fourteen so they won't let her in. He calls me Mrs Vicar too, only it's different. He has lovely teeth.

Go to black.

Come up on Susan in the kitchen near the Aga. Morning.

Once upon a time I had my life planned out...or half of it at any rate. I wasn't clear about the first part, but at the stroke of fifty I was all set to turn into a wonderful woman...the wife to a doctor, or a vicar's wife, Chairman of the Parish Council, a pillar of the WI. A wise, witty and ultimately white-haired old lady, who's always stood on her own feet until one day at the age of eighty she comes out of the County Library, falls under the weight of her improving book, breaks her hip and dies peacefully, continently and without fuss under a snowy coverlet in the cottage hospital. And coming away from her funeral in a country churchyard on a bright winter's afternoon people would say, 'Well, she was a wonderful woman'.

Had this been a serious ambition I should have seen to it I was equipped with the skills necessary to its achievement. How to produce jam which, after reaching a good, rolling boil, successfully coats the spoon; how to whip up a Victoria sponge that just gives to the fingertips; how to plan, execute and carry through a successful garden fête. All weapons in the armoury of any upstanding Anglican lady. But I can do none of these things. I'm even a fool at the flower arrangement. I ought to have a PhD in the subject the number of classes I've been to but still my efforts show as much evidence of art as walking sticks in an umbrella stand. Actually it's temperament. I don't have it. If you think squash is a competitive activity try flower arrangement.

On this particular morning the rota has Miss Frobisher and Mrs Belcher down for the side aisles and I'm paired with Mrs Shrubsole to do the altar and the lectern. My honest opinion, never voiced needless to say, is that if they were really sincere about religion they'd forget flower arrangement altogether, invest in some permanent plastic jobs and put the money towards the current most popular famine. However, around mid-morning I wander over to the church with a few dog-eared chrysanthemums. They look as if they could do with an immediate drink so I call in at the vestry and root out a vase or two from the cupboard where Geoffrey keeps the communion wine.

It not looming very large on my horizon, I assume I am doing the altar and Mrs Shrubsole the lectern, but when I come out of the vestry Mrs S is at the altar well embarked on her arrangement. I said, 'I thought I was doing the altar'. She said, 'No. I think Mrs Belcher will bear me out. I'm down to do the altar. You are doing the lectern. Why'? She smiled sweetly. 'Do you have a preference'? The only preference I have is to shove my chrysanthemums up her nose but instead I practise a bit of Christian forbearance and go stick them in a vase by the lectern. In the best tradition of my floral arrangements they look like the poles of a wigwam, so I go and see if I can cadge a bit of backing from Mrs Belcher. 'Are you using this'? I say, picking up a bit of mouldy old fern. 'I certainly am. I need every bit of my spiraea. It gives it body'. I go over and see if Miss Frobisher has any greenery going begging only she's doing some Japanese number, a vase like a test-tube half filled with gravel, in which she's throttling a lone carnation. So I retire to the vestry for a bit to calm my shattered nerves, and when I come out ready to tackle my chrysanths again Mrs Shrubsole has apparently finished and fetched the other two up to the altar to admire her handiwork. So I wander up and take a look.

Well, it's a brown job, beech leaves, teazles, grass, that school of thought. Mrs Shrubsole is saying, 'It's called Forest Murmurs. It's what I did for my Highly Commended at Harrogate last year. What do you think'? Gert and Daisy are of course speechless with admiration, but when I tentatively suggest it might look a bit better if she cleared up all the bits and pieces lying around she said, 'What bits and pieces'? I said, 'All these acoms and fir-cones and what not. What's this conker in aid of? She said, 'Leave that. The whole arrangement pivots on that'. I said, 'Pivots'? 'When the adjudicator was commenting on my arrangement he particularly singled out the hint I gave of the forest floor'. I said, 'Mrs Shrubsole. This is the altar of St Michael and All Angels. It is not The Wind in the Willows'. Mrs Belcher said, 'I think you ought to sit down'. I said, 'I do not want to sit down'. I said, 'It's all very well to transform the altar into something out of Bambi but do not forget that for the vicar the altar is his working surface. Furthermore', I added, 'should the vicar sink to his knees in prayer, which since this is the altar he is wont to do, he is quite likely to get one of these teazle things in his eye. This is not a flower arrangement. It is a booby trap. A health hazard. In fact', I say in a moment of supreme inspiration, 'it should be labelled HAZFLOR. Permit me to demonstrate'. And I begin getting down on my knees just to prove how lethal her bloody Forest Murmurs is. Only I must have slipped because next thing I know I'm rolling down the altar steps and end up banging my head on the communion rail.

Mrs Shrubsole, who along with every other organisation known to man has been in the St John's Ambulance Brigade, wants me left lying down, whereas Mrs Belcher is all for getting me on to a chair. 'Leave them lying down', says Mrs Belcher, 'and they inhale their own vomit. It happens all the time, Veronica'. 'Only, Muriel', says Mrs Shrubsole, 'when they have vomited. She hasn't vomited'. 'No', I say, 'but I will if I have to listen to any more of this drivel', and begin to get up. 'Is that blood, Veronica'? says Mrs Belcher pointing to my head. 'Well', says Mrs Shrubsole, reluctant to concede to Mrs B on any matter remotely touching medicine, 'it could be, I suppose. What we need is some hot sweet tea'.

'I thought that theory had been discredited', says Mrs Belcher. Discredited or not it sends Miss Frobisher streaking off to find a teabag, and also, it subsequently transpires, to telephone all and sundry in an effort to locate Geoffrey. He is in York taking part in the usual interdenominational conference on the role of the church in a hitherto uncolonised department of life, underfloor central heating possibly. He comes haring back thinking I'm at death's door, and finding I'm not has nothing more constructive to offer than I take a nap.

This gives the fan club the green light to invade the vicarage, making endless tea and the vicar his lunch and, as he puts it, 'spoiling him rotten'. Since this also licenses them to conduct a fact-finding survey of all the housekeeping arrangements or absence of same ('Where does she keep the Duroglit, vicar'?), a good time is had by all. Meanwhile Emily Brontë is laid out on the sofa in a light doze.

I come round to hear Geoffrey saying, 'Mrs Shrubsole's going now, darling'. I don't get up. I never even open my eyes. I just wave and say, 'Goodbye, Mrs Shrubsole'. Only thinking about it as I drift off again I think I may have said, 'Goodbye, Mrs Subsoil'. Anyway I meant the other. Shrubsoil.

When I woke up it was dark and Geoffrey'd gone out. I couldn't find a thing in the cupboard so I got the car out and drove into Leeds. I sat in the shop for a bit, not saying much. Then I felt a bit wanny and Mr Ramesh let me go into the back place to lie down. I must have dozed off because when I woke up Mr Ramesh has come in and started taking off his clothes. I said, 'What are you doing? What about the shop'? He said, 'Do not worry about the shop. I have closed the shop'. I said, 'It's only nine. You don't close till eleven'. 'I do tonight', he said. I said, 'What's tonight'? He said, 'A chance in a million. A turn-up for the books. Will you take your clothes off please'. And I did.

Go to black.

Come up on Susan sitting in the vestry having a cigarette. Afternoon.

You never see pictures of Jesus smiling, do you? I mentioned this to Geoffrey once. 'Good point, Susan', is what he said, which made me wish I'd not brought it up in the first place. Said I should think of Our Lord as having an inward smile, the doctrine according to Geoffrey being that Jesus was made man so he smiled, laughed and did everything else just like the rest of us. 'Do you think he ever smirked'? I asked, whereupon Geoffrey suddenly remembered he was burying somebody in five minutes and took himself off.

If Jesus *is* all man I just wish they'd put a bit more of it into the illustrations. I was sitting in church yesterday, wrestling with this point of theology, when it occurred to me that something seemed to have happened to Geoffrey. The service should have kicked off ages ago but he's still in the vestry. Mr Bland is filling in with something uplifting on the organ and Miss Frobisher, never one to let an opportunity slip, has slumped to her knees for a spot of unscheduled silent prayer. Mrs Shrubsole is lost in contemplation of the altar, still adorned with Forest Murmurs, a trail of ivy round the cross the final inspired touch. Mr Bland now ups the volume but still no sign of Geoff. 'Arnold', says Mrs Belcher, 'there seems to be some hiatus in the proceedings', and suddenly the fan club is on red alert. She's just levering him to his feet when I get in first and nip into the vestry to investigate.

His reverence is there, white-faced, every cupboard open and practically in tears. He said, 'Have you seen it'? I said, 'What'? He said, 'The wine. The communion wine. It's gone'. I said, 'That's no tragedy', and offer to pop out and get some ordinary. Geoffrey said, 'They're not open. Besides, what does it look like'? I said, 'Well, it looks like we've run out of communion wine'. He said, 'We haven't run out. There was a full bottle here on Friday. Somebody has drunk it'.

It's on the tip of my tongue to say that if Jesus is all he's cracked up to be why doesn't he use tap-water and put it to the test when I suddenly remember that Mr Bland keeps a bottle of cough mixture in his cupboard in case any of the choirboys gets chesty. At the thought of celebrating the Lord's Supper in Benylin Geoffrey now has a complete nervous breakdown but, as I point out, it's red and sweet and nobody is going to notice. Nor do they. I see Mr Belcher licking his lips a bit thoughtfully as he walks back down the aisle but that's all. 'What was the delay'? asks Mrs Shrubsole. 'Nothing', I said, 'just a little hiccup'.

Having got it right for once I'm feeling quite pleased with myself, but Geoffrey obviously isn't and never speaks all afternoon so I bunk off Evensong and go into Leeds.

Mr Ramesh has evidently been expecting me because there's a bed made up in the storeroom upstairs. I go up first and get in. When I'm in bed I can put my hand out and feel the lentils running through my fingers. When he comes up he's put on his proper clothes. Long white shirt, sash and what not. Loincloth underneath. All spotless. Like Jesus. Only not. I watch him undress and think about them all at Evensong and Geoffrey praying in that pausy way he does, giving you time to mean each phrase. And the fan club lapping it up, thinking they love God when they just love Geoffrey. Lighten our darkness we beseech thee O Lord and by thy great mercy defend us from all perils and dangers of this night. Like Mr Ramesh who is twenty-six with lovely legs, who goes swimming every morning at Merrion Street Baths and plays hockey for Horsforth. I ask him if they offer their sex to God. He isn't very interested in the point but with them, so far as I can gather, sex is all part of God anyway. I can see why too. It's the first time I really understand what all the fuss is about. There among the lentils on the second Sunday after Trinity.

I've just popped into the vestry. He's put a lock on the cupboard door.

Go to black.

Come up on Susan sitting in the drawing-room of the vicarage. Much smarter than in previous scenes, she has had her hair done and seems a different woman. Evening.

I stand up and say, 'My name is Susan. I am a vicar's wife and I am an alcoholic'. Then I tell my story. Or some of it anyway. 'Don't pull any punches', says Clem, my counsellor. 'Nobody's going to be shocked, believe me, love, we've all been there'. But I don't tell them about Mr Ramesh because they've not been there. 'Listen, people. I was so drunk I used to go and sleep with an Asian grocer. Yes, and you won't believe this. I loved it. Loved every minute'. Dear oh dear. This was a real drunken lady.

So I draw a veil over Mr Ramesh who once, on the feast of St Simon and St Jude (Choral Evensong at six, daily services at the customary hour), put make-up on his eyes and bells on his ankles, and naked except for his little belt danced in the back room of the shop with a tambourine.

'So how did you come to AA'? they ask. 'My husband', I say. 'The vicar. He persuaded me'. But I lie. It was not my husband, it was Mr Ramesh, the exquisitely delicate and polite Mr Ramesh who one Sunday night turned his troubled face towards me with its struggling moustache and asked if he might take the bull by the horns and enquire if intoxication was a prerequisite for sexual intercourse, or whether it was only when I was going to bed with him, the beautiful Mr Ramesh, twenty-six, with wonderful legs, whether it was only with him I had to be inebriated. And was it, asked this slim, flawless and troubled creature, was it perhaps his colour? Because if not he would like to float the suggestion that sober might be even nicer. So the credit for the road to Damascus goes to Mr Ramesh, whose first name turns out also to be Ramesh. Ramesh Ramesh, a member of the community council and the Leeds Federation of Trade.

But none of this I say. In fact I never say anything at all. Only when it becomes plain to Geoffrey (and it takes all of three weeks) that Mrs Vicar is finally on the wagon, who is it gets the credit? Not one of Mr Ramesh's jolly little gods, busy doing everything under the sun to one another, much like Mr Ramesh. Oh no. It's full marks to Geoffrey's chum, the Deity, moving in his well-known mysterious way.

So now everything has changed. For the moment I am a new woman and Geoffrey is a new man. And he brings it up on the slightest pretext. 'My wife's an alcoholic, you know. Yes. It's a great challenge to me and to the parish as extended family'. From being a fly in the ointment I find myself transformed into a feather in his cap. Included it in his sermon on Prayers Answered when he reveals that he and the fan club have been having these jolly get togethers in which they'd all prayed over what he calls 'my problem'. It practically sent me racing back to the Tio Pepe even to think of it. The fans, of course, never dreaming that their prayers would be answered, are furious. They think it's brought us closer together. Geoffrey thinks that too. We were at some doleful diocesan jamboree last week and I'm stuck there clutching my grapefruit juice as Geoffrey's telling the tale to some bearded cleric. Suddenly he seizes my hand. 'We met it with love', he cries, as if love were some all-purpose antibiotic, which to Geoffrey it probably is.

And it goes on, the mileage in it endless. I said to Geoffrey that when I stood up at AA I sometimes told the story about the flower arranging. Result: he starts telling it all over the diocese. The first time was at a conference on The Supportive Parish. Gales of deep, liberated, caring laughter. He's now given it a new twist and tells the story as if he's talking about a parishioner, then at the end he says, 'Friends I want to tell you something. (Deep hush.) That drunken flower-arranger was my wife'. Silence...then the applause, *terrific*.

I've caught the other young, upwardly mobile parsons sneaking looks at me now and again and you can see them thinking why weren't they smart enough to marry an alcoholic or better still a drug addict, problem wives whom they could do a nice redemption job on, right there on their own doorstep. Because there's no stopping Geoffrey now. He grips my hand in public, nay *brandishes* it. 'We're a team', he cries. Looks certain to be rural dean and that's only the beginning. As the bishop says, 'Just the kind of man we're looking for on the bench...someone with a seasoned compassion, someone who's looked life in the face. Someone who's been there'.

Mr Ramesh sold his shop. He's gone back to India to fetch his wife. She's old enough now apparently. I went down there on Sunday. There was a boy writing Under New Management on the window. Spelled wrong. And something underneath in Hindi, spelled right probably. He said he thought Mr Ramesh would be getting another shop, only in Preston.

They do that, of course, Asians, build something up, get it going nicely, then take the profit and move on. It's a good thing. We ought to be more like that, more enterprising.

My group meets twice a week and I go. Religiously. And that's what it is, of course. The names are different, Frankie and Steve, Susie and Clem. But it's actually Miss Frobisher and Mrs Shrubsole all over again. I never liked going to one church so I end up going to two. Geoffrey would call that the wonderful mystery of God. I call it bad taste. And I wouldn't do it to a dog. But that's the thing nobody ever says about God...he has no taste at all.

Fade out.

TRY THIS 4.14

Write a short monologue for a character who has done something illegal, immoral, gross, or unkind. Make us sympathize.

WORKING TOWARD A DRAFT

Pick a character who interests you from one of your journal pieces (fictional, observed, well-known to you—it doesn't matter), and write a letter from this person to yourself, beginning: "You think you know me, but what you don't know about me is...." Write fast. Don't think too much. Let it flow.

5 CHAPTER

Setting

- *As the World*
- *As a Camera*
- *As Mood and Symbol*
- *As Action*

"...place is a definer and a confiner of what I'm doing.... It saves me. Why, you couldn't write a story that happened nowhere."
Eudora Welty

Gerth Roland/Prisma/age fotostock

WARM-UP
Take a page to create this much cold. Write with nouns and verbs, a bare minimum of adjective or adverbs. Remember textures, tastes, smells as part of the atmosphere. Where is this? Who is doing without that car? Make us freeze.

A LOVE OF HOME. A PASSION FOR TRAVEL. THE GRIEF OF EXILE. The fragility of nature. The excitement of the metropolis. A fascination with the past. An obsession with the future. The search to belong. The need to flee. A sense of alienation. The thrill of outer space. The romance of real estate. Fear of the dark. The arctic waste. The swamp. The summit. The sea. The slums. The catacombs. The palace. The rocking chair. The road.

Writer after writer will tell you that **setting** fuels the drive to write. Virtually any writer you ask will profess a profound relation to place and time, whether as patriot, refugee, homebody, adventurer, flâneur, or time traveler; and each will tell you that creating the sensuous particularity of a place and period is crucial to writing. Setting is not merely scenery against which the significant takes place; it is part and parcel of the significant; it is heritage and culture; it is identity or exile, and the writer's choice of detail directs our understanding and our experience of it.

> Like so many Americans raised in suburbia [Deborah Tall writes], I have never really belonged to an American landscape.... The land's dull tidiness was hard to escape, except in the brief adventures of childhood when I could crawl beneath a bush or clothe myself in a willow tree. Before long, tall enough to look out the kitchen window, I saw the tree tamed by perspective, the bush that could be hurdled, my yard effectively mimicked all up and down the block: one house, two trees, one house, two trees, all the way to the vanishing point.
>
> *"Here"*

In rejecting the suburban landscape as her rightful home, Tall creates its oppressive tidiness for us, its suggestive or even symbolic importance to her sense of the "vanishing point." Though the description is of a deliberately static scene, the forceful verbs—*escape, crawl, clothe, tame, hurdle, mimic*—carry the energy of her desire to be gone from it. And readers can connect with the pictures and emotions she evokes in many ways: the image of suburbia itself, the childhood desire to hide, the changing perspective as she grows, the need for independence. For myself, though I grew up in the desert and would have been grateful for two trees, I powerfully identify with the sense of knowing even as a child that the place I lived was not the place I belonged, and the implication that this sense of exile is common among writers.

If a piece of literature does not create the setting for us, if it seems to occur in no-place no-time or in vague-place fuzzy-time, we cannot experience it, or else we must experience that vagueness itself as crucial to the action. Samuel Butler's Utopia is set in *Erewhon* (*nowhere* spelled backward) because the point of such a place, where philosophers reign and children select their parents, is that it cannot exist. Tom Stoppard's heroes in *Rosencrantz and Guildenstern Are Dead* do not know where they are, or where they came from, or where the sun comes up, or what time it is, and therefore *do not know who they are.*

Yet there's a resistance and even a measure of boredom that greets the subject of setting, and I can think of at least two reasons for this. The first is that tedious and sentimental descriptions of nature tend to be part of our early schooling, operating as a sort of admonishment that we should pay less attention to Mickey Mouse and Beyoncé, and more to the (ho-hum) wonders of nature. The other is that in daily life we take our surroundings ninety percent for granted. The world you know is what you're told to write about. What's the big deal? Isn't it everybody's world? Well, no.

Setting as the World

Don't think that any place is "typical."

Steven Schoen

Your routine, your neighborhood, your take on home, history, climate, and the cosmos is unique, like your voice, and inseparable from your voice. As a writer you need to be alert to your own vision and to create for us, even make strange to us, the world you think most familiar. Richard Ford demonstrates the technique in his description of "Seminary Street" in the novel *Independence Day*:

> The 4th is still three days off, but traffic is jamming into Frenchy's Gulf and through the parking lot at Pelcher's Market, citizens shouting out greetings from the dry cleaners and Town Liquors, as the morning heat is drumming up . . . all merchants are staging sidewalk "firecracker sales," setting out derelict merchandise they haven't moved since Christmas and draping sun racks with patriotic bunting and gimmicky signs that say wasting hard-earned money is the American way.

Ford's portrait here of a typical American town is given immediacy and life with names, quotations, and just slightly unexpected diction like *jamming, drumming, staging, "firecracker sales," derelict, sun racks, bunting, gimmicky*. These words and images are deliberate choices on Ford's part to particularize not only the town but our response to it. We may know this street well, but we would not see it well nor would we experience it in any particular way if we were told it was "a typical small town on 4th of July weekend."

If, on the other hand, the world you are writing about is itself in some way exotic, you may want to work in the opposite direction, to make it seem as familiar to us as the nearest mall.

> A server is woken at hour four-thirty by stimulin in the airflow, then yellow-up in our dormroom. After a minute in the hygiener and steamer, we put on fresh uniforms before filing into the restaurant. Our seer and aides gather us around Papa's Plinth for Matins, we recite the Six Catechisms, then our beloved Logoman appears and delivers his Sermon.
>
> Cloud Atlas, *David Mitchell*

Here, the familiar tone and casual delivery help readers accept the futuristic setting as the norm, at least for the duration of this fiction, in spite of the unusual words.

TRY THIS 5.1

Draw the floor plan of the first house you remember living in. Take a mental tour through this house, pausing (and marking on the floor plan) where significant events occurred. Walk through again, making a list of these events. Pick one of them and write about it. Pay attention to the setting and the atmosphere of the event. How does your relation to the space, light, weather, walls, furniture, and objects affect what you are doing and feeling? Does the place represent safety or confinement?

Description has earned a bad rap with overlong, self-indulgent eulogies to wildflowers, furniture, or alien planets. But setting involves everything that supports and impinges on your characters. The props of the world—artifacts and architecture, infrastructure, books, food, fabrics, tools and technology—create and sustain identity. People behaving in relation to their surroundings define both space and time, and reveal much more.

Take the example of a simple stage setting. The stage is bare; it could represent anywhere at any time. Now place on it an ordinary straight-backed chair. What portion of history is now eliminated? How much of the contemporary world can the setting now *not* represent—in what portion of the planet do people not sit on chairs? You don't know the answer. Neither do I. That neither of us knows the answer proves how particular and limited is our vision of the world.

A male actor enters the space. He sits in the chair. He holds his arms and head rigid, as if strapped. Where is he now? What will happen? Or he sweeps in and sits, miming the flinging aside of his robe. Where is he now? To what tradition does the scene belong? He drops a briefcase, slumps in the chair, and slips off his shoes with a toe on the heel of each. Where? What is he feeling? Or he sets the briefcase down, opens it, removes something, clears a space before him and begins to study, frowning. Where? Who is he? He tips back, one fist over the other in front of him, fighting the pull of the thing in his hands. Where? How much do you know about him? He kneels in front of the chair, one hand on his heart. What is he up to? He stands on the chair, fingering his neck, eyeing the ceiling. What is he thinking?

The male actor exits. A female actor enters. What does *she* do in relation to the chair? Which of the above actions would she not be likely to perform? What would she do that he would not?

Each of these actions, in relation to the absolute rock-bottom-simplest setting, represents a narrowing of possibility, an intensifying of situation, a range of emotions, and a shape of story. Each depends on the historical, geographical, psychological, and narrative potential that we have learned throughout a lifetime. Dancers have been so enamored of these possibilities that the use of chairs in dance has become a cliché. When a playwright wishes to indicate the most minimal set imaginable, she will usually indicate something like: *bare stage, three chairs.*

TRY THIS 5.2

Pick some element of the outside world with which you have a special relationship. It may be a room, an object of furniture, a space, a plant, or an element of a landscape. Write about it. Do not tell us how you feel about it, but choose your words, mostly nouns and verbs, so that we know.

In choosing the most minimal stage set, the playwright is relying on the body and mobility of the actor to create the world around the chair, and those represent a powerful collaborative presence. If your medium is poetry, essay, or fiction, you need to supply the whole of that vitality in words. Think of your characters as the point and center of what you write. Setting is everything else. It is the world. You need to make that world for us even as you present your characters, in order to let us care about them. Novelist and short-story writer Ron Carlson nicely catches the necessity and the priority:

> ...[I]f the story is about a man and a woman changing a tire on a remote highway...you've nonetheless got to convince me of the highway, the tire, the night, the margin, the shoulder, the gravel under their knees, the lug nuts, the difficulty getting the whole thing apart and back together, and the smells. You must do that. But that's not what you're there to deliver. That's the way you're going to seduce me...after you've got my shirt caught in the machine of the story and you've drawn me in, what you're really going to crush me with are these hearts and these people. Who are they?
>
> *interview with Ron Carlson by Susan McInnis*

The techniques of setting—"the machine of the story"—are those you have already encountered as image and voice. Create a place by the selection of concrete detail in your particular diction or that of your narrating character. When you focus on offering us the particularity of place, time, and weather, you will also be able to manipulate the mood, reveal the character, and advance the action.

The details you choose to evoke place will also, if you choose them well, signal the period. Albert Einstein invented the word *chronotope* to indicate the "space–time continuum," or the fact that space and time are different manifestations of the same thing. Metaphorically this is true of imagery, and of the imagery of space and time. You will indicate something about period as well as architecture if your characters live in a *hogan, bungalow, cottage, sod house, split-level,* or *high-rise.* Likewise you will tell us something about where and when we are likely to be if your heroine is carrying a *reticule, porte monnaie, poke, duffle,* or *fanny pack.*

> My father walked beside me to give me courage, his palm touching gently the back laces of my bodice. In the low-angled glare already baking the paving stones of the piazza and the top of my head, the still shadow of the Inquisitor's noose hanging above the Tor di Nona, the papal court, stretched grotesquely down the wall, its shape the outline of a tear.

"A brief unpleasantness, Artemisia," my father said, looking straight ahead. "Just a little squeezing."

The Passion of Artemisia, *Susan Vreeland*

This is a voice of relative calm in a situation of high drama. Can you identify the images and the diction that indicate period and locale?

If you have, as a reader, been impatient with description, it is probably either because the author relied on a cliché picture-postcard image to evoke the scene, or else because the description existed as a pedestal for the author's piety or cleverness. The techniques that convincingly create the world are the same as those that create image and character: be alert to the sense impressions of your inner eye (remembering that place and time can be created by smells and sounds, by textures and even tastes as well as the visible). As with character, a single vivid detail may accomplish more than a catalogue. Originality often means a genuine connection with some particularity that you have noticed, and the ability to dream that particularity into your scene, however fictional.

An example from my own ignorance: In a novel set in Mexico in 1914, I needed to establish the threatening atmosphere of a small town. I decided I had better endow the town with a cockfight—everybody knows a cockfight is scary—and went looking for fictional and nonfiction accounts as models. I made notes about factual details, tried several pale drafts, and despaired at the brilliance of Nathaniel West and Ernest Hemingway. I'd never seen a cockfight, but I thought my imagination ought to be up to the task. It was not. Then it occurred to me that what frightened *me* in the desert was Gila monsters. I wrote a scene in which an old man with a Gila monster on a leash taunts the town by tossing frogs and snakes that his lizard paralyzes with its venomous tongue. There was more invention required by this scene than the cockfight I'd been trying to write (so far as I know nobody puts a leash on a Gila monster), but because it came out of my own emotion, feeling, and observation, it moved my character and his story in the direction needed.

TRY THIS 5.3

Write two pages beginning "Get me out of here."

Setting as a Camera

"...[M]y favorite sentence may be, 'Last Wednesday at the Black Cat Night Club.' I mean, I just love knowing where I am."

Ron Carlson

Setting often begins a piece, for the very good reason that this is the first thing we register in life. Entering a place, we take it in as a panorama (sit in a restaurant and watch people enter; their eyes go left and right, even up and down before they fix on the approaching hostess). Waking with the sense "Where am I?" is notoriously disconcerting. It is no less so in literature. This does not mean setting has to be the very first thing writers address, but it does mean that their audience can't go far without some sort of orientation.

As a model, consider the western movie, which typically begins with a *long shot* (the camera at distance) of the horsemen coming over the rise. We get a sense of the landscape, then we see the far-off arrival of the riders. Then there might be a *middle shot*, say four riders in the frame, to give us a sense of the group. Then a *close-up*: this is our hero, his head and shoulders. Screenwriters and directors are taught that they need such an "establishing shot" at the beginning of *each* scene. This parallels the action that often takes place on stage: The curtain opens on an empty room; we register it, read its clues. Someone enters. What is the relationship of this person to this space? Someone else comes in; they begin to talk and the situation is revealed.

Carl Sandburg, in "Good Morning, America," demonstrates the long shot opening:

> In the evening there is a sunset sonata to the cities.
> There is a march of little armies to the dwindling of drums.
> The skyscrapers throw their tall lengths of walls into black bastions on the
> red west.

Only after this cityscape, its sound, sight, and time of day, is established, does he introduce the puny maker of these great structures, man.

The process of orientation somehow takes place in every piece that tells a story. Consider again the beginning of the Housman poem in the last chapter:

> Loveliest of trees, the cherry now
> Is hung with snow along the bough
> And stands about the woodland ride
> Wearing white for Easter tide
>
> Now of my threescore years and ten
> Twenty will not come again...

Notice how this poem follows both the pattern of a film opening (and also, incidentally, the "seduction" process that Ron Carlson describes earlier in this chapter). Actually, we begin with a middle shot (cherry tree, bough with the snow that tells us the season), pull back to a long shot (woodland ride), and then zoom in on the persona in relation to the scene (my whole life, and where I am in it now).

The practice of beginning with a wide angle and moving to closer focus is important for introducing us to an exotic locale:

> The thin light of the approaching daybreak always seemed to emphasize the strangeness and foreignness of our battalion's bivouac area on a country road outside Casablanca. Every morning a heavy mist covered the land just before the sun rose. Then, as the light grew, odd-looking shapes and

things came slowly into view.... Dim, moving figures behind the mist, dressed in ghostly white, materialized as Arabs perched on the hindquarters of spindly donkeys or walking along the road.

"On the Fedala Road," John McNeel

But this technique is no less useful to present a domestic scene:

Throughout my childhood our family's evening meals were expeditious and purposeful, more reliable than imaginative. We were French Canadians, which meant we knew pork and maple syrup. My grandfather liked to eat salt pork, sautéed in a frying pan, or cold, right out of the fridge, with a schmear of horseradish, a side of string beans, and a bottle of Tadcaster ale.

"Nothing to Eat but Food: Menu as Memoir," John Dufresne

Part of the long shot is temporal here, involving the whole sweep of *throughout my childhood.* Then it places us at table (*evening meals*). The diction also begins on a wide scale, with generalizations (*expeditious, purposeful*) narrowing to an ethnicity and a region (*French Canadians*) and then comically to an image (*pork and maple syrup*). The character of grandfather is introduced and the close-up begins, narrowing toward his plate while the details and diction also give us the ethnic oddities of voice and flavor: *sautéed* and *schmear* and *Tadcaster ale.*

TRY THIS 5.4

Pick a scene from your childhood and describe it in three sentences: one long shot, one middle shot, one close-up. How much can you tell us about the feel of your surroundings in this short space?

Of course, it is equally possible, and potentially interesting, to begin with the close-up and then move to middle and long shots—an opening image, say, of a fly crawling up three-days' worth of stubble to disappear into a nostril—only then you had better pull back to show us the bad guy's whole face, and the way he is wedged in the rock, and the wide-sky emptiness of the desert he has to cross. Sandra Cisneros demonstrates the technique in the short story "Salvador Late or Early":

Salvador with eyes the color of a caterpillar, Salvador of the crooked hair and crooked teeth, Salvador whose name the teacher cannot remember, is a boy who is no one's friend, runs along somewhere in that direction where homes are the color of bad weather, lives behind a raw wood doorway, shakes the sleepy brothers awake, ties their shoes, combs their hair with water, feeds them milk and corn flakes from a tin cup in the dim dark of morning.

In this dense miniature portrait, notice how the focus begins on Salvador, then places him in a classroom, then chases him *somewhere in that direction,* so that we know the very vivid images of his poverty are the narrator's invention, impressions of the *dim dark* setting in which he lives.

Or observe, in this excerpt from Michael Ignatieff's memoir, *August in My Father's House,* how a storm is evoked in three sentences, first in middle shot, then close-up, and then sweeping away to a long shot:

> ...A shutter bangs against the kitchen wall and a rivulet of sand trickles from the adobe wall in the long room where I sit. The lamp above my head twirls in the draught. Through the poplars, the forks of light plunge into the flanks of the mountains and for an instant the ribbed gullies stand out like skeletons under a sheet.

Notice also how the energy of the verbs (some of them personifications) mimic the energy of the storm: *bangs, trickles, twirls, plunge, stand out,* and how the scene is capped with a simile that suggests its malevolence: *ribbed gullies...like skeletons.* So active is this storm and the "camera" swinging to capture it, so forcefully does it suggest the emotion of the narrator, that it's unlikely anyone would refer to it as a "description of nature," though it is also that.

As this example shows, the "camera" may record the scene, but it is a subjective, not an impartial observer. The angle and distance are, like the details themselves, a choice made by the author that conveys a sense of viewpoint, of *someone* standing *somewhere* to watch the scene. Also, as with a film, the story will continue to move back and forth among long, middle, and close perspectives, for variety's sake and to allow us both orientation and involvement.

TRY THIS 5.5

Pick a scene from your journal. Describe the setting in the pattern *long shot, middle shot, close-up.* Make sure that you begin with a wide sweep and end with a tight focus.

Pick another scene. Begin with a very small, close image. Widen the lens until you have placed that scene in the context of the entire continent.

Setting as Mood and Symbol

> If the atmosphere is to be foreboding, you must forebode on every page. If it is to be cold, you must chill, not once or twice, but until your readers are shivering.
>
> *Jerome Stern*

Each of the previous scenes creates a **mood** or **atmosphere** for the events that will unfold there—fearful in the Vreeland, majestic in the Sandburg, elegiac in the Housman, mysterious in the McNeel, comic in the Dufresne, poignant in the Cisneros, malevolent in the Ignatieff. (Do you agree with these characterizations? Which words and images are responsible for the mood created?)

Setting in the sense of atmosphere is one of the writer's most adaptable tools. Mood will inevitably contain some element of time and weather—wet or dry, dark or light, winter or summer, calm or storm, and so forth. These, together with the textures and colors of objects, the smells of vegetation, the shapes of buildings, are all rich with the mood from which the unique action and its meaning emerge.

> When we came back to Paris it was clear and cold and lovely. The city had accommodated itself to winter, there was good wood for sale at the wood and coal place across our street, and there were braziers outside of many of the good cafés so that you could keep warm on the terraces.
>
> A Moveable Feast, *Ernest Hemingway*

Mood is a state of mind or emotion, and when we speak of setting as mood, we are speaking of an external manifestation of the inner, the concrete expressing the abstract, the contingent standing for the essential. In this sense, setting is often to some degree **symbolic**. It may be deliberately and specifically so, like the deranged planets that stand for the disordered society in *King Lear*, or the subway that is "the flying underbelly of the city...heaped in modern myth" in Imamu Amiri Baraka's play *Dutchman*.

More often, the setting is suggestive of a larger meaning, reaching out from a particular place and time toward a cosmic or universal reading. In this opening passage from Don DeLillo's *Underworld*, a boy is playing hooky to be at a New York baseball stadium that becomes the symbolic locus of American longing. (Notice the close-up/long-shot/close-up/long-shot structure.)

> It's a school day, sure, but he's nowhere near the classroom. He wants to be here instead, standing in the shadow of this old rust-hulk of a structure, and it's hard to blame him....
>
> Longing on a large scale is what makes history. This is just a kid with a local yearning but he is part of an assembling crowd, anonymous thousands off the buses and trains, people in narrow columns tramping over the swing bridge above the river, and even if they are not a migration or a revolution, some vast shaking of the soul, they bring with them the body heat of a great city and their own small reveries and desperations, the unseen something that haunts the day....

Our relation to place, time, and weather, like our relation to clothes and other objects, is charged with emotion more or less subtle, more or less profound. It is filled with judgment mellow or harsh. And it alters according to what happens to us. In some rooms you are always trapped; you enter them with grim purpose and escape them as soon as you can. Others invite you to settle in, to nestle or carouse. Some landscapes lift your spirits; others depress you. Cold weather gives you energy and bounce, or else it clogs your head and makes you huddle, struggling. You describe yourself as a night person or a morning person. The house you loved as a child now makes you, precisely because you were once happy there, think of loss and death.

TRY THIS 5.6

As a prompt for a memoir, poem, or fiction, choose one of the clichés below. Using concrete details rather than the words of the cliché, create the setting suggested by it. You might begin with a single sharply focused image, then pull back to reveal the larger landscape. Use a persona or introduce a character if you choose.

- a dark and stormy night
- raining cats and dogs
- freeze you to death
- scorching hot
- foggy as pea soup
- balmy weather
- fragrant as new-mown hay

The potential for emotion inherent in place, time, and weather can be used or heightened (or invented) to dramatic effect in your writing. Nothing happens nowhere. Just as significant detail calls up a sense impression and also an abstraction, so setting and atmosphere impart both information and emotion. Just as dialogue must do more than one thing at a time, so can setting characterize, reveal mood, and signal change. Here from Saul Bellow's "Memoir of a Bootlegger's Son" is a picture of the place his father worked after he lost the fortune he brought from Russia:

> The bakery was a shanty. The rats took refuge from the winter there, and drowned in the oil and fished out suffocated from the jelly. The dogs and cats could not police them, they were so numerous. The thick ice did not float leisurely, it ran the swift current. In March and even April the snow still lay heavy. When it melted, the drains couldn't carry off the water. There were gray lagoons in the hollows of old ice; they were sullen or flashing according to the color of the sky.

Bellow's choices of imagery here are so rich with mood that they amount to a prophecy: *refuge, drowned, suffocated, heavy, gray, hollows, old ice.* The impotence of dogs and cats, ice, snow, and drains, the lagoons "sullen or flashing according to the color of the sky" convey not only the scene but also the man's loss of self-determination.

TRY THIS 5.7

On the left is a list of times, places, and/or weather. On the right are words that represent a mood or quality of atmosphere. Pick one item from the left and one from the right. Write a poem or paragraph in which you make the setting suggest the atmosphere. If the connection is not obvious, your piece will be more interesting. Introduce a character if you please.

the city in the rain	sinister
midnight on the farm	sick with love
1890, in the parlor	full of promise
high noon on the river	suicidal
a spring morning	dangerous
in the bar, after hours	suspense
the dusty road	happy-go-lucky
dawn in a foreign place	lonely

Setting as Action

If character is the foreground and setting the background, then there may be harmony or conflict between character and background. The persons of your poem, play, memoir, or fiction may be comfortably at ease in the world around them, or they may be uneasy, uncomfortable, full of foreboding.

> I will wait for her in the yard that Maggie and I made so clean and wavy yesterday afternoon. A yard like this is more comfortable than most people know. It is not just a yard. It is like an extended living room. When the hard clay is swept clean as a floor and the fine sand around the edges lined with tiny, irregular grooves, anyone can come and sit and look up into the elm tree and wait for the breezes that never come inside the house.
>
> *"Everyday Use," Alice Walker*

Here the setting is a place full of comfort and community, and any conflict comes from an outside threat to that balance—perhaps, we suspect, the "her" being waited for. But where there is potential menace in the setting, or conflict between the character and the setting, there is already an element of "story."

> ...The room is so bleak and unwelcoming, he imagines that dozens of desperate people have checked into this place over the years with no other purpose than to commit suicide....The sparseness of the furniture, for example: just one bed and one battered wardrobe stranded in an overly large space. No chair, no phone. The absence of any pictures on the walls. The blank, cheerless bathroom, with a single miniature bar of soap lying in its wrapper on the white sink, a single white hand towel hanging on the rack, the rusted enamel in the white tub.
>
> Man in the Dark, *Paul Auster*

When a character is in harmony with his/her surroundings, the atmosphere suggested is static, and it will take a disruption of some kind to introduce the possibility of change. But when setting and character, background and foreground, are set in opposition to each other, the process of discovery and decision is already in motion, and we know we are in for a seismic or a psychic shift.

One great advantage of being a writer is that you may create the world. Places and the elements have the significance and the emotional effect you give them in language. As a person you may be depressed by rain, but as an author you are free to make rain mean freshness, growth, bounty, and God. You may love winter, but you are free to make the blank white field symbolize oblivion.

As with character, the first requisite of effective setting is to know it fully, to experience it mentally; and the second is to create it through significant detail. What sort of place is this, and what are its peculiarities? What is the weather like, the light, the season, the time of day? What are the contours of the land and architecture? What are the social assumptions of the inhabitants, and how familiar and comfortable are the characters with this place and its lifestyle? These things are not less important in literature than in life, but more, since their selection inevitably takes on significance.

TRY THIS 5.8

Take a road map, close your eyes, and point to it at random. Have a character drive or walk through the nearest town and stop in at a bank, shop, or restaurant. Study the surrounding area on the map if you like. Invent the details.

Or:

Write about a place you can't return to.

More to Read

Baxter, Charles. *Burning Down the House: Essays on Fiction.* St. Paul: Graywolf Press, 1997. Print.

Bickham, Jack M. *Setting.* Cincinnati: Writer's Digest Books, 1994. Print.

READINGS

CREATIVE NONFICTION

JOAN DIDION

At the Dam

Since the afternoon in 1967 when I first saw Hoover Dam, its image has never been entirely absent from my inner eye. I will be talking to someone in Los Angeles, say, or New York, and suddenly the dam will materialize, its pristine concave face gleaming white against the harsh rusts and taupes and mauves of that rock canyon hundreds or thousands of miles from where I am. I will be driving down Sunset Boulevard, or about to enter a freeway, and abruptly those power transmission towers will appear before me, canted vertiginously over the tailrace. Sometimes I am confronted by the intakes and sometimes by the shadow of the heavy cable that spans the canyon and sometimes by the ominous outlets to unused spillways, black in the lunar clarity of the desert light. Quite often I hear the turbines. Frequently I wonder what is happening at the dam this instant, at this precise intersection of time and space, how much water is being released to fill downstream orders and what lights are flashing and which generators are in full use and which just spinning free.

I used to wonder what it was about the dam that made me think of it at times and in places where I once thought of the Mindanao Trench, or of the stars wheeling in their courses, or of the words *As it was in the beginning, is now and ever shall be, world without end, amen.* Dams, after all, are commonplace: we have all seen one. This particular dam had existed as an idea in the world's mind for almost forty years before I saw it. Hoover Dam, showpiece of the Boulder Canyon project, the several million tons of concrete that made the Southwest plausible, the *fait accompli* that was to convey, in the innocent time of its construction, the notion that mankind's brightest promise lay in American engineering.

Of course the dam derives some of its emotional effect from precisely that aspect, that sense of being a monument to a faith since misplaced. "They died to make the desert bloom," reads a plaque dedicated to the 96 men who died building this first of the great high dams, and in context the worn phrase touches, suggests all of that trust in harnessing resources, in the meliorative power of the dynamo, so central to the early Thirties. Boulder City, built in 1931 as the construction town for the dam, retains the ambience of a model city, a new town, a toy triangular grid of green lawns and trim bungalows, all fanning out from the Reclamation building. The bronze sculptures at the dam itself evoke muscular citizens of a tomorrow that never came, sheaves of wheat clutched heavenward, thunderbolts defied. Winged Victories guard the flagpole. The flag whips in the canyon wind. An empty Pepsi-Cola can clatters across the terrazzo. The place is perfectly frozen in time.

But history does not explain it all, does not entirely suggest what makes the dam so affecting. Nor, even, does energy, the massive involvement with power and pressure and the transparent sexual overtones to that involvement. Once when I revisited the dam I walked through it with a man from the Bureau of Reclamation. For a while we trailed behind a guided tour, and then we went on, went into parts of the dam where visitors do not generally go. Once in a while he would explain something, usually in that recondite language having to do with "peaking power," with "outages" and "dewatering," but on the whole we spent the afternoon in a world so alien, so complete and so beautiful unto itself that it was scarcely necessary to speak at all. We saw almost no one. Cranes moved above us as if under their own volition. Generators roared. Transformers hummed. The gratings on which we stood vibrated. We watched a hundred-ton steel shaft plunging down to that place where the water was. And finally we got down to that place where the water was, where the water sucked out of Lake Mead roared through thirty-foot penstocks and then into thirteen-foot penstocks and finally into the turbines themselves. "Touch it," the Reclamation man said, and I did, and for a long time I just stood there with my hands on the turbine. It was a peculiar moment, but so explicit as to suggest nothing beyond itself.

5 There was something beyond all that, something beyond energy, beyond history, something I could not fix in my mind. When I came up from the dam that day the wind was blowing harder, through the canyon and all across the Mojave. Later, toward Henderson and Las Vegas, there would be dust blowing, blowing past the Country-Western Casino FRI & SAT NITES and blowing past the Shrine of Our Lady of Safe Journey STOP & PRAY, but out at the dam there was no dust, only the rock and the dam and a little greasewood and a few garbage cans, their tops chained, banging against a fence. I walked across the marble star map that traces a sidereal revolution of the equinox and fixes forever, the Reclamation man had told me, for all time and for all people who can read the stars, the date the dam was dedicated. The star map was, he had said, for when we were all gone and the dam was left. I had not thought much of it when he said it, but I thought of it then, with the wind whining and the sun dropping behind a mesa with the finality of a sunset in space. Of course that was the image I had seen always, seen it without quite realizing what I saw, a dynamo finally free of man, splendid at last in its absolute isolation, transmitting power and releasing water to a world where no one is.

PAUL THEROUX

The Slow Train to Kandy

One of the happier and more helpful delusions of travel is that one is on a quest. At the end of Avurudu, when the auspicious day for work, for travel, arrived, the one determined by the astrologers and soothsayers, I took the train to Kandy, the capital of the former kingdom, at the center of the island, sitting at a high altitude, where in a famous temple a tooth of the Buddha was enshrined in a gold casket. It was a plane of pilgrimage.

All the trains I took in Sri Lanka were small and slow, possibly the same rolling stock as those I'd taken long ago, but dirtier. Yet the routes were so dramatic, by the blue sea or the green hills, I hardly noticed the condition of the railway cars or my hard bench. And it was only seventy-five miles to Kandy, the line rising from the coast, passing through the gardens and villages on the slopes, the rice terraces full of still, silvery water and mirroring the sky, the rock temples hacked out of cliffs, the monasteries at the higher elevations. Coconut plantations, vegetable farms, pineapple fields, markets overflowing with blossoms: the way to Kandy was strewn with flowers.

Into the cooler air and taller trees, past Ambepussa Station and Polgahawela Junction, with its Buddhist monastery and temple. In the middle of the steep ascent that began at a place called Rambukkana, it began to rain—the first rain I'd seen since Bokhara, over a month before. The train's windows were open, the rain spattered in, but there weren't many passengers, and there was enough room so that we could move to the drier seats.

An older man with a tightly rolled umbrella and a wide-brimmed hat and a briefcase made room for me on one of the benches.

"You are welcome."

His name was Mr. Kumara. He had been a clerk in the Department of Health and was now retired, living on a pension.

"And I have so many other interests." He had a confident manner, and his hat, his umbrella, and his briefcase gave him a look of authority. His calm smile seemed to invite questions.

"What sort of interests?"

"Palmistry and numerology. I make predictions."

"What was your best prediction?"

"That Franklin Roosevelt would be assassinated," he said, and before I could challenge this, he added, "And that a certain woman would leave her husband—and she did."

He asked me for some of my dates, of numbers related to my life. He took out a pad and did some calculations based on my birth date, covering the page with obscure mathematics and crossings-out until he arrived at a single number, which he circled.

"Your number is two," he said. "You look younger than your age. You will have a good sun line. I can tell you that without looking at your palm." He then made a new page of calculations. "Here are the years that fate has decided for you—the significant years. When you were twenty-three, thirty-two, forty-one, and fifty."

I considered these and thought: Africa, Railway Bazaar, disastrous affair, divorce—fateful years. Mr. Kumara was looking at my palm.

"Sun line is there! See, I told you!"

Now, without anything to do except hold on to the stanchions and the straps, the other passengers took an interest and leaned over, as though to double-check the lines on my palm.

"Here is lifeline. You could live to eighty-two or eighty-five," he said, manipulating my thumb flesh. "This is Mount of Jupiter. You are stubborn, self-made man. Determined. Don't bend to anyone. You brook no interference from anyone. You live life by your own self. You are flirtatious, but not good at satisfying your sexual appetite."

This drew murmurs from the other passengers, and I shook my head, trying to cast doubt on this assessment.

"You are a Jupiter, a leader among men," he said, but stated it as a fact—he wasn't impressed. "Your eyesight is bad, yet I see you don't wear glasses."

"I had double cataract surgery."

"What did I say?"

He was speaking to the onlookers.

"You are charitable, but you were cheated by the love of your heart," he said. "People abused your judgment in the past. Not true?"

"All true."

He was on to my left hand now. He said, "Your left hand is more interesting than your right."

"In what way?"

"More irritated," Mr. Kumara said. "You have won the battles with the enemy. In future you do not need to worry about the enemy."

"That sounds good."

"Very much foreign travel in your life," he said.

"Are you saying that because I'm in Sri Lanka?"

"Your living depends on it," he said, twisting my hand, peering at my palm. "You will soon receive unexpected wealth in unexpected ways. And your career is good. Nothing bothers you. But you have bronchial problems and breathing problems."

"That part isn't true."

"They will come," he said confidently. "Before thirty-five you were very upset. Job, marriage, life—very bad."

"That's a fact."

"You will fall in love more than twice."

"Twice more?"

"It seems so." He looked me square in the face and let go of my hand. "You are a judge, a lawyer, a writer. Maybe an ambassador."

"If I were an ambassador, would I be sitting on this train?"

The passengers nearby looked at me for confirmation. I smiled. Apart from the insulting suggestion that I might be a lawyer, he was right on most counts.

I had gotten used to the tsunami damage on the coast, the ruins and the rebuilding. But inland, up these hills, the houses were whole and the villages intact, shining in the gentle rain, the dense green leaves of the foliage going greener in the drizzle.

"This is Peradeniya," Mr. Kumara said, getting up and unfastening the strap on his umbrella. He gave me his card—his name and address. "When you come back to Sri Lanka, please call me. You can meet my family. My wife is an excellent cook."

“And when I come back you’ll be able to verify your predictions. ‘Unexpected wealth.’”

“I tell only what I see,” he said. And stepping out of the coach he said, “Lovely gardens here. You must see them.”

I planned to, by going from Kandy, which was only a few miles away. I felt it would be harder to get a taxi at the gardens.

At Kandy I walked from the station with a growing crowd of pilgrims to the Dalada Maligawa, the Temple of the Tooth, thinking about Mr. Kumara’s prophecies and palmistry. I had assumed that this Buddhist population of Sinhalese would be rational and compassionate. In some forms, Buddhism is like a vapor, an odor of sanctity, the minimalism of self-denial, not a religion at all but a philosophy of generosity and forgiveness.

Odd, then, to see Sri Lankans closely observing the bizarre Avurudu strictures (“Lighting the hearth should be done wearing colorful clothes and facing the south…juice of nuga leaves on the head at 7:39 A.M.…Set off facing the north…”); or being drawn to Mr. Kumara’s numerology—his addition and subtraction and his confident soothsaying. And now in Kandy the panoply of this thickly decorated temple, the gilded pillars, the ribbons and semi-precious stones, the shrouded statues and heavy-lidded gaze of a hundred gesturing Buddhas—and flowers, candles, fruit and flags, relics and flaming tapers, all the paraphernalia I associated with the blood and gold and organ pipes that epitomize the interior decoration of South American cathedrals and the wilder excesses of Catholicism, complete with a swirling fog of warm incense: “That vast moth-eaten musical brocade / Created to pretend we never die.”*

I kicked off my shoes and joined the line of people eager to see the Buddha’s tooth, which in this temple, in its gold casket, was like a saint’s relic, Saint Francis’s skull, a mummy in a catacomb, a splinter from the True Cross. The story of the Buddha’s tooth dates from the fourth century A.D., and there is some question as to whether this is a real canine or a replacement for the tooth (a fake one, said the Sinhalese) that the pious Portuguese burned in Goa as being wicked and idolatrous. The Portuguese who venerated splinters of the True Cross and the skulls of saints, who had all but destroyed Kandy in their time; and what remained of it when the Dutch conquered them, in the sixteenth century, the Dutch had pulled down, leaving very little for the British when they showed up in 1815.

The inner rooms of the temple were crowded and stifling, mobbed with Buddhists propitiating the impassive statues, prostrating themselves, waving lighted tapers, and making passes with their outstretched arms—as though practicing to be Christians.

I walked outside and along the lake, liking this pleasant air at 1,600 feet, and then found a curry house (plate of rice covered with highly seasoned sauce,

*Philip Larkin, “Aubade.”

75 cents), and sat reading the paper, about recent Tamil Tiger actions. In the place where I'd planned to cross from India to Sri Lanka, an armada of heavily armed Tiger watercraft, camouflaged as fishing boats, had attacked some Sri Lankan navy vessels. Eleven Sri Lankan sailors were either dead or missing, and in the retaliatory action, eight rebel boats were sunk, thirty Tigers dead. And in Colombo three Tiger commandos in diving gear, setting mines, had been captured; two of them committed suicide by swallowing cyanide capsules they kept handy for that purpose.

50 A Sri Lankan sitting near me struck up a conversation. Seeing the article I was reading, he said, "Sixty-seven people killed in the last two weeks. And this is during a cease-fire!"

His name was Kaduwella. He had come to Kandy to see the sacred tooth. He said that the Tamil Tigers had attacked the temple.

Of course: a place of such serenity, such glitter and sanctity, it was inevitable that the Tigers would violate it. And why not? In a paragraph that reads like a historical free-for-all, Christopher Ondaatje describes the skirmishes over the Buddha's tooth going on for a thousand years, how Kublai Khan tried but failed to capture it, how the Indians succeeded in snatching it in the thirteenth century but lost it to a Sinhalese king. When the Chinese failed in their attempt to steal the tooth, they took hostages instead—members of the royal family. The Portuguese were fobbed off with a fake tooth. So the Tamil Tigers were the latest in a long list of predators, poachers, and violators of the Temple of the Tooth.

The Kaduwellas lived in Colombo. While his wife and children smiled shyly, Mr. Kaduwella invited me to his house.

"We'll have a good meal," he said with a glance at my plate, as though dismissing it, but he and his family were all eating something similar.

55 I asked him how to get to Peradeniya. He said it was too far to walk, and when we finished lunch he went out of his way to find me a taxi and negotiate the price. And as we parted he repeated his invitation.

In the past I might not have visited Peradeniya Botanic Gardens. More likely I would have visited the Peradeniya Bar and sat there most of the night. But these days, in travel, I seldom went out at night, and got up earlier, and often visited gardens—particularly the gardens that were devised by the British, in which many of the trees were ancient, and some of the specimens planted in the nineteenth century. I got interested in gardening only after I became a householder, and that was as a result of the windfall occasioned by the success of *The Great Railway Bazaar.* I used the money to buy a house, I planted shrubs, I planted flowers, and more recently have been planting various varieties of noninvasive bamboo.

The bamboo groves at Peradeniya were dense, many of the canes gigantic—even named *giganteus* on their labels. What happens to the clumping noninvasive bamboo after one hundred years? The clumps are twenty feet wide and the plant itself grows as tall as a three-story house. The cycads were vast and feathery, the old palms stood tall; in a place like Sri Lanka, a land of procrastination and decline, these great gardens had ripened and flourished. I was reminded of the palms and mangroves on the coast—Bowles called them "triumphant vegetation"—that had resisted the onslaught of the tidal wave and the fury of the flood, and stood, like these trees and ferns and bamboos at Peradeniya, not only unviolated but bigger and more beautiful.

Leonard Woolf had walked here, so Ondaatje said. He had spent a year in Kandy, at the law court, fascinated by the convoluted murder cases and the complex marriage disputes. He had so impressed his overlords he got a better post in Hambantota, where, so he claimed, he would have been happy to spend the rest of his life.

It was easy to see how Sri Lanka could capture your heart, as it had Sir Arthur's. It was especially pleasant to be in a place where not much changed. Yet it was a violated place—the war, the tsunami, had held it back, kept it from improving in any way. The war of Tamil secession had probably had the greatest effect. War is weird in that way: time stops, no one thinks of the future but only of survival or escape.

I left Kandy. And a few days after I left Colombo, just down the street from my hotel, near a park I'd passed many times for its being so pleasant, a large group of pregnant women had lined up to be examined at a prenatal clinic, the weekly "maternity day" offered by the Sri Lankan army. Without warning, one of the women, a member of the Black Tiger Suicide Squad, pretending to be pregnant (her maternity dress bulged with a bomb), blew herself up and took six people with her into oblivion.

TRY THIS 5.9

Describe in less than two pages some ordinary thing you were doing when a shocking event occurred. End, without comment, with the news of the event.

Or:

Write briefly about some instance of superstition, astrology, or the occult that has unsettled you.

FICTION

DONALD BARTHELME

The School

Well, we had all these children out planting trees, see, because we figured that...that was part of their education, to see how, you know, the root systems...and also the sense of responsibility, taking care of things, being individually responsible. You know what I mean. And the trees all died. They were orange trees. I don't know why they died, they just died. Something wrong with the soil possibly or maybe the stuff we got from the nursery wasn't the best. We complained about it. So we've got thirty kids there, each kid had his or her own little tree to plant, and we've got these thirty dead trees. All these kids looking at these little brown sticks, it was depressing.

It wouldn't have been so bad except that just a couple of weeks before the thing with the trees, the snakes all died. But I think that the snakes—well, the reason that the snakes kicked off was that... you remember, the boiler was shut off for four days because of the strike, and that was explicable. It was something you could explain to the kids because of the strike. I mean, none of their parents would let them cross the picket line and they knew there was a strike going on and what it meant. So when things got started up again and we found the snakes they weren't too disturbed.

With the herb gardens it was probably a case of overwatering, and at least now they know not to overwater. The children were very conscientious with the herb gardens and some of them probably... you know, slipped them a little extra water when we weren't looking. Or maybe... well, I don't like to think about sabotage, although it did occur to us. I mean, it was something that crossed our minds. We were thinking that way probably because before that the gerbils had died, and the white mice had died, and the salamander... well, now they know not to carry them around in plastic bags.

Of course we *expected* the tropical fish to die, that was no surprise. Those numbers, you look at them crooked and they're belly-up on the surface. But the lesson plan called for tropical-fish input at that point, there was nothing we could do, it happens every year, you just have to hurry past it.

5 We weren't even supposed to have a puppy.

We weren't even supposed to have one, it was just a puppy the Murdoch girl found under a Gristede's truck one day and she was afraid the truck would run over it when the driver had finished making his delivery, so she stuck it in her knapsack and brought it to school with her. So we had this puppy. As soon as I saw the puppy I thought, Oh Christ, I bet it will live for about two weeks and then... And that's what it did. It wasn't supposed to be in the classroom at all, there's some kind of regulation about it, but you can't tell them they can't have a puppy when the puppy is already there, right in front of them, running around on the floor and yap yap yapping. They named it Edgar—that is, they named it after me. They had a lot of fun running after it and yelling, "Here, Edgar! Nice Edgar!" Then they'd laugh like hell. They enjoyed the ambiguity. I enjoyed it myself. I don't mind being kidded. They made a little house for it in the supply closet and all that. I don't know what it died of. Distemper, I guess. It probably hadn't had any shots. I got it out of there before the kids got to school. I checked the supply closet each morning, routinely, because I knew what was going to happen. I gave it to the custodian.

And then there was this Korean orphan that the class adopted through the Help the Children program, all the kids brought in a quarter a month, that was the idea. It was an unfortunate thing, the kid's name was Kim and maybe we adopted him too late or something. The cause of death was not stated in the letter we got, they suggested we adopt another child instead and sent us some interesting case histories, but we didn't have the heart. The class took it pretty hard, they began (I think, nobody ever said anything to me directly) to feel that maybe there was something wrong with the school. But I don't think there's anything wrong with the school, particularly, I've seen better and I've seen worse. It was just a run of bad luck. We had an extraordinary number of parents passing away, for instance. There were I think two heart attacks and two suicides, one drowning, and four killed together in a car accident. One stroke. And we had the usual heavy mortality rate among the grandparents, or maybe it was heavier this year, it seemed so. And finally the tragedy.

The tragedy occurred when Matthew Wein and Tony Mavrogordo were playing over where they're excavating for the new federal office building. There were all these big wooden beams stacked, you know, at the edge of the excavation. There's a court case coming out of that, the parents are claiming that the beams were poorly stacked. I don't know what's true and what's not. It's been a strange year.

I forgot to mention Billy Brandt's father, who was knifed fatally when he grappled with a masked intruder in his home.

One day, we had a discussion in class. They asked me, where did they go? The trees, the salamander, the tropical fish, Edgar, the poppas and mommas, Matthew and Tony, where did they go? And I said, I don't know, I don't know. And they said, who knows? and I said, nobody knows. And they said, is death that which gives meaning to life? and I said, no, life is that which gives meaning to life. Then they said, but isn't death, considered as a fundamental datum, the means by which the taken-for-granted mundanity of the everyday may be transcended in the direction of—

I said, yes, maybe.

They said, we don't like it.

I said, that's sound.

They said, it's a bloody shame!

I said, it is.

They said, will you make love now with Helen (our teaching assistant) so that we can see how it is done? We know you like Helen.

I do like Helen but I said that I would not.

We've heard so much about it, they said, but we've never seen it.

I said I would be fired and that it was never, or almost never, done as a demonstration. Helen looked out of the window.

They said, please, please make love with Helen, we require an assertion of value, we are frightened.

I said that they shouldn't be frightened (although I am often frightened) and that there was value everywhere. Helen came and embraced me. I kissed her a few times on the brow. We held each other. The children were excited. Then there was a knock on the door, I opened the door, and the new gerbil walked in. The children cheered wildly.

TRY THIS 5.10

Using what you have learned about voice, pick a character who belongs to a certain place—preacher, prisoner, coach, nurse, Little Leaguer, or the like—and write a monologue in which that place is evoked through the voice.

ANGELA CARTER

The Werewolf

It is a northern country; they have cold weather, they have cold hearts.

Cold; tempest; wild beasts in the forest. It is a hard life. Their houses are built of logs, dark and smoky within. There will be a crude icon of the virgin behind a guttering candle, the leg of a pig hung up to cure, a string of drying mushrooms. A bed, a stool, a table. Harsh, brief, poor lives.

To these upland woodsmen, the Devil is as real as you or I. More so; they have not seen us nor even know that we exist, but the Devil they glimpse often in the graveyards, those bleak and touching townships of the dead where the graves are marked with portraits of the deceased in the naïf style and there are no flowers to put in front of them, no flowers grow there, so they put out small, votive offerings, little loaves, sometimes a cake that the bears come lumbering from the margins of the forest to snatch away. At midnight especially on Walpurgisnacht, the Devil holds picnics in the graveyards and invites the witches; then they dig up fresh corpses, and eat them. Anyone will tell you that.

Wreaths of garlic on the doors keep out the vampires. A blue-eyed child born feet first on the night of St John's Eve will have second sight. When they discover a witch—some old woman whose cheeses ripen when her neighbour's do not, another old woman whose black cat; oh, sinister! *follows her about all the time,* they strip the crone, search her for marks, for the supernumary nipple her familiar sucks. They soon find it. Then they stone her to death.

5 Winter and cold weather.

Go and visit grandmother, who has been sick. Take her the oatcakes I've baked for her on the hearthstone and a little pot of butter.

The good child does as her mother bids — five miles' trudge through the forest; do not leave the path because of the bears, the wild boar, the starving wolves. Here, take your father's hunting knife; you know how to use it.

The child had a scabby coat of sheepskin to keep out the cold, she knew the forest too well to fear it but she must always be on her guard. When she heard that freezing howl of a wolf, she dropped her gifts, seized her knife and turned on the beast.

It was a huge one, with red eyes and running, grizzled chops; any but a mountaineer's child would have died of fright at the sight of it. It went for her throat, as wolves do, but she made a great swipe at it with her father's knife and slashed off its right forepaw.

The wolf let out a gulp, almost a sob, when she saw what had happened to it; 10
wolves are less brave than they seem. It went lolloping off disconsolately between the trees as well as it could on three legs, leaving a trail of blood behind it. The child wiped the blade of her knife clean on her apron, wrapped up the wolf's paw in the cloth in which her mother had packed the oatcakes and went on towards her grandmother's house. Soon it came on to snow so thickly that the path and any footsteps, track or spoor that might have been upon it were obscured.

She found her grandmother was so sick she had taken to her bed and fallen into a fretful sleep, moaning and shaking so that the child guessed she had a fever. She felt the forehead, it burned. She shook out the cloth from her basket, to use it to make the old woman a cold compress, and the wolf's paw fell to the floor.

But it was no longer a wolf's paw. It was a hand, chopped off at the wrist, a hand toughened with work and freckled with age. There was a wedding ring on the third finger and a wart on the index finger. By the wart, she knew it for her grandmother's hand.

She pulled back the sheet but the old woman woke up, at that, and began to struggle, squawking, and shrieking like a thing possessed. But the child was strong, and armed with her father's hunting knife; she managed to hold her grandmother down long enough to see the cause of her fever. There was a bloody stump where her right hand should have been, festering already.

The child crossed herself and cried out so loud the neighbours heard her and came rushing in. They knew the wart on the hand at once for a witch's nipple; they drove the old woman, in her shift as she was, out into the snow with sticks, beating her old carcass as far as the edge of the forest, and pelted her with stones until she fell down dead.

Now the child lived in her grandmother's house; she prospered. 15

TRY THIS 5.11
Rewrite a fairy tale for the modern "child." Maximum words: 250

POEMS

SHERMAN ALEXIE

At Navajo Monument Valley Tribal School

from the photograph by Skeet McAuley

the football field rises
to meet the mesa. Indian boys
gallop across the grass, against

the beginning of their body.
On those Saturday afternoons,
unbroken horses gather to watch

their sons growing larger
in the small parts of the world.
Everyone is the quarterback.

There is no thin man in a big hat
writing down all the names
in two columns: winners and losers.

This is the eternal football game,
Indians versus Indians. All the Skins
in the wooden bleachers, fancydancing,

stomping red dust straight down
into nothing. Before the game is over,
the eighth-grade girls' track team

comes running, circling the field,
their thin and brown legs echoing
wild horses, wild horses, wild horses.

HEATHER MCHUGH

Earthmoving Malediction

Bulldoze the bed where we made love,
bulldoze the goddamn room.
Let rubble be our evidence
and wreck our home.

I can't give touching up
by inches, can't give beating up
by heart. So set the comforter
on fire, and turn the dirt

to some advantage—palaces of pigweed,
treasuries of turd. The fist
will vindicate the hand,
and tooth and nail

refuse to burn, and I
must not look back, as Mrs. Lot
was named for such a little—
something in a cemetery,

or a man. Bulldoze the coupled
ploys away, the cute exclusives
in the social mall. We dwell

on earth, where beds
are brown, where swoops
are fell. Bulldoze

the pearly gates:
if paradise comes down
there is no hell.

PHILIP APPLEMAN

Nobody Dies in the Spring

Nobody dies in the spring
on the Upper West Side:
nobody dies.
On the Upper West Side
we're holding hands with strangers
on the Number 5 bus,
and we're singing the sweet
graffiti on the subway,
and kids are skipping patterns through
the bright haze of incinerators
and beagles and poodles are making a happy
ruin of the sidewalks,
and hot-dog men are racing
their pushcarts down Riverside Drive,
and Con Ed is tearing up Broadway
from Times Square to the Bronx,
and the world is a morning miracle
of sirens and horns and jackhammers
and Baskin-Robbins' 31 kinds of litter
and sausages at Zabar's floating
overhead like blimps—oh,
it is no place for dying, not
on the Upper West Side, in springtime.

There will be a time
for the smell of burning leaves at Barnard,
for milkweed winging silky over Grant's Tomb,

for apples falling to grass in Needle Park;
but not in all this fresh new golden
smog: now there is something
breaking loose in people's chests,
something that makes butchers and bus boys
and our neighborhood narcs and muggers
go whistling in the streets—now
there is something with goat feet out there, not
waiting for the WALK light, piping
life into West End window-boxes,
pollinating weeds around
condemned residential hotels,
and prancing along at the head
of every elbowing crowd on the West Side,
singing:
Follow me—it's Spring—
and nobody dies.

TRY THIS 5.12

Write a "list poem" that pays homage to a place you know. The images may be strung together with "and—and—and" or with any word or prepositional phrase you choose. There should also be some element of action, something moving or doing, passing or becoming.

YUSEF KOMUNYAKAA

Nude Interrogation

Did you kill anyone over there? Angelica shifts her gaze from the Janis Joplin poster to the Jimi Hendrix, lifting the pale muslin blouse over her head. The blacklight deepens the blues when the needle drops into the first groove of "All Along the Watchtower." I don't want to look at the floor. *Did you kill anyone? Did you dig a hole, crawl inside, and wait for your target?* Her miniskirt drops into a rainbow at her feet. Sandalwood incense hangs a slow comet of perfume over the room. I shake my head. She unhooks her bra and flings it against a bookcase made of plywood and cinderblocks. *Did you use an M-16, a hand-grenade, a bayonet, or your own two strong hands, both thumbs pressed against that little bird in the throat?* She stands with her left thumb hooked into the elastic of her sky-blue panties. When she flicks off the blacklight, snowy hills rush up to the windows. *Did you kill anyone over there? Are you right-handed or left-handed? Did you drop your gun afterwards? Did you kneel beside the corpse and turn it over?* She's nude against the falling snow. *Yes.* The record spins like a bull's-eye on the far wall of Xanadu. *Yes,* I say. *I was scared of the silence. The night was too big. And afterwards, I couldn't stop looking up at the sky.*

TRY THIS 5.13

Below are some themes associated with setting, suggested by the preceding poems. Pick one, remember or imagine a place it represents in your own experience, and brainstorm a list of things that might be found there—people, activities, images. Write a one-paragraph prose poem based on these images. Use the name of the place as your title, perhaps?

- ghosts of the past live here
- I will destroy this place
- this is a place of hope and life
- history happened there

DRAMA

DAVID IVES

The Philadelphia

This play is for Greg Pliska, who knows what a Philadelphia can be.

Characters

AL: California cool; 20s or 30s
MARK: frazzled; 20s or 30s
WAITRESS: weary; as you will

Setting

A bar/restaurant. A table, red-checkered cloth, two chairs, and a specials board. At lights up, AL is at the restaurant, with the WAITRESS.

WAITRESS: Can I help you?

AL: Do you know you would look fantastic on a wide screen?

WAITRESS: Uh-huh.

AL: Seventy millimeters.

WAITRESS: Look. Do you want to see a menu, or what?

AL: Let's negotiate, here. What's the soup du jour today?

WAITRESS: Soup of the day you got a choice of Polish duck blood or cream of kidney.

AL: Beautiful. Beautiful! Kick me in a kidney.

WAITRESS: (*Writes it down.*) You got it.

AL: Any oyster crackers on your seabed?

WAITRESS: Nope. All out.

AL: How about the specials today? Spread out your options.

WAITRESS: You got your deep-fried gizzards.

AL: Fabulous.

WAITRESS: Calves' brains with okra.

AL: You are a *temptress.*

WAITRESS: And pickled pigs' feet.

AL: Pigs' feet, *I love it.* Put me down for a quadruped.

WAITRESS: If you say so.

AL: Any sprouts to go on those feet?

WAITRESS: Iceberg.

AL: So be it.

(*Waitress exits, as MARK enters, looking shaken and bedraggled.*)

MARK: Al!

AL: Hey there, Marcus. What's up?

MARK: Jesus!

AL: What's going on, buddy?

MARK: Oh man...!

AL: What's the matter? Sit down.

MARK: I don't get it, Al. I don't understand it.

AL: You want something? Want a drink? I'll call the waitress—

MARK: (*Desperate.*) *No!* No! Don't even try. (*Gets a breath.*) I don't know what's going on today, Al. It's really weird.

AL: What, like...?

MARK: Right from the time I got up.

AL: What is it? What's the story?

MARK: Well—just for an example. This morning I stopped off at a drugstore to buy some aspirin. This is at a big drugstore, right?

AL: Yeah...

MARK: I go up to the counter, the guy says what can I do for you, I say, Give me a bottle of aspirin. The guy gives me this funny look and he says, "Oh we don't have *that,* sir." I said to him, You're a drugstore and you don't have any aspirin?

AL: Did they have Bufferin?

MARK: Yeah!

AL: Advil?

MARK: Yeah!

AL: Extra-strength Tylenol?

MARK: Yeah!

AL: But no aspirin.

MARK: No!

AL: Wow...

MARK: And that's the kind of weird thing that's been happening all day. It's like, I go to a newsstand to buy the *Daily News,* the guy never even *heard* of it.

AL: Could've been a misunderstanding.

MARK: I asked everyplace—*nobody* had the *News*! I had to read the *Toronto Hairdresser.* Or this. I go into a deli at lunchtime to buy a sandwich, the guys tells me they don't have any *pastrami*. How can they be a deli if they don't have pastrami?

AL: Was this a Korean deli?

MARK: This was a kosher-from-*Jerusalem* deli. "Oh we don't carry *that*, sir," he says to me. "Have some tongue."

AL: Mmm.

MARK: I just got into a cab, the guy says he doesn't go to Fifty-sixth Street! He offers to take me to Newark instead!

AL: Mm-hm.

MARK: Looking at me like I'm an alien or something!

AL: Mark. Settle down.

MARK: "Oh I don't go *there*, sir."

AL: Settle down. Take a breath.

MARK: Do you know what this is?

AL: Sure.

MARK: What is it? What's happening to me?

AL: Don't panic. You're in a Philadelphia.

MARK: I'm in a what?

AL: You're in a Philadelphia. That's all.

MARK: But I'm in—

AL: Yes, physically you are in New York. But *meta*physically you are in a Philadelphia.

MARK: I've never heard of this!

AL: You see, inside of what we know as reality there are these pockets, these black holes called Philadelphias. If you fall into one, you run up against exactly the kinda shit that's been happening to you all day.

MARK: Why?

AL: Because in a Philadelphia, no matter what you ask for, you can't get it. You ask for something, they're not gonna have it. You want to do something, it ain't gonna get done. You want to go somewhere, you can't get there from here.

MARK: Good God. So this is very serious.

AL: Just remember, Marcus. This is a condition named for the town that invented the *cheese steak*. Something that nobody in his right mind would willingly ask for.

MARK: And I thought I was just having a very bad day...

AL: Sure. Millions of people have spent entire lifetimes inside a Philadelphia and never even knew it. Look at the city of Philadelphia itself. Hopelessly trapped forever inside a Philadelphia. And do they know it?

MARK: Well what can I do? Should I just kill myself now and get it over with?

AL: You try to kill yourself in a Philadelphia, you're only gonna get hurt, babe.

MARK: So what do I do?

AL: Best thing you can do is wait it out. Someday the great cosmic train will whisk you outa the City of Brotherly Love and off to someplace happier.

MARK: *You're* pretty goddamn mellow today.

AL: Yeah well. Everybody has to be someplace.

(*WAITRESS enters.*)

WAITRESS: Is your name Allen Chase?

AL: It is indeed.

WAITRESS: There was a phone call for you. Your boss?

AL: Okay.

WAITRESS: He says you're fired.

AL: Cool! Thanks. (*WAITRESS exits.*) So anyway, you have this problem...

MARK: Did she just say you got *fired*?

AL: Yeah. I wonder what happened to my pigs' feet...

MARK: Al—!? You *loved* your job!

AL: Hey. No sweat.

MARK: How can you be so calm?

AL: Easy. You're in a Philadelphia? *I* woke up in a Los Angeles. And life is beautiful! You know Susie packed up and left me this morning.

MARK: Susie left you?

AL: And frankly, Scarlett, I don't give a shit. I say, go and God bless and may your dating pool be Olympic-sized.

MARK: But your job? The garment district is your life!

AL: So I'll turn it into a movie script and sell it to Paramount. Toss in some sex, add a little emotional blah-blah-*blah,* pitch it to Jack and Dusty, you got a buddy movie with a garment background. Not relevant enough? We'll throw in the hole in the ozone, make it E.C.

MARK: E.C.?

AL: Environmentally correct. Have you heard about this hole in the ozone?

MARK: Sure.

AL: Marcus, I *love* this concept. I *embrace* this ozone. Sure, some people are gonna get hurt in the process, meantime everybody else'll tan a little faster.

MARK: (*Quiet horror.*) So this is a Los Angeles...

AL: Well. Everybody has to be someplace.

MARK: Wow.

AL: You want my advice? *Enjoy your Philadelphia.* Sit back and order yourself a beer and a burger and chill out for a while.

MARK: But I can't order anything. Life is great for you out there on your cosmic beach, but whatever *I* ask for, I'll get a cheese steak or something.

AL: No. There's a very simple rule of thumb in a Philadelphia. *Ask for the opposite.*

MARK: What?

AL: If you can't get what you ask for, ask for the opposite and you'll get what you want. You want the *Daily News,* ask for the *Times.* You want pastrami, ask for tongue.

MARK: Oh.

AL: Works great with women. What is more opposite than the opposite sex?

MARK: Uh-huh.

AL: So. Would you like a Bud?

MARK: I sure could use a—

AL: No. Stop. (*Very deliberately.*) *Do you want…a Bud?*

MARK: (*Also deliberately.*) No. I *don't* want a Bud. (*WAITRESS enters and goes to the specials board.*)

AL: Good. Now there's the waitress. Order yourself a Bud and a burger. But do not *ask* for a Bud and a burger.

MARK: Waitress!

AL: Don't call her. She won't come.

MARK: Oh.

AL: You're in a Philadelphia, so just figure, fuck her.

MARK: Fuck *her.*

AL: You don't need that waitress.

MARK: *Fuck* that waitress.

AL: And everything to do with her.

MARK: *Hey waitress! FUCK YOU!* (*WAITRESS turns to him.*)

WAITRESS: Can I help you, sir?

AL: *That's* how you get service in a Philadelphia.

WAITRESS: Can I help you?

MARK: Uh—no thanks.

WAITRESS: Okay, what'll you have? (*Takes out her pad.*)

AL: Excellent.

MARK: Well—how about some O.J.

WAITRESS: Sorry. Squeezer's broken.

MARK: A glass of milk?

WAITRESS: Cow's dry.

MARK: Egg nog?

WAITRESS: Just ran out.

MARK: Cuppa coffee?

WAITRESS: Oh we don't have *that,* sir. (*MARK and AL exchange a look, and nod. The WAITRESS has spoken the magic words.*)

MARK: Got any ale?

WAITRESS: Nope.

MARK: Stout?

WAITRESS: Nope.

MARK: Porter?

WAITRESS: Just beer.

MARK: That's too bad. How about a Heineken?

WAITRESS: Heineken? Try again.

MARK: Rolling Rock?

WAITRESS: Outta stock.

MARK: Schlitz?

WAITRESS: Nix.

MARK: Beck's?

WAITRESS: Next.

MARK: Sapporo?

WAITRESS: Tomorrow.

MARK: Lone Star?

WAITRESS: Hardy-har.

MARK: Bud Lite?

WAITRESS: Just plain Bud is all we got.

MARK: No thanks.

WAITRESS: (*Calls.*) *Gimme a Bud!* (*To MARK.*) Anything to eat?

MARK: Nope.

WAITRESS: Name it.

MARK: Pork chops.

WAITRESS: (*Writes down.*) Hamburger...

MARK: Medium.

WAITRESS: Well done...

MARK: Baked potato.

WAITRESS: Fries...

MARK: And some zucchini.

WAITRESS: Slice of raw. (*Exits, calling.*) Burn one!

AL: Marcus, that was excellent.

MARK: Thank you.

AL: *Excellent.* You sure you've never done this before?

MARK: I've spent so much of my life asking for the wrong thing without knowing it, doing it on purpose comes easy.

AL: I hear you.

MARK: I could've saved myself a lot of trouble if I'd screwed up on purpose all those years. Maybe I was in a Philadelphia all along and never knew it!

AL: You might've been in a Baltimore. They're practically the same. (*WAITRESS enters, with a glass of beer and a plate.*)

WAITRESS: Okay. Here's your Bud. (*Sets that in front of MARK.*) And one cheese steak. (*She sets that in front of AL, and starts to go.*)

AL: Excuse me. Hey. Wait a minute. What is that?

WAITRESS: It's cheese steak.

AL: No. I ordered cream of kidney and two pairs of feet.

WAITRESS: Oh we don't have *that,* sir.

AL: I beg your pardon?

WAITRESS: We don't have that, sir. (*Small pause.*)

AL: (*To MARK.*) You son of a bitch! *I'm in your Philadelphia!*

MARK: I'm sorry, Al.

AL: You brought me into your fucking Philadelphia!

MARK: I didn't know it was contagious.

AL: Oh God, please don't let me be in a Philadelphia! Don't let me in a—

MARK: Shouldn't you ask for the opposite? I mean, since you're in a Philad—

AL: Don't you tell *me* about life in a Philadelphia.

MARK: Maybe you're not really—

AL: I taught you everything you know about Philly, asshole. Don't tell *me* how to act in a Philadelphia!

MARK: But maybe you're not really in a Philadelphia!

AL: Do you see the cheese on that steak? What do I need for proof? The fucking *Liberty Bell*? Waitress, bring me a glass of water.

WAITRESS: Water? Don't have that, sir.

AL: (*To MARK.*) "We don't have *water*"—? What, you think we're in a sudden drought or something? (*Suddenly realizes.*) Holy shit, I just lost my job...! Susie left me! I gotta make some phone calls! (*To WAITRESS.*) 'Scuse me, where's the pay phone?

WAITRESS: Sorry, we don't have a pay ph—

AL: Of *course* you don't have a pay phone, of *course* you don't! Oh shit, let me outta here! (*Exits.*)

MARK: I don't know. It's not that bad in a Philadelphia.

WAITRESS: Could be worse. I've been in a Cleveland all week.

MARK: A Cleveland. What's that like?

WAITRESS: It's like death, without the advantages.

MARK: Really. Care to stand?

WAITRESS: Don't mind if I do. (*She sits.*)

MARK: I hope you won't reveal your name.

WAITRESS: Sharon.

MARK: (*Holds out his hand.*) Good-bye.

WAITRESS: Hello. (*They shake.*)

MARK: (*Indicating the cheese steak.*) Want to starve?

WAITRESS: Thanks! (*She picks up the cheese steak and starts eating.*)

MARK: Yeah, everybody has to be someplace...(*Leans across the table with a smile.*) So.

BLACKOUT

TRY THIS 5.14

The Greek and Roman method of comedy was to take an absurd idea and follow it very logically, very precisely, and straight-faced to its conclusion. This is the comic form of *The Philadelphia*. If you have a good, really absurd idea, write a ten-minute comedy. (This is a good place to brainstorm *what if...?*)

TRY THIS 5.15

Write a stage direction, using no more than five elements or objects to set the scene onstage. See how much you can tell us with these five things about the place and time and the characters who are likely to enter here.

Or:

Set a short scene in a place as banal or characterless as you can think of. Make the dialogue bizarre.

WORKING TOWARD A DRAFT

Take one page from among the things you have written, and add a passage detailing the place, time, and/or weather. Use all active verbs in your description. Use the passage to intensify the mood.

Or:

Take something you have written and rewrite it setting it in some altogether different space. If it took place in private, set it in public; if in the past, set it in the future; if on a playground, set it in a cemetery, and so forth. Does this displacement offer possibilities for enriching the piece?

CHAPTER 6

Story

- *As a Journey*
- *As a Power Struggle*
- *As Connection and Disconnection*

Act I, get your guy up a tree. Act II, throw rocks at him. Act III, get your guy outta the tree.
Julius Epstein

Larry Downing/Reuters/Corbis

WARM-UP

These are the belongings of a family being evicted. Who are they? How many are they? Give them names. Whose is the stuffed dog? Why are they being turned out? Who do they blame? Where will they go? What awaits them there?

Story as a Journey

The late great novelist and teacher John Gardner used to say that there are only two stories: *someone went on a journey* and *a stranger came to town.*

I once ran into a poet at the Yaddo writers' colony who reduced the formula still further: "You fiction writers," he said. "Everything you write is the same: two worlds collide; a love story."

The novelist Chaim Potok used to say that the only subject he wanted to write about was a clash between cultures, The Insider encountering The Other.

These are all ways of expressing the fundamental form of a story. When worlds (cultures, generations, genders, 'hoods) encounter each other, conflict will inevitably occur (in a thousand different guises). When conflict occurs, human beings will band together in some form of love. Sometimes allies, families, races, gangs, nations, will draw closer together to repel a common antagonist. Sometimes connection will be made across the divide of *self* and *other.*

In Chapter 3, I said that a dynamic character is someone capable of change. The encounter or collision of one character with others will force such change, and the story is the process of that change. The altered state may be from alive to dead, from ugly to beautiful, from ignorant to wise, callous to compassionate, from certain to uncertain or vice versa. But the change occurs because the character confronts a situation that will challenge her/his assumptions and somehow shake up the easy beliefs—hence the prevalence, in such a formulation, of strangers, journeys, and worlds. I like the metaphor of the two worlds, too, because it suggests both the importance of setting and the necessity of discovery and decision. The new world that the character discovers may be the house next door, it may be a different set of assumptions or the next stage of life (puberty is a foreign country, marriage is an undiscovered planet)—but the story will always end in an altered state in at least the character whose point of view we share. Usually the character will have his or her scope enlarged—but not always. Usually the story will result in greater wisdom, compassion, or understanding—though it can end in diminishment or narrowing. As *readers,* however, we will *always,* if the story succeeds, have our capacity for empathy enlarged by having lived in the character's skin for the duration. Every story is in this important human sense a "love story."

A story is a journey is only one of many useful metaphors for the shape of a story, but it is the one almost always used by actors and directors when they set out to produce a play. Where does the protagonist want to go (what does she/he desire)? What are the obstacles encountered (what discoveries are made, what conflicts arise)? What does she/he do to overcome these obstacles (what decisions are made)? Is the goal reached? Is it as expected? Sometimes the journey of the story ends in fulfillment, sometimes not; sometimes the goal is reached and proves not worth the trip; sometimes a detour leads to paradise.

Here is a **short-short story** (only 101 words) about a long journey. Written in the diction of a five-year-old, it manages to give a panorama in space and time, as well as details that particularize both the setting and the characters. What change takes place in the character? How does the single line of dialogue at the end show this change?

> I've never been this far from home. I've never stayed up this late. I'm out west.
>
> We rode the train. I slept upstairs. You put your clothes in a hammock. They have Dixie cups.
>
> The world has mountains on the edge, where the sun sets, big black things, and that's where we're going.
>
> I'm in the front seat with my mother. I'm five. We're going to a dude ranch. There will be cowboys.
>
> There's a soft green glow on the dash board. My mother wears perfume.
>
> I'm traveling. I've never been this old.
>
> "The stars are ablaze," I tell my mother.

"Frontiers," John M. Daniel

TRY THIS 6.1

Write a two-page memoir or a short-short story about a journey. Give us the setting and at least two characters. They discover something that causes trouble. Let the main character make a decision and take an action.

Or:

Write about a time that you started out on a trip but failed to arrive at your destination. What was the obstacle—weather, accident, mechanical failure, human failure, human conflict? Characterize both the people involved and the setting through significant detail; give us a sense of the trip itself. What changed from the beginning expectations? How did you change?

Story as a Power Struggle

Another, perhaps the most common, way of looking at story structure is in terms of **conflict, crisis,** and **resolution,** a shape that comes from Aristotle's insistence on *a beginning, a middle,* and *an end.*

This model acknowledges that, in literature, only trouble is interesting. *Only* trouble is interesting. This is not so in life. Life offers periods of comfortable communication, peaceful pleasure, and productive work, all of which are extremely interesting to those involved. But passages about such times make for dull reading; they cannot be used as a plot.

Suppose, for example, you go on a picnic. You find a beautiful deserted meadow with a lake nearby. The weather is splendid and so is the company. The food's delicious, the water's fine, and the insects have taken the day off. Afterward, someone asks you how your picnic was. "Terrific," you reply, "really perfect." No story.

But suppose the next week you go back for a rerun. You set your picnic blanket on an anthill. You all race for the lake to get cold water on the bites, and one of your friends goes too far out on the plastic raft, which deflates. He can't swim and you have to save him. On the way in you gash your foot on a broken bottle. When you get back to the picnic, the ants have taken over the cake and a possum has demolished the chicken. Just then the sky opens up. When you gather your things to race for the car, you notice a bull has broken through the fence. The others run for it, but because of your bleeding heel the best you can do is hobble. You have two choices: try to outrun him or stand perfectly still and hope he's interested only in a moving target. At this point, you don't know if your friends can be counted on for help, even the nerd whose life you saved. You don't know if it's true that a bull is attracted by the smell of blood.

A year later, assuming you're around to tell about it, you are still saying, "Let me *tell* you what happened last year." And your listeners are saying, "What a story!"

This pattern of trouble and the effort to overcome it is repeated in every story on a larger or smaller scale. It may seem, for example, that the five-year-old in the previous short-short is not in much trouble. But look at the huge dangers he faces: *never been this far from home, never up this late; mountains on the edge, big black things where we're going.* The clear and intense desire to get to the dude ranch is countered by the awesome strangeness of the adventure. Two worlds collide, in fact.

In the conflict-crisis-resolution model, story is seen as a power struggle between two nearly equal forces, a **protagonist** or central character and an **antagonist,** who represents the obstacles to the protagonist's desires and may be another human being or some other force—God, nature, the self, and so forth. If the antagonist is some abstract force, then, like the character's desire, it will also have a very specific manifestation: not "nature" but "seven miles of white water rapids on the lower Colorado"; not "the supernatural" but "a mutant reptile embryo capable of hatching in a human middle ear."

It is crucial that the opposing forces have approximately equal force, so that our uncertainty about the outcome keeps us reading. We begin with a situation in which the power is with the protagonist or the antagonist. Something happens, and the power shifts to the other. Something else, and it shifts back again. Each time the power shifts, the stakes are raised, each battle is bigger, more intense than the last, until (at the crisis moment) one of the two opposing forces manifests its power in a way that the other cannot match.

Here is another short-short story (a lavish 232 words this time), also in a child's voice, in which the conflict-crisis-resolution pattern is intense.

Watching Joey pop the red berries into his mouth like Ju-Ju Bees and Mags only licking them at first, then chewing, so both of their smiles look bloody and I laugh though I don't eat even one... then suddenly our moms are all around us (although mine doesn't panic till she looks at the others, then screams along with them things like *God dammit did you eat these?* and shakes me so my "No" sounds like "oh-oh-oh") and then we're being yanked toward the house, me for once not resisting as my mother scoops me into her arms, and inside the moms shove medicine, thick and purple, down our throats in the bathroom; Joey in the toilet, Mags in the sink, me staring at the hair in the tub drain as my mom pushes my head down, and there is red vomit everywhere, splashing on the mirror and powder-blue rugs, everywhere except the tub where mine is coming out yellow, the color of corn muffins from lunch, not a speck of red, *I told you,* I want to scream, and then it is over and I turn to my mother for a touch or a stroke on the head like the other moms (but she has moved to the doorway and lights a cigarette, pushes hair out of her eyes) and there is only her smeared lips saying, *This will teach you anyway.*

"This Is How I Remember It," Elizabeth Kemper French

In this classical pattern, the story begins with an **exposition,** or statement of the situation at the beginning of the action, which is typically, as here, a state of unstable equilibrium (*I laugh, though I don't eat even one...*). **Conflict** arrives with the mothers, and that conflict undergoes a series of **complications** involving force, blame, mistake, submission, anger, and so forth. The power struggle between mother and daughter escalates through a change of setting. Details build the contrast between the kinds of *mom* and the kinds of vomit. The **crisis action** occurs as a moment of martyred triumph for the narrator (*I told you*) and then there is a **falling action** or **denouement** in which the mother and daughter retreat to their respective corners and settle back into what (we know by now) is their habit of being. This is the **resolution.** Some questions to consider: Why did the author choose to tell this story in a single sentence? What does the narrator want? Who wins? Is it worth it?

This very short story is very much of the twentieth century, in that the crisis occurs in the mind of the narrator and the "resolution" does not offer a "solution." The completion of the action has changed the characters not by a dramatic reversal, but by moving them deeper into their *impasse.*

Order is a major value that literature offers us, and order implies that the subject has been brought to closure. In life this never quite happens. Even the natural "happy endings," marriage and birth, leave domesticity and child-rearing to be dealt with; the natural "tragic endings," separation and death, leave trauma and bereavement in their wake. Literature absolves us of these nuisances. Whether or not the lives of the characters end, the story does, and we are left with a satisfying sense of completion. This is one reason we enjoy crying or feeling terrified or even nauseated by fiction; we know in advance that it's going to be over, and by contrast with the continual struggle of living, all that ends, ends well.

TRY THIS 6.2

Write a short story on a postcard. (Write small.) Make sure it has a conflict, a crisis, and a resolution. Send it to a friend in another place (meaning you have published it), or to yourself (when it arrives you will be able to see it fresh).

Or:

A story, a memoir, or a play: Place two characters in a dangerous setting. Each has half of something that is no good without the other half. Neither wants to give up his/her half. What happens?

Story as Connection and Disconnection

> Connection is human substance, the substance of story. Its gain and loss provides the emotional power.
>
> *Claudia Johnson*

Every story presents some sort of journey, literal or psychological or both, that results in a change in the central character. Every story shows a pattern of conflict between approximately equal forces, which leads to a crisis and a resolution. Every story also offers a pattern of connection and disconnection between human beings, which is the source of meaning and significance in the story. Conflict is exciting; it keeps the reader wondering what will happen next. But conflict itself is sterile unless it is given human dimension through the connections and disconnections of the characters.

Therefore, boy meets girl, boy loses girl, boy gets girl (connection, disconnection, connection). Therefore, Hamlet's father dies (disconnects), but comes back (connects) as a ghost, Hamlet rages against his mother (disconnects), welcomes his school friends (connects), breaks off with Ophelia (disconnects), kills her father (disconnects), betrays his school friends (disconnects), kills his stepfather (disconnects) and, in the arms (connects) of his best friend, dies (disconnects). It will be evident that a story that ends in disconnection, especially death, tends toward tragedy, and one that ends in connection, traditionally marriage, is a comedy. Examine any story that makes you care, and you will see that people *who matter to each other* perform, as in life, patterns of love and hate, alienation and community, anger and forgiveness, connection and disconnection. As Claudia Johnson puts it, "The conflict and surface events are like waves, but underneath is an emotional tide—the ebb and flow of human connection."

Even in the very short compass of the two short-short stories earlier in the chapter, these patterns occur. In "Frontiers," the boy is frighteningly separated from home, but his mother is there with him, to take him to the glamorous and grown-up connection with *cowboys*. In "This Is How I Remember It," the girl is connected to her friends, but not so close that she will dare the bloodred berries;

the moms arrive to connect, each with her own child; but the heroine deeply disconnects from her punitive and unjust mother.

TRY THIS 6.3

Write down a memory of a time you seriously disconnected from someone close to you. Know that the person will never read it.

Or:

Write a poem about a death, a breakup, a divorce, a quarrel, or leaving a house. Find some small positive aspect of the disconnection.

It is useful to think of story shape as an inverted check mark, rising from left to right and ending in a short downswing. The story begins with an *exposition* of the opening situation, develops a conflict through a series of complications in which the power changes back and forth, and culminates in a crisis. Then there is a brief walking-away (falling action or denouement), leading to resolution.

If we take the familiar tale of Cinderella, we can see how even this simple children's story relates to each of the models—as journey, as power struggle, and as pattern of connection/disconnection.

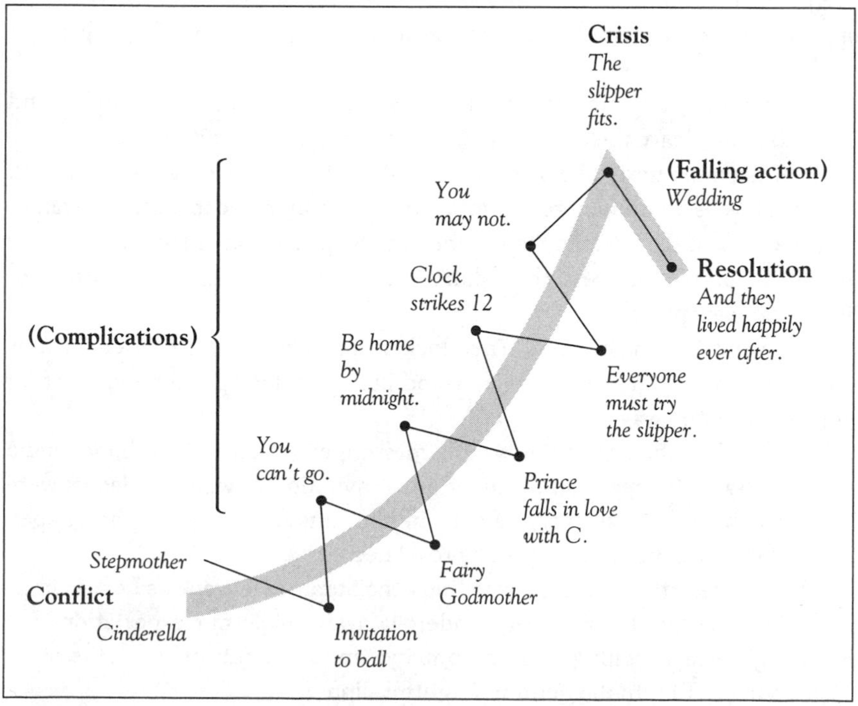

At the opening of the tale we're given the basic conflict: Cinderella's mother has died, and her father has married a brutal woman with two waspish daughters. Cinderella is made to do all the menial work, and she weeps among the cinders. Her journey is, on the literal level, from the hearth to the palace, and on the mythic level from slave to Princess. Along the way she encounters the obstacles of powerlessness, evil, short-lived magic, and chance. With the aid of goodness, beauty, magic, and chance, she also reaches her goal.

Next consider the story in relation to the "check mark" in terms of a power struggle. The Stepmother has on her side the strength of ugliness and evil (two very powerful qualities in literature as in life). With her daughters she also has the strength of numbers, and she has parental authority. Cinderella has only beauty and goodness, but (in literature and life) these are also very powerful.

At the beginning, the power is on the Stepmother's side. But the first event of the story is that an invitation arrives from the Prince explicitly stating that *all* the ladies of the land are invited to a ball. Notice that Cinderella's desire is not to triumph over her Stepmother (though she eventually will, much to our satisfaction); such a desire would diminish her goodness. She simply wants equality, so that the Prince's invitation, which specifically gives her a right equal to the Stepmother's and Stepsisters', shifts the power to her.

The Stepmother takes the power back by force: You may not go; you must get us ready to go. Cinderella does so, and the three leave for the ball.

Then what happens? The Fairy Godmother appears. It is very powerful to have magic on your side. The Fairy Godmother offers Cinderella a gown, glass slippers, and a coach with horses and footmen, giving her more force than she has yet had.

But the magic is not all-potent. It will last only until midnight, and Cinderella must leave the ball before then or risk exposure and defeat.

What happens next? She goes to the ball and the Prince falls in love with her—and love is an even more powerful weapon than magic in a literary war. In some versions of the tale, the Stepmother and Stepsisters are made to marvel at the beauty of the princess they don't recognize, pointing to the irony of Cinderella's new power.

And then? The magic quits. The clock strikes twelve, and Cinderella runs down the steps in her rags to her rats and pumpkin, losing a slipper, bereft of her power in every way.

But after that, the Prince sends out a messenger with the glass slipper and a dictum (a dramatic repetition of the original invitation in which all ladies were invited to the ball) that every female in the land is to try on the slipper. Cinderella is given her rights again by royal decree.

What happens then? In most retellings, the Stepmother repeats her assumption of brute authority by hiding Cinderella away, while our expectations are tantalizingly delayed with grotesque comedy: One sister cuts off a toe, the other a heel, trying to fit into the heroine's rightful slipper.

Cinderella tries on the slipper and it fits. *This is the crisis action.* Magic, love, and royalty join to recognize the heroine's true self; evil, numbers, and authority are powerless against them. At this point, the power struggle has been decided. When the slipper fits, no further action can deprive Cinderella of her desire. The change in the lives of all concerned is significant and permanent. The tale then has a brief falling action: The Prince sweeps Cinderella up on his white horse and gallops away to their wedding, and comes to closure with the classic resolution of all comedy: They lived happily ever after.

In many of the finest modern short stories and novels, the true territory of struggle is the main character's mind, and so the real crisis action must occur there. Yet it is important to grasp that any mental reversal that takes place in the crisis of a story must be triggered or shown by an action. The slipper must fit. It would not do if the Stepmother just happened to change her mind and give up the struggle; it would not do if the Prince just happened to notice that Cinderella looked like his love. The moment of recognition must be manifested in an action.

The *crisis,* also referred to as the *turning point* or *climax* of a story, is often the most difficult for beginning writers to identify and to produce. It is likely to be the moment of greatest emotional intensity in the story, and it is by definition the point at which the change in the protagonist is decisive and inevitable.

In "Red Sky in the Morning," a memoir that tells a story in the Readings section of this chapter, the crisis moment occurs quite early, as an "indelible bittersweetness," on which the rest of the essay reflects. In the story "Incarnations of Burned Children," also in this chapter, the action begins at high pitch, in the middle of what we would surely call a crisis in life, but the crisis of the story occurs with the discovery "and they saw where the real water'd fallen," at which point the end is inevitable.

If we look at "Cinderella" in terms of connection/disconnection we see a pattern as clear as that represented by the power struggle. The first painful disconnection is that Cinderella's mother has died; her father has married (connected with) a woman who spurns (disconnects from) her; the Prince's invitation offers connection, the Stepmother's cruelty alienates again. The Fairy Godmother connects as a magical friend, but the disappearance of the coach and gown disconnect Cinderella temporarily from that grand and glorious fairy tale union, marriage to the Prince. If we consult the emotions that this tale engenders—pity, anger, hope, fear, romance, anticipation, disappointment, triumph—we see that both the struggle between antagonist/protagonist and the pattern of alienation/connectedness are necessary to ensure, not only that there is an action, but also that we care about its outcome.

Forms of imaginative writing are not mutually exclusive. Often a memoir is dramatic, dialogue can be lyrical, narrative turns to poetry. Above all, many essays, poems, and plays have the fundamental form of story. This form—in its incarnations as journey, conflict-crisis-resolution, and connection/disconnection—is so prevalent in human culture that scarcely any communication is free of it. The most casual conversation includes anecdotes of destination and detour. The company report boasts of obstacles overcome. The trip to school shapes up as power struggle between protagonist child and antagonist mom, resolved with a connecting hug or a parting blast. Awareness of these shapes can inform any genre of writing and help to bridge the gap between mind and mind, helping to achieve the first desire of any writer: connection with that intimate stranger, the reader.

TRY THIS 6.4
Write a memory that tells a story.

Or:

Write a dialogue that is a poem.

More to Read

Burroway, Janet. *Writing Fiction: A Guide to Narrative Craft.* New York: Longman, 2011. Print.
Forster, E. M. *Aspects of the Novel.* New York: Harcourt Brace Jovanovich, 1972. Print.

READINGS

CREATIVE NONFICTION

PATRICIA HAMPL

Red Sky in the Morning

Years ago, in another life, I woke to look out the smeared window of a Greyhound bus I had been riding all night, and in the still-dark morning of a small Missouri river town where the driver had made a scheduled stop at a grimy diner, I saw below me a stout middle-aged woman in a flowered housedress turn and kiss full on the mouth a godlike young man with golden curls. But I've got that wrong: *he* was kissing *her*. Passionately, without regard for the world and its incomprehension. He had abandoned himself to his love, and she, stolid, matronly, received this adoration with simple grandeur, like a socialist-realist statue of a woman taking up sheaves of wheat.

Their ages dictated that he must be her son, but I had just come out of the cramped, ruinous half sleep of a night on a Greyhound and I was clairvoyant: This was that thing called love. The morning light cracked blood red along the river.

Of course, when she lumbered onto the bus a moment later, lurching forward with her two bulging bags, she chose the empty aisle seat next to me as her own. She pitched one bag onto the overhead rack, and then heaved herself into the seat as if she were used to hoisting sacks of potatoes onto the flatbed of a pickup. She held the other bag on her lap, and leaned toward the window. The beautiful boy was blowing kisses. He couldn't see where she was in the dark interior, so he blew kisses up and down the side of the bus, gazing ardently at the blank windows. "Pardon me," the woman said without looking at me, and leaned over, bag and all, to rap the glass. Her beautiful boy ran back to our window and kissed and kissed, and finally hugged himself, shutting his eyes in an ecstatic pantomime of love-sweet-love. She smiled and waved back.

Then the bus was moving. She slumped back in her seat, and I turned to her. I suppose I looked transfixed. As our eyes met she said, "Everybody thinks he's my son. But he's not. He's my husband." She let that sink in. She was a farm woman with hands that could have been a man's; I was a university student, hair down to my waist. It was long ago, as I said, in another life. It was even another life for the country. The Vietnam War was the time we were living through, and I was traveling, as I did every three weeks, to visit my boyfriend who was in a federal prison. "Draft dodger," my brother said. "Draft resister," I piously retorted. I had never been kissed the way this woman had been kissed. I was living in a tattered corner of a romantic idyll, the one where the hero is willing to suffer for his beliefs. I was the girlfriend. I lived on pride, not love.

My neighbor patted her short cap of hair, and settled in for the long haul as 5
we pulled onto the highway along the river, heading south. "We been married five years and we're happy," she said with a penetrating satisfaction, the satisfaction that passeth understanding. "Oh," she let out a profound sigh as if she mined her truths from the bountiful, bulky earth, "Oh, I could tell you stories." She put her arms snugly around her bag, gazed for a moment, apparently made pensive by her remark. Then she closed her eyes and fell asleep.

I looked out the window smudged by my nose which had been pressed against it at the bus stop to see the face of true love reveal itself. Beyond the bus the sky, instead of becoming paler with the dawn, drew itself out of a black line along the Mississippi into an alarming red flare. It was very beautiful. The old caution—*Red sky in the morning, sailor take warning*—darted through my mind and fell away. Remember this, I remember telling myself, hang on to this. I could feel it all skittering away, whatever conjunction of beauty and improbability I had stumbled upon.

It is hard to describe the indelible bittersweetness of that moment. Which is why, no doubt, it had to be remembered. The very word—*Remember!*—spiraled up like a snake out of a basket, a magic catch in its sound, the doubling of the m—*re memmemem*—setting up a low murmur full of inchoate associations as if a loved voice were speaking into my ear alone, occultly.

Whether it was the unguarded face of love, or the red gash down the middle of the warring country I was traveling through, or this exhausted farm woman's promise of untold tales that bewitched me, I couldn't say. Over it all rose and remains only the injunction to remember. This, the most impossible command we lay upon ourselves, claimed me and then perversely disappeared, trailing an illusive silken tissue of meaning, without giving a story, refusing to leave me in peace.

Because everyone "has" a memoir, we all have a stake in how such stories are told. For we do not, after all, simply *have* experience; we are entrusted with it. We must do something—make something—with it. A story, we sense, is the only possible habitation for the burden of our witnessing.

The tantalizing formula of my companion on the Greyhound—*oh, I could tell you stories*—is the memoirist's opening line, but it has none of the delicious promise of the storyteller's "Once upon a time..." In fact, it is a perverse statement. The woman on the bus told me nothing—she fell asleep and escaped to her dreams. For the little sentence inaugurates nothing, and leads nowhere after its *dot dot dot* of expectation. Whatever experience lies tangled within its seductive promise remains forever balled up in the woolly impossibility of telling the-truth-the-whole-truth of life, any life.

Memoirists, unlike fiction writers, do not really want to "tell a story." They want to tell it *all*—the all of personal experience, of consciousness itself. That includes a story, but also the whole expanding universe of sensation and thought that flows beyond the confines of narrative and proves every life to be not only an isolated story line but a bit of the cosmos, spinning and streaming into the great, ungraspable pattern of existence. Memoirists wish to tell their mind, not their story.

The wistfulness implicit in that conditional verb—*I could tell*—conveys an urge more primitive than a storyteller's search for an audience. It betrays not a loneliness for someone who will listen but a hopelessness about language itself and a sad recognition of its limitations. How much reality can subject-verb-object bear on the frail shoulders of the sentence? The sigh within the statement is more like this: I could tell you stories—if only stories could tell what I have in me to tell.

For this reason, autobiographical writing is bedeviled. It is caught in a self which must become a world—and not, please, a narcissistic world. The memoir, once considered a marginal literary form, has emerged in the past decade as the signature genre of the age. "The triumph of memoir is now established fact," James Atlas trumpeted in a cover story on "The Age of the Literary Memoir" in the *New York Times Magazine*. "Fiction," he claimed, "isn't delivering the news. Memoir is."

With its "triumph," the memoir has, of course, not denied the truth and necessity of fiction. In fact, it leans heavily on novelistic assumptions. But the contemporary memoir has reaffirmed the primacy of the first-person voice in American imaginative writing established by Whitman's "Song of Myself." Maybe a reader's love of memoir is less an intrusive lust for confession than a hankering for the intimacy of this first-person voice, the deeply satisfying sense of being spoken to privately. More than a story, we want a voice speaking softly, urgently, in our ear. Which is to say, to our heart. The voice carries its implacable command, the ancient murmur that called out to me in the middle of the country in the middle of a war—remember, remember (*I dare you, I tempt you*).

Looking out the Greyhound window that red morning all those years ago, 15
I saw the improbable face of love. But even more puzzling was the cryptic remark of the beloved as she sat next to me. I think of her more often than makes sense. Though he was the beauty, she was the one who comes back. How faint his golden curls have become (he also had a smile, crooked and charming, but I can only remember the idea of it—the image is gone). It is she, stout and unbeautiful, wearing her flowery cotton housedress with a zipper down the middle, who has taken up residence with her canny eye and her acceptance of adoration. To be loved like that, loved improbably: of course, she had stories to tell. She took it for granted in some unapologetic way, like being born to wealth. Take the money and run.

But that moment before she fell asleep, when she looked pensive, the red morning rising over the Mississippi, was a wistful moment. *I could tell you stories*—but she could not. What she had to tell was too big, too much, too *something*, for her to place in the small shrine that a story is.

When we met—if what happened between us was a meeting—I felt nothing had ever happened to me and nothing ever would. I didn't understand that riding this filthy Greyhound down the middle of bloodied America in the middle of a mutinous war was itself a story and that something *was* happening to me. I thought if something was happening to anybody around me it was happening to people like my boyfriend: They were the heroes, according to the lights that shined for me then. I was just riding shotgun in my own life. I could not have imagined containing, as the farm woman slumped next to me did, the sheer narrative bulk to say, "I could tell you stories," and then drifting off with the secret heaviness of experience into the silence where stories live their real lives, crumbling into the loss we call remembrance.

The boastful little declaration, pathetically conditional (not "I'll tell you a story" but "I could") wavered wistfully for an instant between us. The stranger's remark, launched in the dark of the Greyhound, floated across the human landscape like the lingering tone of a struck bell from a village church, and joined all the silence that ever was, as I turned my face to the window where the world was rushing by along the slow river.

TRY THIS 6.5

Recall an experience that changed you. Write about it with one of the traditional openings of story:

- Once upon a time...
- Long ago and far away...
- In the beginning...
- Let me tell you a story...
- Listen!
- It all began...

FICTION

DAVID FOSTER WALLACE

Incarnations of Burned Children

The Daddy was around the side of the house hanging a door for the tenant when he heard the child's screams and the Mommy's voice gone high between them. He could move fast, and the back porch gave onto the kitchen, and before the screen door had banged shut behind him the Daddy had taken the scene in whole, the overturned pot on the floortile before the stove and the burner's blue jet and the floor's pool of water still steaming as its many arms extended, the toddler in his baggy diaper standing rigid with steam coming off his hair and his chest and shoulders scarlet and his eyes rolled up and mouth open very wide and seeming somehow separate from the sounds that issued, the Mommy down on one knee with the dishrag dabbing pointlessly at him and matching the screams with cries of her own, hysterical so she was almost frozen. Her one knee and the bare little soft feet were still in the steaming pool, and the Daddy's first act was to take the child under the arms and lift him away from it and take him to the sink, where he threw out plates and struck the tap to let cold wellwater run over the boy's feet while with his cupped hand he gathered and poured or flung more cold water over the head and shoulders and chest, wanting first to see the steam stop coming off him, the Mommy over his shoulder invoking God until he sent her for towels and gauze if they had it, the Daddy moving quickly and well and his man's mind empty of everything but purpose, not yet aware of how smoothly he moved or that he'd ceased to hear the high screams because to hear them would freeze him and make impossible what had to be done to help his own child, whose screams were regular as breath and went on so long they'd become already a thing in the kitchen, something else to move quickly around. The tenant side's door outside hung half off its top hinge and moved slightly in the wind, and a bird in the oak across the driveway appeared to observe the door with a cocked head as the cries still came from inside. The worst scalds seemed to be the right arm and shoulder, the chest and stomach's red was fading to pink under the cold water and his feet's soft soles weren't blistered that the Daddy could see, but the toddler still made little fists and screamed except maybe now merely on reflex from fear, the Daddy would know he thought it possible later, small face distended and thready veins standing out at the temples and the Daddy kept saying he was here he was here, adrenaline ebbing and an anger at the Mommy for allowing this thing to happen just starting to gather in wisps at his mind's extreme rear and still hours from expression. When the Mommy returned he wasn't sure whether to wrap the child in a towel or not but he wet the towel down and did, swaddled him tight and lifted his baby out of the sink and set him on the kitchen table's edge to soothe him while the Mommy tried to check the feet's soles with one hand waving around in the area of her mouth and uttering objectless words while the Daddy bent in and was face to face with the child on the table's checked edge repeating the fact that he was here and trying to calm the toddler's cries but still the child breathlessly screamed, a high pure shining sound that could stop his heart and his bitty lips and gums now tinged with the light blue of a low flame the Daddy thought, screaming as if almost still under the tilted pot in pain. A minute, two like this that seemed much longer, with the Mommy at the Daddy's side talking singsong at the child's face and the lark on the limb with its head to the side and the hinge going white in a line from the weight of the canted door until the first seen wisp of steam came lazy from under the wrapped towel's hem and the parents' eyes met and widened—the diaper, which when they opened the towel and leaned their little boy back on the checkered cloth and unfastened the softened tabs and tried to remove it resisted slightly with new high cries and was hot, their baby's diaper burned their hand and they saw where the real water'd fallen and pooled and been burning their baby boy all this time while he screamed for them to help him and they hadn't, hadn't thought and when they got it off and saw the state of what was there the Mommy said their God's first name and grabbed the table to keep her feet while the father turned away and threw a haymaker at the air of the kitchen and cursed both himself and the world for not the last time while his child might now have been sleeping if not for the rate of his breathing and the tiny stricken motions of his hands in the air above where he lay, hands the size of a grown man's thumb that had clutched the Daddy's thumb in the crib while he'd watched the Daddy's mouth move in song, his head cocked and seeming to see way past him into something his eyes made the Daddy lonesome for in a sideways way. If you've never wept and want to, have a child. Break your heart inside and something will a child is the twangy song the Daddy hears again as if the radio's lady was almost there with him looking down at what they've done, though hours later what the Daddy most won't forgive is how badly he wanted a cigarette right then as they diapered the child as best they could in gauze and two crossed handtowels and the Daddy lifted him like a newborn with his skull in one palm and ran him out to the hot truck and burned custom rubber all the way to town and the clinic's ER with the tenant's door hanging open like that all day until the hinge gave but by then it was too late, when it wouldn't stop and they couldn't make it the child had learned to leave himself and watch the whole rest unfold from a point overhead, and whatever was lost never thenceforth mattered, and the child's body expanded and walked about and drew pay and lived its life untenanted, a thing among things, its self's soul so much vapor aloft, falling as rain and then rising, the sun up and down like a yoyo.

TRY THIS 6.6

Recall an experience that frightened you. Write about only the last fifteen minutes of it—no more than two pages. You will have to jump into the action quickly and you will have time for few explanations. Can you nevertheless make clear the crisis moment, after which the outcome was inevitable?

NAGUIB MAHFOUZ

Half a Day

Translated by Denys Johnson-Davies

I proceeded alongside my father, clutching his right hand, running to keep up with the long strides he was taking. All my clothes were new: the black shoes, the green school uniform, and the red tarboosh. My delight in my new clothes, however, was not altogether unmarred, for this was no feast day but the day on which I was to be cast into school for the first time.

My mother stood at the window watching our progress, and I would turn toward her from time to time, as though appealing for help. We walked along a street lined with gardens; on both sides were extensive fields planted with crops, prickly pears, henna trees, and a few date palms.

"Why school?" I challenged my father openly. "I shall never do anything to annoy you."

"I'm not punishing you," he said, laughing. "School's not a punishment. It's the factory that makes useful men out of boys. Don't you want to be like your father and brothers?"

5 I was not convinced. I did not believe there was really any good to be had in tearing me away from the intimacy of my home and throwing me into this building that stood at the end of the road like some huge, high-walled fortress, exceedingly stern and grim.

When we arrived at the gate we could see the courtyard, vast and crammed full of boys and girls. "Go in by yourself," said my father, "and join them. Put a smile on your face and be a good example to others."

I hesitated and clung to his hand, but he gently pushed me from him. "Be a man," he said. "Today you truly begin life. You will find me waiting for you when it's time to leave."

I took a few steps, then stopped and looked but saw nothing. Then the faces of boys and girls came into view. I did not know a single one of them, and none of them knew me. I felt I was a stranger who had lost his way. But glances of curiosity were directed toward me, and one boy approached and asked, "Who brought you?"

"My father," I whispered.

"My father's dead," he said quite simply.

I did not know what to say. The gate was closed, letting out a pitiable screech. Some of the children burst into tears. The bell rang. A lady came along, followed by a group of men. The men began sorting us into ranks. We were formed into an intricate pattern in the great courtyard surrounded on three sides by high buildings of several floors; from each floor we were overlooked by a long balcony roofed in wood.

"This is your new home," said the woman. "Here too there are mothers and fathers. Here there is everything that is enjoyable and beneficial to knowledge and religion. Dry your tears and face life joyfully."

We submitted to the facts, and this submission brought a sort of contentment. Living beings were drawn to other living beings, and from the first moments my heart made friends with such boys as were to be my friends and fell in love with such girls as I was to be in love with, so that it seemed my misgivings had had no basis. I had never imagined school would have this rich variety. We played all sorts of different games: swings, the vaulting horse, ball games. In the music room we chanted our first songs. We also had our first introduction to language. We saw a globe of the Earth, which revolved and showed the various continents and countries. We started learning the numbers. The story of the Creator of the universe was read to us, we were told of His present world and of His Hereafter, and we heard examples of what He said. We ate delicious food, took a little nap, and woke up to go on with friendship and love, play and learning.

As our path revealed itself to us, however, we did not find it as totally sweet and unclouded as we had presumed. Dust-laden winds and unexpected accidents came about suddenly, so we had to be watchful, at the ready, and very patient. It was not all a matter of playing and fooling around. Rivalries could bring about pain and hatred or give rise to fighting. And while the lady would sometimes smile, she would often scowl and scold. Even more frequently she would resort to physical punishment.

15 In addition, the time for changing one's mind was over and gone and there was no question of ever returning to the paradise of home. Nothing lay ahead of us but exertion, struggle, and perseverance. Those who were able took advantage of the opportunities for success and happiness that presented themselves amid the worries.

The bell rang announcing the passing of the day and the end of work. The throngs of children rushed toward the gate, which was opened again. I bade farewell to friends and sweethearts and passed through the gate. I peered around but found no trace of my father, who had promised to be there. I stepped aside to wait. When I had waited for a long time without avail, I decided to return home on my own. After I had taken a few steps, a middle-aged man passed by, and I realized at once that I knew him. He came toward me, smiling, and shook me by the hand, saying, "It's a long time since we last met—how are you?"

With a nod of my head, I agreed with him and in turn asked, "And you, how are you?"

"As you can see, not all that good, the Almighty be praised!"

Again he shook me by the hand and went off. I proceeded a few steps, then came to a startled halt. Good Lord! Where was the street lined with gardens? Where had it disappeared to? When did all these vehicles invade it? And when did all these hordes of humanity come to rest upon its surface? How did these hills of refuse come to cover its sides? And where were the fields that bordered it? High buildings had taken over, the street surged with children, and disturbing noises shook the air. At various points stood conjurers showing off their tricks and making snakes appear from baskets. The there was a band announcing the opening of a circus, with clowns and weight lifters walking in front. A line of trucks carrying central security troops crawled majestically by. The siren of a fire engine shrieked, and it was not clear how the vehicle would cleave its way to reach the blazing fire. A battle raged between a taxi driver and his passenger, while the passenger's wife called out for help and no one answered. Good God! I was in a daze. My head spun. I almost went crazy. How could all this have happened in half a day, between early morning and sunset? I would find the answer at home with my father. But where was my home? I could see only tall building and hordes of people. I hastened on to the crossroads between the gardens and Abu Khoda. I had to cross Abu Khoda to reach my house, but the stream of cars would not let up. The fire engine's siren was shrieking at full pitch as it moved at a snail's pace, and I said to myself, "Let the fire take its pleasure in what it consumes." Extremely irritated, I wondered when I would be able to cross. I stood there a long time, until the young lad employed at the ironing shop on the corner came up to me. He stretched out his arm and said gallantly, "Grandpa, let me take you across."

TRY THIS 6.7

Write a short-short story in which time expands, contracts, or turns back on itself.

ROBERT HASS

A Story About the Body

The young composer, working that summer at an artist's colony, had watched her for a week. She was Japanese, a painter, almost sixty, and he thought he was in love with her. He loved her work, and her work was like the way she moved her body, used her hands, looked at him directly when she made amused and considered answers to his questions. One night, walking back from a concert, they came to her door and she turned to him and said, "I think you would like to have me. I would like that too, but I must tell you that I have had a double mastectomy," and when he didn't understand, "I've lost both my breasts." The radiance that he had carried around in his belly and chest cavity—like music—withered very quickly, and he made himself look at her when he said, "I'm sorry. I don't think I could." He walked back to his own cabin through the pines, and in the morning he found a small blue bowl on the porch outside his door. It looked to be full of rose petals, but he found when he picked it up that the rose petals were on top; the rest of the bowl—she must have swept them from the corners of her studio—was full of dead bees.

TRY THIS 6.8

"Nude Interrogation" on page 158 and "A Story About the Body" above are **prose poems,** poems that are not written in lines but continue to the margins of the page like prose. Earlier in this chapter you read two short-short stories within the text—"Frontiers" and "This Is How I Remember It." The borderline between a prose poem and a short-short story is very fine, and you could (probably not very fruitfully) argue about whether any given piece is one or the other. In a general way, you could say that a prose poem will pay central attention to the language and its pattern of sound, whereas a short-short story will be first of all structured on the narrative arc conflict-crisis-resolution. You will, however, find many exceptions to this general—not even rule, but—observation. If you contrast "Nude Interrogation" and "Frontiers," you will see the difference relatively clearly.

Write either a prose poem or a short-short story such that no one would claim it was the other. If a poem, dwell on the language but tell *no story.* If a story, plainspeak a plot.

ALBERT GOLDBARTH

Columbine High School/Littleton, CO

Here, thirteen high school students died,
murdered by two other high school students
—the memorial consists

of fifteen crosses. In this photograph, a woman
rests her head against one upright beam
as if decanting
(*trying* to) everything that's in her brain
—only the wood, only something
inhuman now, could hold what flows from her.
This grief's too vast for us, a color of its own,
not from our limited strip of the spectrum.
Really all that makes this picture comprehensible
to us—to we who view, but haven't
lived, this news—is the take-out cup
for her cola. You know, with the plastic lid
and the straw. A summer movie
advertised around it. Droplets
on the side, from where its ice and the heat
of the afternoon commune.
It's a large. You've had it
on maybe a thousand occasions. Any of us
might hold this drink,
might take it into our systems.

TRY THIS 6.9

Write a poem or a few paragraphs about a photograph of a horrific event. Focus as Goldbarth does on a mundane detail. What point can you make, what effect can you achieve, what story can you tell, with this contrast between horrific and mundane?

ELLEN BRYANT VOIGT

Short Story

My grandfather killed a mule with a hammer,
or maybe with a plank, or a stick, maybe
it was a horse—the story varied
in the telling. If he was planting corn
when it happened, it was a mule, and he was plowing
the upper slope, west of the house, his overalls
stiff to the knees with red dirt, the lines
draped behind his neck.
He must have been glad to rest
when the mule first stopped mid-furrow;
looked back at where he'd come, then down
to the brush along the creek he meant to clear.
No doubt he noticed the hawk's great leisure
over the field, the crows lumped

in the biggest elm on the opposite hill.
After he'd wiped his hatbrim with his sleeve,
he called to the mule as he slapped the line
along its rump, clicked and whistled.

My grandfather was a slight, quiet man,
smaller than most women, smaller
than his wife. Had she been in the yard,
seen him heading toward the pump now,
she'd pump for him a dipper of cold water.
Walking back to the field, past the corncrib,
he took an ear of corn to start the mule,
but the mule was planted. He never cursed
or shouted, only whipped it, the mule
rippling its backside each time
the switch fell, and when that didn't work
whipped it low on its side, where it's tender,
then cross-hatched the welts he'd made already.
The mule went down on one knee,
and that was when he reached for the blown limb,
or walked to the pile of seasoning lumber; or else,
unhooked the plow and took his own time to the shed
to get the hammer.
                                        By the time I was born,
he couldn't even lift a stick. He lived
another fifteen years in a chair,
but now he's dead, and so is his son,
who never meant to speak a word against him,
and whom I never asked what his father
was planting and in which field,
and whether it happened before he married,
before his children came in quick succession,
before his wife died of the last one.
And only a few of us are left
who ever heard that story.

MAXINE KUMIN

Woodchucks

Gassing the woodchucks didn't turn out right.
The knockout bomb from the Feed and Grain Exchange
was featured as merciful, quick at the bone
and the case we had against them was airtight,
both exits shoehorned shut with puddingstone,
but they had a sub-sub-basement out of range.

Next morning they turned up again, no worse
for the cyanide than we for our cigarettes
and state-store Scotch, all of us up to scratch.
They brought down the marigolds as a matter of course
and then took over the vegetable patch
nipping the broccoli shoots, beheading the carrots.

The food from our mouths, I said, righteously thrilling
to the feel of the .22, the bullets' neat noses.
I, a lapsed pacifist fallen from grace
puffed with Darwinian pieties for killing,
now drew a bead on the littlest woodchuck's face.
He died down in the everbearing roses.

Ten minutes later I dropped the mother. She
flipflopped in the air and fell, her needle teeth
still hooked in a leaf of early Swiss chard.
Another baby next. O one-two-three
the murderer inside me rose up hard,
the hawkeye killer came on stage forthwith.

There's one chuck left. Old wily fellow, he keeps
me cocked and ready day after day after day.
All night I hunt his humped-up form. I dream
I sight along the barrel in my sleep.
If only they'd all consented to die unseen
gassed underground the quiet Nazi way.

LI-YOUNG LEE

The Hammock

When I lay my head in my mother's lap
I think how day hides the stars,
the way I lay hidden once, waiting
inside my mother's singing to herself. And I remember
how she carried me on her back
between home and the kindergarten,
once each morning and once each afternoon.

I don't know what my mother's thinking.

When my son lays his head in my lap, I wonder:
Do his father's kisses keep his father's worries
from becoming his? I think, *Dear God,* and remember
there are stars we haven't heard from yet:
They have so far to arrive. *Amen,*
I think, and I feel almost comforted.

I've no idea what my child is thinking.

Between two unknowns, I live my life.
Between my mother's hopes, older than I am
by coming before me, and my child's wishes, older than I am
by outliving me. And what's it like?
Is it a door, and good-bye on either side?
A window, and eternity on either side?
Yes, and a little singing between two great rests.

TRY THIS 6.10

Several of the preceding poems are also memoirs. All of them tell a story. Write a poem of no more than a dozen lines with the title of one of the traditional tales below. Make it contemporary. Can you base it on your own experience?

- Beauty and the Beast
- Ugly Duckling
- Mulan
- Baba Yaga
- Humpty Dumpty
- Noah's Ark
- Three Little Pigs
- Aladdin's Lamp

DRAMA

MICHAEL GOLAMCO

Heartbreaker

Characters

Vuthy, male, sixteen
Ra, female, twenty-two

Setting

A small, empty apartment bedroom in Long Beach, California. The present.

■ ■ ■

A small, empty bedroom. Vuthy (pronounced "woo-tee"), sixteen, Cambodian American, carries in a duffle bag of his things; he has thick-ass glasses and is so skinny that they probably keep him from blowing away.

He's followed in by his sister Ra, twenty-two, normal. She's got another box of his stuff, puts it down.

RA: So you got all your things...And Aunt Tizz is gonna drive you to pick up your computer later.

(*He sits, doesn't say anything.*)

RA: Hey, look at all this space. Nice...Window. Finally some sunlight for you. Lotsa blank walls for whatever you wanna put up on them—

VUTHY: I need my computer now.

RA: She's gonna drive you to pick it up later. I gotta go, traffic on the Five's gonna get crazy if I don't leave right now—

(*She hugs him.*)

VUTHY: She isn't even our aunt.

RA: You know how much of a big heart she's gotta have to open up her home to you?

VUTHY: She isn't even related to us. She's just a lady that Ma used to play mahjong with—

RA: You gotta start being more grateful. Social services isn't gonna let a sixteen-year-old kid live by himself—

VUTHY: I'm mature for my age.

RA: You still buy toys—

VUTHY: VINTAGE TIN ROBOTS. VINTAGE TIN ROBOTS and they're still in their boxes which makes me a collector of vintage tin robots. I don't *play*, Ra.

RA: Sure.

(*Short pause.*)

VUTHY: It smells like mothballs and cat pee in here. And I gotta get my computer—

RA: It wouldn't hurt you to stay off that thing for a coupla days, y'know. Lay off the video games.

VUTHY: I don't play video games. I told you: I only do pen-and-paper role playing. It's more visceral. I gotta get it 'cause I wanna see if I got any e-mail from Bert.

RA: The e-mail from Bert can wait. I gotta go.

(*She hugs him again.*)

VUTHY: Hey I heard they have this real great comic book store in Berkeley—

RA: Vuthy—

VUTHY: That's run by this crazy beardo hippie who's all nazi with the comics, and this place is like a museum of art-Fort-Knox—they got the 1940 All American with the first appearance of The Green Lantern under glass. An if the hippie doesn't like how you look he hits a button and it drops down underneath a blast shield—

RA: It's the middle of the school year.

VUTHY: So what?

RA: It would be bad to move you right now, put you in a brand-new school—

VUTHY: So what.

RA: So you gotta stay here with Aunt Tizz and then we'll see—

VUTHY: I don't care if I move, Ra. I wanna move. They hate me at Lakewood High. You remember how Justin Vu accidentally stabbed me with a pencil?

RA: Yeah.

VUTHY: It wasn't an accident. I'm pretty sure I'm gonna be murdered by senior year.

RA: You've got friends.

VUTHY: Bert moved. See I'm too Cambodian for the black and Latino kids and I'm not Cambodian enough for the Cambodian kids.

RA: What does that mean?

VUTHY: *Look at me,* Ra. And they got the mad dogg stare down—that whatchoo lookin at sucka stare down—but whenever I try to do it my gently arching eyebrows betray me.

RA: My place in Berkeley's just one room and a hot plate. We sleep on a futon, and Glenn's got all his stuff packed in there—

VUTHY: Oh yeah, you're living with the whitest white man from Orange Country—

RA: (*Defensively.*) He's not that white—

VUTHY: "Glenn" with two *n*'s? Oh yeah he is. He's so white that I'm still not exactly sure what he looks like 'cause he appears as this huge blinding silhouette—

RA: So you know there's no space what with His Blindingness in there. You gotta stay here, Vuthy. I can't take you.

VUTHY: Ra—

RA: I can't.

(*Ra unzips his duffle bag, begins to unpack it.*)

RA: Look, you got an even better setup here than you did back in our old place. You got more space, it's closer to the library—OH SHIT—

(*She whips her hand away from his bag; he leans over to see—*)

VUTHY: What? Oh, that.

RA: What the fuck is that?!

(*Vuthy reaches into the bag—*)

VUTHY: OK, remember three years ago, I was thirteen and you were a senior and we went on that Khmer group trip to Choeung Ek, and they had that temple in the middle of the field—

RA: Oh my god, Vuthy—

VUTHY: And inside, they had all these racks inside, like right there in front of you. And on them there were hundreds, thousands of them, these—

RA: Please tell me you didn't—

VUTHY: Close enough to touch. One of them just seemed outta place, Ra. It was just a little one, and I coulda sworn I heard it call to me. It was like, *Hey kid—*

RA: Fuck, Vuthy!

VUTHY: *I been here too long, kid. My eyes been seeing the same sad faces... They look into me always expectin' to see sorrow back... I wanna run. Take me with you—I wanna see this place called Long Beach...*

So when no one was looking I—

(*He produces a human skull.*)

VUTHY: Popped it into my backpack.

RA: Do you know how totally monstrous and insane that is?

VUTHY: No.

RA: VUTHY. That was someone's fucken head. Someone's bodily remains—you had no right—

VUTHY: I take good care of it, Ra.

RA: I don't care!... Oh my god!

VUTHY: You gotta care for the dead.

RA: So this is what you do? You steal their skulls?

VUTHY: (*Thinking.*) This is somebody who ran. They ran and got caught. Ma ran and didn't get caught, and that's how come you and me can go back and see what they did, see all the people that ran and got caught—

RA: So what.

VUTHY: So when this one said, "Take me with you," I had to take it, Ra. Had to.

RA: It's a crime.

VUTHY: What?

RA: Importing human remains, bones, over international... Whatever—you gotta bury it, Vuthy. Do something, please.

VUTHY: OK, Ra—

RA: Shit—do you know how many times I prayed to have a normal little brother? God, Jesus, please give me a normal little brother that I don't have to worry about. But for some reason you don't know how to be normal—

VUTHY: I'm trying as hard as I can—

RA: You made Ma sick by gettin' picked on all the time, by being weird, by having no friends. Sick with worry. You broke her heart with worry.

VUTHY: I just wanted to help somebody run away—

RA: For once, OK, put away the heartache, leave the past behind, stop talking about shit that happened a long time ago. "They ran." So what.

(*A pause.*)

VUTHY: ... You didn't want to go. Three years ago, when we went to Cambodia, you didn't want to go.

RA: But I had to go.

VUTHY: At Choeung Ek, you stayed outside the temple.

(Beat.)

You wouldn't go in.

RA: ...Ma made me go.

VUTHY: You didn't wanna go? You said that you did.

RA: That's the past. That's...

VUTHY: You seemed like you did.

RA: Ma didn't want you to go alone. But you of course wanted to go, so I had to go with you.

VUTHY: You didn't have to.

RA: Yeah I did, Vuthy.

VUTHY: Oh...Thanks, Ra.

(Beat.)

Hey, Ra...

(Re: the skull)

I didn't steal it from the temple at Choeung Ek. I bought it offa the Internet—museum quality replica, thirty-nine dollars shipped.

(She punches him in the arm twice.)

VUTHY: Ow ow.

RA: I hate you so.

VUTHY: *(Grinning.)* You believed though.

RA: Why the fuck can't you be normal?

VUTHY: I don't know, I don't think about it.

(A beat, then re: the skull.)

Though when I look at this I remember Choeung Ek. I think about Ma running, all by herself with wet feet through the long grass.

(Beat.)

Been thinking about that a lot lately...I think about all those skulls on the rack lookin' at me askin' me what I did to deserve Ma's gettin' away.

RA: You think too much.

VUTHY: I got no friends since Bert moved. Got nothing to do but think.

RA: Yeah, well...I just wanna be happy, Vuthy. That's all.

VUTHY: Livin' with the whitest white man from Orange County.

RA: *(Laughs.)* He's not that white.

VUTHY: He's polar bear white. Translucent-North-Pole-snowman-style. He got a carrot for a nose.

RA: He makes me laugh. And he hasn't made me cry.

VUTHY: Yet.

RA: Yet.

(Ra suddenly picks up Vuthy's box of things.)

RA: C'mon. Get your stuff. We're going.

VUTHY: Really, Ra? Really really?

RA: Get your stuff before I change my mind.

(Vuthy grabs his duffle bag.)

VUTHY: What about my computer?

RA: We'll swing by, get it right now.

(He hugs her. Her arms are full of his things. She starts to head out—)

RA: But.

VUTHY: But what?

RA: You gotta promise me: Don't turn me into Ma. Do not make me worry. I'm not like she was—I can't take it. Can you promise me that?

VUTHY: Ra...

RA: Can you?

VUTHY: You know me. I can't promise anything.

RA: Then...I guess we'll just have to see.

(Ra exits.)

(Vuthy regards the skull.)

VUTHY: All right. We shall see this place called Berkeley...And believe-you-me, we're gonna test the hell outta this comic book nazi!

(He exits with his duffle bag.)

END OF PLAY

TRY THIS 6.11

Write a one-paragraph description of a character, including at least the information from the sentence in the middle of page 89 and a brief physical description. Make a copy. Exchange the copy with someone else who has also written such a paragraph. Invent a situation in which these two characters might meet and find themselves in conflict. Each of you write an opening stage direction specifying the place. Write three pages of dialogue between the two characters. Compare the two scenes that result. Is there a journey suggested? Is there conflict? A crisis? A resolution? Connection and disconnection? At this point, the important thing is not whether these things are in the script, but whether you can recognize them.

WORKING TOWARD A DRAFT

Identify a passage in your journal that might be made into a story. Write a three-paragraph outline of what the story would be like: a beginning (What is the situation? What happens to disturb the equilibrium?), a middle (How does the conflict play out between the protagonist and antagonist?), and an end (How is the conflict resolved?).

Write another paragraph (or single sentence) describing the journey of the main character.

Write another describing the main connections and disconnections.

This may seem a sterile exercise, but it will accustom you to the thinking of the structure. Very likely none of what you do here will appear in the final manuscript. Do it, put it away, and don't consult it if and when you come to write the story.

7 CHAPTER

Development and Revision

- *Developing a Draft*
- *Structuring*
- *Research*
- *Revision*
- *Editing*
- *The Workshop*

Ultimately my hope is to amaze myself.
Jerry Uelsmann

(clockwise from top left) Macduff Everton/Corbis; Chris Carroll/ Corbis; Ken Seet/Corbis; William Karel/Sygma/Corbis

WARM-UP

One of these people is a respected, accomplished, and successful writer; you decide which one. Write a brief description of the sort of thing he or she writes. Visualize him or her wherever that writing takes place—desk, table, plane, park. What does it feel like to be this person, in this place, writing? Now: somewhere in your journal is a piece you care about, but you don't know how to develop or enrich it; you don't know where it's going. Hand it over to this person. For the next fifteen minutes she or he is going to write it for you.

IMAGINATIVE WRITING HAS ITS SOURCE IN DREAM, RISK, mystery, and play. But if you are to be a good—and perhaps a professional—writer, you will need discipline, care, and ultimately even an obsessive perfectionism. As poet Paul Engle famously said, "Writing is rewriting what you have rewritten."

Just as a good metaphor must be both apt and surprising, so every piece of literary work must have both unity and variety, both craft and risk, both form and invention. Having dreamt and played a possibility into being, you will need to sharpen and refine it in action, character, and language, in a continual process of development and revision. You may need both to research and to re-dream. This will involve both disciplined work and further play, but it won't always be that easy to tell one from the other. Alice Munro describes the duality of a process in which seeking order remains both mysterious and a struggle:

> So when I write a story, I want to make a certain kind of structure, and I know the feeling I want to get from being inside that structure. . . . There is no blueprint for this structure. . . . It seems to be already there, and some unlikely clue, such as a shop window or a bit of conversation, makes me aware of it. Then I start accumulating the material and putting it together. Some of the material I may have lying around already, in memories and observations, and some I invent, and some I have to go diligently looking for (factual details), while some is dumped in my lap (anecdotes, bits of speech). I see how this material might go together to make the shape I need, and I try it. I keep trying and seeing where I went wrong and trying again. . . . I feel a part that's wrong, like a soggy weight; then I pay attention to the story, as if it were happening somewhere.

The concept of "development" seems to contain the notion of making something longer and fuller, whereas that of "revision" suggests mere changing or polishing. But in fact both terms are part of a continual process toward making the piece the best that it can be, and it isn't always easy to say which comes first or even which is which. Sometimes adding a paragraph to a character description will suggest a whole new theme or structure; sometimes a single word change proves a clue to a core meaning. Once when I had a fictional character describing her sister, she said, "She needs to be important," and for no reason but the rhythm I added, "especially if it means being dangerous." I didn't at once know what I meant, but I'm afraid that small addition led, two hundred pages later, to the sister's death. Much of development and revision, especially in the early stages, relies on your being receptive to the small interior voice that nudges you in this direction or feels vaguely unsatisfied with that paragraph.

Developing a Draft

Your journal is now a warehouse of possibilities, and you probably already have a sense of the direction in which many of its entries might be developed. Consider the following suggestions as you choose the form best suited to bring out the strengths of your journal work.

- If you wrote of a memory or an event that seems to you to contain a point or to lead toward reflection, if you came up with ideas that mattered to you and that you wanted both to illustrate and to state, then you probably have creative nonfiction, perhaps a memoir or personal essay in the works.
- If a journal entry has a strong setting, with characters who engage each other in action and dialogue, whose thoughts and desires may lead them into conflict and toward change, perhaps a short story is brewing.
- If the sound and rhythm of the language seem integral to the thought, if the images seem dense and urgent, if the idea clusters around imagery and sound rather than playing itself out in a sequence of events, then a poem is probably forming.
- If you have characters who confront each other in dialogue, especially if they are concealing things that they sometimes betray in word or action, and if they face discovery and decision that will lead to change in one or more of their lives, then you very likely have a play.

TRY THIS 7.1

Go quickly through your journal and identify the passages that seem to you on first sight to belong to the genres of creative nonfiction, fiction, poetry, and drama. Star those that interest you most. What is it about each of those pieces that seems worth more development? Make notes to yourself in the margin; circle or highlight ideas, images, connections you might want to pursue.

Chapters 8 through 11 of this book will discuss the techniques peculiar to each of the four forms—creative nonfiction, fiction, poetry, and drama—and you'll want to look at those chapters as you work toward a finished draft. In the meantime, there are a number of ways to develop your ideas in order to find your direction. Some of these are repetitions or adaptations of ideas you have already used for play.

TRY THIS 7.2

Take a journal entry you like and highlight any word that seems particularly evocative, that seems to capture the spirit of the whole. Free-associate around that word. Freewrite a paragraph on the subject.

And:

Pick another journal piece. Read it over, set it aside, and begin writing, starting every sentence with the words, "It's like...It's like...It's like..." Sometimes the sentence will evoke colors, sometimes memories, sometimes metaphors, and so forth. Keep writing, fast, until you're moderately tired.

Or:

Pick a journal entry that does not depend on setting, and give it a setting; describe the place and atmosphere in detail. Think of "setting" loosely. Perhaps the setting of a piece is someone's face. Perhaps the weather is internal.

When I was eight or nine, my brother, who was four years older, made up wonderful stories with which he used to pass the hot boring afternoons of Arizona summer. I would whine and beg for another episode. At some point he got tired of it and decided I should make up stories on my own. Then he would drill me by rapping out three nouns. "Oleanders, wastebasket, cocker spaniel!" "Factory, monkey bars, chop suey!" I was supposed to start talking immediately, making up as I went along a story about a dog who used to scrounge around in the garbage until one day he made the mistake of eating a poison flower...or a tool and die worker who went to a Chinese restaurant and left his son on the playground....My brother was the expert writer (and eventually went on to become an editor at the *Los Angeles Times*). I myself had not considered storytelling—I wrote ill-advised love letters and inspirational verse—and was amazed that I could—almost always—think of some way to include his three arbitrary things in a tale of mystery, disaster, or romance.

Neither of us knew that my brother had stumbled on a principle of literary invention, which is that creativity occurs when things not usually connected are seen as connected. It is the *unexpected* juxtaposition that generates literature. A more sophisticated version of this game is used in film writing. Screenwriter Claudia Johnson tells me that she and collaborator Pam Ball once went to a restaurant to celebrate the finishing of a film script. They had no idea what they were going to write next and decided to test the nimbleness of their plotting by outlining a film based on the next three things they overheard. The three conversations turned out to concern a cigarette, a suicide in Chicago, and origami. By the time they had their coffee they had a treatment for the next film.

Novelist Margaret Drabble describes the same process as organic and largely unconscious. "It's an accumulation of ideas. Things that have been in the back of my mind suddenly start to swim together and to stick together, and I think, 'Ah, that's a novel beginning.'"

TRY THIS 7.3

Pick, without too much thought about it—random would be fine—three entries in your journal. Take one element from each (a character, an image, a theme, or a line of dialogue perhaps) and write a new passage that combines these three elements. Does it suggest any way that the three entries might in fact be fused into a single piece and be enriched by the fusion?

Or:

Take one of your journal entries and rewrite it in the form of one of the following: an instruction pamphlet, a letter to the complaints department, a newspaper item, a television ad, a love song. Does the new juxtaposition of form and content offer any way to enrich your idea?

Structuring

Once you've identified a piece you want to develop, there are basically two ways to go about structuring the finished work—though they are always in some way used in combination.

Outlining

At one extreme is the **outline.** You think through the sequence of events of a story or drama, the points of an essay, the movement of a poem. Then when you have an outline roughly in mind (or written down in detail), you start at the beginning and write through to the end of a draft.

Do not underestimate the power and usefulness of this method. However amorphous the vision of the whole may be, most writers begin with the first sentence and proceed to the last. Though fiction writer/essayist Charles Baxter has mourned the "tyranny of narrative," his stories and novels show the most careful attention to narrative sequence. (That one of them, *First Light,* presents its events in reverse order makes precise sequencing all the more necessary.) E. M. Forster spoke of writing a novel as moving toward some imagined event that loomed as a distant mountain. Eudora Welty advised a story writer to take walks pondering the story until it seemed whole, and then to try to write the first draft at one sitting. Though playwrights may first envision a climactic event and poets may start with the gift of a line that ends up last in the finished poem, still, the pull is strong to write from left to right and top to bottom.

TRY THIS 7.4

Take a pack of 3 × 5 cards and jot down, only a few words per card, any images, scenes, reflections you have in mind for a particular piece. Arrange them in a possible sequence. What's missing? Dream or freewrite or ponder what might be needed. Put each of these possible additions on a card and place them in sequence. Now you have a rough outline. You may want to write it down in outline or list form or you may not. Perhaps the cards, which can be reshuffled as you and the piece evolve, are what you need.

Quilting

At the opposite end of the spectrum from the outline is *quilting*, or "piece work," in which you carry on writing without attention to shape or structure. To use this method, you decide that this paragraph or verse or incident is the kernel of the thing you're going to write, and you continue to doodle and noodle around it, seeing what will emerge. You freewrite a dialogue passage, sketch in a description of the setting, try it in this character's voice and then as an omniscient narrator, let yourself go with a cascade of images. Two or three time a day, sit down and dash out a potential section of such a piece—a few lines, a paragraph, a monologue, images, a character sketch. Talk to yourself in your journal about what theme or idea matters to you, what you'd like to accomplish, what you fear will go wrong. If you do this for several days, you will have roughed out a sizeable portion of your project.

When you have a small mountain of material (I like to write or copy it into a single computer file I label a "ruff," then identify each paragraph by page number so I can find it easily), you print it, chop it into sections, spread it out on a large surface, and start moving pieces around till you seem to have a composition. Tape the sections together and make notes on them, discarding what seems extraneous, indicating what's missing, what needs rewriting, where a transition is in order, and so forth. Then cut and paste on the computer to put them in that order, noting the needed changes. When you print out this version, you have a rough shape of your piece.

TRY THIS 7.5

Doodle a series of lists—of the characteristics of someone you have written about, or of phrases and idioms that character would use; or of objects associated with a person, place, profession, or memory you have written about. Generate, rapidly, a list of metaphors for some central object in a piece you want to develop.

This jot-cut-and-sort system can work for any genre, and it's worth getting used to the process. However, sometimes it works better than others, and sometimes it just isn't the best way. The advantages of the outline method tend to be clarity, unity, and drive; of the cut-and-paste method, richness, originality, and surprise. The problem with writing from an outline is that the piece may seem thin and contrived; the trouble with piece work is that it can end up formless, diffuse, and dull.

You will already have a sense of which method is your natural tendency, and I'd urge you, whichever it is, to work in the opposite direction. The methods are not mutually exclusive, and each can benefit from the particular discipline of the other.

If you start with a clear sense of direction, a determination to follow a plan, then detour from time to time. Too tight a rein on the author's part, too rigid a control of where the imagery is headed, what the protagonist will do next, how the remembered event exactly happened—any of these can squeeze the life out of the work. When you feel the action or the language becoming mechanical, stop and freewrite a monologue, a list of images, an exploration of character, or conflict, or the weather. One freeing trick, if you find your piece flat, is to go through and put some arbitrary line or sentence in each paragraph or verse, something that absolutely does not belong and that you would never put there. Then go away from it for a while, and when you go back, see if there's anything in the nonsense that might in fact improve the sense.

If, on the other hand, you can generate lovely stuff but have trouble finding a through-line for it, if you find yourself in successive drafts generating new possibilities and never settling on a form or sequence, then you probably need to focus on a plan and push yourself through one draft based on it. Set your quilt aside and consider the questions of unity and shape: What is the heart of this piece? What is its emotional core? What, in one word, is it *about*? How can I focus on that, make each part illuminate it, raise the intensity, and get rid of the extraneous?

And don't give up. "The big secret," says fiction writer Ron Carlson, "is the ability to stay in the room. The writer is the person who stays in the room. ...People have accused me...'You're talking Zen here.' And I just say, 'Zen this: The secret is to stay in the room.'"

TRY THIS 7.6

Practice in brief form each of the methods described. Pick an entry in your journal—not one you intend to make into a finished work. Before lunch, write an outline of a piece based on that entry. In late afternoon or evening, take *no more than one hour* to write a draft of the piece that covers the whole outline. Your work will have holes, cracks, and sloppy writing. Never mind; get through to the end. Leave it for a day or two, then make marginal notes on what you would want to do in the next draft.

Pick another entry and over the next two or three days, freewrite something or other about it every four hours. Print, cut, and arrange into a sequence or shape. Print out the result and make marginal notes on what the next draft would need.

Discuss in class what you learned from the two methods. Which would suit you best when you come to write an essay, a story, a poem, a play?

Research

Any piece of writing, to be convincing and rich with detail, needs solid knowledge of its subject matter. Nothing more undermines a reader's trust than to be told a character is a doctor when it's clear he doesn't know a stethoscope from a stegosaur. For any genre of writing there will come a time when you need to research through library, interview, Internet, or some other way.

But research for imaginative writing has a rather different nature and purpose than the research you've been taught. Whereas the "research paper" has as its first requirement a rigorous attention to both facts and sources, the watchword of imaginative research is *immersion.* Depending on the kind of piece you're writing, you may need accuracy, and you may need to credit or quote someone, but you certainly need the flavor, the imagery, and the atmosphere of whatever you seek to know. If you make yourself wholly available to whatever information you seek, what you need will be there when you come to write about it.

I once had the luck, just as I was starting on a novel set in Mexico and Arizona in 1914, to hear a lecture by the great novelist Mary Lee Settle. She offered three rules for historical fiction research:

- Don't read *about* the period; read *in* the period. Read letters, journals, newspapers, magazines, books written at the time. You will in this way learn the cadences, the turn of mind and phrase, the obsessions and quirks of the period.
- Don't take notes. If you save everything that interests you, you'll be tempted to use it whether it fits or not, and your fiction will smell of research. Immerse yourself and trust that what you need will be there.
- Don't research beyond the period you're writing about. If you know too much about the future, your characters will inevitably know it too.

Now, these rules are particular to historical fiction, but I think the spirit of them is applicable to any sort of imaginative research.

You may need to interview someone in order to write a piece about your family, and you may want to quote exactly. But don't take down everything, and don't think you have to use everything. Much more important than notes is to listen with an absolutely open mind. Hear the rhythms and the images of the particular voice. Sponge up the sounds and the peculiarities.

For any genre of imaginative work, you may need to search the library or the Internet for information on an object, a profession, a region, a building, a kind of clothing, and so forth. Read ravenously. Reread, read a second book or site. Look into a third that suggests something vaguely connected. But understand that you are reshaping the information into something that is not primarily information, and the crucial thing is to absorb it, toss it on the compost of your imagination, and let it feed your piece, not devour it.

TRY THIS 7.7

Bring your research skills to your imaginative work. Identify something in a piece that you aren't sure about. You don't know the facts, don't understand the process or the equipment, aren't clear on the history or the statistics, don't know the definition. Find out. Consult books, reference works, newspapers, the Internet; interview someone, email someone, ask the experts.

Revision

> *Interviewer:* Was there some technical problem? What was it that had stumped you?
> *Hemingway:* Getting the words right.

Most people dread revision and put it off; and most find it the most satisfying part of writing once they are engaged in it and engaged by it. The vague feelings of self-dissatisfaction and distress that accompany an imperfect draft are smoothed away as the pleasure of small perfections and improvements comes.

To write your first draft, you banished the internal critic. Now make the critic welcome. The first round of rewrites is probably a matter of letting your misgivings surface. Revision is a holistic process, unique to each piece of writing, and though this chapter includes questions you might use as a guide, there is no substitute for your own receptivity and concentration. What do *you* think is needed here? What are you sure of, and where are you dissatisfied?

Focus for a while on what seems awkward, overlong, undeveloped, flat, or flowery. Tinker. Tighten. Sharpen. Let that small unease surface and look at it squarely. More important at this stage than finishing any given page or phrase is that you're getting to know your piece in order to open it to new possibilities. Novelist Rosellen Brown says, "What I love about being in the revision stage is that it means you've got it. It's basically there. And so then you've got to chip away at it, you've got to move things around, you've got to smooth it down. But the fact of the matter is, you've got it in hand."

It is when you have a draft "in hand" that you will experience development and revision as a continuum of invention and improvement, re-seeing and chiseling. Sometimes the mere altering of punctuation will flash forth a necessary insight. Sometimes inspiration will necessitate a change of tense or person. To find the best way of proceeding, you may have to "see again" more than once. The process involves external and internal insight; you'll need your conscious critic, your creative instinct, and readers you trust. You may need each of them several times, not necessarily in that order. Writing gets better not just by polishing and refurbishing, not only by improving a word choice here and image there, but by taking risks with the structure, re-envisioning, being open to new meaning itself. Sometimes, Annie Dillard advises in *The Writing Life,* what you must do is knock out "a bearing wall." "The part you jettison," she says, "is not only the best written part; it is also, oddly, that part which was to have been the very point. It is the original key passage, the passage on which the rest was to hang, and from which you yourself drew the courage to begin."

There are many kinds of work and play that go under the name of "revision." It would be useful to go back to the film metaphor—long shot, middle shot, close-up—in order to think of ways of re-visioning your work. You will at some point early or late need to step back and view the project as a whole, its structure and composition, the panorama of its tones: Does it need fundamental change, reversal of parts, a different shape or a different sweep? At some point you will be working in obsessive close-up, changing a word to alter the coloration of a mood, finding a fresher metaphor or a more exact verb, even changing a comma to a semicolon and changing it back again. Often you'll be working in middle shot, moving this paragraph from page one to page three, chopping out an unnecessary line or verse, adding a passage of dialogue to intensify the atmosphere. Read each draft of your piece aloud and listen for rhythm, word choice, unintended repetition. You'll move many times back and forth among these methods, also walking away from the piece in order to come back to it with fresh eyes.

TRY THIS 7.8

Choose a character in one of your journal pieces and make a list of things this character fears. Try arranging the fears from the least to the largest; does that suggest a story shape? Now play with the arrangement and language of the list toward making a poem.

Or:

Show a character doing something genuinely dangerous. But the character or persona is not afraid. Why not?

If you feel stuck on a project, put it away. Don't look at it for a matter of days or weeks, until you feel fresh again. In addition to getting some distance on your work, you're mailing it to your unconscious. You may even discover that in the course of developing a piece, you have mistaken its nature. I once spent a year writing a screenplay—which I suppose I thought was the right form because the story was set in an Arizona cow town in 1914—finally to realize that I couldn't even *find out* what the story was until I got inside the characters' heads. Once I understood this, that story became a novel.

As you plan your revisions and as you rewrite, you will know (and your critics will tell you) what problems are unique to your piece. You may also be able to focus your own critique by asking yourself these questions:

What is this piece about? The answer may be different according to the genre, may involve a person, an emotion, an action, or a realization rather than an idea. But centering your consciousness on what the piece is about will help to center the piece itself.

TRY THIS 7.9

State your central subject or idea in a single sentence. Reduce it to a word. Express it in an image. Express it in a line of dialogue that one of your characters might say. Probably none of these things will appear in your finished piece, but they will help you focus. Are you clear about what you're writing about? Does it need thinking and feeling through again?

Is the language fresh? Have you used concrete imagery, the active voice to make the language vivid? Are these abstractions necessary? Does your opening line or sentence make the reader want to read on?

TRY THIS 7.10

Go through your work and highlight generalizations in one color, abstractions in another, clichés in a third. Replace each of them with something specific, wild, inappropriate, far-fetched. Go back later to see if any of these work. Replace the others, working toward the specific, the precise, and the concrete.

Is it clear? Do we know who, what, where, when, what's happening? Can we see the characters, keep their names straight, follow the action?

TRY THIS 7.11

Go through your manuscript and highlight the answers to these questions: *Where are we? When are we? Who are they? How do things look? What period, time of year, day or night is it? What's the weather? What's happening?* If you can't find the answers in your text, the reader won't find them either. Not all of this information may be necessary, but you need to be aware of what's left out.

Where is it too long? The teacher William Strunk, long revered for his little book *The Elements of Style*, used to bark at his students, "Omit unnecessary words!" Do so. Are there too many adjectives, adverbs, flowery descriptions, explanations—as perhaps there are in this sentence, since you've already got the point?

TRY THIS 7.12

Carefully save the current draft of your piece. Then copy it into a new document on which you play a cutting game—make your own rules in advance. Cut all the adjectives and adverbs. Or remove one line from every verse of a poem. Delete a minor character. Fuse two scenes into one. Cut half of every line of dialogue. Or simply require yourself to shorten it somehow by a third. You will have some sense of what tightening might improve your work. Compare the two drafts. Does the shortened version have any virtues that the longer one does not?

Where is it underdeveloped? This question may simply involve the clarity of the piece: What necessary information is in your head that has not made it to the page, and so to the mind of the reader? But underdevelopment may also involve depth or significance, what memoirist Patricia Foster calls "the vertical drop... when an essay drops deeper—into character, into intimacy, into some sense of the hidden story."

TRY THIS 7.13

In any first, second, or third draft of a manuscript there are likely to be necessary lines, images, or passages that you have skipped or left skeletal. Make notes in your margins wherever you feel your piece is underdeveloped. Then go back and quickly freewrite each missing piece. At this point, just paste the freewrites in. Then read over the manuscript (long shot) to get a feel for how these additions change, add, or distort. Are some unnecessary after all? Do some need still fuller expanding? Should this or that one be reduced to a sentence or image? Do some suggest a new direction?

Does it end? The ending of a piece is its most powerful point in terms of its impact on the reader (the beginning is the second most important). So it matters that it should have the effect you want. Does the character change? Does the essay reveal? Does the poem offer a turn or twist on its image? Does the drama move? (Actually, any of these questions might apply to any genre.) This is not to say that the piece should clunk closed with a moral or a stated idea. Novelist Elizabeth Dewberry puts it this way: "When you get to the end you want to have a sense that you understand for the first time—and by *you* I mean the writer and the reader and even the characters—for the first time, how the whole story fits together."

TRY THIS 7.14

As an experiment only, end your piece with a poetic line, a line of dialogue, or a paragraph that is the direct opposite of the meaning or effect you want. You might try ending by repeating the opening (which can, in fact, turn out to be effective if the line or paragraph takes on a new and changed meaning). Consider the impact of what you have done. Does it help to clarify what the ending should be?

Editing

Just as there is no clear line between development and revision, so revision and editing are part of the same process, helping the piece to be as good as it can possibly be. Editing addresses such areas as clarity, precision, continuity, and flow. One way to see the distinction is that editing can be done by an editor, someone other than the author, whereas revision is usually turned back to the author. (For example, noting a lack of transition from the last section to this one, my editor has just asked, "Can you insert a short paragraph here explaining the relationship between revision and editing, and the difference between editing and line editing?") Line editing is the last in the care-and-feeding process of the manuscript, a line-by-line check that spelling, grammar, and punctuation—including agreement, comma placement, quotation marks, modifiers, and so forth—are accurate (and perhaps in the "style" of the publication or press). Although these jobs can be invaluably done by an editor and copyeditor, and many a genius has been saved from embarrassment by their intervention, it's also true that the more carefully you edit and **line edit** your own manuscript the more professional you will appear, and that "clean copy" is most likely to be given serious consideration. Appendix B looks more closely at line editing.

Spelling, grammar, and punctuation are a kind of magic; their purpose is to be invisible. If the sleight of hand works, we will not notice a comma or a quotation mark but will translate each instantly into a pause or an awareness of voice; we will not focus on the individual letters of a word but extract its sense whole. When the mechanics are incorrectly used, the trick is revealed and the magic fails; the reader's focus is shifted from the story to its surface. The reader is irritated at the author, and of all the emotions the reader is willing to experience, irritation at the author is not one.

There is no intrinsic virtue in standardized mechanics, and you can depart from them whenever you produce an effect that adequately compensates for the attention called to the surface. But only then. Unlike the techniques of narrative, the rules of spelling, grammar, and punctuation can be coldly learned anywhere in the English-speaking world—and they should be learned by anyone who aspires to write.

No one really has an eagle eye for his/her own writing. It's harder to keep your attention on the mechanics of your own words than any other's—for which reason a friend or a copyeditor with the skill is invaluable. In the meantime, however, try to become a good surface editor of your work. Reading aloud always helps.

TRY THIS 7.15

Particularly frequent problems in grammar and punctuation are these: dangling modifiers, unclear antecedents of pronouns, the use of the comma in compound sentences, the use of *lay* and *lie*. If you're unsure of yourself with regard to any of these giveaway errors, look them up in a standard grammar text. Spend the time to learn them—the effort will repay itself a hundredfold throughout your writing life.

Then:

What follows is a passage with at least three punctuation mistakes, three spelling mistakes, one dangling modifier, four typos, two awkward repetitions, one unclear antecedent, two misused words, and a cliché (though some may fit more than one category and a few may cause disagreement—that is the nature of proofreading). Spot and correct them. Make any necessary judgment calls.

Together, Lisel and Drakov wondered through Spartanvilles noisy, squalid streets. Goats clogged the noisy streets and the venders cursed them. Walking hand in hand, the factory generater seemed to send it's roar overhead at the level of a low plane.

A homeless man leared up at them crazy as a cuckoo. They were astonished to see the the local police had put up a barrier at the end of Main Street, plus the government were making random passport checks at the barrier.

"What could they be looking for on a georgeous day like this"? Lisel wondered.

Drakov said, "Us, Maybe."

Then:

Your manuscript, as you present it to your workshop, an agent, or an editor, is dressed for interview. If it's sloppy it'll be hard to see how brilliant it really is. Groom it. Consult the end of each genre chapter for the traditional and professional formats.

Line Edit: Check through for faulty grammar, inconsistent tenses, unintended repetitions of words, awkwardness. Consult Appendix B.

Proofread: Run a spell check (but don't rely on it entirely). Read through for typos, punctuation errors, any of those goblins that slip into a manuscript. If you are in doubt about the spelling or meaning of a word, look it up.

The Workshop

Whatever can't be taught, there is a great deal that can, and must, be learned.

Mary Oliver

Once you have a draft of a piece and have worked on it to the best of your ability, someone else's eyes can help refresh the vision of your own. That's where the workshop can help. Professionals rely on their editors and agents in this process, and as Kurt Vonnegut has pointed out, "A creative writing course provides experienced editors for inspired amateurs. What could be simpler or more dignified?"

In preparation for the workshop, each class member should read the piece twice, once for its content, a second time with pen in hand to make marginal comments, observations, suggestions. A summarizing end note is usual and helpful. This should be done with the understanding that the work at hand is *by definition* a work in progress. If it were finished then there would be no reason to bring it into the workshop.

Keep in mind that the goal of the workshop is to make the piece under consideration *the best that it can be.* The group should continue to deal, first, in neutral and inquiring ways with each piece before going on to discuss what does and doesn't "work." It's often a good idea to begin with a detailed summary of what the poetry, story, essay, or drama actually says—useful because if class members understand the characters or events differently, find the imagery confusing, or miss an irony, this is important information for the author, a signal that she has not revealed what, or all, she meant. The exploratory questions suggested in the introduction may still be useful. In addition, the class might address such questions as:

- What kind of piece is this?
- What other works does it remind you of?
- How is it structured?
- What is it about?
- What does it say about what it is about?
- What degree of identification does it invite?
- How does its imagery relate to its theme?
- How is persona or point of view employed?
- What effect on the reader does it seem to want to produce?

Only then should the critique begin to deal with whether the work under consideration is successful in its effects: *Is the language fresh, the action clear, the point of view consistent, the rhythm interesting, the characters fully drawn, the imagery vivid?* Now and again it is well to pause and return to more substantive matters: *What's the spirit of this piece, what is it trying to say, what does it make me feel?* Take another look also at the suggestions for workshop etiquette on pages 11 and 12 of Chapter 1, "Invitation to the Writer." Your workshop leader will also have ground rules for the conducting of the workshop.

If the process is respectfully and attentively addressed, it can be of genuine value not only to the writer but to the writer-critics, who can learn, through the articulation of their own and others' responses, what "works" and what doesn't, and how to face similar authorial problems. In workshop discussion, disagreements are often as instructive as consensus; lack of clarity often teaches what clarity is.

For the writer, the process is emotionally strenuous, because the piece under discussion is a sort of baby on the block. Its parent may have a strong impulse to explain and plead. Most of us feel not only committed to what we have put on the page, but also defensive on its behalf—wanting, really, only to be told that it is a work of genius or, failing that, to find out that we have gotten away with it. We may even want to blame the reader. If the criticism is: *this isn't clear,* it's hard not to feel: *you didn't read it right*—even if you understand that although the workshop members have an obligation to read with special care, it is not up to them to "get it" but up to the author to be clear. If the complaint is: *this isn't credible,* it's very hard not to respond: *but it really happened!*—even though you know perfectly well that credibility is a different sort of fish than fact. There is also a self-preservative impulse to keep from changing the core of what you've done: *Why should I put in all that effort?*

The most important part of being a writer in a workshop is to learn this: Be still, be greedy for suggestions, take everything in, and don't defend. The trick to making good use of criticism is to be utterly selfish about it. Ultimately you are the laborer, the arbiter, and the boss in any dispute about your story, so you can afford to consider any problem and any solution. Therefore, the first step toward successful revision is learning to hear, absorb, and accept criticism.

It *is* difficult. But only the effort of complete receptivity will make the workshop work for you. The chances are that your draft really does not say the most meaningful thing inherent in it, and that most meaningful thing may announce itself sideways, in a detail, a parenthesis, an afterthought, a slip. Somebody else may spot it before you do. Sometimes the best advice comes from the most surprising source. The thing you resist the hardest may be exactly what you need.

After the workshop, the writer's obligation alters slightly. It's important to take the written critiques and take them seriously, let them sink in with as good a will as you brought to workshop. But part of the need is also not to let them sink in too far. Reject without regret whatever seems on reflection wrong-headed, dull, destructive, or irrelevant to your vision. Resist the impulse to write "for the workshop" what you think your peers or teacher will praise. It's just as important to be able to discriminate between helpful and unhelpful criticism as it is to be able to write. It is in fact the same thing as being able to write. So listen to everything and receive all criticism as if it is golden. Then listen to yourself and toss the dross.

More to Read

Bell, Susan. *The Artful Edit: On the practice of editing yourself.* New York: Norton, 2007. Print.

Carlson, Ron. *Ron Carlson Writes a Story.* St. Paul, Minnesota: Graywolf Press, 1997. Print.

Fiske, Robert Hartwell and Laura Cherry. *Poem, Revised.* Oak Park, Illinois: Marion St. Press, 2007. Print.

Strunk, William, Jr., and E. B. White. *The Elements of Style*, Fourth Edition. New York: Longman, 2000. Print.

And to Watch

Burroway, Janet. *So Is It Done? Navigating the Revision Process.* Chicago: Elephant Rock Productions, 2005. DVD.

EXAMPLES

What follows in this chapter are several examples of revision, four of them with a narrative by the author explaining what changes were made in the manuscripts and why. Most are poems that change their forms; one is the opening of a novel.

Elizabeth Bishop: First and Final Drafts of "One Art"

The first and final drafts of Elizabeth Bishop's poem "One Art" show an evolution from a focused freewrite toward the very intricate poetic form of a **villanelle,** in which the first and third lines are repeated at the end of alternating successive verses and as a couplet at the end. In spite of this very demanding scheme, the finished version is about half the length of the freewrite. Notice how the ideas are increasingly simply stated, the tone of the final version calm and detached until the burst of emotion in the last line. In these two drafts, Bishop plays with various points of view, trying "one" and "I" and "you" before settling on the final combination of instruction and confession. The title, too, works toward simplicity, from "How to Lose Things," "The Gift of Losing Things," and "The Art of Losing Things" to the most concise and understated "One Art."

THE FIRST DRAFT

HOW TO LOSE THINGS /? / THE GIFT OF LOSING THINGS?

[Draft 1]

One might begin by losing one's reading glasses
oh 2 or 3 times a day - or one's favorite pen.

THE ART OF LOSING THINGS

The thing to do is to begin by "mislaying".

Mostly, one begins by "mislaying":
keys, reading-glasses, fountain pens
- these are almost too easy to be mentioned,
and "mislaying" means that they usually turn up
in the most obvious place, although when one
is making progress, the places grow more unlikely
- This is by way of introduction. I really
want to introduce myself - I am such a
fantastic lly good at losing things
I think everyone shd. profit from my experiences.

You may find it hard to believe, but I have actually lost
I mean lost, and forever two whole houses,
one a very big one. A third house, also big, is
at present, I think, "mislaid" - but
maybe it's lost, too. I won't know for sure for some time.
I have lost one/~~long~~ peninsula and one island.
I have lost - it can never be has never been found -
a small-sized town on that same island.
I've lost smaller bits of geography, like   and many smaller bits of geogfaphy or scenery
a splendid beach , and a good-sized bay.
Two whole citiees, two of the
world's biggest citiies (two of the most beautiful
although that's beside the point)
A piece of one continent -
and one entire continent.   All gone, gone forever and ever.

One might think this would have prepared me
for losing one average-sized not ~~especially~~------- exceptionally
beautiful or dazzlingly intelligent person
(except for blue eyes)   (only the eyes were exceptionally beautiful and
But it doesn't seem to have, at all...   the hands looked intelligent)
the fine hands

a good piece of one continent
and another continent - the whole damned thing!
He who loseth his life, etc. - but he who
loses his love - neever, no never never never again -

A
B

THE FINAL DRAFT

ELIZABETH BISHOP

One Art

The art of losing isn't hard to master;
so many things seem filled with the intent
to be lost that their loss is no disaster.

Lose something every day. Accept the fluster
of lost door keys, the hour badly spent.
The art of losing isn't hard to master.

Then practice losing farther, losing faster:
places, and names, and where it was you meant
to travel. None of these will bring disaster.

I lost my mother's watch. And look! my last, or
next-to-last, of three loved houses went.
The art of losing isn't hard to master.

I lost two cities, lovely ones. And, vaster,
some realms I owned, two rivers, a continent.
I miss them, but it wasn't a disaster.

—Even losing you (the joking voice, a gesture
I love) I shan't have lied. It's evident
the art of losing's not too hard to master
though it may look like (*Write it!*) like disaster.

A detailed comparison of the many drafts of this poem appears in the fine essay "A Moment's Thought" in Ellen Bryant Voigt's, The Flexible Lyric (Athens and London, The University of Georgia Press, 1999).

Notice also that "One Art" is a "list poem" or "catalogue poem," built on a list of things that can be lost. It's almost impossible to overstate the importance of the list in literature. You can use lists of images to build a description or a portrait, extend a metaphor by listing the aspects of a comparison, or structure an essay as a list of ways to look at your subject. (Margaret Atwood's "The Female Body," on page 250, is structured in such a way.) It could even be argued that a story is based on a list of events one after the other.

TRY THIS 7.16

Choose one of the lists in your journal and play around with it, extending each item on the list into a sentence or two, adding an image, an idea, a memory. When you

(continued)

(*Try This 7.16 continued*)

have a page or so, look it over and see what repeated images or ideas emerge. What do the parts have in common? What do you seem to be saying? Can you give it a title? If so, you may have a theme. Try arranging the parts into lines. Now try cutting whatever seems extraneous to your theme. Are you partway to a poem?

PATTY SEYBURN

Anatomy of Disorder

This is the first thorough draft of the poem:

12:19 a.m.

Open your primers to Shape, the fourth chapter
in the Anatomy of Disorder, writ yore,
and you'll find a daguerrotype of my eyelids—
beneath, fibers capable of exponential
reproduction, renegade begetting, vanishing

their trellis, as should good vines.
Don't get me wrong—I know the minions
of the Angel of Death crouch beneath my drapes,
eager to filch my soul from my animate
frame, should my breath hesitate. I know

that longing listens to the surf report:
("Don't bother. No waves. But there's hope
on the northwest horizon") and burrows its head
in Psyche's sand, emerging as a castle with turrets,
drawbridge and moat, subject to fits of mutability.

Remember: Capability Brown reshaped
the English Garden from contrivance
to the articulated wild. In his perfect hermitage,
he was overheard chiding a local child:
"You can't escape landscape."

I always loved the reiteration of lilac
and city block, pastel stock and power line,
thistle and used car lot with chrome hopes.
A triangle implies. Stairs have convictions;
the oval, qualities. When a trapezoid is present,

one can make predictions. The valentine has graciously
figured the human heart into a bi-valve container
with angles and curves for the furies
to tour with rhyming guidebooks, and there you are
on the back road to beauty and the sublime,

where the service is terrible—they have no
work ethic, those two, always Me Me Me.
We said: pipe down, you're nothing special
but they keep emerging—bedraggled, buoyant
with threat and decree. When Virginia Woolf

put stones like literature in her pockets
to weigh down her corpus, and took a constitutional
into the waves that broke and broke
and broke, each stone had its own shape,
its own responsibility—complicit,

along with the sea.

This poem began as a much longer poem—that's often the trajectory of a poem, for me. I write an original draft that goes on expanding for a while, at which time it hits critical mass and I realize that I've added one too many appositions, one too many clauses, dragged out a sentence as long as it can possibly go. In the case of this poem, it started as part of a series of poems with times for titles. I feel like these poems are obliquely about parenting, mostly because I wrote them when I had insomnia during pregnancy, and odd images related to parturition and my physical condition would sneak into the poems. I also figured that I would not be awake if I weren't pregnant, so there had to be some psychic connection between my child and the poem; of course, poems are children, I think, both in that we parent them and they have the charm and indiscretion we wish we could display as adults (and get away with).

So I was looking around my bedroom—I tended to think that if I actually got out of bed, I'd never get back to sleep, so I kept a pen and pad on the dresser, and would reach up and scribble, nearly illegibly, in the dark. Sometimes the accidents of my penmanship were fortuitous (such as my student who wrote, "There is no escaping the inedible"). In this case, I lie awake looking at the various shapes in my room, and so thought this poem would be a diatribe on those: the shape of things, of ideas, and how they shift.

What I came to realize was that the shapes were, to use Richard Hugo's idea of "the triggering town," triggers for the real subject of the poem, which would seem to be something about...I'm really not sure. Perhaps about the tentative imposition of order on chaos, the impossibility of doing so, and/or the notion that we must take control of our own internal disorder, or else it will win out. Not to sound like a "cop-out," but I have gained some comfort with Keats's "Negative Capability," which is to say, I'm okay with not knowing everything about what I write. In any case, I found out that the first two stanzas of the poem were functioning as "warm-up," which makes them initially useful and ultimately dispensable—necessarily so, to make the poem "go." To find the "final" beginning of the poem, I looked for the line that I thought was most alive, and being a new Californian, originally a Detroiter, that would seem to be about surfing. I've glanced at the "Surf Reports" on the weather page of the *LA Times,* and they often use phrases that sound sort of existential, more about the human condition than the waves' condition.

So I cut the first two stanzas and pulled the middle stanzas of the poem almost verbatim from the earlier draft (I'll get back to the almost), and then I cut the fifth and sixth stanzas and I re-entered the older version at the very end of the sixth stanza. In other words: I started with an eight-stanza poem of five-line stanzas, and ended up with a poem of seven tercets: a poem of half the size. But poetry is about economy, right? When I said "almost" about keeping the middle of the poem, there's one notable word excision. In the old version, I had the word *Remember* between "mutability" and "Capability." For musical reasons, I wanted those two words together, so "remember" went under the redacting knife and did not emerge. Incidentally or not so, I encountered Capability Brown from two places: when I toured the English countryside with my husband, we learned about the wild English garden and their owners' penchant for the hermitage, complete with hermit. I also heard about this when seeing Tom Stoppard's play *Arcadia,* which is one of my favorite plays. I made up the phrase: "You can't escape landscape." Of course, that's the way a landscape architect would feel, I think.

I cut the fifth and sixth stanzas—enough, already, about shape. The word *buoyant* triggered the reference to Virginia Woolf that begins the conclusion of the poem—still in England, I suppose—and the notion of shape does emerge in the end—part of me still thinks of the final version of the poem as a study of shape, which everything has, even longing: giving a physical coherence to an idea. The poem begins and ends with the water, which, I suppose, is an obsession I've taken on as a converted Californian. The phrase "broke and broke / and broke" comes from Tennyson's poem, titled "Break, Break, Break," which I love. I keep trying to call a book by that title, but have not succeeded in writing that book, yet.

As far as the length and shape of the stanzas, I'll admit an affection for tercets: they don't seem as stodgy as quatrains (which I also love, but they do carry their history with them), and tercets are less "naked" than a couplet: I tend to feel that I should have something very important to say in a couplet, though contemporary poets often use couplets as exactly the opposite sort of container, a repository for the casual. I liked the two short lines beginning the tercet, and the longer third line—I get disappointed in poets who use a consistently short line; it seems like a cop-out to me: stretch out! I usually take my lineation cues from a couple of lines in the poem that seem to be working well. I didn't want "longing" and "listens" on the same line—too much alliteration—ending the line on longing seems a good invitation to keep reading, but together, the *l* sound would dominate and distract.

Looking back at the first draft, it's easy to see why I made certain decisions, generally favoring the internal music of the line. So "chide" and "child," "moat" and "mutability" (which also earned its keep due to Shelley's poem titled

"Mutability"—with all the reference to landscape, for me "Anatomy" grounds itself in the Romantic tradition—I was probably reading Shelley when I wrote the first draft), "city block" and "pastel stock" (which did not survive the chopping block), "curves" and "furies" (sigh—will it find its way into another poem? Perhaps). What's more, I have a penchant for stretching out a line as long as it will go, and a little farther, not just for the sake of "information" or content, but to achieve a sort of breathlessness, as though the container of the poem will just barely hold; I want poems to do a great deal of work in relatively little space.

Here's where the poem ended up:

Anatomy of Disorder

I know that longing
listens to the surf report:
("Don't bother. No waves. Hope on the Northwest horizon")

and burrows its head
in Psyche's sand, emerging
a castle with turrets, drawbridge and moat, subject to fits

of mutability. Capability Brown
reshaped the English Garden
from contrivance to the articulated wild. In his perfect hermitage,

he was heard chiding a child:
"You can't escape landscape,"
and there you are on the back road to beauty and the sublime,

where the service is terrible—
they have no work ethic,
those two, always *Me Me Me.* We say: pipe down, you're nothing

special, but they keep
emerging—bedraggled,
buoyant with threat and decree. When Virginia Woolf put stones

like literature
in her pockets
to weigh down her corpus, and took a constitutional into the waves

that broke and broke
and broke, each stone
had its own shape, its own responsibility—complicit, along with the sea.

I like the sounds in a poem to intensify toward the end, so "sea" ideally echoes "decree" and "Me Me Me," though they are not too close together, so the poem doesn't get sing-songy. I don't use too many metaphors and similes: the only one in this poem is "stones like literature." Of course, Woolf did put stones in her pockets, and I wanted them in the poem, as well, because they are part of Capability Brown's landscaping. But I also wanted the notion that literature, which I like to believe can save us, can also weigh us down. Ideally, it can do both, in moderation: provide us with gravitas, with substance, reasons to live, keep us from floating away.

TRY THIS 7.17

The poems by both Elizabeth Bishop and Patty Seyburn begin in long versions and are cut and tightened over the course of their revisions. Take a poem you have written, tighten it, and recast it in both fewer and shorter stanzas. Is it better? What do you learn?

Or:

Identify a single sentence summary in a prose passage you have written. Lengthen it; develop it; turn it into a scene.

JANET BURROWAY

The Opening of *Indian Dancer*: A Revision Narrative

As I write this, I am still in the process of revising a novel, *Indian Dancer.* The novel tells the story of a girl born in Belgium in 1930, who escapes to England during the World War II and later emigrates to America. Most of the novel deals with her adolescent and adult life, but after I had written many of the later scenes, it seemed to me that the novel should begin with an image of that childhood escape, which affects everything she later does. I felt "inspired" when I woke up one morning and tapped out this:

Always,

> she retained one image from the boat, too fleeting for a memory but too substantial for a dream, like a few frames clipped from a kinetoscope. She was standing in the stern, embraced from behind by a woman who was wrapping her in rough blanket stuff. Her shoes and the hem of her coat above her knees were wet. She knew that the woman was kind, but the smell of anxiety and too many nights' sweat filled her with dark judgment. There was no moon at all, which was the point, but all the same she could watch the wake of the boat widening behind them. She also knew, in a cold, numbed way, that her father was bleeding on the shore, but what presented itself as monstrous was the wake, dark and glutinous, ever spreading toward the land, as if she herself were a speck being washed from a wound. *I will never go back. I will never.* This was experienced as grief, not yet a vow.

After a day or so I felt this was melodramatic—that "dark judgment," her father "bleeding on the shore," the "monstrous" and "glutinous" sea. I noticed that "kinetoscope" stuck out like a piece of show-off research. I thought there should be more sense of the woman trying to help her, and of the others on the boat. The past tense also troubled me. If she "always retained," then wouldn't the memory be in the present?

Always,

> also, she is standing in the stern, embraced from behind by a woman who swaddles her in coarse blanket stuff. Her shoes and the hem of her coat above her knees are wet. There is no moon—which is the point—but all the same she can see the wake widening in the Channel, and close beside her on the deck the boy who broke his shin, the bone stub moving under the flesh like a tongue in a cheek. The man—his father?—still has the boy's mouth stuffed with a forearm of loden coat to keep him from crying out, although they are far enough from shore that the oars have been shipped and the motor roped into life. It sputters like a heart. Behind her the people huddle—you can't tell heroes from refugees—over flasks of tea and Calvados whose fireapple smell flings up on the smell of sea. She will never see any of these people again. The woman's armpit cups her chin, old wet wool and fear. She knows unflinchingly that her father has been left behind. What presents itself as monstrous is the wake—dark, glutinous—which seems to be driving them from the land on its slubbed point as if the boat is a clot being washed from a wound.
>
> *I will never go back. I will never.* This is experienced as grief, not yet a vow.

I fiddled with this a lot, still dissatisfied with its tone, which seemed to set the book on a loftier course than I intended, but it was several months before it struck me that *the woman should tell this scene.* I think it was the image of the boy's broken bone "like a tongue in a cheek" that gave me the first hint of the woman's voice. She was a British woman; I imagined her as working class, one of the accidental heroes of the Resistance, a practical, solid sort. This revelation must have occurred to me on an airplane (the disembodied feeling of airplanes *always* sets me writing) because I scribbled on a page of a yellow pad:

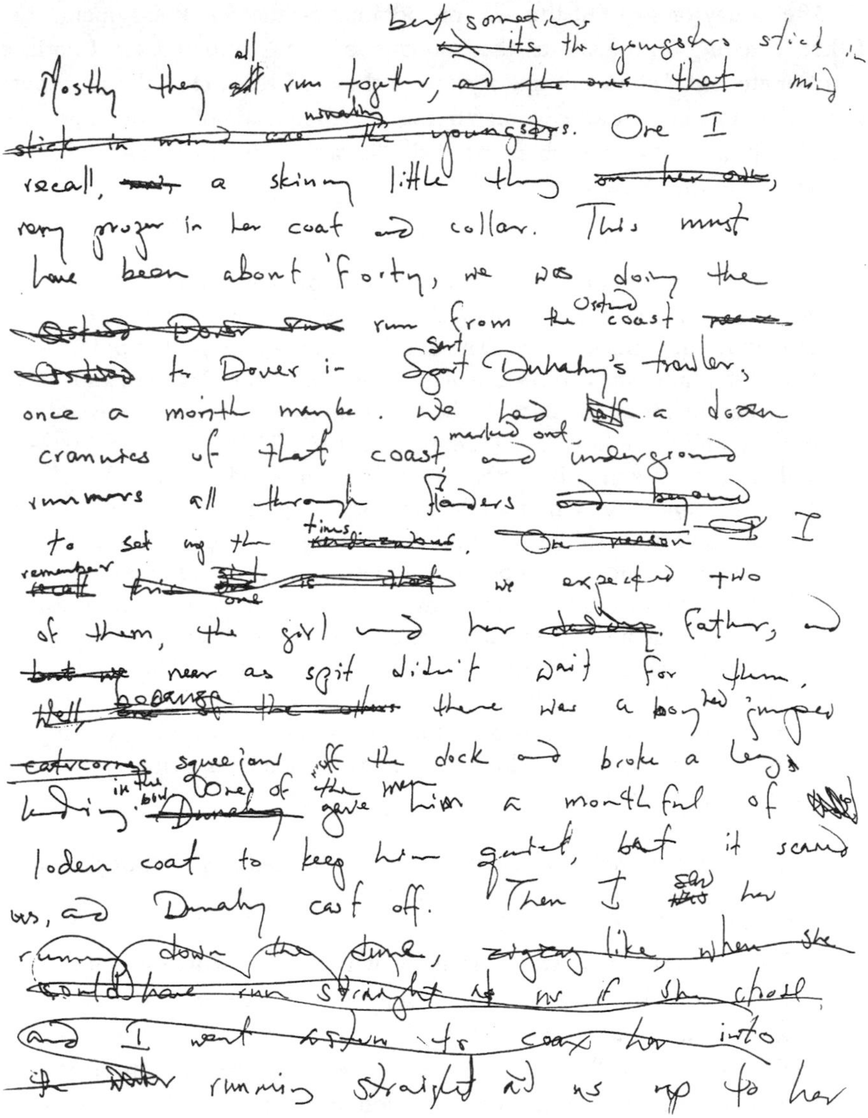
Mostly they all run together, but sometimes its the youngsters stick in mind. One I recall, a skinny little thing, very proper in her coat and collar. This must have been about 'forty, we was doing the run from the Ostend coast to Dover in Sart Duhaney's trawler, once a month maybe. We had a dozen crannies of that coast marked out and underground runners all through Flanders to set up the times. I remember we expected two of them, the girl and her father, and near as spit didn't wait for them. There was a bony lad jumped squeejaw off the dock and broke a leg landing in the boat. One of the men gave him a mouthful of loden coat to keep him quiet, but it scared us, and Duhaney cast off. Then I saw her running straight at us up to her

Now I started over, putting the scene back in chronological order but always chasing the woman's voice, also reading up on the period and the events of the war, checking out British expressions with my son who lives in London:

This must have been about 'forty, the Vicar and I were coming down from Teddington maybe once a month to make the crossing from Dover to Ostend and back again. We had the use of Duck Henley's trawler and half a dozen meeting points along the coast, underground runners all through that part of Flanders setting up the times. ~~Usually they came on foot, talk about misery and scared, and~~ They mostly run together, only it's the children that stick out in your mind.

They came in all sorts, talk about misery a scared, and I never saw a one of them again.

~~Sometimes they were that dumb brave.~~ ~~There were babies never made a peep, and~~ I remember one boy landed squeejaw off the dock and broke his shin so the bone rolled under his skin like a tongue in a cheek. It was maybe the same trip we ~~was~~ were expecting a girl and her father and nearly pushed off without them when we saw her running ~~all by herself~~ down the rocks, straight into the water up to her coat hem. O'Hannaughy swung his arm signalling her to go round the dock and lowered her down with her shoes full of water. I wrapped her up and she says po-faced, "My Father sends me to come ahead." She says, "My fah-zer."

or maybe another

What I remember ~~about her~~ is, we had a little bunsen and usually when you got out far enough to rope the motors alive, they were all glad to hunker down over a cuppa. But this one didn't leave the stern six, maybe eight hours of rough crossing, looking back where we'd come from, ~~It was black dark—we always picked nights with no moon—but all the same you could see the wake~~ in the dark. Very polite she was in her soggy shoes, but couldn't be budged. ~~I knew not to ask about her father~~. And I remember I tucked the blanket around her, which she let me, and I thought the way we must have looked to God, that greasy little trawler in the black ~~water~~ wake, like a clot being washed ~~out of~~ from a wound.

in the ~~black~~ dark. ~~with no moon~~.

arrives not. He ~~keeps back but~~ ~~is~~ ~~not able~~ to

Over the course of several months I kept coming back to this scene, trying to imagine it more fully, to heighten the sense of danger as the little boat flees the mines and U-boats, but to keep it in the chatty, down-to-earth voice of the woman who was—when? I asked myself suddenly; why?—telling this story—to whom? At some point, having spent perhaps a couple of full-time work weeks on this tiny but crucial scene, it came to me that the woman was being interviewed on television, for one of those anniversary documentaries of the war. At once, though I do not describe the scene of the interview, I could see and hear her more clearly.

The book now begins this way:

Transit: Ostend–Dover

All that spring and summer we brought back boatloads of the refugees. The Vicar organized us. They didn't mind I was a woman because I was able-bodied. We traveled down from Teddington once a month to make the crossing, and we had the use of Duck Henley's trawler and half a dozen meeting points along the Flemish coast. Underground runners all through Belgium setting up the rendezvous.

It's a wonder what you remember. Great swollen blanks, and then some daft thing bobs up like flotsam. Such as, I'd never worn a pair of trousers, and what I couldn't get used to was the twill going swish between my thighs. Is that camera running? Don't show me saying *thighs,* will you? Anyway, that and the smells. Tar, old fish in the wet boards. Seasick, of course. And off your own skin a bit of metal smell, with a sourness like fireworks. When they say "sweating bullets" I expect that's what they mean.

The ones we ferried came in every sort—rich man, poor man, tinker, tailor. I never saw a one of them again. Now and then I cross via Newhaven over to Normandy for the shopping, and I look around and think: they're not so different, take away their pocket books and their sunburn. What struck me, in Teddington everybody got raw noses from the cold and spider veins from the fire, but those ones were always drained-looking like they hadn't been out of doors, although most had been living rough or walking nights. You probably think I misremember it from a newsreel—not that we ever made it into the Movietone—but I said it at the time: every one of them gray, and eyes like drain holes that the color washed right down.

It's the children stick in your mind—a wee tiddler with its eyes wide open and its mouth tight shut. I remember one boy landed crooked off the dock and broke his shin, so the bone stub rolled under the skin like a tongue in a cheek. Somebody gave him a mouthful of coat sleeve to keep him quiet.

It was that same trip we were expecting a father and daughter that didn't show up, and we about pushed off without them. We'd heard dogs, and you never knew the meaning of dogs—it could be the patrols, or just somebody's mutt in a furore. One thing I've never understood, you pick a night with no moon and a piece of shore without a light—a disused lighthouse this was, great dark lump in the dark—and you can't see a whit, *can not see.* And then there's a click, like, in the back of your eyes, and you can. Sandiford was pressing off the piling, and the Vicar said, *no, steady on.* Duck was reluctant—you couldn't know when the boy would yell out—and then he felt it too and had them put up the oars. The waves were thick as black custard, and the black shore, and now, click! there's this girl, maybe ten or twelve, gawky little tyke, slogging straight into the water up to her coat hem. Sandiford swung his arm signaling her to go round the dock and fetched her down with her shoes full of water. She's got one hand done up in a fist against her collar bone. I wrapped her up, and she says po-faced, "My father arrives not. I arrive alone." She says, "My fah-zer." I knew better than to ask.

From there across—you understand, nobody said *U-boats.* Nobody said *mines.* Mostly you didn't keep an eye out, except for Duck and Sandiford whose job it was, because you were superstitious you would call them up. All the same that's what was in everybody's mind. You just hoped the kiddies didn't know the odds.

What I remember is, we had a little paraffin stove, and usually when you got out far enough to rope the motors into life, they were all glad to settle down over a cuppa. But this one didn't leave the stern maybe eight hours of rough crossing, looking back where we'd come from in the dark. She held that one hand tight as lockjaw, and I thought she had some money in there, maybe, or a bit of jewelry, something she'd been told to keep from harm. You'd think you wouldn't be curious under the circumstances, but eight hours is a long time to be standing, your mind must be doing something. I remember I tucked the blanket tighter around her and held it there, which she let me, and for most of the way we just stood till it was lightening a little down by the horizon. She dozed, I thought. She sagged against me and bit by bit her hand relaxed over the top of the blanket. There was nothing in it. Not a thing. I cupped it in my own and chafed it back to life a little. And I thought the way we must have looked to God, that greasy little trawler in the black wake, like a clot being washed from a wound.

My folder of drafts of this passage now runs to forty pages, excessive and obsessive perhaps, but it is after all the beginning of the book and must be right. I have noticed over the years that my digging at, fiddling with, scratching away at a scene will often turn up something much more fundamental than a new image or a livelier verb. In this case, I gradually realized that the reason the scene must be in somebody else's voice is that *the heroine does not remember it.* Traumatized by her flight, she cannot recall witnessing her father's death until she is nearly fifty years old. When I realized that, I understood much better what story I was telling and how the plot could be shaped and resolved. I had the delicious chance to let my heroine see the television documentary in the 1980s—in a twenty-year-old rerun—and let that chunk of interview, which contained the reader's first view of her, finally jog her memory.

TRY THIS 7.18

Choose a scene in your journal, either of fiction or memoir, and rewrite it from another point of view, in another voice. Try to choose a character as different from the original voice as possible, so that we get not just a change of "person" (from *he* or *she* to *I*), but a different set of attitudes, a different take on the events. Under what circumstances would this character be telling the story? To whom? Set the scene if you like.

Or:

Interview one of your characters. Write the questions out as if you were in fact conducting a radio, television, or newspaper interview, and then answer them.

Or:

Trade brief character descriptions with another writer. Make up a list of questions for that writer's character, then trade lists and write your own character's answers to the questions.

MARK VINZ

The Penitent

As many of my poems do, this one began with a prose version, which simply tries to reconstruct an incident that, for no apparent reason, crept into my head one morning as I lay awake during one of my recurring stretches of insomnia. The incident itself went back to a time many years before when I was traveling in South Dakota with two other poets, taking part in a series of workshops and readings—another time when I was having trouble sleeping. What came to me first was the vivid image of a large black dog and the severed duck heads that he bore around his neck (and where I probably first discovered the meaning of the term *hang-dog look*). Especially to one who had spent very little time on farms, that image was startling. I had to wonder why I hadn't used it in a poem years before, and how it had managed to get lost, so to speak. Anyway, as I sat with my morning coffee that day, I tried to reconstruct the experience in a journal entry before it disappeared again:

> When they found out I hadn't been sleeping, Craig and Daniel dropped me off at their friends' farm so I might get a nap—we had a workshop to do that night and were 60 miles from our motel. All I really remember about that afternoon was the dog, a big black lab, with three severed duck heads tied around his neck—for punishment, the farmer told us, for killing the ducks in the muddy farmyard. He also said it was the only way that dog would ever learn. All afternoon I lay in the bed upstairs but I couldn't sleep. Maybe it was the unseasonable spring heat. Every so often I'd look out the window at the farmyard and whenever I did, that dog seemed to be looking up at me, duck heads swaying around his neck as he circled.

As Richard Hugo says in *The Triggering Town*, poems tend to have two subjects—what triggers or generates them and what the author discovers they're really about, which is what emerges through the process of revision. My first attempt to recreate the experience thus focused on a lot of information about what occasioned the poem—information that was important to me in the poem's genesis but wouldn't, finally, matter to a reader and would thus needlessly bog the poem down at the outset. As a result, the information about my friends disappeared quickly, once a poem began to emerge from my drafts, though the presence of insomnia did remain in some way important to the poem.

Insomniac (Fourth or Fifth Draft)

This morning I remember a farm I visited once,
where there was a huge and hulking black labrador
wearing three severed duck heads, tied
around his neck with baling wire for punishment,

the farmer said, for killing mallards
which the family raised to sell.
It was a late March day as I remember,
and everybody went about their muddy business
except for me and that dog, watching each other
while he circled among the waddling ducks and geese,
heads flopping under his throat.

Why today should I remember that?
The angle of spring sun and thawing yard
I look out on? Or something else—
circling with lowered eyes, wearing some stubborn
grief it doesn't understand. The only way,
the farmer said, that some of us ever learn a thing.

As I worked through this draft, deciding to begin simply with "This morning I remember" to cut away that unnecessary exposition and move quickly to the image of the dog, I also sensed that this was an opening line that was flat and would soon have to be dealt with. But I was also discovering what the poem was really about, which seemed to begin with the line "Why today should I remember that?" (which wasn't in my first couple of drafts). The more I revised, the more it seemed this was why I was really writing the poem—to explore the question of why we retain such images, why they spring back into our heads long after they've been (supposedly) forgotten. And that seemed to be directly connected to the idea of *penance*—a penance I certainly didn't understand any more than the dog did. In this version, the penance, the "grief," is something "it" (the dog) "doesn't understand." As the revision process progressed, however, my focus became a *human* inability to understand, a link between what the dog was going through and what all of us have to go through in one way or another—bearing our own kinds of grief. Perhaps I was aware of a faint echo of Coleridge's ancient mariner at this point, too.

I also noticed, of course, some of the places where the language could be much improved—"hulking," for instance, is something better shown than labeled; likewise, ducks always "waddle," and the literal "heads flopping" is eventually to become the metonymy "penance flopping" (discovered long after the fact when pointed out by a friend). The poem's central subject has fully emerged at this point, calling for a new title. Insomnia still plays a part in the poem, though smaller than in earlier drafts; perhaps I saw insomnia itself as a kind of penance.

Looking back on this draft again, I can't stress the importance of the revision process enough; indeed, one of my favorite quotes is this one, from Dana Gioia: "Revision is an essential part of the creative act. Enter into revision with the same openness to inspiration you had while jotting down first lines. Remember, a first draft is a kind of doorway to a room where the poem is waiting in one of the corners." What happened in my own drafting process involved a lot of wandering through the house, so to speak, till I found the room I didn't know I was looking for.

The Penitent

What drives me from bed at first light is
a farm I visited once, and a huge black labrador
who wore three severed duck heads
tied around his neck with baling wire—
for punishment, the farmer said, for killing
the mallards his family raised to sell.

It was a late March day, as I recall, and
everybody went about their muddy business
except for me and that dog, watching
each other as he circled, head down
among those trusting ducks and geese,
penance flopping against his throat.

Why today should I remember that? Perhaps
it's the angle of spring sun and thawing ground
I look out upon. Perhaps it's something else,
circling with lowered eyes, bearing some stubborn,
incomprehensible grief—as that farmer kept repeating,
the only way that some of us will ever learn a thing.

The poem went through a few more drafts, a lot of tinkering, and this "final" version was eventually published in *Prairie Schooner* magazine (Spring 1998) as the last poem in a four-poem sequence called "Morning Watch"—which has to do with insomnia-provoked early-morning recollections in some way involving startling animals, as is also indicated by "drives me from bed" in the new first line. So, insomnia is still there as a "generator," and as I wrote more poems in some way relating to insomnia, I found I indeed had a small group that seemed to work together, though I think "The Penitent" is the strongest of the four and certainly the one I'm most attached to; that perhaps has something to do with the way it came to me.

Finally, in this version, I've also paid a lot more attention to form—for example, the six-line stanzas—and sounds, such as the rhythmic parallel provided by "Perhaps" in the third stanza, as well more regular four-beat lines, and even the almost onomatopoeic effect of the word *incomprehensible,* which is probably the biggest word I've ever used in a poem!

I've also paid more attention to the *s* consonance and alliteration that provides an aural pattern, especially in the third stanza. The last line has become strongly iambic, too, which adds, I think, to its finality.

As Michelle Boisseau points out, "Though it uses meter and rhyme nonsystematically..., free verse is still organized around technical constraints." In my experience, these matters of technical constraint are what the final stages of the revision process focus on, once the basic movement and imagery have become apparent. Looking back on the poem, I have to wonder how conscious I was of those technical constraints in the early stages, being guided mainly by some sense of what "feels right" and then, in later drafts, paying more conscious attention to sounds and rhythms.

Finally, I believe what Paul Valéry said: "A poem is never finished, only abandoned." That's why, when it comes to poems, I always put the words *final* and *finished* in quotes. Poets can always do more tinkering with their poems.

TRY THIS 7.19

Pick a passage from your journal that is written in prose. Write a sentence or two about what the passage tries to say. Circle the images that seem resonant to you. Beginning with one of these, try turning the passage into a poem. Has the meaning altered?

RITA MAE REESE

A History of Glass

When God closes a door, we break a window.
Sorry I say to the landlord who replaces it. *Sorry*
I say the next morning to the neighbor who

complains about the noise. An accident. She
waits for more of an explanation. So I
start at the beginning. The history of glass is a history

of accidents. Long ago and far away: a woman, a pot, a fire.
Her lover surprises her from behind, kisses her
until the pot glows, smoke rising like a choir.

She snatches it from the hearth
& drops it on the floor covered in sand
& ashes. (She is a good cook but not tidy.) Her lover

throws water on the whole mess: the sand hisses, her hand
burns. She can hardly see the hard new miracle
forming for the tears in her eyes, at her feet a new obsidian

spreads, clear & eddied. It will be 2000 years until
a tradesman molds by hand the small green & blue
glass animals (housed today on the second floor of a local

museum), & nearly 4000 before sheet glass in 1902.
(Many accidents happen during this period.) One hundred years
later the glass animals in the museum are visited by two

women: one marvels at their wholeness, except for an ear
or a nose or a paw; one does not marvel. She says, "They
survived because they're small." They stop for dinner,

mostly wine. They stumble home. Were there
eyewitnesses at that late hour when they embraced & fell?
Once inside there is a window of sheet glass & a bare

bulb burning out. In the darkness of the stairwell
they sink, dark coats spreading around them. The wind
rushes in. Remember the glass animals? They tell

a history of accidents too, accidents waiting to happen.

A History of "A History of Glass"

At a glass art exhibit, I remember being particularly drawn to a pair of glass shoes, nothing like Cinderella's slippers but rather a pair of loafers made of frosted green glass. I thought I would eventually write a poem about them but I never did. I read all of the placards in the exhibit, one of which detailed the origins of glass. It said Phoenician merchants discovered glass when they placed cooking pots on blocks of nitrates they had placed near their fire, from which flowed a translucent liquid that hardened when cooled into a translucent solid.

A few years later, I was living in Madison, Wisconsin, and had a fellowship that allowed me time to do more writing than I'd ever been able to do before. For a few months I'd been working on a poem about windows because I like the word itself so much, but that hadn't gone anywhere, in part, I think, because it was about the idea of windows rather than an actual window. And then quite luckily I broke a window one night, and a neighbor confronted me about it. I gave a briefer explanation than is outlined here and then immediately went to my desk and started writing this poem.

I'd been looking at Lewis Turco's *The New Book of Forms* and was interested in trying a terza rima, and this seemed like a good choice for the poem that was developing in my mind—it would give it some structure and also allow for whatever length I chose. I broke with the form at the ending, providing a single rhymed line rather than a couplet, in part because the broken quality fit the poem and also because a rhymed couplet would, I felt, provide too much finality. I did a bit of research online, mostly on Wikipedia and found the facts about sheet glass. I also learned that the history I had discovered at the exhibit was most likely not accurate, reminding me that history is even less reliable than eyewitness accounts. So I felt free to make up my own story of the origin of glass and to create a history that, like other histories, is a combination of facts, perceptions and wishful thinking.

When I wrote "A History of Glass," I spent the overwhelming majority of my time taking long walks and reading and writing poetry. I wrote dozens of poems during that time that I have since abandoned, even after working on them for weeks or even months. Since then, I have come to realize that in order to write one lasting poem, I have to write at least ten to twenty failed poems and twenty or thirty competent ones. I dread this part of the process and dream of avoiding it. But then every failed and competent poem is worth it when the words, feeling and form come together in one place, at virtually one sitting, as it did with this poem. The only thing I remember changing about the poem was the final line; originally I had written "a history of accidents too, accidents that are yet to happen." I didn't like the stiff sound of "yet to happen." I thought for a while that I should break the form further by disrupting the rhyme scheme at the end but all of the alternative lines I came up with wouldn't work. Finally, I went back to the rhyme and changed the line to "accidents waiting to happen," which now seems terribly obvious but took a long time to get to.

Since this poem first appeared in *The Nation* many people have mentioned it to me. They all seem to have a personal relationship with it. It's like a grown child's friends telling you about your own child. I feel shy about it, pleased that it has friends, but lost in the associations it has made since it left me.

TRY THIS 7.20

Identify something you have mentioned in a journal entry, poem, story, or essay that you don't really know much about—a historical figure, a manufactured object, an occupation, an event, a place. Research it. Interview someone, search the Internet, go to the library. Incorporate *some* of what you learn. How much inspires and enriches? How much is too much?

WORKING TOWARD A DRAFT

By now you have a pretty clear idea of what genre your first whole piece will be—creative nonfiction, fiction, poem, or play—and how long you have to complete a draft. You have a fair idea of which journal piece you will pursue. Make that choice. Make journal notes on what you think you have yet to accomplish. Freewrite a few passages where you think development is needed. Write a quick outline. Print out what you have, cut the paragraphs apart, and spread them out on a table.

What do *you* think is the next step?

When you are ready for the final close reading of your piece, you will find a series of proofreader's marks and an example of line editing in Appendix B, page 374.

8 CHAPTER

Creative Nonfiction

- *The Essay and Creative Nonfiction*
- *Memoir and the Personal Essay*
- *Techniques of Creative Nonfiction*
- *Fact and Truth*
- *Creative Nonfiction Format*

The essay is a pair of baggy pants into which nearly anyone and anything can fit.
Joseph Epstein

Laurie Lipton

WARM-UP
Write, quickly, a personal memory of either: swimming, or: a time you were totally happy, or: a time you believed you could fly, or: a time you were deluded about your own power.

The Essay and Creative Nonfiction

Just about anyone who goes through high school in America gets some practice in basic forms of the **essay**—expository, descriptive, persuasive, and so forth. The tradition of the essay is that it is based in fact, and that the reader has a right to expect that the facts presented will be accurate and truthful.

But the word *essay* itself comes from the French for *try*, and "A Try" captures the modest and partial nature of the form. Anything in the world is potential subject matter, and anything you say about it is an attempt to be accurate, to be interesting, to offer a perspective.

Any or all forms of the essay may be enlivened and made more meaningful through attention to imagery, voice, character, setting, and scene—the elements of imaginative writing. Such essays may be called **literary nonfiction** or **creative nonfiction,** terms to describe the kinds of essays that may begin with a personal experience or the merely factual, but which reach for greater range and resonance.

Writer–editor Lee Gutkind sees creative nonfiction as allowing the writer "to employ the diligence of a reporter, the shifting voices and viewpoints of a novelist, the refined wordplay of a poet, and the analytical modes of the essayist," and he sees as a requirement that the essays should "have purpose and meaning beyond the experiences related."

In one sense, the rules for meaning-making are more relaxed in the essay form than in poetry, fiction, or drama, in that you may tell as well as show; you may say in so many words what the significance is for you. Sometimes the process of gathering information becomes part of the story. Sometimes an object of research leads to a personal discovery. Sometimes the essay begins in personal memory, but aspires to a truth about the human condition. In any of these cases the essay will move back and forth from the intellectual to the emotional, and from the specific to the general.

Creative nonfiction is capacious, malleable, forthright, and forgiving. Unlike the conventional academic essay all students are expected to write in freshman composition, creative nonfiction does not need to follow the standard thesis–topic-sentence–conclusion outline. Instead, it can easily borrow from any form you choose: story, monologue, lesson, list, rondel, collage. The trick is to find the right shape for the idea you have to present. At the end of this chapter are two essays that represent two extremes of possible form. "Margot's Diary" is a meditative recreation of a document that does not exist; "Jack Culberg, 79" is an **oral history** entirely in the recorded words of its subject. Each focuses on an actual person; neither intrudes the author into the story; yet in each the imaginative mark of the author is evident—in the former through artful but honest invention, in the latter through artful inquiry and arrangement.

TRY THIS 8.1

At some point in your school life you were asked to write an essay that made you angry or anxious. (You needed the grade? You hated the subject? You didn't have time? You were in love?) As an exercise in showing yourself the difference between that school essay and creative nonfiction, write two pages about writing that essay. See it as a chance to tell the (personal, emotional, atmospheric, judgmental?) truths that had no place in the essay you were assigned.

Memoir and the Personal Essay

Two familiar and attractive essay forms, differing more in emphasis than in kind, are memoir and the personal essay. A **memoir** is a story retrieved from the writer's memory, with the writer as protagonist—the *I* remembering and commenting on the events described in the essay. Memoir tends to place the emphasis on the story, and the "point" is likely to emerge, as it does in fiction, largely from the events and characters themselves, rather than through the author's speculation or reflection.

Example: In the essay "Sundays," from his memoir *What I Can't Bear Losing,* poet Gerald Stern describes his boyhood in Pittsburgh in a Jewish neighborhood surrounded by Calvinist Christians. The emphasis is on the pattern of his Sundays: his parents' quarrels, his walks with his father, later his long walks alone through the hills of the city, the concerts of the Pittsburgh Symphony Orchestra, the ethnic clubs, an early romance. But as he recalls these days he paints a resonant picture of the ethnic, religious, and economic demarcations of the city. His overt analyses are few and light, but he evokes by implication the tensions underlying a divided society.

The **personal essay** also usually has its origin in something that has happened in the writer's life, but it may be something that happened yesterday afternoon, or it may represent an area of interest deliberately explored, and it is likely to give rise to reflection or intellectual exploration.

Example: I took a photograph out of an old frame to put in a picture of my new husband and stepdaughter. Because the frame was constructed in an amazingly solid way, I thought about the man whose photo I was displacing; his assumptions about permanence; how we use frames to try to capture and hang onto moments, memories, families, selves that are in fact always in flux; how we frame our cities with roads, our shoreline with resorts, our dead with coffins—marking our territory, claiming possession. In this instance a very small task led me to write about the nature of impermanence and enclosure.

Both memoir and personal essay grow out of some degree of autobiographical experience and are usually (though there are exceptions) written in the first person. The distinction between them is not always clear, although it may be said that the memoir sets up a dialogue between the writer and his/her past, while the emphasis of the personal essay is likely to be a relationship, implied or sought, between the writer and the reader. Philip Lopate, in the brilliant introduction to his anthology *The Art of the Personal Essay,* dissects the tone in terms of its intimacy, its "drive toward candor and self-exposure," the conversational dynamic and the struggle for honesty.

The personal essay is a form that allows maximum mobility from the small, the daily, the domestic, to the universal and significant. Essayist Philip Gerard says, "The subject has to carry itself and also be an elegant vehicle for larger meanings." What makes it "creative" is that though you may take the subject matter of research or journalism, there is "an apparent subject and a deeper subject. The apparent subject... is only part of what we are interested in."

Example: Whereas you might write a newspaper article about the Little Miss Blue Crab Festival of Franklin County, naming the contestants, the organizers, and the judges, describing the contest, announcing the winner—if you undertook this same subject matter as a piece of creative nonfiction, your main focus would not be the event itself but the revelation of something essential about the nature of beauty contests, or children in competition, or the character of the fishing village, or coastal society, or rural festivals. In a first-person essay, the focus might be on how you personally fit or don't fit into this milieu, what memories of your own childhood it calls up, how it relates to your experience of competition in general, or other structures in your life and, by extension, life in general. You would have "distance on it," a perspective that embraces not just the immediate event but its place in a human, social, historical, even cosmic context. Because creative nonfiction has this deeper (or wider, or more universal, or significant) subject, it won't necessarily date in the manner of yesterday's newspaper.

TRY THIS 8.2

Begin with the conventional notion of titling an essay:

On ________ .

- Make a list of at least six titles that represent things you might like to write about, things that interest you and that you feel confident you know something about. These may be either abstractions or specifics, *On Liberty* or *On Uncle Ernie's Saddle.*
- Then make a list of six subjects you do *not* want to write about, and wouldn't show to anybody if you did. (*On* ________.)
- Make a list of six titles in which the preposition "on" could be a pun: *On Speed. On the 'Net. On My Feet.*
- Make a list of six titles dealing with subjects about which you know "nothing at all." For me such a list might include: *On Brain Surgery. On Refrigerator Repair. On Tasmania.*

If you choose to write an essay from the first list, you are embarking on an honorable enterprise. If you choose from the second list, you are very courageous. If you choose

(continued)

(Try This 8.2 continued)

from list three, you'll probably have a good time—and remember that such an essay should deal with both aspects of the pun: *On My Feet* should deal with toenails, calluses, pain, or podiatry, and also with courage or persistence. The last list offers the wildest ride and may turn up something original, comic (Dave Barry makes a living in this territory), or unexpectedly true. Remember that your intent is not to deceive: signal or confess your ignorance when appropriate. Any of the four lists may, like focused freewrites, unlock subject matter that you didn't know you had in you.

Techniques of Creative Nonfiction

Memory has its own story to tell.

Tim O'Brien

Creative nonfiction tells a true story. How does it tell a story? (I'll deal with the "true" part below.)

Every writerly technique that has been discussed in these pages can be used in the essay form, and just as a character will be most richly drawn when presented by more than one method, so a variety of techniques will enrich the texture of nonfiction. As an essayist you may (and should) employ image, metaphor, voice, dialogue, point of view, character, setting, scene, conflict, human connection—and you are also free to speak your mind directly, to "tell" what you mean and what matters. The success of your essay may very well depend on whether you achieve a balance between the imaginative and the reflective. Often, the story and its drama (the showing) will fill most of the sentences—that is what keeps a reader reading—and the startling or revelatory or thoughtful nature of your insight about the story (the telling) will usually occupy less space.

Image and Voice

When writing academic research essays, you generally try for an authoritative, abstract, and impersonal voice: "Howard Dilettante was born of humble parentage. . . ." or "The next four centuries were characterized by international strife. . . ." But creative nonfiction calls for a conversational tone, a personal "take," and it is largely through your choice of concrete detail that you will carry the reader into the confidence of this persona.

> The park is hardly a block away, where lighted ball diamonds come into view on ducking through branches. There, too, is a fenced acre for unleashed dogs, a half dozen tennis courts with yellow balls flying and, close by, a game of summertime hoops under the lights, a scrambling, squeaking, stampede of sweat and bodies on green tarmac.

"Hoop Sex," Theodore Weesner

Here Weesner introduces us to a persona at the same time as he declares the topic of summer night sports. The author is somebody who ducks through branches, who notices dogs and flying balls, who knows basketball as "hoops," and who is comfortable with, excited by, sweat and scramble. The same scene would come to us in a different choice of imagery from the pen of a horticulturalist or a reminiscing mother.

TRY THIS 8.3

Tell your life story in three incidents involving hair.

Scene

Like a story, creative nonfiction needs scenes. If you are working from a remembered period of your life, it may present itself as summary, and summary will have its place in your essay; but when you get to what mattered—what changed you, what moves us—it will need the immediacy of detailed action, of discovery and decision.

> Just down from the mountains, early August. Lugging my youngest child from the car, I noticed that his perfectly relaxed body was getting heavier every year. When I undressed his slack limbs, he woke up enough to mumble, "I like my own bed," then fell back down, all the way down, into sleep. The sensation of his weight was still in my arms as I shut the door.

"Images," Robert Hass

Notice that Hass begins with a brief summary (or long shot) of the situation, then moves at once into the sensual apprehension of the action, the boy's body relaxed, heavy, slack, while the father takes care of him.

TRY THIS 8.4

Pick the five photographs that you would want to illustrate your life so far. Choose one of them to write about.

Character

Like a story, creative nonfiction depends on character, and the creation of character depends on both detail and dialogue. Dialogue is tricky because the memory does its own editing, but you can re-create a voice from memory no less than from imagination. Write, remembering as truly as you can, then test in your mind whether the other person involved would agree: *What we said was like this.*

Whatever looks I had were hidden behind thick cat-eyed glasses and a hearing aid that was strapped to my body like a dog halter. My hallucinatory visions would sometimes lift me up and carry me through the air. When I told my mother that I was afraid of the sky, she considered it a reasonable fear, even though she said, "Well, the sky isn't something I could ever be afraid of."

"Falling in Love Again," Terry Galloway

TRY THIS 8.5

Write about the loss of a friendship you have experienced, whether by anger, change, death, moving away—whatever reason. Use the skills you have to create the characters of both yourself and the friend you lost. Speculate on what this loss teaches you about yourself, or about your life, or about life.

Setting

Like a story, creative nonfiction needs the context and texture of setting. Frequently an encounter with setting is the point and purpose of the piece, whether that encounter is with an exotic foreign country or your own backyard. If you're stuck for a way to begin, you might remember the long shot–middle shot–close-up pattern.

It's past eleven on a Friday night in the spring of 1955. Here comes a kid down the length of Eighteenth Street in the Midwood section of Flatbush, in Brooklyn, New York. He passes the kept lawns and tidy hedges under big leafy sycamores and maples. The middle class is asleep, and most of the houses attached to the lawns are dark, though an occasional window pulses with blue-gray television light. Streetlamps shine benignly, and Mars is red in the sky. The kid is on his way home from the weekly meeting of Troop 8, Boy Scouts of America. . . .

"For the Love of a Princess of Mars," Frederick Busch

Interpretation

Unlike a story, creative nonfiction involves a balance of dramatization and overt reflection. This doesn't mean that the balance needs to be the same in all essays. On the contrary, a memoir that leaves us with a vivid image of an aging relative or a revelation of an error in judgment may be absolutely appropriate, whereas a piece on a walk in the woods may need half its space to analyze and elucidate the discoveries you have made. Sometimes an essay will convey its personal intensity precisely through the force of its abstractions.

I have had with my friend Wes Jackson a number of useful conversations about the necessity of getting out of movements—even movements that have seemed necessary and dear to us—when they have lapsed into self-righteousness and self-betrayal, as movements seem almost invariably to do. People in movements too readily learn to deny to others the rights and privileges they demand for themselves. They too easily become unable to mean their own language, as when a "peace movement" becomes violent.

"In Distrust of Movements," Wendell Berry

One part of the purpose of an essay will always be to inform or teach, either by presenting new knowledge or by combining old facts in a new way. Often the essay seduces the reader with a personal note into an educational enterprise. The nature essayist Barry Lopez demonstrates the technique again and again; he places himself in relation to the landscape, and later in the piece slips in the history, archeology, or biology. So a typical essay will begin, "I am standing at the margin of the sea ice called the floe edge at the mouth of Admiralty Inlet. . . ." or "We left our camp on Pingok Island one morning knowing a storm was moving in from the Southwest. . . ." Later in each piece, more factual or speculative paragraphs begin, "Three million colonial seabirds, mostly northern fulmars, kittiwakes, and guillemots, nest and feed here in the summer," and, "Desire for wealth, for spiritual or emotional ecstasy, for recognition—strains of all three are found in nearly every arctic expedition." Lopez immediately involves the reader in the human drama, but he also wants to teach us what he knows. He exhibits the range of the personal essay: involvement and intellectual enlargement, both operating at full stretch. He wants to have and to offer both the experience and the knowledge.

Research

If your essay asks for research, it may be very different, and vastly more inclusive, than what you usually mean by research. Taking a walk in your old neighborhood or getting on a surfboard for the first time, phoning or e-mailing friends and family members, recording an interview, reading old letters including your own, digging among photographs or mementos or recipes—any of these may be exactly what you need to research a memoir. If your subject takes you into areas you need to know more about, you may spend as much time in interview and legwork as on the Internet or in the library.

When it comes to the writing, an essay may be researched and still be "personal," either by making the research (including interview, observation, and detective work) part of the essay, or by allowing the reader to share the emotions you as writer experienced in the process. How does it *feel* to watch a kidney operation? What emotions pass among the athletes in the locker room? How did your interview of Aunt Lena change your view of your family?

TRY THIS 8.6

Write a personal essay about a building you care about. Choose one of which you have strong memories, then research the place itself. This research might, if it's a house or school in your hometown, consist of calling people to interview them. If it's a church or municipal building of some sort, it might be archival or library research. You will know what's appropriate. How does your memory of the place contrast with, or how is it qualified by, what you have learned? Is there an idea to be mined in the difference between them?

Although the personal essay offers an insight into the writer's life and thought, that doesn't necessarily mean that it must be written in the first person. It may be that the story you have to tell or the drama you have witnessed can be best conveyed (as in a short story) by focusing on that experience, implying rather than spelling out how it has moved you. George Plimpton wrote sports stories in the first person because his point was to expose the emotions of an amateur among the pros; whereas Roger Angell writes occasionally in the first person, and sometimes in the collective "we," but most often in the third person, focusing on the players but putting on their stories the stamp of his style. If in doubt, try a few paragraphs in first and then in third person; fool around with the perspective of fly-on-the-wall and with myself-as-participant. Usually the material will reveal its own best slant, and the experiment may help you find out what you have to say.

Transitions and Focus

Transitions are particularly important in creative nonfiction because of the needed rhythm back and forth between scene and summary, abstraction and detail. We expect a degree of direction and interpretation that in fiction would be called **authorial intrusion.** An essayist is allowed and encouraged to employ intrusion to a degree, and we expect and ask for the generalization that says, in effect: *This is what I think.* I find it useful, when I find myself getting a little wound up or mixed up in the writing, to type in "What's my point?" and try to answer the question right then. The question can come out later. Often the answer can, in some form or other, stay. Even if you end up cutting it, it may help you find your way.

In the past, when writing a critical or research essay, you've been told to pick a confined and specific subject and explore it thoroughly. The same advice holds for creative nonfiction. Don't try to write about "my family," which will overwhelm you with vagaries and contradictions, just as if your subject were "Shakespeare." Write about one afternoon when things changed. Focus on one kid in the fifth grade who didn't fit in. Write about your first encounter with language, oysters, God, hypocrisy, race, or betrayal. Creative nonfiction tells a story, and like a story it will describe a journey and a change; it will be written in a scene or scenes; it will characterize through detail and dialogue. The difference is not only that it is based on the facts as your research or your memory can dredge them up, but that you may interpret it for us as you go along or at the end or both: *This is what I learned, this is how I changed, this is how I relate my experience to the experience of the world, and of my readers.*

TRY THIS 8.7

Pick a piece from your journal that represents an observation or a memory. Copy it. Begin a new paragraph, "What's the point?" and answer the question. Does the answer suggest there's an essay here?

Fact and Truth

> I never want to discover, after reading a piece of nonfiction, that I have not read a piece of nonfiction.
>
> *Joe Mackall*

"Essays," says novelist and travel writer Edward Hoagland, "are how we speak to one another in print—caroming thoughts not merely in order to convey a certain packet of information but with a special edge or bounce of personal character in a kind of public letter. ... More than being instructive, as a magazine article is, an essay has a slant. ..."

How do you balance the information against the slant? How, in that *caroming*, do you judge when edge or bounce has overwhelmed instruction?

This is an interesting issue because in the latter half of the twentieth century readers became intensely interested in "what really happened," and memoirs, personal experience, biography, and autobiography are now more marketable than fiction or poetry. Television and film offer us an endless buffet of drama, and perhaps we are tired of being overfed with formulaic dramatic plots.

But it's not always clear what is fact and what is fiction. Recent years have seen several scandals when authors were caught passing off fictional exploits as their own. TV news raises the question of how much "entertainment" enters journalistic decisions. Is a docudrama documentary or drama? If a memoir "remembers" dialogue from forty years ago, is it memory or fiction? If a living person is shielded from recognition in a biography, is the piece dishonest? If you have taken seven trips in a fishing boat and you want to write about it as personal experience, do you have to go through seven trips, or can you conflate them into one trip and still call it fact? How much dramatizing may be said to reveal rather than distort the truth?

At some point every writer of memoir and personal essay has to grapple with these issues. Luckily, they don't have to be grappled with in first draft. Having accepted that the mere fact of putting something into words *changes* it, begin by putting into words as clearly and vividly as you can something that you know about, care about, or that has happened to you. Look for your particular purpose. Consider how to raise the tension and the drama. Be scrupulously honest about the facts and, beyond that, explore the essential truth of what you have to say. There will inevitably be changes of emphasis and balance in the shaping of both rough draft and revisions.

The distance between "facts" and "essential truth," of course, can be troubling. What and how much is it fair to make up? Let's say I'm writing a piece about my mother, and I want to give an accurate image of her. When I try to remember the things she wore, what stands out are the unusual things, the embroidered yellow wedding coat she kept for special occasions, the pink satin housecoat that was too precious to wear often. These are in my memory precisely because they were uncharacteristic of her, whereas the kind of housedress she wore every day is a blur of composite images, a mnemonic generalization. As a writer I concentrate on this vagueness and bring it into focus in my imagination *as if* it were fiction. *She wore a cap-sleeve cotton house dress, a plaid of lavender and yellow crisscrossing on faded gray.* Or: *She wore a cotton house dress with piping around the collar, sprigs of lily-of-the-valley tied with a pink bow on a pale gray ground.* I don't know whether these images came from somewhere deep in my memory, or whether I "made them up." They are true to the image of my mother I am trying to capture, and therefore they partake of "essential truth," whereas if I said she wore bikinis or Armani, I would be honoring neither fact nor truth.

Fiction writers also grapple with the level of historical or regional fact that is necessary to their truth, and like essayists, they answer it differently. James Joyce wanted every Dublin bus route and ticket price accurate in *Ulysses*; E. L. Doctorow invented the events of several famous real lives in *Ragtime.* In the only historical novel I have written, I decided that I could harmlessly put an ice house in a rural Arizona town seven years before there was actually such a thing, but that I couldn't blow off the arm of a famous Mexican general two years before, historically, it happened.

The delicacy of this issue is slightly augmented for an essayist, and I think the touchstone is: an absence of the intent to deceive. A fiction writer is in the clear to the extent that a reader understands from the beginning that the story is "made up"—yet must on whatever level of reality convince us to suspend disbelief. Since a reader of essays expects factual truth, you are under some obligation to signal its absence. It can add to both the authenticity and the interest of a piece (as long as it isn't too repetitive), to say in effect: I don't remember exactly, but I seem to see... Or: So-and-so says it was this way, but I think... Or: I am imagining that it must have been...

> I know nothing about how they meet. She is a schoolgirl. He is at work, probably a government clerk in a building near her school. At the hour when the school and the office are out for lunch their lives intersect at sandwich counters, soft-drink stands, traffic lights, market squares. Their

eyes meet or their bodies collide at one of these food queues. He says something suggestive, complimentary. She suppresses a smile or traps one beneath her hands.

"A Son in Shadow," Fred D'Aguilar

TRY THIS 8.8

Write a personal essay about your parents' courtship. It may be totally imaginary (in which case, that you are making it up becomes part of the subject matter and the truth of your essay); or you may write it from facts you already know (acknowledging where you fill in, leave out, or speculate); or you may "research" it by interviewing family members (in which case your research may become the subject of the essay, the family members become characters, and their interviews become dialogue). You may choose any method you like, based on whatever quantity of information you have or choose to use, but it must remain an essay; that is, with a basis in fact, so that where you invent, you acknowledge "I imagine...I guess...I'm inventing here."

"When you use memories as a source," says E. L. Doctorow, "they're no different from any other source—the composition still has to be made." Memory is imperfect; that is its nature, and you are responsible only for the honest attempt and the honest presentation. No two siblings will remember their mother, or even Christmas dinner, in the same way. One of the leaps of faith you must make to write from memory is that the process of writing itself will yield that essential truth. Sometimes clarifying a quotation, compressing several conversations or events into one, exaggerating one physical detail while omitting another, or transposing a scene from one locale to another—any of these can honor (and reveal) an essential truth when the literal truth would distort. If you get the color of your childhood wagon wrong, it will not damage that truth. If you sentimentalize an emotion, it will.

It is likely that the most troubling conflict you face as a writer of memoir and personal essay will be between your essential truth and obligation to those you know. When does honesty require that you reveal an ugly fact? Is it arrogance to suppose that anything you write is worth wounding someone else? There is no answer to this dilemma, or there are as many answers as there are works in a lifetime or paragraphs in a work. As a rough rule of thumb, I would say that the cost of honesty might be the loss of your own labor. That is: write your truth. You are under no obligation to publish it, and you may find yourself under the pressure of personal integrity not to. If you need to alter details in order to conceal a living person, let it be later. It may or may not work, but it will be easier to alter identifying details than to censor yourself as you write.

TRY THIS 8.9

Write an anonymous memoir about someone you dislike or someone you are afraid of. The surer you are that nobody is going to know who wrote it, the freer you are to write; but also, strangely! the more freely you write, the less likely anybody is to know who wrote it. You have angers and fears that nobody has ever suspected, right? Write.

More to Read

Gutkind, Lee. *The Art of Creative Nonfiction*. New York: John Wiley & Sons, 1997. Print.

Zinsser, William. *On Writing Well*. New York: HarperCollins, 2001. Print.

READINGS

GAYLE PEMBERTON

Do He Have Your Number, Mr. Jeffrey?

During the fall of 1984 I worked for three weekends as a caterer's assistant in Southern California. Like lots of others seeking their fortunes in L.A., I was working by day as a temporary typist in a Hollywood film studio. I was moonlighting with the caterer because, like lots of others, I was going broke on my typist's wages.

Though the job was not particularly enjoyable, the caterer and her husband were congenial, interesting people who certainly would have become good friends of mine had I stayed in California. I spent my three weekends in basic scullery work—wiping and slicing mushrooms, mixing batters, peeling apples, tomatoes, and cucumbers, drying plates, glasses, and cutlery. Greater responsibilities would have come with more experience, but I had brushed off California's dust before I learned any real catering secrets or professional gourmet techniques.

One exhausting dinner party, given by a rich man for his family and friends, turned out to be among the reasons I brushed off that California dust. This dinner was such a production that our crew of five arrived the day before to start preparing. The kitchen in this house was larger than some I've seen in fine French restaurants. Our caterer was one of a new breed of gourmet cooks who do all preparation and cooking at the client's house—none of your cold-cut or warming-tray catering. As a result, her clients had a tendency to have loads of money and even more kitchen space.

Usually her staff was not expected to serve the meal, but on this occasion we did. I was directed to wear stockings and black shoes and I was given a blue-patterned apron dress, with frills here and there, to wear. Clearly, my academic lady-banker pumps were out of the question, so I invested in a pair of trendy black sneakers—which cost me five dollars less than what I earned the entire time I worked for the caterer. Buying the sneakers was plainly excessive but I told myself they were a necessary expense. I was not looking forward to wearing the little French serving-girl uniform, though. Everything about it and me were wrong, but I had signed on and it would have been unseemly and downright hostile to jump ship.

One thing I liked about the caterer was her insistence that her crew not 5
be treated as servants—that is, we worked for her and took orders from her, not from the clients, who might find ordering us around an emboldening and socially one-upping experience. She also preferred to use crystal and china she rented, keeping her employees and herself safe from a client's rage in case a family heirloom should get broken. But on this occasion, her client insisted that we use his Baccarat crystal. We were all made particularly nervous by his tone. It was the same tone I heard from a mucky-muck at my studio typing job: cold, arrogant, a matter-of-fact "you are shit" attitude that is well known to nurses and secretaries.

I had never served a dinner before that one—that is, for strangers, formally. I had mimed serving festive meals for friends, but only in a lighthearted way. And, when I was a child, my family thought it a good exercise in etiquette—not to mention in labor savings—to have me serve at formal dinners. "It's really fun, you know," they would say. I never handled the good china, though.

I didn't mind cutting up mushrooms or stirring sauce in some foul rich man's kitchen for pennies, but I certainly didn't like the idea of serving at this one's table. I saw our host hold up one of his goblets to a guest, showing off the fine line and texture. There were too many conflicting images for me to be content with the scene. He was working hard on his image for his guests; I was bothered by the way I looked to myself and by what I might have looked like to the assembled crew, guests, and host. I couldn't get the idea of black servility to white power out of my mind.

The food was glorious. I recall serving quenelles at one point, followed by a consommé brunoise, a beef Wellington with a carrot and herb based sauce that I stirred for a short eternity, vegetables with lemon butter, and a variety of mouth-watering pastries for dessert. We worked throughout the meal, topping up wine and coffee, removing plates, bumping into each other. As long as I was doing this absurd thing I decided to make some kind of mental work attend it. I made the entire scene a movie, and as I served I created a silent voice-over. At one point, after the quenelles and the entrée and before the coffee, the table of eight sat discussing literature—a discussion of the "what'd you think of…" variety. My professorial ears pricked up. I discovered that one member of the party had actually read the book in question, while a few others had skimmed condensed versions in a magazine. My voice-over could have vied, I thought, with the shrillest Bolshevik propaganda ever written.

Pemberton (*Voice-over*)
(*haughtily*)

> You self-satisfied, rich, feeble-brained, idiotic, priggish, filthy maggots! You, you sit here talking literature—why, you don't even know what the word means. This is high intellectual discourse for you, isn't it? High, fine. You are proud to say, "I thought the theme honest." What, pray tell, is an honest theme? It might be better to consider the dishonesty of your disgusting lives. Why, here I am, a PhD in literature, listening to this garbage, making a pittance, while you illiterate pig-running-dogs consume food and non-ideas with the same relish.

Oh, I did go on. My script was melodramatic, with great soliloquies, flourishes, and, for verisimilitude, an eastern European accent. My comeuppance came as I dried the last of the Baccarat goblets. The crystal, no doubt responding to the dissonance and intensity of my sound track, shattered as I held it in my hand. The rest of the crew said they'd never seen anyone look as sick as I did at that moment. The goblet was worth more than the price of my trendy sneakers and my night's work combined. I decided to go home.

I drove slowly back to my room near Culver City; it was well past midnight. I had the distinct sense that I was the only sober driver on the Santa Monica Freeway that night, but given the weaving pattern of my driving—to avoid the other weavers—I fully expected to be picked up and jailed. Then, some alcohol residue from the broken goblet would have transported itself magically into my bloodstream to make me DWI, just as the goblet had reacted to my thoughts and sacrificed itself in the name of privilege, money, and mean-spiritedness. I made it home, feeling woozy as I left my car.

I didn't have to pay for the goblet; the caterer did. She was insured. I worked another party for her—another strange collection of people, but a more festive occasion—and I didn't have to wear the French maid's outfit. I got to stand happily behind a buffet, helping people serve themselves. I think back on my catering experience the way people do who, once something's over, say that they're glad they did it—like lassoing a bull, riding him, then busting ribs and causing permanent sacroiliac distress. The job was just one of many I've had to take to make me believe I could survive when it was obvious that I was going further and further into the hole. I never had more than ten dollars in my wallet the entire time I lived in L.A., and not much more than that in the bank. Perhaps there's something about L.A. that makes working unlikely jobs—jobs your parents send you to college to keep you from having to do—all right and reasonable, since very little makes sense there anyway, and surviving means bellying up to the illusion bar and having a taste with everyone else.

L.A. has been like that for a long time. It did not occur to me that night, as I moved from one dinner guest to another dressed in that ludicrous outfit, that I might have created some other kind of scenario—linking what I was doing to what my mother had done nearly fifty years before, probably no farther than ten miles away.

It was in the middle thirties, Los Angeles. My mother's employers supplied her with a beige uniform with a frilled bib, short puff sleeves, and a narrow, fitted waist. The skirt of the dress was narrow, stopping just below the knee. She wore seamed stockings and low pumps, black. And her job, as far as she could ascertain, was to just be, nothing else. The couple who employed her—the husband wrote screenplays—had no children, and did not require her services to either cook or clean. I suppose they thought that having a maid was a requirement of their social position. So, Mother got the job. She is fair-skinned, and at that time she wore her dark, wavy hair long, in large curls that gathered just below her neck. I've seen pictures from those days and see her most enviable figure, an old-fashioned size ten, held up by long legs that, doubtless, were enhanced by the seamed stockings and pumps. Her employers were quite proud of her and thought she looked, they said, "just like a little French girl." When I was very young and filled with important questions, Mother explained to me that she thought it "damned irritating that whites who knew full well who they were hiring and talking to went to such lengths to try to make blacks into something else. If they wanted a little French girl, why didn't they go out and get one?" Ah, the days before *au pairs*. Well, I knew the answer to that one too.

Mother had moved to L.A. with her mother. Nana had decided to leave Papa, tired of his verbal abusiveness and profligacy. There were various cousins in California, and I am sure the appeal of the West and new beginnings at the start of the Depression made the choice an easy one. Both of my parents told me that they didn't feel the Depression all that much; things had never been financially good and little changed for them after Wall Street fell. The timing seemed right to Nana. Her other daughter, my aunt, had recently married. My mother had finished her third year at the university and, I bet, got an attack of wanderlust. She went with Nana to help her—and also to get some new air. The circumstances accommodated themselves.

I remember my shock when I learned that Mother had worked as a maid. 15
I had always known that she had lived in California, but as a child, it never occurred to me that she would have had to "do something" there. It was not so much that my middle-class feathers were ruffled by the revelation as that I found it difficult to see her in a role that, on screen at least, was so demeaning and preposterous. Mother simply did not fit the stereotype I had been fed. And, to make matters worse, Grandma had taken pains to inform my sister and me when we were little girls that we should avoid—at all costs—rooming with whites in college or working in their homes. Her own stints as a dance-hall matron had convinced her, she said, that whites were the filthiest people on earth. The thought of my mother cleaning up after them made me want to protect her, to undo the necessity for that kind of work by some miraculous feat of time travel, to rescue her from the demeaning and the dirty.

Mother's attitude about her past employment was more pragmatic, of course. She explained to me—as if I didn't know—that there were really no avenues for black women apart from "service," as it was called, prostitution, and, perhaps, schoolteaching. Nana had no higher education and Mother's was incomplete, so service was the only route they could take. Mother also assured me that she had not cleaned unimaginable filth, but rather, with nothing else to do, had sat all day long reading novels, memorably *Anthony Adverse* by Hervey Allen, a big best-seller of 1934. My image of Mother became brighter, but in some ways more curious: there she was, imagined as a French maid by her employers, but really a black coed, lolling around a Los Angeles home reading *Anthony Adverse*. That's one far cry from Butterfly McQueen as Prissy in *Gone with the Wind*.

All good things must come to an end, as they say, and Mother's job did one day. She had been dating a man, she says, "who was very handsome, looked Latin, like Cesar Romero, but he was black too." Talk about images. He arrived to pick her up for a date as she got off work. He inquired after her at the front door—oops—and there went the job. Seems the little French maid's Spanish-looking boyfriend should have realized that no matter what black might appear to be, it better not act other than what it was. A slip in racial protocol, a lost novel-reading employ. "So it went," Mother said. After that incident she decided to look for a different kind of work and she began selling stockings for the Real Silk Hosiery Company, door-to-door.

Mother was lucky. I suspect that she and Nana might have had a tougher time if they had been brown-skinned, for contrary to many images from movies, white employers—if they were going to hire blacks at all—preferred the lighter-skinned variety. This was true of professions as diverse as chorus girls, maids, schoolteachers, waitresses, and shop clerks, an implied greater worth as blackness disappears drop by drop into ginger, to mocha, to "high yellow," to white. This scale was intraracially internalized too, making a shambles of black life from the earliest slave days to the present. These gradations also made color-line crossing a popular black sport, particularly since white America seemed to be at once so secure and satisfied in its whiteness and so ignorant of who's who and who's what. Blacks existed only as whites saw them, blackness affirming white racial self-consciousness and nothing else. This is what Ralph Ellison's invisibility is all about; it is what we have all lived.

In the evenings and on weekends, Mother and Nana used to go to the movies; they both were hooked and on location for Hollywood's Golden Age. I love movies too. It is on the gene, as I frequently remind myself as I sit watching a vintage B from the forties for the fifth time or so when I ought to be reading a book. A major chunk of my misspent youth involved watching them. When I should have been reading, or studying mathematics, or learning foreign languages—like my more successful academic friends—I was hooked on three-reelers.

20 During my youth Mother was my partner in all this. When I was in kindergarten and first grade on half-day shifts, I never missed a morning movie. When

we watched together I would barrage her with important questions: "Who is that?" "Is he dead?" "Is she dead?" "Who was she married to?" "Is this gonna be sad?" Mother was never wrong, except once. We were watching an early Charles Bickford movie and I asked the standard heady question: "Is he dead?" Mother said, "Oh, Lord, yes. He died years ago." Several years later I came home triumphantly from a drive-in and announced that I had seen Bickford in *The Big Country* and that he looked just fine and alive to me.

Of course, hopeless romanticism is the disease that can be caught from the kind of movie-going and movie-watching my mother and I have done. There she was, with her mother, frequently a part of the crowd being held behind the barricades at Hollywood premiers, sighing and pointing with agitation as gowned and white-tied stars glided from limousines into rococo movie-houses. Both she and Nana read screen magazines—the forerunners to our evening news programs—that detailed the romantic, hedonistic public and private exploits of Hollywood's royalty. It was a time when my mother, as French maid reading *Anthony Adverse*, had to wait only a few months before the novel burst onto the screen, with glorious illusionary history and Frederic March swashbuckling his way into the hearts of screaming fans. The stars were part of the studio system and could be counted on to appear with frequency, even if the roles appeared to be the same and only the titles, and a few plot twists, changed. (I am convinced, for example, that the 1934 *Imitation of Life* was remade as *Mildred Pierce* in 1945, the major change being that the relatively good daughter of the former becomes the monster of the latter. Louise Beavers and Fredi Washington in the black theme of *Imitation of Life* only slightly alter the major plot.)

Mother's was the perfect generation to see Hollywood movies when they were fresh, new, and perhaps more palpable than they are now—when comedies of remarriage, as Stanley Cavell calls them, and historical adventures and melodramas dominated the screen, when westerns and political dramas were self-consciously mythologizing the American past and present, and when young French maids and their mothers, along with the impoverished, the disillusioned, the lost, and even the comfortable and secure, could sit before the silver screen and see a different world projected than the one they lived in. And they could dream. Mother loves to sketch faces and clothing, using an artistic talent inherited from Papa. She marveled at the stars and their sculpted (sometimes) faces, and would draw from memory the costume designs that made the likes of Edith Head, Cecil Beaton, and Irene famous.

Hopeless romanticism was the threat, but neither Nana nor Mother—nor I completely—succumbed to it. They never confused reality with anything they saw on either the big or the small screen. And they taught me what they believed. They both warned me, in different ways and at different times, to be wary of the type of people who wake up to a new world every day (and I've met some)—people with no memory, ingenuous, incapable of seeing either the implications or the connections between one event and another, people who willingly accept what the world makes of them on a Tuesday, forget as night falls, and wake up on Wednesday ready to make the same mistakes. It might have been some of that ingenuousness that produced my feelings of discomfort when I learned that Mother had been a maid, and she understood how I felt.

My mother always deplored the depiction of blacks on screen. She saw their roles as demeaning and designed to evoke either cheap sentimentality, cheap laughter, or cheap feelings of superiority in the white audiences they were aimed at. And, although she says she didn't see many of them, Mother loathed the all-black B movies Hollywood made for the "colored" audience, where the stereotypes were broader and more offensive to her, and where the musical interludes did no justice to real talent, she said, but trivialized it. She even hated musical interludes featuring black performers in the standard white A and B movies. She was—and still is—cold to arguments that say talented black performers needed to take any work they could get, and that black audiences were encouraged and happy to see black Hollywood stars no matter what they were doing. Mother countered that Hattie McDaniel's acceptance speech, when she won an Oscar for her role as Mammy in *Gone with the Wind,* was written for her, and that McDaniel was denied the status of eating dinner with her peers that night.

We have talked about all of this many, many times, particularly when I have felt it necessary to sort out my own complex and conflicting reactions to Hollywood movies. Like Mother, I have seen as nothing but illusion the world projected on the screen. But as Michael Wood notes in *America in the Movies*: "All movies mirror reality in some way or other. There are no escapes, even in the most escapist pictures.... The business of films is the business of dreams... but then dreams are scrambled messages from waking life, and there is truth in lies, too." Mother may have recoiled from black images on screen because they affirmed a reality she did not like. She could suspend her disbelief at white characters and their predicaments, she could enter the dream worlds of aristocrats and chorus girls living happily ever after, or dying romantic, drawn-out deaths, because there was some measure of inner life given these portrayals. The audience demanded some causal foundation to acts ranging from heroism and self-sacrifice to murder, duplicity, and pure cussedness. But black characters on screen, no matter how polished their roles, were ultimately as invisible as she was in her own role as French maid—a projection only of what the white world wanted to see, robbed of the implication of inner lives, nothing but glorified surfaces that really said everything about whiteness and nothing at all about blackness. It didn't matter to Mother if the characters were maids or butlers, lawyers or doctors, simpletons or singers. I knew there was an inner life, a real person in my mother—passionate and shy, lacking self-confidence but projecting intense intelligence and style—and that she had no business being anybody's French girl. The "truth in lies" was that Hollywood rent from us our human dignity while giving us work, as it sought to defuse and deflect our real meaning—a potentially dangerous meaning—in American life.

Mother found these invisible blacks painful to watch because they were so effective as images created in white minds. These complex feelings are on the gene too. I find Shirley Temple movies abominable, notwithstanding the dancing genius of Bill "Bojangles" Robinson. In *The Little Colonel* young Shirley has just been given a birthday party; there are hats and horns and all sorts of scrubbed white children celebrating with her. At some moment—I refuse to watch the film again to be precise—she gets up and takes part of her cake to a group of dusty and dusky children who are waiting outside in the backyard of the house. The only reason for their existence is to be grateful for the crumbs and to sing a song. There can be no other motivation, no reason to exist at all, except to show the dear Little Colonel's largesse and liberal-mindedness, befitting someone not quite to the manor born but clearly on her way to the manor life.

I was watching an Alfred Hitchcock festival not long ago. Hitchcock films are some of Mother's favorites. She likes the illusions and twists of plots, the scrambling of images light and dark. I realized that I hadn't seen *Rear Window* since I was a little girl, and that at the time I hadn't understood much of what had taken place in the movie. I was very interested in it this time around. There was James Stewart, as Jeffries, in the heaviest makeup ever, with his blue eyes almost enhanced out of his face, looking at evil Raymond Burr through binoculars in the apartment across the way. I was letting the film take me where it would; I created an *explication de texte,* noting how the film raises questions about voyeurism and images. Indeed, Stewart, in looking at the world from his temporary infirmity, is only content when he places a narrative line on the lives of the people on the other side of his binoculars. He is, in a sense, reacting to images and attempting to order them—as we all do.

At a crucial moment in the movie, Stewart realizes that he is in danger. The evil wife-murderer and dismemberer, Burr, knows that Stewart has figured out the crime. Stewart hobbles to the telephone, trying to reach his friend, Wendell Corey. Corey isn't in, but Stewart gets the babysitter on the line—who speaks in a vaudevillian black accent. He asks her to have Corey call him when he returns. The babysitter asks, "Do he have your number, Mr. Jeffrey?"

I called my mother to tell her that I had an interesting bit of trivia from *Rear Window*. She became angry when she heard it, said she was appalled. "He should have been ashamed of himself," she said of Hitchcock. Into the white world of *Rear Window* and questions of imagery, it was necessary to place a familiar black image—and this time it didn't even have a face.

Mother and Nana left L.A. in 1937. Working in service and selling silk stock- 30
ings could not provide enough money for them to survive. They went back to the frozen North. Mother married in 1939; Nana returned to Papa and stayed with him until he died in 1967.

Nana and Papa both moved to L.A. in 1950, Papa then a semi-retired architect. They had a beautiful home on West Fourth Avenue. It was right in the middle of a two-block area that became part of the Santa Monica Freeway. One morning, on my way to a catering job, I drove my car as far as I could, to the fence above the freeway. I got out and thought long and hard about what had been lost—beyond a house, of course, but their lives gone, part of my youth as a little girl visiting in summers, and dreams about what life could be in the semi-tropical paradise of Southern California where they made dreams that seduced the whole world.

TRY THIS 8.10

Write a memoir about a job you have held. Show (and tell) why this job did not lead to a lifelong career.

MARGARET ATWOOD

The Female Body

...entirely devoted to the subject of "The Female Body." Knowing how well you have written on this topic...this capacious topic...
letter from Michigan Quarterly Review

1.

I agree, it's a hot topic. But only one? Look around, there's a wide range. Take my own, for instance.

I get up in the morning. My topic feels like hell. I sprinkle it with water, brush parts of it, rub it with towels, powder it, add lubricant. I dump in the fuel and away goes my topic, my topical topic, my controversial topic, my capacious topic, my limping topic, my nearsighted topic, my topic with back problems, my badly behaved topic, my vulgar topic, my outrageous topic, my aging topic, my topic that is out of the question and anyway still can't spell, in its oversized coat and worn winter boots, scuttling along the sidewalk as if it were flesh and blood, hunting for what's out there, an avocado, an alderman, an adjective, hungry as ever.

2.

The basic Female Body comes with the following accessories: garter belt, panti-girdle, crinoline, camisole, bustle, brassiere, stomacher, chemise, virgin zone, spike heels, nose ring, veil, kid gloves, fishnet stockings, fichu, bandeau, Merry Widow, weepers, chokers, barrettes, bangles, beads, lorgnette, feather boa, basic black, compact, Lycra stretch one-piece with modesty panel, designer peignoir, flannel nightie, lace teddy, bed, head.

3.

The Female Body is made of transparent plastic that lights up when you plug it in. You press a button to illuminate the different systems. The circulatory system is red, for the heart and arteries, purple for the veins; the respiratory system is blue; the lymphatic system is yellow; the digestive system is green, with liver and kidneys in aqua. The nerves are done in orange and the brain is pink. The skeleton, as you might expect, is white.

The reproductive system is optional, and can be removed. It comes with or without a miniature embryo. Parental judgment can thereby be exercised. We do not wish to frighten or offend.

4.

He said, I won't have one of those things in the house. It gives a young girl a false notion of beauty, not to mention anatomy. If a real woman was built like that she'd fall on her face.

She said, If we don't let her have one like all the other girls she'll feel singled out. It'll become an issue. She'll long for one and she'll long to turn into one. Repression breeds sublimation. You know that.

He said, It's not just the pointy plastic tits, it's the wardrobes. The wardrobes and that stupid male doll, what's his name, the one with the underwear glued on.

She said, Better to get it over with when she's young. He said, All right, but don't let me see it.

She came whizzing down the stairs, thrown like a dart. She was stark naked. Her hair had been chopped off, her head was turned back to front, she was missing some toes and she'd been tattooed all over her body with purple ink in a scrollwork design. She hit the potted azalea, trembled there for a moment like a botched angel, and fell.

He said, I guess we're safe.

5.

The Female Body has many uses. It's been used as a door knocker, a bottle opener, as a clock with a ticking belly, as something to hold up lampshades, as a nutcracker, just squeeze the brass legs together and out comes your nut. It bears torches, lifts victorious wreaths, grows copper wings and raises aloft a ring of neon stars; whole buildings rest on its marble heads.

It sells cars, beer, shaving lotion, cigarettes, hard liquor; it sells diet plans and diamonds, and desire in tiny crystal bottles. Is this the face that launched a thousand products? You bet it is, but don't get any funny big ideas, honey, that smile is a dime a dozen.

It does not merely sell, it is sold. Money flows into this country or that country, flies in, practically crawls in, suitful after suitful, lured by all those hairless pre-teen legs. Listen, you want to reduce the national debt, don't you? Aren't you patriotic? That's the spirit. That's my girl.

She's a natural resource, a renewable one luckily, because those things wear out so quickly. They don't make 'em like they used to. Shoddy goods.

6.

One and one equals another one. Pleasure in the female is not a requirement. Pair-bonding is stronger in geese. We're not talking about love, we're talking about biology. That's how we all got here, daughter.

Snails do it differently. They're hermaphrodites, and work in threes.

7.

Each Female Body contains a female brain. Handy. Makes things work. Stick pins in it and you get amazing results. Old popular songs. Short circuits. Bad dreams.

Anyway: each of these brains has two halves. They're joined together by a thick cord; neural pathways flow from one to the other, sparkles of electric information washing to and fro. Like light on waves. Like a conversation. How does a woman know? She listens. She listens in.

The male brain, now, that's a different matter. Only a thin connection. Space over here, time over there, music and arithmetic in their own sealed compartments. The right brain doesn't know what the left brain is doing. Good for aiming though, for hitting the target when you pull the trigger. What's the target? Who's the target? Who cares? What matters is hitting it. That's the male brain for you. Objective.

This is why men are so sad, why they feel so cut off, why they think of themselves as orphans cast adrift, footloose and stringless in the deep void. What void? she asks. What are you talking about? The void of the universe, he says, and she says Oh and looks out the window and tries to get a handle on it, but it's no use, there's too much going on, too many rustlings in the leaves, too many voices, so she says, Would you like a cheese sandwich, a piece of cake, a cup of tea? And he grinds his teeth because she doesn't understand, and wanders off, not just alone but Alone, lost in the dark, lost in the skull, searching for the other half, the twin who could complete him.

Then it comes to him: he's lost the Female Body! Look, it shines in the gloom, far ahead, a vision of wholeness, ripeness, like a giant melon, like an apple, like a metaphor for "breast" in a bad sex novel; it shines like a balloon, like a foggy noon, a watery moon, shimmering in its egg of light.

Catch it. Put it in a pumpkin, in a high tower, in a compound, in a chamber, in a house, in a room. Quick, stick a leash on it, a lock, a chain, some pain, settle it down, so it can never get away from you again.

TRY THIS 8.11

You have by this time generated a number of lists in your journal. Pick one of them and add to it. See if your list has room for a memory, a song, a metaphor, a fantasy, a machine, a sarcasm, a dream, a grand idea. Pick seven items on the list and write a paragraph about each. Do they add up to a rough draft of an essay?

S. L. WISENBERG

Margot's Diary

PHOTOS: ANNE, 1941; MARGOT, 1941:

They both part their hair on the left side, wear a watch on the same wrist, have the same eyebrows, same open-mouthed smile. Their noses and eyes are different, the shape of their faces, the cut of their hair, the fall of it. Books are open in front of each of them. One photo we glance past. Because she is unknown. We don't care what she looks like—she's vaguely familiar. Not the real one. She is the sister of. The shadow. The first child who made way for the second, the important one. Who is more alive. Whose photo is crisp in contrasts, not blurry.

THE DIARIES:

Margot kept one, you know. She was the daughter known to be smart, studious, reflective. Hers was lost. Among the many items lost in the war, among millions. Perhaps her diary was darker—she was older, quieter, frailer. More naturally introspective. Perhaps she did not write that she believed that people were good at heart. (Which is something Anne believed only some of the time, anyway.) Perhaps Margot did not rejoice in nature. Perhaps she wrote: "There must be something wrong with us or else they would not be after us. We are cooped up here like mice. Anne is the only one who seems not to know we are doomed but she may be the bravest of all. We learn our French for what. In order to learn our French. We will be so warped upon our exit here that if we ever do escape, if there ever is freedom, we will not be able to live among the others. We shall be marked more than by the outline of the yellow badges."

WHY WE LIKE THEM:

They were suburban and then urban. They had bicycles and birthday parties. We know how to put both of those things together. Or whom to call to arrange them. The girls were just like us—the thrill of the avalanche missed.

Not that we would ever sacrifice someone else—

IN THE ANNE FRANK *HUIS*, AMSTERDAM:

Which was not a house, but an apartment over the office where her father 5
had been in business selling pectin for making jellies, and spices for making sausages. In July 1992 a young girl on a tour smiles in recognition of Anne's familiar face in a photo. On the wall are French vocabulary words Anne copied out:

la poudre à canon
le voleur
la maison de commerce
le conseil
de retour
le gluie (het glure)
le musée
la cause
le bouquet
l'éducation
envie
après-demain
avant-hier
le sang

[gunpowder
thief
business-firm?
advice
returning back
glue?
museum
cause
bouquet
education
desire
the day after tomorrow
the day before yesterday
blood]

Five thousand visitors a year stream into the old narrow house. Often, there are lines.

In Frankfurt:

There's a plaque on the door of the duplex that was the first Anne Frank house, which the family left the year of Hitler's election. They went west, to Aachen, then Amsterdam, for safety. Someone lives in the house still; it's private, not open to the public. The neighborhood is outside the center city, an area where young families set up hopeful households in the late 1920s and early 1930s. Streets named for poets, three-storey stucco buildings. Cars are parked all along both sides of the street. You can hear TVs, dogs, birds, children playing. Occasionally a bike rider glides past. I wonder if it was as leafy sixty years ago. There should be plaques on houses throughout Europe: A Jew lived here and was taken away.

Anne was four when they left in 1933; Margot was six.

Perhaps Margot remembered:

"Frankfurt, the house, the neighborhood, the protected feeling of it, safe, bright, like in the country, but the excitement, too, the newness of it. The best of everything, said my mother: Brand-new sturdy outside, delicate antiques inside. In Amsterdam, we learned to see vertically, to look up and down. All is narrow and the streets are crooked and thin. Contained. I was sorry to move away from everything familiar. From my native language. Everything in Amsterdam is approximate. And old. Compare and contrast. In Amsterdam we find what is already here. Someone else has already named everything. Anne, I don't think, really understands what is happening. We brought our old grandfather clock with us here, because it too is tall and thin. Ticks like a soft heartbeat, brooding over us."

Perhaps Margot grieved:

"July 1942. To leave yet again another house, in Amsterdam. They have named me. The Nazis have found me. They know I am here. A post card ordering me to pack my winter clothes and appear for a transport to Germany. Instead I left the house, rode my bicycle with Miep to what became the Annex. Rain protected us; no one stopped us. And we arrived. I was the first one in the family to enter it that day. The boxes were already there. Night fell.

"July 1943. Over time I grew quieter and quieter, they said. My thoughts raged inside then slowed. Everything slowed. I followed the course for French, for shorthand. At night we went downstairs to file and alphabetize for the company—for its benefit, for ours, a slender thread connecting us to the real world, commerce.

"We could not get away from the chime of the Westertoren clock, every quarter hour. It surprised me each time; nothing seemed predictable about it. I missed the steady ticking of our clock at home, imagined it slowing down to match the winding down of my thoughts. My stomach throbbed, my head. My heartbeat pounded in code: It is time to die. That's why I was so quiet, in order to hear the heart's message. I couldn't tolerate Anne's chatter. I abhorred singing."

Margot also didn't write:

"Of the day they came for us, August 4, 1944. It was late morning, happened fast. I gathered some bread, a Bible, a threadbare sweater—buttons missing. We tramped out, like machines set in motion. The sun hit us for a moment before we were herded into the car. Silent, of course, on the way to the station. Anne couldn't bear to look out the window. I did. Hungry for the familiar but impersonal landmarks. Signs in Dutch and German. German, the language we no longer memorized. Everyone was thin. But their hair shone. Wind riffled through skirts. That's what we'd been missing: the benign unpredictability of the breeze.

"You can imagine the rest."

At Bergen-Belsen, Winter 1945

Margot ran out of language. Everything seeped from her. She was barely eighteen. Her name appeared on lists of people who didn't come back. The day of death unmarked. She left no papers behind that were gathered up and stored in a file drawer in a *maison de commerce* in Amsterdam, then translated, published. Of her family, only her father came *de retour*. The Annex is now a *musée*. It is a center for *l'éducation*, to search for *la cause*. Margot has lost her *envie*. It no longer matters if it is *aprés-demain* or *avant-hier*, she has lost today, the glue that binds one minute to the next, as once marked by the German-made grandfather clock. Her *sang* is as dry as *poudre à canon*. Time is the *voleur*. She offers no *conseil*. This is not her bouquet.

TRY THIS 8.12

Pick a photograph from an occasion when you were not present—it can be from your family collection or from any other source. Describe it in at least half a page of detail. Then, acknowledging that you are now in the realm of speculation or guess, interpret the situation in the photo.

STUDS TERKEL

Jack Culberg, 79

The corporation is a jungle. It's exciting. You're thrown in on your own and you're constantly battling to survive. When you learn to survive, the game is to become the conqueror, the leader.

Larry Ross (pseudonym for Jack Culberg), Working, *1970*

He is now a corporate consultant in Chicago. Over the years, he has served as CEO of several conglomerates.

We're a new generation. When we grew up anybody fifty or sixty was considered old. I remember as a young boy, thirteen, fourteen, attending the twenty-fifth wedding anniversary of my mother and father. Everybody was dancing and singing and having a wonderful time. I remember saying to myself: "What are they so happy about? They're on the verge of dying." They were maybe fifty-five.

There's a new breed now. I'm going to be seventy-nine in July and I don't for a second consider myself old. I still play a good game of golf, and I exercise and swim and am active in business. There are many corporations out there that feel you're old and should be out of it, no matter how you look or feel. You have to quit at sixty-five or seventy. You can't be on the board. I don't feel that way at all. I'm still involved. I don't feel any older than them in any way. I feel I have more vitality than those who call me an old man. You turn around and want to know who the hell they're talking about.

What I said about the corporate jungle twenty-five years ago still goes. I've been in it ever since 1942. When you suddenly leave it, life is pretty empty. I was sixty-five, the age people are supposed to retire. I started to miss it quite a bit. The phone stops ringing. The king is dead. You start wanting to have lunch with old friends. At the beginning, they're nice to you, but then you realize that they're busy, they're working. They've got a job to do and just don't have the time to talk to anybody where it doesn't involve their business. I could be nasty and say, "Unless they can make a buck out of it"—but I won't. [Chuckles.] You hesitate to call them.*

You get involved in so-called charity work. I did a lot of consulting for not-for-profit organizations. It was encouraging for a while, but the people who run that world are a different breed. They're social workers who've become managers. The great curse of business is amateurs running things. They can't make it. It's amazing how much money is foolishly wasted in charitable organizations.

5 But Jobs for Youth is something else. It's a sensational group. It takes dropouts from high school, ages seventeen to twenty-one. We train them, get them a diploma,

*It was Gaylord Freeman's last year as chairman of the board of the First National Bank of Chicago. A successor had already been chosen. "As soon as Bob was designated as my successor, it was inevitable that people say, 'Gale Freeman's a nice guy, but Bob's the fella we should be talking to.' I find now that every couple of weeks I have a free luncheon engagement. Where will I have lunch? I had a magnificent dining room here. I'll go to a club. I won't be in demand. I'll be seeking company rather than being sought."

From American Dreams: Lost and Found, *1980*

counseling, and jobs. We place eight hundred to nine hundred a year. I'm still on the board.

As for the corporate jungle, it's even worse today. The circle of power is becoming smaller and smaller with fewer and fewer dominant people in control. IBM can lay off fifty thousand, or General Motors. They're not talking about blue-collar workers necessarily. They're talking about middle management who aspire to become CEOs. Today lots more people are fired or forced to retire before they reach the fifty percent mark on the way to the top. The jungle has become worse. You can smell the insecurity and fear all over the place. And the people who lose those jobs have nowhere else to go.

Most big corporations suggest early retirement. It isn't as much pension as you'd get if you lived out the entire thing. You take it. A genteel form of being fired.*

Of course, you're more afraid now than when we last met, twenty-five years ago. If you lost your job then, there were many more opportunities to find another. Today there are fewer companies. I'm talking about middle management and up. Let's say you're the manager of a company division and they're merged or bought out. They cut down on the bureaucrats and you're fired. Where do you go? A lot of them are taking lesser jobs.

Most of these people live on their investments or whatever they saved up. The interest rate is so low, they're having great difficulty. Let's say you have a million dollars saved. In the old days, it was an astronomical amount of money. If you're getting an interest of three percent, that's $30,000 a year. You can't live on that. So you have to go into the principal. It's very uneasy now. In the old days, it didn't mean a hell of a lot because nobody lived that long. The longer the life span, the more the insecurity—for the great majority.

I happen to be one of the lucky ones. When I retired at the age of sixty-five, 10
I thought I had enough money to live comfortably. If things hadn't happened for me during my retirement, I'd have a rough time now. With retirement, I started doing some consulting. I wasn't satisfied just playing golf or spending winters in Florida. I was too involved in the business world because it was exciting. It had been my whole life.

So I started dabbling around. The LBO† swing came in. One of the top men in the business is someone I've known for years. I found some businesses for him. For at least nine years, I've been involved with these companies. I'm still the chairman of one. In the last seven, eight years, I've made myself an awful lot of money—I was able to work three to four days a week and have a ball. Now I spend maybe two days a month. I still have a hand in. I have a fax machine at home and daily reports, but I'm not in active management.

*A neighbor of mine, an executive of a large consulting firm, had just touched fifty-five. It was suggested—astonishing him—that he accept early retirement. There had been no forewarning at all; he had been expecting a promotion. "They made me an offer I couldn't refuse," he deadpanned. "They had a younger guy in the wings, for about half my salary and none of my benefits..."

†Leveraged buy-out.

Because you're a top businessman, you don't stop being a human being. Human frailties exist in the corporate world as they do outside. The top executive is the loneliest guy in the world because he can't talk confidentially to the board of directors. They expect him to be strong and know everything. They don't want a guy that's doubtful or weak. He can't talk to the people working for him because he's got a guy who'll say yes to anything he says and the other guy wants his job. So he doesn't have anybody to talk to. So he becomes insecure and makes the decisions covering his ass.

The board of directors will never take the blame. They're heads of big corporations and don't have time to spend on this particular one. It's more or less a social thing.

With fewer companies, the tension is at its greatest in fifty years. There's a joke that someday there will be one manufacturing and one retailing concern. The retailer will say to the manufacturer, "I don't like your line." And the business dies. There used to be a business saying: "Eighty-twenty." Eighty percent of your volume comes from twenty percent of your customers. Eighty percent of the work is done by twenty percent of the workers. Today I think it's changed to ninety-five-five. Today, Wal-Mart, K-Mart, Target, Service Merchandise. People aren't buying less. There are as many places to buy, but they're controlled by fewer people.

15 Youngsters are coming up now and want a crack at the big jobs. In the old days, to become president of a company, top man, you had to be in your fifties and sixties. Today, you've got CEOs that are thirty-seven years old, twenty-nine. When I started out in the jungle, you were considered a baby at forty-one.

Also, there's a new way of doing business. A lot of older people didn't keep up with the modern ways. It's difficult, too, because computers are running the world. Yet people are still vigorous at seventy, seventy-five.

Ageism is a tremendous problem today. Investment bankers will tell you they're very uncomfortable with old people running anything. Business analysts don't give a good rating if a seventy-five-year-old guy is running the company. What the hell, he's going to die any minute, a change in management, an upset. It starts getting dangerous at sixty, sixty-five.

A guy was saying the other day, "You people on Medicare are making it awful tough. The costs are unbelievable." There is that feeling: taxes wouldn't be so high if it weren't for the old geezers.

As for me, if I didn't work, I'd deteriorate and die. My doctor tells me to keep active, keep your brain going, keep your body going. Some people my age have hobbies—painting, gardening. That keeps them alive. Unfortunately, I'm not one of these. I love golf, I love swimming, but that doesn't stimulate the mind. I need something else.

20 Power, age, greed. These are human qualities. They don't disappear when you become a CEO. Having the telephone constantly ring, all the perks, people catering to you, asking your opinions, asking you on boards. It's very flattering and ego-building. Many of the top executives start to believe their publicity and

think they walk on water. Many of the business failures today are the result of top executives feeling that they walk with God.

People of my age are a lost generation. What's left for him to do if he's not creating? Every businessman feels he's doing something creative. What the hell are you alive for? It's nice being a great father and a great grandfather—but they're a different generation, your kids, no matter how close you are to them. I don't know what's to be done.

We're living longer and we're cursed with such things as Alzheimer's, heart attacks, and strokes. That's the great fear with us. But if you're busy running a business, you don't sit around and think about your sicknesses. You have this big struggle not to deteriorate. When you create and contribute, you feel marvelous.

One of the nice things at this age is the luxurious morning. Before, you had to get up, get out, get going. Now, I can lay around, read the paper, *Wall Street Journal*, trade magazines, take my time with breakfast, go over the mail. Then I talk on the phone, spend time with my investment counselor. If it's a nice day, play golf or find someone to have lunch with. I'll take long walks, walk the treadmill, swim at about four o'clock, and then I'm ready for dinner. [Pauses.] It sounds pretty dull.

Yeah, I get a little bored. The pain of being unneeded and unwanted is uncomfortable at every stage. There are some guys who are unneeded 100 percent of the day. That would drive me absolutely insane. There are some guys who play golf in the morning, play cards in the afternoon, go out for dinner at night, spend the summers here and winters in Florida or Palm Springs, do the same things there. I don't know how they live.

When you're CEO, people are always after you. [Snaps his fingers.] What are 25
we gonna do here? What are we gonna do there? What do you think about this guy? That guy? Mr. Culberg, so-and-so called and wants to have lunch with you at two o'clock. You're being wanted always. That ties in with being needed. That's a massive human desire.

When you're a CEO, my goodness, you're at the office at eight o'clock. You have meetings going on, correspondence, phone, this guy calls you, that guy calls you, planning for a board meeting, people problems, manufacturing problems. And they need somebody for a final decision.

Your social circle has diminished by the deaths. Mostly what's left of your social world are the widows. [Chuckles.] You read the obituaries by habit now.*

As for politics, I've become a cynical old man. I don't believe in miracles anymore. I don't believe anybody walks on water. It's kind of a hopeless feeling. There's a lot to be done, but I don't think it can ever be done because the people will never allow it. I don't think the human species has changed since it was created. The

*"I wake up in the morning and dust off my wits,
I grab the newspaper and read the obits.
If I'm not there, I know I'm not dead,
So I have a good breakfast and go back to bed."

From a turn-of-the-century parlor song

horrors of centuries ago are still happening today. What have we learned? The human failing. And the CEO is no different than the rest of us.

In my opinion, the world is in a worse mess than it's ever been. I know it's been said of every generation, but this time it's really true. I wasn't this cynical when I was younger. I thought we were helping save the world. I have no regrets for those feelings.

I envy the young their rage but not their future. I think they're in for some rough times. You see it in their daily lives. A small percentage of young executives will hit the top and make far more money than we did. But there will be far less opportunities for the majority. The great middle class is going to be less and less. There will be extreme wealth and extreme poverty. I hope I'm completely wrong. I'd be the happiest guy in the world, even if I'm not around. Personally, I look forward to some years of health, and when my time comes, to go immediately.

TRY THIS 8.13

Either:

Interview someone at least a generation older than you are about an event that took place before you were born. Make the interview the scene of your personal essay, and let the event emerge through the conversation and your reflections on it.

Or:

Conduct an interview, recording at least half an hour of question and answer. Make a transcript of the answers. Subject the transcript to the "quilting" process, cutting paragraphs apart and rearranging them to make a coherent whole. Strive to make this rearrangement a truer picture of the interviewee than the transcript itself presents. Will you need to restore some of the questions to accomplish this? Preface the resulting oral history with a paragraph describing the person and the scene.

TRY THIS 8.14

Write two pages about a vegetable. Let it characterize your neighborhood, your childhood, or your family.

ACCOMPLISHING A DRAFT

Choose among your writings so far the piece that seems most promising as creative nonfiction. Over the course of a few days add to what you already have in various ways: computer research, meditation and reflection, details of character, setting, dialogue, and so forth. Try a paragraph challenging your point. Add something illogical or only vaguely relevant—you can toss these later and they may spark an interesting idea. Then, using either the outline or the quilting method described in Chapter 7, rough out a draft. Try various beginnings: Begin with the most intense action, begin with a general statement, begin with dialogue, with setting. Which works best?

Creative Nonfiction Format

"Clean copy" is the first and very visible sign of the professional. Your manuscript should be carefully proofread, neatly printed or copied, and stapled or paper clipped in the upper left-hand corner. Your particular teacher, group leader, or editor may have format requirements. To cut copying costs, some teachers will ask you to omit a cover page, and/or to single space. Otherwise, title and author's name and address (or class identification) should appear on a cover page, and your name need appear only there. Page numbering can be done in the upper or lower center or right corner of the page.

Manuscripts should be double-spaced, with generous (approximately one inch) margins, on one side of 8 1/2 × 11-inch white paper. The first page of the essay should begin about one-third of the way down the page.

Copyrighting of literary manuscripts is not necessary—essays, stories, poems, and plays are, alas, rarely worth money enough to be attractive to thieves. If your work is published, the magazine or publisher will apply for copyright, and you will have a contract that specifies what rights belong to you.

Always keep a copy of your work.

ROUGHING IT

by Mark Twain

Creative Nonfiction 101
Prof. Becky Thatcher
Hannibal State University
October 15, 1872

1

My brother had just been appointed Secretary of Nevada Territory—an office of such majesty that it concentrated in itself the duties and dignities of Treasurer, Comptroller, Secretary of State, and Acting Governor in the Governor's absence. A salary of eighteen hundred dollars a year and the title of "Mr. Secretary" gave to the position an air of wild and imposing grandeur.

I was young and ignorant, and I envied my brother. I coveted his distinction and his financial splendor, but particularly and especially the long, strange journey he was going to make, and the curious new world he was going to explore. He was going to travel! I never had been away from home, and that word "travel" had a seductive charm for me. Pretty soon he would be hundreds and hundreds of miles away on the great plains and deserts, and among the mountains of the Far West, and would see buffaloes and Indians, and prairie dogs, and antelopes, and have all kinds of adventures, and may be get hanged or scalped, and have ever such a fine time.

9 CHAPTER

Fiction

- *Story and Plot*
- *Scene and Summary*
- *Backstory and Flashback*
- *Text and Subtext*
- *Fiction Format*

The writer of any work . . . must decide two crucial points: what to put in and what to leave out.
Annie Dillard

Andrew Fox/Corbis/Corbis

WARM-UP
Whose scooter is this? Where is he? She? Who is that across the street? What happens next? What's the story? Tell it in exactly 250 words.

YOU HAVE A STORY TO WRITE. YOU HAVE A CHARACTER IN mind. The character has a desire. A situation presents itself. That the situation will lead to fulfillment of the desire is possible, but uncertain. How do you proceed?

Aristotle, the Greek philosopher who was also the first critic in Western literature, famously said that a story must have a beginning, a middle, and an end. This is less obvious than it looks. As the author, the questions you must answer are: Where shall I begin? Where will I end? What is in between? When you have made these decisions, you have made a choice between *story* and *plot*.

Story and Plot

Humphry House, in his commentaries on Aristotle, defines **story** as everything the reader needs to know to make coherent sense of the plot, and **plot** as the particular portion of the story the author chooses to present—the "present tense" of the narrative.

The story of *Oedipus Rex,* for example, begins before Oedipus's birth, with the oracle predicting that he will murder his father and marry his mother. It includes his birth, his abandonment with hobbled ankles, his childhood with his foster parents, his flight from them, his murder of the stranger at the crossroads, his triumph over the Sphinx, his marriage to Jocasta and his reign in Thebes, his fatherhood, the Theban plague, his discovery of the truth, and his self-blinding and self-banishment.

When Sophocles set out to plot a play on this story, he began the action at dawn on the very last day of it. All the information about Oedipus's life is necessary to understand the plot, but the plot begins with the conflict: How can Oedipus get rid of the plague in Thebes? Because the plot is so arranged, it is the revelation of the past that makes up the action of the play, a process of discovery that gives rise to the significant theme: Who am I? Had Sophocles begun with the oracle before Oedipus's birth, no such theme and no such significance could have been explored.

E. M. Forster, in *Aspects of the Novel,* makes substantially the same distinction between plot and story. A story, he says, is:

> ...the chopped off length of the tape worm of time...a narrative of events arranged in their time sequence. A plot is also a narrative of events, the emphasis falling on causality. "The king died, and then the queen died," is a story. "The king died, and then the queen died of grief," is a plot. The time sequence is preserved, but the sense of causality overshadows it. Or again: "The queen died, no one knew why, until it was discovered that it was through grief at the death of the king." This is a plot with a mystery in it, a form capable of high development. It suspends the time sequence; it moves as far away from the story as its limitations will allow. Consider the death of the queen. If it is in a story we say, "and then?" If it is in a plot we ask, "why?"

The human desire to know why is as powerful as the desire to know what happened next, and it is a desire of a higher order. Once we have the facts, we inevitably look for the links between them, and only when we find such links are we satisfied that we "understand." Rote memorization in a science bores almost everyone. Grasp and a sense of discovery begin only when we perceive *why* "a body in motion tends to remain in motion" and what an immense effect this actuality has on the phenomena of our lives.

The same is true of the events of a story. Random incidents neither move nor illuminate; we want to know why one thing leads to another and to feel the inevitability of cause and effect.

Arranging for Plot

A *story* is a series of events recorded in their chronological order. A *plot* is a series of events deliberately arranged so as to reveal their dramatic, thematic, and emotional significance.

Here, for example, is a series of uninteresting events chronologically arranged.

Ariadne had a bad dream.
She woke up tired and cross.
She ate breakfast.
She headed for class.
She saw Leroy.
She fell on the steps and broke her ankle.
Leroy offered to take notes for her.
She went to a hospital.

This series of events does not constitute a plot, and if you wish to fashion it into a plot, you can do so only by letting us know the meaningful relations among the events. We first assume that Ariadne woke in a temper because of her bad dream, and that Leroy offered to take notes for her because she broke her ankle. But why did she fall? Perhaps because she saw Leroy? Does that suggest that her bad dream was about him? Was she, then, thinking about his dream-rejection as she broke her egg irritably on the edge of the frying pan? What is the effect of his offer? Is it a triumph or just another polite form of rejection when, really, he could have missed class once to drive her to the X-ray lab? All the emotional and dramatic significance of these ordinary events emerges in the relation of cause to effect, and where such relation can be shown, a possible plot comes into existence.

Ariadne's is a story you might very well choose to tell chronologically. It needs to cover only an hour or two, and that much can be handled in the compressed form of the short story. But such a choice of plot is not inevitable even in this short compass. Might it be more gripping to begin with the wince of pain as she stumbles? Leroy comes to help her up and the yolk yellow of his T-shirt fills her field of vision. In the shock of pain she is immediately back in her dream....

Choosing Where to Begin

Here is another example of a quite standard story: A girl grows up bossed by her older sister, who always tells her she's fat and a nerd. She ends up with "low self-esteem," poor grades, and a stutter. She has "social anxiety"; she stays at her computer most of the time. Her mother takes her to a series of therapists, but nothing brings her out of her shell. She's not asked to the big basketball dance, and won't go alone, but on the night of the game the computer system that runs the gym lighting breaks down, and the coach, who knows she's a computer whiz, gives her a call. She fixes the program and catches the eye of the handsome Center (who probably takes off her glasses and lets down her hair, right?). And they live happily ever after.

This Cinderella story line shows up over and over again in film and print. The question is, how can you make it fresh and interesting? Where should your *plot* begin?

You may start, if you like, with the immigration of the heroine's grandparents from Lithuania. But if you do, it's going to be a very long story and we may close the book before she's born. You may begin it, like your childhood tale of Cinderella, with the background situation of the family, but then you must summarize, generalize, and focus on minor characters; and you may have a hard time holding our attention. Begin with the announcement of the dance? Better. If so, you'll somehow have to let us know all that has gone before, either through dialogue or through the girl's memory; but you have only a few days to cover and you have an opportunity to show the sisters in conflict. Suppose you begin with the telephone call from the coach? Is that perhaps best of all? An urgent dramatic scene, an immediate conflict that must lead to a quick and striking crisis?

TRY THIS 9.1

By now you have from your journal entries an idea for a short story. Take fifteen minutes to list all the events of this story in their chronological order. List *everything* we will need to know in order to make sense of it. If Seth's fear of water results from the time his cruel half-brother held him under when he was five—and we will need to know this in order to understand why he won't go out in a boat at twenty—then list the bullying incident in its chronological place.

- Find the item exactly halfway down your list. Write the first paragraph of your story beginning it there.
- Take the last item on your list. Write the first paragraph of the story beginning it there.
- Pick the *right* item on your list for the beginning of the story. Try these: Begin with a line of dialogue. Begin with an action. Begin with an image of danger. Begin with the weather. Begin with the protagonist's thought. Begin with a long shot. Begin with a closeup.

It is a cliché of critical reaction—and not just for the work of beginners!—that "your story actually begins on page three." I think there is good reason that this failure of technique afflicts even professional writers. When you begin a story you are very properly feeling your way, getting to know your characters, bringing the setting into focus, testing the sorts of voice and action that will work. Since you're a little unsteady on your literary feet at this point, it's tempting to fiddle with the dialogue, alter this phrase, perfect that image. The writing, thus polished, starts to look valuable—so it's hard to see that the reader doesn't need the same extended orientation that you did. Sometimes you need a few weeks' distance, or somebody else's insight, to recognize that you can move farther faster.

TRY THIS 9.2

Take the manuscript you worked on in Try This 9.1. Toss out page one. Try beginning with the first whole paragraph on page two. Doesn't work?

Then:

Condense the first three pages to a paragraph. How much of the lost information can, in fact, be done without?

Scene and Summary

A child in a tantrum screams, throws toys, lies on the floor, and kicks in the air. The parents say, "You're making a scene!"

Jerome Stern

Summary and **scene** are methods of treating time in fiction. A summary covers a relatively long period of time in relatively short compass; a scene deals at length with a relatively short period of time.

Summary is a useful and often necessary device: to give information, fill in a character's background, let us understand a motive, alter pace, create a transition, leap moments or years.

Scene is *always* necessary to fiction. Scene is to time what concrete detail is to the senses; that is, it is the crucial means of allowing your reader to experience the story with the characters. A confrontation, a turning point, or a crisis occurs at given moments that take on significance as moments and cannot be summarized. The form of a story requires confrontation and change, and therefore requires scenes. As Jerome Stern points out in *Making Shapely Fiction,* when you want everyone's full attention you "make a scene" like a child in a tantrum, using the writer's full complement of "dialogue, physical reactions, gestures, smells, sounds, and thoughts."

It is quite possible to write a short story in a single scene, without any summary at all. It is not possible to write a successful story entirely in summary. One of the most common errors beginning fiction writers make is to summarize events rather than to realize them as moments.

One quite common and effective technique in fiction is to orient us with a short summary and then move to a scene when the action begins. In the following paragraphs from Margaret Atwood's *Lady Oracle*, the narrator has been walking home from her Brownie troop meeting with older girls who tease and terrify her with threats of a bad man.

> The snow finally changed to slush and then to water, which trickled down the hill of the bridge in two rivulets, one on either side of the path; the path itself turned to mud. The bridge was damp, it smelled rotten, the willow branches turned yellow, the skipping ropes came out. It was light again in the afternoons, and on one of them, when for a change Elizabeth hadn't run off but was merely discussing the possibilities with the others, a real man actually appeared.
>
> He was standing at the far side of the bridge, a little off the path, holding a bunch of daffodils in front of him. He was a nice-looking man, neither old nor young, wearing a good tweed coat, not at all shabby or disreputable. He didn't have a hat on, his taffy-colored hair was receding and the sunlight gleamed on his high forehead.

The first paragraph of this quotation covers the way things changed over a period of a few months and then makes a transition to one of the afternoons; the second paragraph specifies a particular moment. Notice that although summary sets us at a distance from the action, sensory details remain necessary to its life: *snow, path, bridge, willow branches, skipping ropes.* The scene is introduced when an element of conflict and confrontation occurs. That the threatened bad man does appear and that he is surprisingly innocuous promises a turn of events and a change in the relationship among the girls. We need to see the moment when this change occurs.

Throughout *Lady Oracle,* which is by no means unusual in this respect, the pattern recurs: a summary leading up to, and followed by, a scene that represents a turning point.

> My own job was fairly simple. I stood at the back of the archery range, wearing a red leather change apron, and rented out the arrows. When the barrels of arrows were almost used up, I'd go down to the straw targets. The difficulty was that we couldn't make sure all the arrows had actually been shot before we went down to clear the targets. Rob would shout, Bows DOWN, please, arrows OFF the string, but occasionally someone would let an arrow go, on purpose or by accident. This was how I got shot. We'd pulled the arrows and the men were carrying the barrels back to the line; I was replacing a target face, and I'd just bent over.

The summary in the second excerpt describes the general circumstances during a period of time—this is how things were, this is what usually or frequently happened: *I'd go down to the straw targets. Rob would shout.* Again, when the narrator arrives at an event that changes her circumstance (*I got shot*), she focuses on a particular moment: *I was replacing a target face, and I'd just bent over.* Notice that the pattern summary-to-scene parallels in time the spatial pattern of long shot-to-close-up.

Since the changes in your story will take place in fully developed scenes, it's important to limit the *number* of scenes, and summary can be useful to get you from one to another. Frequently, the function of summary is precisely to heighten scene. It is in the scene, the "present" of the story, that the drama, the discovery, the decision, the potential for change, engage our attention.

TRY THIS 9.3

Look at the list of your story's events. How many of them belong in summary? How *few* scenes would it be possible to use and still tell the story? Those three dinners with dad—could they be conflated to one? The quarrel on the morning after—could it happen the same night? Which of them involve moments of discovery or decision and should be scenes? List the events of the story that represent its essential scenes.

Pick a scene and write it quickly, in no more than two pages. Then rewrite it beginning with a method or a mood you've never used before. Begin with a cliché. Begin with a line of angry dialogue. Begin tenderly. Begin with an action no bigger than a breadbox. Begin with the outcome of the scene and then go back to get us there.

In Chapter 6, I said that the crisis point of a story must always be manifested in an action. Another way of saying this is that the crisis is always a scene. At the moment the protagonist's situation will change, we as readers must *be there.* What is important about this crisis action is not that it be violent or even external, but that its intensity signal a turning point in the character's fortune or outlook. Often, the intensity of the moment will require that all the senses come into play.

Consider, for example, David Foster Wallace's "Incarnations of Burned Children," (p. 180–182). This story is written entirely at a high pitch of emotion. Nevertheless there comes a moment that irrevocably seals the outcome:

> "...and leaned their little boy back on the checkered cloth and unfastened the softened tabs and tried to remove it resisted slightly with new high cries and was hot, their baby's diaper burned their hand and they saw where the real water'd fallen and pooled and been burning their baby boy all this time...."

The tragedy here has been going on all along, but "they saw" presents us with the moment of terrible discovery, after which the parents can feel nothing other than shame and grief.

TRY THIS 9.4

Identify the crisis of the story you are working on. Describe that moment with details involving at least three senses.

Backstory and Flashback

Clearly, if you are going to begin *in medias res* (in the middle of the action), then parts of your story will have to be brought in later. **Backstory** is a relatively new term, which started out in film meaning a *prequel,* but has come to refer to any information about the past—whatever has occurred before the plot begins and is necessary to make the story coherent. Such information can be revealed in dialogue, or in the character's thoughts, or in the narrative itself. When the narrative actually travels back from its current action to depict the past in scenes, it is called a **flashback**—also a term borrowed from film.

There is, I think, one cardinal rule about the past in fiction: don't give us more than we need. As with opening paragraphs, so with backstory: As the author you need to know so much about your characters in order to make them real and complex that you may think we readers need to know just as much. But if your characters are interesting and credible, we probably don't. Especially in the twenty-first century—accustomed to the quick cuts of film, inundated with the lessons of psychology—we will understand causal connections, accept odd behavior, and tolerate a degree of inconsistency without needing a whole lot of psychological explanation. On the other hand, our primal desire to get on with the story is as powerful as it was around the prehistoric campfire, and we are likely to be impatient with too much background information.

When intrusive passages of childhood, motivation, and explanation tend to come early in the story, before we are caught up in the action, we wonder whether there is any story on its way. Dialogue, brief summary, a reference, or a detail can often tell us all we need to know, and when that is the case, a flashback becomes cumbersome and overlong. If, four pages into your story, you find there is more action happening in the character's memory than in the present action, you may not yet have found where the story lies.

TRY THIS 9.5

Find a place in your story where you either do or could use a flashback. Instead, use your journal for exploring background. Write down everything, fast. Then take a hard look at it to decide just how little of it you can use, how much of it the reader can infer, how you can sharpen an image to imply a past incident or condense an emotion into a line of dialogue.

Frequently it's best to trust the reader's experience of life to understand events from action and attitude, and to keep the present of the story moving.

That said, flashback is still one of the most magical of fiction's contrivances. Effectively used to *reveal* at the *right time*, it does not so much take us from, as contribute to, the central action of the story, so that as readers we suspend the forward motion of the narrative in our minds as our understanding of it deepens. Because the reader's mind is a swifter mechanism for getting into the past than anything that has been devised for stage or even film, all you must do is give the reader smooth passage into the past, and the force of the story will be time-warped to whenever and wherever you want it.

A connection between what's happening in the present and what happened in the past will often best transport the reader, just as it does the character. Where possible avoid blatant transitions such as "Henry thought back to the time," and "I drifted back in memory." Assume the reader's intelligence and ability to follow a leap back, as in this excerpt from Nadine Gordimer's *July's People*, where the protagonist and her husband Bamford have escaped an African uprising to hide in the village of their former servant:

> The black man looked over the three sleeping children bedded-down on seats taken from the vehicle. He smiled confirmation: "They all right."
>
> "Yes, all right." As he dipped out under the doorway: "Thank you, July, thank you very much."
>
> She had slept in round mud huts roofed in thatch like this before. In the Kruger Park, a child of the shift boss and his family on leave, an enamel basin and ewer among their supplies of orange squash and biscuits on the table coming clear as this morning light came. Rondavels, adapted by Bam's ancestors on his Boer side from the huts of the blacks. They were a rusticism true to the continent; before air-conditioning, everyone praised the natural insulation of thatch against heat. Rondavels had concrete floors, thickly shined with red polish, veined with trails of coarse ants....

Here both a memory from her childhood and a historical vignette, each sketched with a few details, points up the irony of her situation without impeding the flow of the narrative.

When you end a flashback, make it clear that you are catching up to the present again. Repeat an action or image that the reader will remember belongs to the basic time period of the story. Often simply beginning the paragraph with "Now..." will accomplish the reorientation. Gordimer accomplishes it by returning from the general to the specific hut:

> This one was a prototype from which all the others had come and to which all returned: below her, beneath the iron bed on whose rusty spring they had spread the vehicle's tarpaulin, a stamped mud and dung floor....

TRY THIS 9.6

Put your character in motion, on foot or in a vehicle, in urgent search of something. What does he or she need? Why so urgently? Let us know in a flashback of no more than three sentences. Avoid the words *remembered, recalled, thought back to,* and others of their ilk.

Add a character. In dialogue, let us know some important thing from the past.

Add music. Let the music trigger a memory good or bad, in thought or dialogue. Let the memory reveal something we didn't know before, in no more than two sentences.

Text and Subtext

As a writer you are always trying to mean more than you say. You want dialogue to convey information and character, you want setting to convey mood and propel the action, you want clothing to indicate politics, and gesture to betray thought.

You can do this, and your reader can understand it, because people operate this way in their daily lives. We express ourselves in many ways besides words, sometimes by choice and sometimes in self-betrayal, sometimes trying to conceal for the sake of friendship and sometimes in fear or contempt. How many times have you sat through a meal in which the dialogue was all polite, anecdotal, and bland, but everybody was *desperate* with boredom, anger, anxiety, or the need to control?

The *text* is what is stated in any situation; the *subtext* is whatever remains unstated—with the usual implication that the unstated is what's really going on.

Imagine a restaurant scene in which Bill asks his friend Lex to pass the shrimp. Lex passes them by way of his wife, Sara, who takes a handful on the way. There are none left for Bill's wife, Jane, who says she didn't want any more anyway. Imagine how the dialogue, gestures, glances, facial expressions, tones of voice differ in this scene if Lex suspects that Bill is having an affair with Sara; and/or Jane is pregnant, which Sara knows but her husband doesn't; and/or Jane feels herself to be superior to the rest of them, including her husband; and/or Sara and Lex had a quarrel just before they left home in which Lex accused her of selfishness; and/or Jane is trying to get home early to intercept a phone call from Bill's mother, who may have cancer; and/or Bill wrote a report that he suspects will get Lex fired. Any combination of these complications probably means that all four of them are sick of the friendship anyway, and looking for a way to end it. Yet they may not. Situations of this complexity occur every day.

Here is a passage from Barbara Kingsolver's *Poisonwood Bible,* in which an American Baptist minister and his family sit with a Bantu council in the Belgian Congo:

> Father tried to interrupt the proceedings by loudly explaining that Jesus is exempt from popular elections. But people were excited, having just recently got the hang of democratic elections. The citizens of Kilanga were ready to cast their stones....

Anatole, who'd sat down in his chair a little distance from the pulpit, leaned over and said quietly to Father, "They say you thatched your roof and now you must not run out of your house if it rains."

Father ignored this parable. "Matters of the spirit are not decided at the marketplace," he shouted sternly. Anatole translated.

"*Á bu, kwe?* Where, then?" asked Tat Nguza, standing up boldly. In his opinion, he said, a white man who has never even killed a bushbuck for his family was not the expert on which god can protect our village.

When Anatole translated that one, Father looked taken aback. Where we come from, it's hard to see the connection.

Father spoke slowly, as if to a half-wit, "Elections are good, and Christianity is good. Both are good." We in his family recognized the danger in his extremely calm speech, and the rising color creeping toward his hairline.

In this passage, while a controlled form of political negotiation goes on, the participants vie for status, and we have a dozen or more clues to the political and personal subtext. The contrast between the Congolese's parables and the American's abstractions, the conflicting logic, the gestures, bodily movements and expressions, the genuine calm of the translator as opposed to the bottled-fury calm of the father—all these reveal the unspoken meanings. In addition, they are interpreted through the point of view of a daughter who, in spite of her youth and relative innocence, has reason to understand the signs.

TRY THIS 9.7

Choose three characters from your story-in-progress and put them in a scene where they must decide on a name for something (a pet, a brochure, a dessert, a building...) Write the dialogue and their actions, in play form if you like, because this scene will probably not find its way into your story, but it will help you identify their attitudes and feelings toward each other.

Subtext is a necessary result and cost of civilization—if everyone went around saying what they meant all the time there would be fewer friends and a lot more pain—but it offers a glorious opportunity for art. When your characters let us know by action, tone, thought, gesture, hesitation, slip of the tongue, contradiction, or backtracking that they are leaving an iceberg's worth of the truth submerged, the reader reads their truth as well as the words.

TRY THIS 9.8

All of the following are the opening lines of published short stories, some of them famous. Pick one and write the first few paragraphs of a story. Write fast.

- The house was all wrong for them.
- It was Sunday—not a day, but rather a gap between two other days.

- Mother says that when I start talking I never know when to stop.
- During my holidays from school, I was allowed to stay in bed until long after my father left for work.
- I have a photo of a man whose name I don't know.
- Jane's husband, Martin, works for the fire department.
- He had no body hair.
- I read about it in the paper, in the subway, on my way to work.

More to Read

Gardner, John. *The Art of Fiction.* New York: Vintage Books, 1991. Print.
Stern, Jerome. *Making Shapely Fiction.* New York: W.W. Norton, 2000. Print.

READINGS

AMY BLOOM

The Story

You wouldn't have known me a year ago.

A year ago I had a husband, and my best friend was Margeann at the post office. In no time at all my husband got cancer, house prices tumbled in our part of Connecticut, and I got a new best friend. Realtors' signs came and went in front of the house down the road: from the elegant forest green-and-white FOR SALE BY OWNER, nicely handmade to show that they were in no hurry and in no need, to MARTHA BRAE LEWIS AND COMPANY, realtors who sold only very expensive houses and rode horses in the middle of the day when there was nothing worthwhile on the market and then down, down to the big national relocator company's fiberboard sign practically shouting, "Fire Sale, You Can Have This House for Less Than They Paid for It." My place was nothing special compared to my neighbor's, but it did have the big stained-glass windows Ethan had made, so beautiful, sightseers drove right up our private road, parked by the birches, and begged to come in, just to stand there in the rays of purple and green light, to be charmed by twin redheaded mermaids flanking the front door, to run their fingers over the cobalt blue drops sprayed across the hall, bezel set into the plaster. They stood between the cantering cinnabar legs of the centaur in the middle of the kitchen wall and sighed. After coffee and cookies they would order two windows or six or, one time, wild with real estate money, people from Gramercy Park ordered a dozen botanical panels for their new house in Madison, and Ethan always said, "Why do you do that?" I did it for company and for money, since I needed both and Ethan didn't care. When he asked for the mail, without looking up, or even when he made the effort to ask about my bad knee, not noticing that we'd last spoken two full days ago, it was worse than the quiet. If I didn't ask the New Yorkers for money, he'd shuffle around in his moccasins, picking at his nails until they made an insulting offer or got back in their cars, baffled and rich.

Six months after Ethan caught cancer like a terrible cold and died; I went just once to the Unitarian widows group in which all the late husbands were much nicer than mine had been and even the angriest woman only said, "Goddamn his smoking," and I thought, His smoking? Almost all that I liked about Ethan was his stained glass, his small, wide hands, and the fact that he was willing to marry Plain Jane me when I thought no one would, and willing to stay by me when I lost the baby. That was such a bad time I didn't leave the house for two months and Ethan invited the New Yorkers in just to get me out of bed. Other than that, I only thought that if you didn't hate your silent, moody husband after twenty years, and he didn't seem to hate you and your big blob of despair, you could call it a good thing, no worse than other marriages. That last month was like the honeymoon we never took, and when strangers talk to me now, I sound like a woman who lost her beloved and grieves still.

I have dead parents—the best kind, I think, at this stage of life—two sisters, whom I do love at a little distance, a garden that is as close to God as I need it to be, and a book group I've been in for fourteen years, which also serves as mastectomy hot line, menopause watch, and PFLAG. I don't mind being alone, having been raised by hard-drinking, elderly parents, a German and a Swede, with whom I never had a fight or a moment's pleasure, and I took off for college at sixteen, with no idea of what to say to these girls with outerwear for every season (fall coats and spring jackets and pale blue anoraks) and underwear that was nicer than my church clothes. Having made my own plain, dark way, and having been with plain, dark but talented Ethan such a long time, I've been pleasantly surprised in middle age, to have yoga and gardening for my soul, and bookkeeping to pay the bills. Clearly, my whole life was excellent training for money managing of all kinds, and now I do the books for twenty people like Ethan, gifted and without a clear thought in their heads about organizing their finances or feeding their families, if they're lucky enough to have more than a tiny profit to show for what they do.

5 I didn't call my new neighbors the Golddust Twins. Margeann, our postmaster, called them that. She nicknamed all the New Yorkers, and preread their magazines and kept the catalogues that most appealed to her. Tallblondgorgeous, she said. And gobs of money, she said. Just gobs of money, and Mr. Golddust had a little sense but she had none and they had a pretty little blond baby who would grow up to be hell on wheels if the mother didn't stop giving her Coca-Cola at nine in the morning and everything else she asked for. And they surely needed a bookkeeper, Margeann said, because Doctor Mrs. Golddust was a psychiatrist and he did something mysterious in the import and export of art. I could tell, just

from that, that they would need me, the kind of bookkeeper and accountant and paid liar who could call black white and look you straight in the eye. I put my business card in their mailbox, which they (I assumed she) had covered in bits of fluorescent tile, making a rowdy little work of art, and they called me that night. She invited themselves over for coffee on Sunday morning.

"Oh my God, this house is gorgeous. Completely charming. And that stained glass. You are a genius, Mrs. Baker. Mrs.? Not Ms.? Is Janet all right? This is unbelievable. Oh my God. And your garden. Unbelievable. Miranda, don't touch the art. Let Mommy hold you up to the light. Like a fairy story."

Sam smiled and put out his hand, my favorite kind of male hand, what I would call shapely peasant, auburn hairs on the first joint of each finger and just a little ginger patch on the back. His hands must have been left over from early Irish farmers; the rest of him looked right out of a magazine.

"I know I'm carrying on, but I can't help it. Sam, darlingdarling, please take Miranda so Janet and I can just explore for two minutes."

We walked out to the centauries, and she brushed her long fingers against their drooping blue fringe.

"Can I touch? I'm not much of a gardener. That card of yours was just a gift from God. Not just because of the bookkeeping, but because I wanted to meet you after I saw you in town. I don't think you saw me. At the Dairy Mart."

I had seen her, of course.

"Sam, Janet has forgiven me for being such a loony. Maybe she'll help us out of our financial morass."

Sam smiled and scooped Miranda up just before she smacked into the coffee table corner. He said he would leave the two of us to it and any help at all would be better than what he had currently. He pressed my hands together in his and put two files between them, hard clear plastic with "MoBay Exports, Incorporated" embossed across the front and a manila folder with stationery from Dr. Sandra Saunders sticking out of it. I sent them away with blueberry jam and a few begonia cuttings. Coming from New York, she thought any simple thing you could do in a garden was wonderful.

Sandra called, "I can tell Miranda's fallen in love with you. Could you possibly watch her tomorrow? Around five? Just for a half hour? Sam has to go to the city."

After two tantrums, juice instead of Coke, stories instead of videos, and no to her organdy dress for playing in the sandbox, it was seven o'clock, then eight. I gave Miranda dinner and a bath. She was, in fact, a very sweet child, and I thought that her mother, like mine, meant well but seemed not to have what was called for. When Sandra came home, Miranda ran to her but looked out between her legs and blew me a kiss.

"Say 'We love you, Janet,'" Sandra said.

"We love you, Jah-net."

"Say 'Please come tomorrow for drinks, Janet.'"

Miranda sighed. "Drinks, Jah-net," she said, indulgently.

20 I kissed them both good-bye. I had never had such fresh, sweet skin under my lips, Miranda's peach and Sandra's apricots-and-cream moisturizer, and although I wasn't attracted to women or girls, I could see why a person would be.

I planted a small square garden near Sam's studio, sweet William and campanula and Violet Queen asters with a little rosemary bonsai that Miranda could put her pinkie-sized plastic babies around. Sandra was gone more than Sam was. He worked in the converted barn with computers and screens and two faxes and four phone lines, and every time I visited, he brought me a cup of tea and admired our latest accomplishments.

He said, "It's very good of you to do this."

"I don't mind," I said.

"We could always get a sitter," he said, but he knew I knew that wasn't true, because I had done their books.

25 Can I say that the husband was not any kind of importer? Can I say that he was what he really was, a successful cartoonist? That they lived right behind me, in a house I still find too big and too showy, even now that I am in it?

I haven't even described the boyfriend, the one Sandra went off to canoodle with while I baby-sat. Should I write him as tall and blond when in fact he was dark and muscular, like the husband? It will be too confusing for readers if both men are dark and fit, with long ponytails, but they both were. And they drove the same kind of truck, making for more confusion.

I've given them blandly wholesome, modern names, wishing for the days of Aunt Ada Starkadder and Martin Chuzzlewit and Pompeo Lagunima. Sam's real name conveys more of his rather charming shy stiffness and rectitude, but I keep "Sam," which has the advantage of suggesting an unlikely, misleading blend of Jewish and New England, and I'll call the boyfriend "Joe," suggesting a general good-natured lunkishness. Sandra, as I've named her, actually was a therapist, just as I've written her, but not a psychiatrist, and I disliked her so much, I can't bear to make you think, even in this story, that she had the discipline and drive and intellectual persistence to become a physician. She had nothing but appetite and brass balls, and she was the worst mother I ever saw. Even now, I regard her destruction as a very good thing, which may undermine the necessary fictive texture of deep ambiguity, the roiling ambivalence that gives tension to the narrator's affection.

Sandy pinched her child for not falling asleep quickly enough; she gave her potato chips for breakfast and Slurpees for lunch; she cut her daughter's hair with pinking shears and spent two hundred dollars she didn't have on her own monthly Madison Avenue haircuts. She left that child in more stores than I can remember, cut cocaine on her changing table, and blamed the poor little thing for every disappointment and heartache in her own life, until Miranda's eyes welled up at the sound of her mother calling her name. And if Sandy was not evil, she was worse than foolish, and sick, and, more to the point, incurable. If Sandra were smooshed inside a wrecked car splattered against the inside of a tunnel, I wouldn't feel even so sad for her as I did for Princess Diana, for whom I felt very little indeed.

I think the opening works, and the part about the widows group is true, although I've left out the phone call I got a week after the group met, when the nicest widow, an oversized Stockard Channing, invited me to a dinner with unmistakable overtones and I didn't go. I wish I had gone; that dinner and its aftermath might make a better story than this one I've been fooling with.

I don't want to leave out the time Sandra got into a fistfight with Joe's previous girlfriend, who knocked Sandra down into the middle of her own potato salad at the Democrats annual picnic, or the time Joe broke into the former marital home after Sandra moved out and threw Sam's library into the fire, not realizing that he was also destroying Sandra's collection of first editions. And when he was done, drunk and sweating, I sat on my porch, watching through my late husband's binoculars ("Ethan" is very much my late husband, a sculptor, not a glassmaker, but correct in the essentials of character; my husband wasn't dead before I met them; he died a year later, and Sam was very kind and Sandra was her usual charming, useless self). I saw Joe trip on little Miranda's Fisher-Price roller skate and slide down the ravine. I went to sleep, and when Sam called me the next day, laughing and angry, watching an ambulance finally come up his long gravel drive and the EMTs put splints all over Joe the Boyfriend, I laughed too and brought over corn chowder and my own rye bread for Sam and Miranda.

I don't have any salt-of-the-earth-type friends like Margeann. Margeanns are almost always crusty and often black and frequently given to pungent phrases and earth wisdom. Sometimes, they're someone's grandmother. In men's stories they're either old and disreputable drinking buddies, someone's tobacco-chewing, trout-fishing grandpaw, or the inexplicably devoted sidekick-of-color, caustic and true.

My friends in real life are two other writers—the movie critic for our nearest daily newspaper and a retired home-and-garden freelancer I've been playing tennis with for twenty years. Estelle, my tennis buddy, has more the character of the narrator than I do, and I thought I could use her experience with Sandra to make a story line. Sandra had sprinkled her psychobabble all over poor Estelle, got her coming three times a week, cash on the table, and had almost persuaded her to leave Dev, her very nice husband, in order to "explore her full potential." Estelle's entire full potential is to be the superb and good-natured tennis partner she is, a gifted gardener (which is where I got all that horticultural detail), and a poor cook and worse housekeeper for an equally easygoing, rosy-cheeked man who inherited two million dollars when he was fifty and about whom I can say nothing worse than at eighty-three Dev's not quite as sharp as he was—although he's nicer. I could not imagine how else Estelle's full potential, at seventy-seven, with cataracts in her left eye, bad hearing, and not the least interest in art, theater, movies, or politics, would express itself. I persuaded Dev to take her on a fancy cruise, two weeks through the canals of France, and when they came back, beaming pinkly, a little chubby, and filled with lively remarks about French bread and French cheese, Estelle said nothing more about her underdeveloped potential and nothing more about meeting with Sandra.

I see that I've made Sam sound more affably dodgy than he really is. He wouldn't have caught my eye in the first place if he was no more than the cardboard charmer I describe, and he was tougher than Joe, in the end. Even if Sandra hadn't been a bad mother, I might have imagined a complex but rosy future with Sam and Miranda, if I was capable of imagining my future.

I don't know what made Sandra think I would be her accomplice. If you are thin and blondly pretty and used to admirers, maybe you see them wherever there are no rivals. But, hell, I read the ladies' magazines and drove all the way to Westport for a new haircut and spent money on clothes, and although she didn't notice that I was coming over in silk knit T-shirts and black jeans, Sam did. When Sandra called me, whispering from Joe's bed, "Ohmigod, make something up, I lost track of time," I didn't. I walked over with dinner for Sam and Miranda, and while Miranda sat in front of her computer, I said, "I'm a bad liar. Sandra called from Joe's. She asked me to make something up, but I can't."

There is no such thing as a good writer and a bad liar.

After she moved out, she called me most mornings, just to report on the night before. She was in heaven. Joe was wonderful in every way but terribly jealous of Sam. Very silly, of course. Very flattering.

I called Joe in the late afternoons. I said, "Oh, Sandy's not there? Oh, of course." Joe was possibly the most easily led person God ever made. I didn't even have to drop a line, I just dangled it loosely and flicked. I said, "She's not at the office. She must be at home. I mean, at Sam's. It's great that they're getting along, for Miranda's sake. Honestly, I think they're better friends now that they're separated."

I did that twice a week, making up different reasons for calling. Joe hit her, once. She told me and I touched the round bruise on her jaw, begging her to press charges, but she didn't.

The part where Joe drove his truck into the back of Sam's house is too good to leave out, and tells funnier than it really was, although the rear end of his pickup sticking out through acres of grape arbor was pretty funny, as was the squish-squish of the grapes as Joe tried to extricate himself, and the smell of something like wine sweeping over us as he drove off, vines twirling around his tires.

I reported Sandy to the ethics committee of the Connecticut Association of Family Counselors. All the things she shouldn't have told me—how she did things in her office, and her financial arrangements with her patients, and the stock tips they gave her, and her insistence on being paid in cash in advance—and the fact that I, who was no kind of therapist at all, knew all these things and all their names, was enough to make them suspend her license for six months.

Sophisticated readers understand that writers work out their anger, their conflicts, their endless grief and rolling list of loss, through their stories. That however mean-spirited or diabolical, it's only a story. That the darkness in the soul is shaped into type and lies there, brooding and inert, black on the page but active, dangerous, only in the reader's mind. Actually, harmless. I am not harmless.

The story I had hoped to write would have skewered her, of course. Anyone who knew her would have read it, known it was her, and thought badly of her while reading. She would have been embarrassed and angry. That really was not what I had in mind. I wanted her skin like a rug on my floor, her slim throat slit, heart still beating behind the newly bricked-up wall. In stories, when someone behaves uncharacteristically, we know a meaningful, even pivotal, moment has come. If we are surprised too often, we either vacillate or just give up and close the book. In real life, when people think they know you, know you well enough not only to say, "It's Tuesday, she must be helping out at the library today," but well enough to have said to the librarian, after you've left the building, "You know, she just loves reading to the four-year-olds. I think it's been such a comfort to her since her little boy died"—when they know you like that, you can do almost any bad, secretive thing and if they hear about it, they will, as readers do, simply disbelieve the narrator.

I find that I have no sympathy with the women who have nannies, on top of baby sitters on top of beepers and pagers and party coordinators, or with the older ones who want to give back their damaged, distressing adopted children, or with the losers who sue to get their children back when they had given them to adequate and loving parents three years before. In my world, none of them would be allowed to be mothers, and if they had slipped through my licensing bureau, their children would be promptly removed and all traces of their maternal claims erased.

As Sandra's dear friend and reliable baby sitter, it was easy to hire Joe to do a little work on my front porch, easy to have him bump into my research assistant, the two of them as much alike as a pair of pretty quarter horses, easy to fuel Sandra's sudden wish to move farther out of town. Easy to send the ethics committee the information they needed to remove her license permanently, easy to suggest she manage Joe's business, easy to suggest that children need quality time not quantity, and that young, handsome lovers need both, easy to wave Sandra and Joe off in their new truck (easy to arrange a ten-thousand-dollar loan when you are such a steady customer of the local bank and own your home outright).

I can't say I didn't intend harm. I did and would not have minded even death, and if death is beyond my psychological reach, then disappearance, which is worse because it's not permanent but better, because there is no body.

And I am like a wife now to this lovely, appreciative man who thinks me devoted and kind, who teases me for trembling at dead robins on the patio, for crying openly at AT&T commercials. And I am like a mother to this girl as rapacious and charming and roughly loving as a lion cub. The whole house creaks with their love, and I walk the floors at night, up and down the handsome distressed pine stairs, in and out of the library and the handmade-in-England kitchen through a family room big enough for anything but contact sports. In the daylight, I make myself garden—fruit trees, flowers, and herbs—and it's no worse than doing the crossword puzzle, as I used to. I have taken a bookkeeping class; we don't need an accountant anymore. I don't write so much as an essay for the library newsletter, although I still volunteer there and at Miranda's school, of course, and I keep our nice house nice. I go to parties where people know not to ask writers how it's going and I still play tennis. Although I feel like a fool and worry that the Tai Chi teacher will sense that I am not like the others, I go twice a week, for whatever balance it will give me.

I slip into the last row and I do not look at the pleasant, dully focused faces of the women on either side of me. *Bear Catching Fish,* she says, and moves her long arms overhead and down, trailing through the imaginary river. *Crane,* and we rise up on one single, shaky leg. At the end of class, we are all sweating lightly, lying in the dusty near-dark of the Lyman School gym. The floor smells of boys and rubber and rosin, and I leave before they rise and bow to each other, hands in front of sternum, ostentatiously relaxed and transcendent.

In the farthest northwest corner of our property, on the far side of the last stand of skinny maples, I put up an arbor and covered it with Markham's Pink clematis and Perle d'Azur. The giant heart-shaped leaves of Dutchman's pipe turn my corner into a secret place. I carried the pieces of a large cedar bench down there one night last fall and assembled it by flashlight.

There is no one in this world now who knew my baby or me, when I was twenty-eight, married four years and living in the graduate student apartments of the University of California at Berkeley. Our apartment was next to a pale, hunched engineer from New Jersey, who lived next to an anguished physicist from Chad and his good-natured Texan wife, baking Derby pie and corn bread for the whole floor, and we were all across from the brilliant Indian brothers, both mathematicians, both with gold-earringed little girls and wives so quick with numbers that when Berkeley's power went out, as it often did during bad weather, the cash registers were replaced by two thin, dark women in fuchsia and turquoise saris rustling over their raw silk *cholis,* adding up the figures without even a pencil. Our babies and toddlers played in the courtyard and the fathers watched and played chess and drank beer and we watched and brushed sand out of the children's hair and smoked Marlboros and were friends in a very particular, young, and hopeful way.

When Eddie died, they all came to the little funeral at the university chapel and filled our apartment with biscuits and samosas and brisket and with their kindness and their own sickening relief. We left the next day, like thieves. I did not finish my Ph.D. in English literature. My husband did not secure a teaching position at the University of San Francisco, and when I meet people who remember Mario Savio's speeches on the steps of Sproul Hall and their cinder-block apartments on Dwight Way, I leave the room. My own self is buried in Altabates Hospital, still between the sheet and the mattress of his peach plastic Isolette, twisted around the tubes that wove in and out of him like translucent vines, trapped inside that giant ventilator, four times Eddie's size without being of any use to him or his little lungs.

I have made the best and happiest ending that I can, in this world, made it out of the flax and netting and leftover trim of someone else's life, I know, but I made it to keep the innocent safe and the guilty punished, and I made it as the world should be and not as I have found it.

ERNEST HEMINGWAY

A Very Short Story

One hot evening in Padua they carried him up onto the roof and he could look out over the top of the town. There were chimney swifts in the sky. After a while it got dark and the searchlights came out. The others went down and took the bottles with them. He and Luz could hear them below on the balcony. Luz sat on the bed. She was cool and fresh in the hot night.

Luz stayed on night duty for three months. They were glad to let her. When they operated on him she prepared him for the operating table; and they had a joke about friend or enema. He went under the anæsthetic holding tight on to himself so he would not blab about anything during the silly, talky time. After he got on crutches he used to take the temperatures so Luz would not have to get up from the bed. There were only a few patients, and they all knew about it. They all liked Luz. As he walked back along the halls he thought of Luz in his bed.

Before he went back to the front they went into the Duomo and prayed. It was dim and quiet, and there were other people praying. They wanted to get married, but there was not enough time for the banns, and neither of them had birth certificates. They felt as though they were married, but they wanted every one to know about it, and to make it so they could not lose it.

Luz wrote him many letters that he never got until after the armistice. Fifteen came in a bunch to the front and he sorted them by the dates and read them all straight through. They were all about the hospital, and how much she loved him and how it was impossible to get along without him and how terrible it was missing him at night.

After the armistice they agreed he should go home to get a job so they 5
might be married. Luz would not come home until he had a good job and could come to New York to meet her. It was understood he would not drink, and he

did not want to see his friends or any one in the States. Only to get a job and be married. On the train from Padua to Milan they quarrelled about her not being willing to come home at once. When they had to say good-bye, in the station at Milan, they kissed good-bye, but were not finished with the quarrel. He felt sick about saying good-bye like that.

He went to America on a boat from Genoa. Luz went back to Pordonone to open a hospital. It was lonely and rainy there, and there was a battalion of arditi quartered in the town. Living in the muddy, rainy town in the winter, the major of the battalion made love to Luz, and she had never known Italians before, and finally wrote to the States that theirs had been only a boy and girl affair. She was sorry, and she knew he would probably not be able to understand, but might some day forgive her, and be grateful to her, and she expected, absolutely unexpectedly, to be married in the spring. She loved him as always, but she realized now it was only a boy and girl love. She hoped he would have a great career, and believed in him absolutely. She knew it was for the best.

The major did not marry her in the spring, or any other time. Luz never got an answer to the letter to Chicago about it. A short time after he contracted gonorrhea from a sales girl in a loop department store while riding in a taxicab through Lincoln Park.

TRY THIS 9.9
Choose a moment when your protagonist is feeling something intensely. Write, headlong, an "interior monologue," that is, a monologue of his or her thoughts.

TOBIAS WOLFF

Powder

Just before Christmas my father took me skiing at Mount Baker. He'd had to fight for the privilege of my company, because my mother was still angry with him for sneaking me into a nightclub during his last visit, to see Thelonious Monk.

He wouldn't give up. He promised, hand on heart, to take good care of me and have me home for dinner on Christmas Eve, and she relented. But as we were checking out of the lodge that morning it began to snow, and in this snow he observed some rare quality that made it necessary for us to get in one last run. We got in several last runs. He was indifferent to my fretting. Snow whirled around us in bitter, blinding squalls, hissing like sand, and still we skied. As the lift bore us to the peak yet again, my father looked at his watch and said, "Criminy. This'll have to be a fast one."

By now I couldn't see the trail. There was no point in trying. I stuck to him like white on rice and did what he did and somehow made it to the bottom without sailing off a cliff. We returned our skis and my father put chains on the Austin-Healey while I swayed from foot to foot, clapping my mittens and wishing I was home. I could see everything. The green tablecloth, the plates with the holly pattern, the red candles waiting to be lit.

We passed a diner on our way out. "You want some soup?" my father asked. I shook my head. "Buck up," he said. "I'll get you there. Right, doctor?"

I was supposed to say, "Right, doctor," but I didn't say anything.

A state trooper waved us down outside the resort. A pair of sawhorses were blocking the road. The trooper came up to our car and bent down to my father's window. His face was bleached by the cold. Snowflakes clung to his eyebrows and to the fur trim of his jacket and cap.

"Don't tell me," my father said.

The trooper told him. The road was closed. It might get cleared, it might not. Storm took everyone by surprise. So much, so fast. Hard to get people moving. Christmas Eve. What can you do.

My father said, "Look. We're talking about five, six inches. I've taken this car through worse than that."

The trooper straightened up. His face was out of sight but I could hear him. "The road is closed."

My father sat with both hands on the wheel, rubbing the wood with his thumbs. He looked at the barricade for a long time. He seemed to be trying to master the idea of it. Then he thanked the trooper, and with a weird, old-maidy show of caution turned the car around. "Your mother will never forgive me for this," he said.

"We should have left before," I said. "Doctor."

He didn't speak to me again until we were in a booth at the diner, waiting for our burgers. "She won't forgive me," he said. "Do you understand? Never."

"I guess," I said, but no guesswork was required; she wouldn't forgive him.

"I can't let that happen." He bent toward me. "I'll tell you what I want. I want us all to be together again. Is that what you want?"

"Yes, sir."

He bumped my chin with his knuckles. "That's all I needed to hear."

When we finished eating he went to the pay phone in the back of the diner, then joined me in the booth again. I figured he'd called my mother, but he didn't give a report. He sipped at his coffee and stared out the window at the empty road. "Come on, come on," he said, though not to me. A little while later he said it again. When the trooper's car went past, lights flashing, he got up and dropped some money on the check. "Okay. Vamanos."

The wind had died. The snow was falling straight down, less of it now and lighter. We drove away from the resort, right up to the barricade. "Move it," my father told me. When I looked at him he said, "What are you waiting for?" I got out and dragged one of the sawhorses aside, then put it back after he drove through. He pushed the door open for me. "Now you're an accomplice," he said. "We go down together." He put the car into gear and gave me a look. "Joke, son."

20 Down the first long stretch I watched the road behind us, to see if the trooper was on our tail. The barricade vanished. Then there was nothing but snow: snow on the road, snow kicking up from the chains, snow on the trees, snow in the sky; and our trail in the snow. Then I faced forward and had a shock. The lay of the road behind us had been marked by our own tracks, but there were no tracks ahead of us. My father was breaking virgin snow between a line of tall trees. He was humming "Stars Fell on Alabama." I felt snow brush along the floorboards under my feet. To keep my hands from shaking I clamped them between my knees.

My father grunted in a thoughtful way and said, "Don't ever try this yourself."

"I won't."

"That's what you say now, but someday you'll get your license and then you'll think you can do anything. Only you won't be able to do this. You need, I don't know—a certain instinct."

"Maybe I have it."

25 "You don't. You have your strong points, but not this. I only mention it because I don't want you to get the idea this is something just anybody can do. I'm a great driver. That's not a virtue, okay? It's just a fact, and one you should be aware of. Of course you have to give the old heap some credit, too. There aren't many cars I'd try this with. Listen!"

I did listen. I heard the slap of the chains, the stiff, jerky rasp of the wipers, the purr of the engine. It really did purr. The old heap was almost new. My father couldn't afford it, and kept promising to sell it, but here it was.

I said, "Where do you think that policeman went to?"

"Are you warm enough?" He reached over and cranked up the blower. Then he turned off the wipers. We didn't need them. The clouds had brightened. A few sparse, feathery flakes drifted into our slipstream and were swept away. We left the trees and entered a broad field of snow that ran level for a while and then tilted sharply downward. Orange stakes had been planted at intervals in two parallel lines and my father steered a course between them, though they were far enough apart to leave considerable doubt in my mind as to exactly where the road lay. He was humming again, doing little scat riffs around the melody.

"Okay then. What are my strong points?"

30 "Don't get me started," he said. "It'd take all day."

"Oh, right. Name one."

"Easy. You always think ahead."

True. I always thought ahead. I was a boy who kept his clothes on numbered hangers to insure proper rotation. I bothered my teachers for homework assignments far ahead of their due dates so I could draw up schedules. I thought ahead, and that was why I knew that there would be other troopers waiting for us at the end of our ride, if we even got there. What I did not know was that my father would wheedle and plead his way past them—he didn't sing "O Tannenbaum," but just about—and get me home for dinner, buying a little more time before my mother decided to make the split final. I knew we'd get caught; I was resigned to it. And maybe for this reason I stopped moping and began to enjoy myself.

Why not? This was one for the books. Like being in a speedboat, only better. You can't go downhill in a boat. And it was all ours. And it kept coming, the laden trees, the unbroken surface of snow, the sudden white vistas. Here and there I saw hints of the road, ditches, fences, stakes, but not so many that I could have found my way. But then I didn't have to. My father was driving. My father in his forty-eighth year, rumpled, kind, bankrupt of honor, flushed with certainty. He was a great driver. All persuasion, no coercion. Such subtlety at the wheel, such tactful pedalwork. I actually trusted him. And the best was yet to come—switchbacks and hairpins impossible to describe. Except maybe to say this: if you haven't driven fresh powder, you haven't driven.

TRY THIS 9.10

If the story you are writing is in the first person or in third person giving us the thoughts of a character, recast a few paragraphs in the objective point of view. How much is still conveyed?

Or:

If your story is already written from the objective viewpoint, write a paragraph or two of your protagonist's interior monologue.

In either case, the exercise may help you to see how successful you are in "showing" the interior reality of your character through sensory detail.

RON CARLSON

Bigfoot Stole My Wife

The problem is credibility.

The problem, as I'm finding out over the last few weeks, is basic credibility. A lot of people look at me and say, sure Rick, Bigfoot stole your wife. It makes me sad to see it, the look of disbelief in each person's eye. Trudy's disappearance makes me sad, too, and I'm sick in my heart about where she may be and how he's treating her, what they do all day, if she's getting enough to eat. I believe he's being good to her—I mean I feel it—and I'm going to keep hoping to see her again, but it is my belief that I probably won't.

In the two and a half years we were married, I often had the feeling that I would come home from the track and something would be funny. Oh, she'd say things: *One of these days I'm not going to be here when you get home,* things like that, things like everybody says. How stupid of me not to see them as omens. When I'd get out of bed in the early afternoon, I'd stand right here at this sink and I could see her working in her garden in her cut-off Levis and bikini top, weeding, planting, watering. I mean it was obvious. I was too busy thinking about the races, weighing the odds, checking the jockey roster to see what I now know: he was watching her too. He'd probably been watching her all summer.

So, in a way it was my fault. But what could I have done? Bigfoot steals your wife. I mean: even if you're home, it's going to be a mess. He's big and not well trained.

5 When I came home it was about eleven-thirty. The lights were on, which really wasn't anything new, but in the ordinary mess of the place, there was a little difference, signs of a struggle. There was a spilled Dr. Pepper on the counter and the fridge was open. But there was something else, something that made me sick. The smell. The smell of Bigfoot. It was hideous. It was...the guy is not clean.

Half of Trudy's clothes are gone, not all of them, and there is no note. Well, I know what it is. It's just about midnight there in the kitchen which smells like some part of hell. I close the fridge door. It's the saddest thing I've ever done. There's a picture of Trudy and me leaning against her Toyota taped to the fridge door. It was taken last summer. There's Trudy in her bikini top, her belly brown as a bean. She looks like a kid. She was a kid I guess, twenty-six. The two times she went to the track with me everybody looked at me like how'd I rate her. But she didn't really care for the races. She cared about her garden and Chinese cooking and Buster, her collie, who I guess Bigfoot stole too. Or ate. Buster isn't in the picture, he was nagging my nephew Chuck who took the photo. Anyway I close the fridge door and it's like part of my life closed. Bigfoot steals your wife and you're in for some changes.

You come home from the track having missed the Daily Double by a neck, and when you enter the home you are paying for and in which you and your wife and your wife's collie live, and your wife and her collie are gone as is some of her clothing, there is nothing to believe. Bigfoot stole her. It's a fact. What should I do, ignore it? Chuck came down and said something like well if Bigfoot stole her why'd they take the Celica? Christ, what a cynic! Have you ever read anything about Bigfoot not being able to drive? He'd be cramped in there, but I'm sure he could manage.

I don't really care if people believe me or not. Would that change anything? Would that bring Trudy back here? Pull the weeds in her garden?

As I think about it, no one believes anything anymore. Give me one example of someone *believing* one thing. I dare you. After that we get into this credibility thing. No one believes me. I myself can't believe all the suspicion and cynicism there is in today's world. Even at the races, some character next to me will poke over at my tip sheet and ask me if I believe that stuff. If I believe? What is there to believe? The horse's name? What he did the last time out? And I look back at this guy, too cheap to go two bucks on the program, and I say: it's history. It is historical fact here. Believe. Huh. Here's a fact: I believe everything.

Credibility. 10

When I was thirteen years old, my mother's trailer was washed away in the flooding waters of the Harley River and swept thirty-one miles, ending right side up and nearly dead level just outside Mercy, in fact in the old weed-eaten parking lot for the abandoned potash plant. I know this to be true because I was inside the trailer the whole time with my pal, Nuggy Reinecker, who found the experience more life-changing than I did.

Now who's going to believe this story? I mean, besides me, because I was there. People are going to say, come on, thirty-one miles? Don't you mean thirty-one feet?

We had gone in out of the rain after school to check out a magazine that belonged to my mother's boyfriend. It was a copy of *Dude,* and there was a fold-out page I will never forget of a girl lying on the beach on her back. It was a color photograph. The girl was a little pale, I mean, this was probably her first day out in the sun, and she had no clothing on. So it was good, but what made it great was that they had made her a little bathing suit out of sand. Somebody had spilled a little sand just right, here and there, and the sand was this incredible gold color, and it made her look so absolutely naked it wanted to put your eyes out.

Nuggy and I knew there was flood danger in Griggs; we'd had a flood every year almost and it had been raining for five days on and off, but when the trailer bucked the first time, we thought it was my mother come home to catch us in the dirty book. Nuggy shoved the magazine under the bed and I ran out to check the door. It only took me a second and I hollered back *Hey no sweat, no one's here,* but by the time I returned to see what other poses they'd had this beautiful woman commit, Nuggy already had his pants to his ankles and was involved in what we knew was a sin.

If it hadn't been the timing of the first wave with this act of his, Nuggy might have gone on to live what the rest of us call a normal life. But the Harley had crested and the head wave, which they estimated to be three feet minimum, unmoored the trailer with a push that knocked me over the sofa, and threw Nuggy, already entangled in his trousers, clear across the bedroom. 15

I watched the village of Griggs as we sailed through. Some of the village, the Exxon Station, part of it at least, and the carwash, which folded up right away, tried to come along with us, and I saw the front of Painters' Mercantile, the old porch and signboard, on and off all day.

You can believe this: it was not a smooth ride. We'd rip along for ten seconds, dropping and growling over rocks, and rumbling over tree stumps, and then wham! the front end of the trailer would lodge against a rock or something that could stop it, and whoa! we'd wheel around sharp as a carnival ride, worse really, because the furniture would be thrown against the far side and us with it, sometimes we'd end up in a chair and sometimes the chair would sit on us. My mother had about four thousand knickknacks in five big box shelves, and they gave us trouble for the first two or three miles, flying by like artillery, left, right, some small glass snail hits you in the face, later in the back, but that stuff all finally settled in the foot and then two feet of water which we took on.

We only slowed down once and it was the worst. In the railroad flats I thought we had stopped and I let go of the door I was hugging and tried to stand up and then swish, another rush sent us right along. We rammed along all day it seemed, but when we finally washed up in Mercy and the sheriff's cousin pulled open the door and got swept back to his car by water and quite a few of those knickknacks, just over an hour had passed. We had averaged, they figured later, about thirty-two miles an hour, reaching speeds of up to fifty at Lime Falls and the Willows. I was okay and walked out bruised and well washed, but when the sheriff's cousin pulled Nuggy out, he looked genuinely hurt.

"For godsakes," I remember the sheriff's cousin saying, "The damn flood knocked this boy's pants off!" But Nuggy wasn't talking. In fact, he never hardly talked to me again in the two years he stayed at the Regional School. I heard later, and I believe it, that he joined the monastery over in Malcolm County.

My mother, because she didn't have the funds to haul our rig back to Griggs, worried for a while, but then the mayor arranged to let us stay out where we were. So after my long ride in a trailer down the flooded Harley River with my friend Nuggy Reinecker, I grew up in a parking lot outside of Mercy, and to tell you the truth, it wasn't too bad, even though our trailer never did smell straight again.

Now you can believe all that. People are always saying: don't believe everything you read, or everything you hear. And I'm here to tell you. Believe it. Everything. Everything you read. Everything you hear. Believe your eyes. Your ears. Believe the small hairs on the back of your neck. Believe all of history, and all of the versions of history, and all the predictions for the future. Believe every weather forecast. Believe in God, the afterlife, unicorns, showers on Tuesday. Everything has happened. Everything is possible.

I come home from the track to find the cupboard bare. Trudy is not home. The place smells funny: hairy. It's a fact and I know it as a fact: Bigfoot has been in my house.

Bigfoot stole *my* wife.

She's gone.

Believe it.

I gotta believe it.

TRY THIS 9.11

Take a few paragraphs of the story you are writing and substitute an animal or a monster for one of the characters. What sort of creature will it be? How will it behave? What can this teach you about your character?

ACCOMPLISHING A DRAFT

Write a quick draft of the story you are working on as a short-short. If you had to condense it into a page or two, what would you retain? This exercise may help you whenever a story seems amorphous or sprawling—when you don't, in fact, quite know what it's about.

Fiction Format

As with creative nonfiction, "clean copy" is the first and very visible sign of the professional. Your manuscript should be carefully proofread, neatly printed or copied, and stapled or paper clipped in the upper left-hand corner. Your particular teacher, group leader, or editor may have format requirements. To cut copying costs, some teachers will ask you to omit a cover page, and/or to single space. Otherwise, title and author's name and address (or class identification) should appear on a cover page, and your name need appear only there. Page numbering can be done in the upper or lower center or right corner of the page.

Manuscripts should be double-spaced, with generous (approximately one inch) margins, on one side of $8\frac{1}{2} \times 11$-inch white paper. The first page of the story should begin about one-third of the way down the page.

Copyrighting of literary manuscripts is not necessary—essays, stories, poems, and plays are, alas, rarely worth money enough to be attractive to thieves. If your work is published, the magazine or publisher will apply for copyright, and you will have a contract that specifies what rights belong to you.

Always keep a hard copy of your work.

THE YELLOW WALLPAPER

by Charlotte Perkins Gilman

1001 Herland Street
Pasadena, CA 91101
(626) 123–6543
cpgilman@mindspring.com
www.cpgilman.com

It is very seldom that mere ordinary people like John and myself secure ancestral halls for the summer. A colonial mansion, a hereditary estate, I would say a haunted house, and reach the height of romantic felicity—but that would be asking too much of fate.

Still I will proudly declare that there is something queer about it. Else why should it be let so cheaply? And why stood so long untenanted? John laughs at me, of course, but one expects that in marriage.

John is practical in the extreme. He has no patience with faith, an intense horror of superstition, and he scoffs openly at any talk of things not to be felt and seen and put down in figures. John is a physician, and perhaps (I would not say it to a living soul, of course, but this is dead paper and a great relief to my mind)—perhaps that is one reason I do not get well faster.

You see he does not believe I am sick!

And what can one do?

If a physician of high standing, and one's own husband,

10 CHAPTER

Poetry

- *Formal and Free Verse*
- *Working with Sound*
- *The Poetic Line*
- *Imagery, Connotation, and Metaphor*
- *Density and Intensity*
- *Poetry Format*

Every poetry tradition is a formal exercise, and every fully made poem is formally complete.
Charlie Smith

The poem is insane.
It ties tin cans to its tail.
Alicia Ostriker

Jerry Uelsmann

WARM-UP
This photomontage is a visual metaphor—but representing what? Is the woman a victim of the fist or is she the fist? Write a poem about her. Develop the metaphor in some way.

THERE ARE HUNDREDS OF DEFINITIONS OF POETRY, RANGING from the religious to the flippant, from the sentimental to the psychological. Poetry is "the natural language of all worship," "devil's wine," "an imitation of an imitation," "more philosophic than history," "painting that speaks," "a criticism of life," "a way of taking life by the throat," "an escape from emotion," "the antithesis to science," "the bill and coo of sex," "a pause before death."

Unlike the essay or drama, poetry can take shapes that bear little or no resemblance to each other. Individual poems may aspire to freeze a single image like a painting or to spin off musical variations like a jazz riff. Unlike the novel or the short story, length has nothing at all to do with whether a thing may be called poetry; epics may cover many hundreds of pages or take hours to recite, while the haiku is seventeen syllables.

Perhaps the most comprehensive and least confining definition is W. H. Auden's: *Poetry is memorable speech.*

This memorably succinct sentence contains the two essentials: Poetry is meant to be heard aloud in the human voice, and it is meant to be remembered. All of the techniques that belong to this genre—imagery, metaphor, repetition, meter, stress, rhythm, assonance, consonance, alliteration, rhyme—all these aid speech or memory or both. In the process of manipulating language, the poet works toward that state of art in which sound is inseparable from meaning.

Formal and Free Verse

> Make the sound an echo to the sense.
> *Alexander Pope*

For several decades of the century just past, poets, readers, and teachers made an easy distinction between "formal" and "free" verse. In this view, "formal" meant time-honored set patterns of rhythm and rhyme, and "free" was pretty much anything else. It was acknowledged that the danger of formal poetry was that it should fall into the singsong of greeting card verse, and of free verse that it might consist of no more than chopped-up prose.

But this way of speaking about poetry has fallen into disfavor. Poets point out that the notion of "free" verse implies there is no discipline in the rhythm and sound patterns of poetry that does not follow a predetermined form. This is far from the case. If anything, verse that must find its own unique pattern is more rigorous. Is the poem enhanced with correspondences of sound? Is every syllable necessary? Is the line-break with its "half-comma" of hesitation meaningful?

"Free verse," says poet Mary Oliver, "is of course not free."

Interestingly, and increasingly, contemporary writers speak of language as a physical pleasure. Here is Eudora Welty:

> In my sensory education I include my physical awareness of the *word*. Of a certain word, that is; the connection it has with what it stands for. At around age six, perhaps, I was standing by myself waiting for supper... There comes a moment, and I saw it then, when the moon goes from flat to round. For the first time it met my eyes as a globe. The word "moon" came into my mouth as though fed to me out of a silver spoon.

Many poets now insist on this centrality of physical pleasure to their art form. Robert Pinsky puts it this way:

> The medium of poetry is the human body: the column of air inside the chest, shaped into signifying sounds in the larynx and the mouth. In this sense, poetry is just as physical an act as dancing.

TRY THIS 10.1

Find a word or phrase with a meaning you consider negative, but of which you like the sound. Write a brief paragraph describing that sound. Make up a fantasy meaning for it. For example, "coronary thrombosis" to me suggests drums reverberating through the tops of trees.

Or:

Try writing a line that sounds like an explosion but does not describe an explosion; like a train, but does not mention a train; like a crying baby, but without the baby; like a storm, not about a storm; like tapping fingernails—but, look Ma, no hands.

Poetry is older than prose. It grew out of an oral tradition in which word play and patterns of repetition were **mnemonic** devices, making it possible to remember, and so possible repeatedly to perform, long histories of gods, peoples, their trials and heroic battles. Now we have many technologies for preserving stories, but poetry retains its original nature: spoken sound made memorable through the poet's art.

In the early traditions of Greek and Latin verse, a means of measuring poetry came into being, counting syllables with short and long vowel sounds—a distinction we still make in English: the long sound of *a* as in *play* as opposed to the short sound of *a* as in *cat*; the long *e* in *sweet*, the short *e* in *sweat*. These designations of length in Greek and Latin are absolute. A vowel is either short or long.

But English, a mishmash of Teutonic and Latinate sources, is an accentual language: Some syllables are given more stress in speech than others, and stress is not an absolute measure. It involves vowel length, yes, but also pitch, volume, and duration. Some syllables will be loud but short, or low but long, others higher in pitch, softer in tone, or rushed over so as to be barely heard. The same syllable in a different context will have a different weight. Consider for example the one-syllable word *on* in the following sentences. Say the sentences aloud, emphasizing their emphases:

Put it on the table, please.
I will fall like an ocean on that court!
He went on and on.
Enough, already! I'm on it!

To my ear (and it represents a relevant complexity of the English language that we might disagree on this), the *on* gets a little more emphasis (accent or stress) in each succeeding sentence.

PUT it on the TABle, *please.*
i will FALL like an O-cean *on* that COURT.
He went *on* and ON.
e-NOUGH, already! i'm ON it!

(My clumsy attempt here to capture more than two levels of stress indicates the difficulty. In prosody notation, stressed, unstressed, and semi-stressed syllables might appear like this: H̋e wĕnt ón ăňd ón. (A discussion of English **prosody** and the **poetic feet**, including the marking of stress, will be found in Appendix A.)

When the Greek and Latin system of notation with its strict long/short vowels was adopted for English, it worked imperfectly and was eventually felt to straitjacket the language. For centuries, poets continued to count their meters in stressed and unstressed syllables, adapting them to the greater variety of English in many ways. Since English is rich in syllables but short on rhymes, Shakespeare and others loosened the rhyme scheme of the sonnet. The best poets devised ways to exploit the system by working the rhythm of the sense against or across the rhythm of the form. Through four centuries the formal patterns persisted, poets in the mystical seventeenth seeking by them to "echo a celestial music," in the scientific eighteenth to celebrate God-given rationality ("Whatever is, is right"), and in the romantic nineteenth to go in quest of an unreachable ideal.

Toward the end of the nineteenth century a few great poets, quite isolated from each other, rebelled against the forms. Gerard Manley Hopkins in England devised (or as he said, "discovered") a poetic line that had a set number of stressed or accented syllables but any number of unstressed or unaccented:

I caught this morning morning's minion, king-
    dom of daylight's dauphin, dapple-dawn-drawn Falcon in his riding...

Walt Whitman rejected regular meter and incorporated a rolling, sonorous voice into the rhythms of ordinary American speech:

My tongue, every atom of my blood, formed from this soil, this air,
Born here of parents born here from parents the same, and their parents the
    same...

Emily Dickinson took another route, writing in short lines and recognizable stanzas but working with slant-rhymes or not-quite-rhymes that surprise and disorient:

> I've known her from an ample nation
>   Choose one.
> Then shut the valves of her attention
>   Like stone.

In the twentieth century the search for "free" verse began in earnest. Robert Frost, who wrote in a way that combined fixed forms with the cadences of ordinary speech, spoke of English as an "onomatopoeic" language—one, that is, in which the words tend to sound like what they mean. Frost heard this sound-as-sense not only in single words like "buzz" and "murmur," "stop" and "sprawl," but also in what he called "sentence sound," claiming that we could understand through a closed door, in English, the meaning of such sentences as:

> Open the door!
> It's freezing out here!
> What, are you nuts?
> What is the matter with you?

It was Ezra Pound who influentially declared that a poet should "compose in the sequence of the musical phrase, not the metronome." This makes eminent sense, not only because the equation with music suggests the infinite possibilities of speech sound, but also because musical notation, like the stresses in the English language but unlike poetic notation, takes into account duration, pitch, and volume as well as emphasis.

Working with Sound

How are you to begin? Robert Pinsky says, "There are no rules. But..."

There are some guidelines, some principles, and some techniques of which you need to become aware:

Write in full sentences. Use standard punctuation. Too often, beginning poets feel that a string of adjectival phrases amounts to a mood, or that sentence fragments conjure up drama. It doesn't and they don't. On the contrary, if poetry is memorable speech, like articulate speech it will be built of strong sentences. Likewise, as in all imaginative writing, prefer the concrete over the abstract and the active over the passive voice.

Since writing is learned first of all in the doing, I propose that you go about writing poems by borrowing from other genres in which you are more practiced and adept, and at the same time begin to *play* with sound and rhythm. This chapter will suggest some possibilities for such play, and the "Basic Prosody" in Appendix A will lead you to invent others of your own. Meanwhile, read widely in both formal (rhymed and metered) and **informal** (free) verse, with particular attention to metaphor and patterns of sound. Imitate what you like; imitation, which has been called the sincerest form of flattery, is also the most teaching form of play.

TRY THIS 10.2

Write a poem that takes advantage of your earlier exercises in one of these ways:

- That presents an image in terms of all five senses, how it looks, smells, sounds, tastes, feels
- As a dialogue between two people who see some object in very different ways
- In the form of a list
- About a memory, in the voice and from the point of view of someone other than yourself
- In the form of a letter saying good-bye

Then, there are a number of concepts of which you should be aware, and learn to hear in the poems you read. Often, people who complain that a poem doesn't rhyme do so because they are unaware of the rich variety of rhyming English sounds. For example, the very short excerpt from an early Alicia Ostriker poem at the head of this chapter seems to make a claim for verse "free" to the point of dementia. Nothing could be farther from "formally complete," right?

> The poem is insane.
> It ties tin cans to its tail.

But the lines are intricately tied together with sound. Look at the relationship of the ending consonants in *-sane, tin, can* (this is called **consonance**). Look at the matching vowel sounds in the ending words *-sane* and *tail* and in the words *is, in-, it, tin, its* (**assonance**). Consider the beginning consonants *ties, tin, to, tail* (**alliteration**). In fact "...is insane. It ties tin cans to it tail" is a playful jumble of *t, s,* and *n* sounds that do indeed sound a little crazy. By contrast, "The poem" stands at the beginning, a mellow open sound, unrelated to such antics.

Of course, not all poems will ask for, or want, sound-play as dense as in this example. Nevertheless, it is useful to have some of these poetic tools at hand. (Again, others will be taken up in Appendix A, "A Basic Prosody.")

Alliteration is the repetition of an initial consonant:

> "I've **g**ot a stubborn **g**oose whose **g**ut's
> Honeycombed with **g**olden eggs,
> Yet won't lay one.

"Rhyme," Sylvia Plath

Assonance is the repetition of a vowel sound between consonants that may or may not match:

At the retr**ea**t, L**ee** wasn't allowed
to sp**ea**k or r**ea**d for ten days…

"Nirvana," Alan Tate

Consonance is the repetition of the consonant that concludes a word or syllable:

We say a heart brea**ks**—li**ke**
a sti**ck**, maybe…

"We Say," Reginald Gibbons

A **true rhyme** is the matching sound familiar from childhood, in which both the vowel and the consonant of the last accented syllable (and everything thereafter) corresponds, like "Little Miss Muffet / Sat on a tuffet…" but such a rhyme may also be **internal**, which means that the end of one line rhymes into the beginning or middle of another:

My grandfather died one morning in **damp**ness,
tamping, watering the roses for the coming season…

"Him, His Place," Liam Rector

Or:

…the lights dance on the dark water,
our president, of **late** of Water**gate**,
is spozed to fly above the flooded areas
and esti**mate** how much damage has been done…

"A Poem to Galway Kinnell," Etheridge Knight

Many contemporary poets also, like Emily Dickinson, use the slightly discordant sounds of **off-rhyme,** also called **near-rhyme, half-rhyme,** or **slant rhyme,** which often involves consonance:

Why should I let the toad **work**
　　Squat on my **life**?
Can't I use my wit as a pitch**fork**
　　And drive the brute **off**?

Many of these techniques you already know in a way that, if not instinctive, has come to you by a combination of imitation, context, and repetition, through nursery rhymes, songs, and jingles. But there is a sense in which things only come into existence when they are learned and can't be clearly thought without being defined. In Alexander Pope's line, "When Ajax strives some rock's vast weight to throw," you can feel the muscularity and effort. But to understand and be able to employ the effect, it helps to know that it's achieved by a combination of **spondees** and **consonant clusters.** Or again: William Butler Yeats's line, "I walk through the long schoolroom questioning." Why is this line so long? Because it uses **long vowels,** many **consonants,** and an unusual number of heavy **stresses.**

TRY THIS 10.3

Make a quick list of terms that relate to any subject you know well (you can go back and add to it at any time)—kinds of fish or shoes, baseball terms, car parts, fabrics, tools, instruments—whatever falls in your area of expertise. Try to list at least twenty or thirty words. Here, for example, is a list of some spices on my spice shelf:

ginger	turmeric	parsley
cinnamon	oregano	arrowroot
cardamom	rosemary	cayenne
pepper	cumin	fennel
peppercorns	dill weed	coriander
paprika	poppy seed	curry
cloves	sesame seed	cilantro
bay leaves	thyme	chili

Comb your list for instances of alliteration, consonance, assonance, rhyme, and off-rhyme.

Write an ode to the subject of your list, being aware of these sounds and the pattern they make.

The Poetic Line

> The line, when a poem is alive in its sound, measures: it is a proposal about listening.
>
> *Robert Hass*

The **line,** common to nearly all poetry, is a unit of verse ending in a typographical break. It visually represents a slight oral pause or hesitation, what poet Denise Levertov calls "a half-comma," so that both the word at the end of the line and the one at the beginning of the next receive a slight extra emphasis. The line operates *not as a substitute* for the sentence, but in addition to it. The line directs the breath; the rhythm of the line is played off against the rhythm of the sense, and this is one of the ways that poets alter, stress, and redirect their meaning. Here is the famous beginning of Milton's *Paradise Lost*:

> Of man's first disobedience, and the Fruit
> Of that immortal tree...

Notice how that fatal apple is given prominence by its position at the end of the line. In general, it may be said that the end of just about anything—line, paragraph, stanza, story—is the strongest position, and the beginning is the second strongest.

A **caesura** is a pause that occurs within the line (above, after *disobedience*), and can help manipulate the rhythm, as can **enjambment,** the running-on of the sense from one line to another (*and the Fruit / Of that immortal tree...*). A line that is **end-stopped,** meaning that the line break coincides with a pause in the sense, ends with greater finality:

> An elegy is really about the wilting of a flower,
> the passing of the year, the falling of a stone.
>
> *"A Lecture on the Elegy,"* William Stafford

The added emphasis of the line break, playing the sentence rhythm against the meter, is capable of many and powerful effects. Amateur actors are inclined to speak Shakespeare's blank verse (iambic pentameter) lines according to the singsong of the form, and such a reading betrays their amateurism:

> To BE or NOT to BE; that IS the QUEStion.

Such a reading is intolerable to our experience of the language and exhausting to the ear. First-rate professionals understand the way the verse rhythm plays the sense against the iambic rhythm, and this gives the actor room for interpretation, by choosing among myriad possible readings. As long as the emphasis in the line makes sense, the actor can emphasize nearly any word: *be, or, not, be, that, is, the, quest-*. In each choice there will be not two weights, accented and unaccented, but many, in subtle shadings that affect each other. And in every case the underlying blank verse rhythm will remain, as resonance, residue, or trace, due to its having been established as the base rhythm of the verse.

TRY THIS 10.4

Take the ode of the previous exercise (or any poem you have written that you consider finished) and play with the line breaks. Combine every line-and-a-half into a single line. Break every line in half. Place the line breaks so that there are no caesuras. Place the line breaks so that there are *no* end-stopped lines. Read each version aloud. What do you learn about the power of the line? Which version will you keep? Why?

Imagery, Connotation, and Metaphor

Because poetry attempts to produce an emotional response through heightened evocation of the senses, imagery holds a central place among its techniques. John Keats famously advised, "...be more of an artist, and load every rift of your subject with ore," which illustrates his advice with a weighty metaphor.

But remember that not all images are metaphors. Sometimes, as Robert Hass put it, "they do not say *this is that,* they say *this is.*"

> O Western wind, when wilt thou blow,
> That the small rain down can rain?
> Christ, that my love were in my arms
> And I in my bed again!

This most famous of anonymous poems, disputedly from the thirteenth to the fifteenth centuries, contains no metaphors. Its simple images are wind, rain, lover, arms, and bed. The poem says, "I am stuck here in an ugly climate with no chance of getting out any time soon, and I'm lonely and miserable and miss my girl." But it says all that with a good deal more force partly because of the way the first line evokes the sound of the wind (all those *w*'s, the breath of *wh*, the vowel length of blow-oh-oh) and partly because it uses images rich in connotation.

Denotation and Connotation

Words have **denotation**—a literal or primary meaning (usually the first definition in the dictionary)—and also **connotation,** which refers to the layers of suggestion and implication they acquire through usage. Words can be richly encrusted with all we have heard, read, seen, felt, and experienced in their name. In the anonymous poem above, *love* implies longing, lust, romance, affection, tenderness, and, for each of us, further images of all these and more. *Bed* evokes sex, but also warmth, safety, comfort, home. *Wind* has connotations of wailing and loneliness and, in this poem, in combination with its sounds, becomes a lament, a cry of yearning. The "small rain" evokes gentleness by contrast with both the implied harshness of the climate and the force of the exclamation, "*Christ! That my love...*" The word *Christ* itself, its implicit gentleness and faith set against its use as a curse, offers a high tension of contradictory connotation.

Connotation is partly personal, which means that no two readers ever read exactly the same poem. Since I grew up in the desert, the first image that comes to my mind in the poet's plea for "small rain" is a parched barren landscape. Someone who grew up in New England might think of long winter and the gentler promise of spring.

Metaphor, Cliché, and Conceit

Imagery is necessary to poetry for the same picture-making reason it is necessary to all literary writing, but poetry also asks for and usually receives the special intensity of metaphor. Metaphor has a strong hold on the imagination because of its dual qualities of surprise and precision. Emily Dickinson described in a letter to a friend how she had studied the scriptures to learn the "mode of juxtaposing elements of concrete things with equally fundamental ideas and feelings—grass, stone, heart, majesty, despair." This principle yielded Dickinson's signature style:

> "Hope" is the thing with feathers—
> That perches in the soul—
> And sings the tune without the words—
> And never stops—at all—

Metaphor (including simile) has as its central function to make concrete, so that even if one member of the comparison is an abstraction, its comparison to a thing or a sensory detail will vivify and particularize—Dickinson's "Hope" as a "thing with feathers," or "the purple terricloth robe of nobility," or "like a diver into the wretched confusion."

Most metaphors, however, compare two sensory images and let the abstraction remain unvoiced but present in the tension between them ("electric eel blink like stringlight," "a surf of blossoms," "rooms cut in half hang like flayed carcasses"). The function of comparison is not to be pretty, but to be exact, evocative, and as concrete as the sidewalk. Or as Ted Hughes's "Thistles," which:

> ...grow grey, like men.
> Mown down, it is a feud. Their sons appear,
> Stiff with weapons, fighting back over the same ground.

Learning to recognize and flee clichés, to find metaphors that are both surprising and apt, can only be achieved through attention and a fair amount of trial and error. The ability to spot clichés, as Jerome Stern points out, is "not in the genetic code." But this is one place in your apprenticeship where the practice of brainstorming, freeassociating, and freewriting can continue to help, because the attention we pay to the poetic image allows for free, extreme, even wild connection. The less you clamp down on your dreaming, the less you concede to logic, the less you allow your internal critic to shut you up, the more likely you are to produce the startling, dead-on comparison. Cut logic loose; focus on what you see, taste, touch. Freewrite, and let the strangeness in you surface.

From time to time you may even come up with a good **conceit,** which is a comparison of two things radically and startlingly unlike—in Samuel Johnson's words, "yoked by violence together." A conceit compares two things that have no evident similarity; the author must explain to us, sometimes at great length, why these things can be said to be alike. When John Donne compares a flea to marriage, the two images have no areas of reference in common, and we don't understand. He must explain to us that the flea, having bitten both the poet and his lover,

> ...Our marriage bed, and marriage temple is;
> Though parents grudge, and you, we're met
> And cloistered in these living walls of jet.

TRY THIS 10.5

Make a list of abstract concepts like *love, ego, persistence, sloth...* Make the list longer. Make a list of common objects. Point blind at one term on each list. Write no more than five lines making the object a metaphor for the abstraction. Try it again. Again.

Idiom and Dead Metaphor

The process of learning what's fresh and what's stale is complicated—and in no language more so than English—by the fact that not all familiar phrases are clichés. Many have settled down into the language as **idioms,** a "manner of speaking." English is so full of idioms that it is notoriously difficult for foreigners to learn. Try explaining to a non-native speaker what we mean by: *put 'em up, can you put me up? put 'er there, don't let me put you out, does she put out?, he put it off, I was put off, he put in!*

Moreover, English is full of **dead metaphors,** comparisons so familiar that they have in effect ceased to be metaphors; they have lost the force of the original comparison and acquired a new definition. Fowler's *Modern English Usage* uses the word "sift" to demonstrate the dead metaphor, one that has "been used so often that speaker and hearer have ceased to be aware that the words used are not literal."

> Thus, in *The men were sifting the meal* we have a literal use of sift; in *Satan hath desired to have you, that he may sift you as wheat, sift* is a live metaphor; in *the sifting of evidence,* the metaphor is so familiar that it is equally possible that either *sifting* or *examination* will be used, and that a sieve is not present to the thought.

English abounds in dead metaphors. *Abounds* is one, where the overflowing of liquid is not present to the thought. When a person *runs* for office, legs are not present to the thought, nor is an arrow when we speak of someone's *aim,* hot stones when we go through an *ordeal,* headgear when someone *caps* a joke. Unlike clichés, dead metaphors enrich the language. There is a residual resonance from the original metaphor but no pointless effort on the part of the mind to resolve the tension of like and unlike.

Alert yourself to metaphors, idioms, and dead metaphors in your reading and in your writing; eventually the recognition will become second nature, and you will develop a powerful background awareness in your craft. Meanwhile *keep your eyes peeled* and *give it your best shot,* because *it's not whether you win or lose, it's how you play the game. Go for it; because—It's show time!*

TRY THIS 10.6

Go back to the list of clichés you made for Try This 2.6 (p. 24) 1. Add to it. Make a list of dead metaphors. Then choose a phrase from either list that you find particularly vivid (or detestable) and write a short poem in which you take it *literally.* Focus on, imagine, dream the images as if they were real. Some poor exhausted fellow is *running for office?* What must it feel like to have *a nose to the grindstone? Sifting the evidence? A vale of tears?*

Density and Intensity

The meaning in a poetic line is *compressed.* Whereas a journalist may treat it as a point of honor to present information objectively, and a legal writer may produce pages of jargon in an attempt to rule out any ambiguity, subjectivity and ambiguity are the literary writer's stock in trade; you are at constant pains to mean more than you say. This is why dialogue must do more than one thing at a time, why an image is better than an abstraction, and why an action needs to represent more than mere movement. Especially and to a heightened degree in poetry, this **density,** this more-than-one-thing-at-a-time, raises the **intensity** of feeling. Poet Donald Hall observes that, "In logic no two things can occupy the same point at the same time, and in poetry that happens all the time. This is almost what poetry is for, to be able to embody contrary feelings in the same motion." Notice, for example, the paradoxical effect of newspaper rhetoric in these lines from "Epithalamion":

> Child-eyed among the Brooklyn cousins,
> Leanne, *the bride, wore cotton lace*
> *Caught in a bow of peau de soie, and dozens*
> *Of pearls* of sweat adorned her face
> At the upper lip...

Not only imagery but each of the elements discussed in this book—voice, character, setting, and story—will be relevant to achieving this compression, and each in a particular and particularly heightened way. The techniques of good prose make for good poetry—only more so. Active verbs are crucial. Nouns will do more work than adjectives. Specific details will move more than abstractions. Vocabulary, word choice, syntax, and grammar take on added importance; you will spend a good deal of time cutting vague verbiage and looking for the phrases that strike with special vividness or suggest double meaning or vibrate or *resonate* with widening significance.

Poetic Voice

Voice will have a special importance in your poetry not only because of the likelihood or inevitability that you will adopt a persona, but also because in the concentrated attention we pay to the language, diction *becomes* content, and poets reveal their way of looking at the world the moment they open their mouths. Since poetry is meant to be said and heard aloud it will have a particularly close relationship to the tone of the implied speaker. Imamu Amiri Baraka says, "the first thing you look for is the stance." "Stance" is another way of saying *point of view,* in both the sense of opinion and the sense that the poem reveals who is standing where to watch the scene, which in turn reminds us of Philip Roth's statement that voice "begins around the back of the knees and reaches well above the head."

The elements of poetic voice are the same as those in prose—word choice, syntax, rhythm, pace—but because poetry is such a dense and compact form, the tone or attitude implied will be announced at once, usually in the first line. Some lines hurl themselves at the reader, some muse and meander, some put the face of calm on rage or grief. Compare the voices in these first lines from poems in this book:

When I lay my head in my mother's lap...
Sometimes it's all about how you wear your poncho...
Life, friends, is boring. We must not say so...
I have wanted excellence in the knife throw...

These are lines of roughly equal length; each has four or five accented syllables; all use language and syntax familiar to us. But in each case, we as readers have instant insight into the attitude or tone of the speaker, and could probably identify the facial expression, even the physical stance, taken by the speaker of each. Here are three further first lines all couched in the form of a command:

Remove clothes and put to one side...
Bulldoze the bed where we made love...
Don't look at his hands now...

Yet in this swift compass we hear the rhetoric of three very different emotions. Spoken aloud each will, literally, invite a particular tone of voice.

Doubleness

Poet David Kirby points out that when you "...link convincingly two unrelated objects or ideas...follow through to its logical conclusion and then push it past logic into meaningful *non sequiture*, you are doing what you came to do in the first place: thinking and feeling in fresh, original ways, with heart and mind working together."

What makes for literary freshness—the combination of two things not usually combined—also makes for density. There is great poetic potential in all sorts of doubleness: not only "mixed emotions" and the larger ironies of life, but also the **pun** (a play on two meanings of the same word, as *the pun is mightier than the sword*), the **paradox** (a seeming contradiction that may nevertheless be true, as *the trap of too many options*), and the **oxymoron** (the pairing of contradictory terms, as a *deafening silence*).

Here is a poem by Sharon Olds in which image, voice, character, setting, story, and wordplay are compressed, into vivid and resonant "contrary feelings":

When I take my girl to the swimming party
I set her down among the boys. They tower and
bristle, she stands there smooth and sleek,
her math scores unfolding in the air around her.
They will strip to their suits, her body hard and
indivisible as a prime number,

they'll plunge in the deep end, she'll subtract
her height from ten feet, divide it into
hundreds of gallons of water, the numbers
bouncing in her mind like molecules of chlorine
in the bright blue pool. When they climb out,
her ponytail will hang its pencil lead
down her back, her narrow silk suit
with hamburgers and fries printed on it
will glisten in the brilliant air, and they will
see her sweet face, solemn and
sealed, a factor of one, and she will
see their eyes, two each,
their legs, two each, and the curves of their sexes,
one each, and in her head she'll be doing her
wild multiplying, as the drops
sparkle and fall to the power of a thousand from her body.

"The One Girl at the Boys Party"

This poem marries puberty and mathematics—a conceit, because we can't immediately apprehend any similarity. The strange combination begins prosaically enough, with some tension in the contrast between the boys' bristling and the girl's smoothness, and develops into an extended metaphor as the poem progresses. We are surprised by the image "her math scores unfolding in the air around her" and then the power struggle inherent in the numbers begins to unfold, the "body hard and indivisible," the "plunge in the deep end," the "pencil lead down her back," the "power of a thousand" laying out for us an absolutely generic American scene in terms that render it alive and new. As for "embodying contrary feelings in the same motion," here we have a portrait of a girl who has all the power of refusal—*smooth, sleek, indivisible, sweet, solemn,* and *sealed.* But what is the effect of those hamburgers and fries glistening on her suit? What of her wild multiplying?

And consider the voice. How would this poem be altered if it were in the voice of the girl herself, rather than the mother? If it were from the viewpoint of one of the boys? The poem has very much the tone of personal experience: Suppose it were an essay rather than a poem. How would language have to change? What points made by the imagery would be made in explanatory or confessional prose? How *long* would it have to be?

TRY THIS 10.7

Recast "The One Girl at the Boys Party" as an essay. Untangle the syntax, supply the missing reasoning and reflection, develop the point of view of the mother.

Write the poem from the daughter's viewpoint.

Write it from a boy's viewpoint.

Write a poem, in exactly one hundred words, about a scene familiar to you, developing a metaphor or conceit.

Cut it to fifty words, leaving in all the meaning.

Poetic Action

Caroline Kizer voices the perhaps surprising requirement that "in a poem something happens." Her mentor Theodore Roethke even advised thinking of a poem "as a three-act play, where you move from one impulse to the next, and then there is a final breath, which is the summation of the whole." Kizer points out that Roethke's poem, "I Knew a Woman" (p. 119), contains the line "She taught me Turn, and Counter-turn, and Stand," which is "the essence of the dramatic structure. It's what a long poem has to do. It doesn't require physical action, but there has to be some mental or emotional movement that carries through the poem." Another way of saying this is that a poem will have a beginning, a middle, and an end—and as in a story the beginning will somehow lay out a situation, the middle will somehow develop that situation, and the end will find it somehow changed. In a poem what happens may be huge, historical, mythical, or it may be mental or microscopic. It need not involve an overt action; it may be a shift of perspective, a movement of the mind—but as in a story it will involve some discovery and also at the very least the decision to accept a new perspective. To the extent that the poem involves decision and discovery, it will also tell a story.

If a poem mimics dramatic structure and involves movement, it will need like a story or drama to achieve conclusion. In Roethke's description, this achievement is the "final breath," or in his line above, the "and Stand" of the poem. Poet Maxine Kumin uses the metaphor of a closing door to argue that at the end of a poem there needs to be "if not the slam...then at least the click of the bolt in the jamb," and she disparages "the poem that ends by simply falling off the page in an accident of imbalance, so that the reader, poor fish, doesn't actually know the poem has ended."

Kumin identifies four kinds of ending that make the poem click like a bolt in the jamb:

1. A poem that comes full circle, like Phillip Larkin's "Annus Mirabilis," (page 313) which begins and ends with the four lines:

   ...Nineteen sixty-three
   (Which was rather late for me)—
   Between the end of the *Chatterly* ban
   And the Beatles' first LP.

2. The poem that ends in a startling understatement, of which Grace Paley's "Fathers" on page 314 is an example:

   ...as the women and children who
   will surely be in the way.

3. By contrast, a poem that culminates in an apocalyptic statement, as at the end of William Trowbridge's "Kong Looks Back on His Tryout with the Bears" in Chapter 3, page 80, which ends:

   ...and here I am, panty sniffer, about to die a clown,
   who once opened a hole you could drive Nebraska through.

4. A poem that ends with an aggressive shift of balance; read through Donald Hall's "To a Waterfowl" on pages 315–316 and observe how the last stanza, and especially the last line, turn the poem radically outward to the reader:

Not you, not you, not you, not you, not you.

Kumin's classifications seem to me helpful toward seeing the possibilities of poetic closure. On the other hand, like most systems, they run the risk of narrowing your vision. So try this:

TRY THIS 10.8

Choose three published poems that especially speak to you. Ponder the effect of the last line or lines and write a sentence or two describing that effect. Give it a name.

Now choose a poem you have written, preferably one with which you are not quite satisfied, and experiment with radically altering the last line or the last few lines. Try repeating the opening. Try understatement, apocalypse, or some means of sharply shifting balance. Try to give the poem one or another of the effects you have described. Chances are you will see the poem in a new light, and may be ready to tackle it again.

The rules of scansion are outlined in Appendix A, "A Basic Prosody," together with some suggestions for stanza form; at the end of this chapter are some suggestions for still further study. If it is your intention, your calling, and your destiny to be a poet, then you probably drink in this technical trivia with an unslakable thirst, like a sports fan after baseball statistics or a train spotter with a schedule in hand. W. H. Auden observed that the best poets often start out with a passion, not for ideas or people, but for the possibilities of sound. It is surely true that the love of language can be practiced in the throat, the ear, the heartbeat, and the body; whatever you have or may in future have to say, the saying of it starts there.

TRY THIS 10.9

Write a dozen lines of verse about the (real or imaginary) boring or marvelous things you did yesterday. When you've done that, look through your lines to find at least one example of alliteration, one example of assonance, and one internal rhyme. Find at least one end-stopped line, one run-on line, and one caesura. If you don't find any one of these things, alter the lines to put it there. Read the lines aloud and do anything you feel necessary to make them *sound* better. Don't make sense. Make music.

More to Read

Pinsky, Robert. *The Sounds of Poetry*. New York: Farrar, Strauss, Giroux, 1998. Print.
Fussell, Paul. *Poetic Meter and Poetic Form*. New York: McGraw-Hill, 1979. Print.
Hirshfield, Jane. *Nine Gates: Entering the Mind of Poetry*. New York: Harper Perennial, 1997. Print.

GERALD STERN

Columbia the Gem

I know that body standing in the Low Library,
the right shoulder lower than the left one, the lotion sea lotion—
his hold is ended.
Now the mouths can slash away in memory
of his kisses and stupefying lies.
Now the old Reds can walk with a little spring
in and around the beloved sarcophagi.
Now the Puerto Ricans can work up another funny America
and the frightened Germans can open their heavy doors a little.
Now the River can soften its huge heart
and move, for the first time, almost like the others
without silence.

TRY THIS 10.10

The Replacement Poem. One way to demonstrate for yourself the density of poetic techniques is to write a "replacement poem." In this form of play, you take any poem you admire and replace all the nouns, verbs, adjectives, and adverbs with other words that are in each case the same part of speech. Other parts of speech—conjunctions, prepositions, articles—you may leave or change as you please. "Columbia the Gem," above, is a damning portrait, made forceful by sense images and energetic verbs, compressed in its rhythm to a kind of poignant anger. If I replace all the major parts of speech (and some prepositions and conjunctions), the mood and meaning will change, but the energy will remain. Here is my replacement poem:

They bless this mother bending in her plastic kitchen,
the crooked knee redder than the straight one, the Clorox stink Pine Sol—
her shine is glorious.
Soon the peppers will leap aloft in celebration
of her moans and hypocritical hypochondria.
Then the fat flowers will jump to the black waters
over and under the hysterical linoleum.
Then the giant corporations will buy out another weeping mom-and-pop
and the laughing Coke-folk will crank her rusted icemaker a while.
Then the stove will burst its stinking flame
and collapse, in its last meal, very near the drains,
for reconciliation.

Write a replacement poem. Choose any poem from anywhere in your reading, but make it one that you truly admire. You needn't worry about making sense; the poem will do it for you. You can fiddle afterward if you want to move it nearer your meaning.

TRY THIS 10.11

Get together with three or four other students and decide on a poem you will all replace. Separately, write the replacement poems. Get together again to discuss how different are your voices and your visions. What do the replacements have in common?

SYLVIA PLATH

Stillborn

These poems do not live: it's a sad diagnosis.
They grew their toes and fingers well enough,
Their little foreheads bulged with concentration.
If they missed out on walking about like people
It wasn't for any lack of mother-love.

O I cannot understand what happened to them!
They are proper in shape and number and every part.
They sit so nicely in the pickling fluid!
They smile and smile and smile and smile at me.
And still the lungs won't fill and the heart won't start.

They are not pigs, they are not even fish,
Though they have a piggy and a fishy air—
It would be better if they were alive, and that's
    what they were.
But they are dead, and their mother near dead
    with distraction,
And they stupidly stare, and do not speak of her.

STEVE KOWIT

The Grammar Lesson

A noun's a thing. A verb's the thing it does.
An adjective is what describes the noun.
In "The can of beets is filled with purple fuzz"

of and *with* are prepositions. *The's*
an article, a *can's* a noun,
a noun's a thing. A verb's the thing it does.

A can *can* roll—or not. What isn't was
or might be, *might* meaning not yet known.
"Our can of beets *is* filled with purple fuzz"
is present tense. While words like *our* and *us*
are pronouns—i.e., *it* is moldy, *they* are icky brown.
A noun's a thing; a verb's the thing it does.

Is is a helping verb. It helps because
filled isn't a full verb. *Can's* what *our* owns
in "*Our* can of beets is filled with purple fuzz."

See? There's almost nothing to it. Just
memorize these rules... or write them down!
A noun's a thing, a verb's the thing it does.
The can of beets is filled with purple fuzz.

TRY THIS 10.12

These two preceding poems are **self-reflexive;** they are about language and writing, one of them in the very intricate poetic form of a **villanelle.** Write a self-reflexive poem, either about your own poetry or about some technical point of language. If you like, try making the poem comic, choosing a formal pattern in which to do it.

PHILIP LARKIN

Annus Mirabilis

Sexual intercourse began
In nineteen sixty-three
(Which was rather late for me)—
Between the end of the *Chatterly* ban
And the Beatles' first LP.

Up till then there'd only been
A sort of bargaining,
A wrangle for a ring,
A shame that started at sixteen
And spread to everything.

Then all at once the quarrel sank:
Everyone felt the same,

And every life became
A brilliant breaking of the bank,
A quite unlosable game.

So life was never better than
In nineteen sixty-three
(Though just too late for me)—
Between the end of the *Chatterly* ban
And the Beatles' first LP.

TRY THIS 10.13
Write four funny verses about one of these:
sex
religion
birth
war

GRACE PALEY

Fathers

Fathers are
more fathering
these days they have
accomplished this by
being more mothering

what luck for them that
women's lib happened then
the dream of new fathering
began to shine in the eyes
for free women and was irresistible

on the New York subways
and the mass transits
of other cities one may
see fatherings of many colors
with their round babies on
their laps this may also
happen in the countryside

these scenes were brand-new
exciting for an old woman who

had watched the old fathers
gathering once again in
familiar Army camps and comfortable war rooms to consider
the necessary eradication of
the new fathering fathers
(who are their sons) as well
as the women and children who
will surely be in the way.

TRY THIS 10.14

Write four serious free-verse stanzas about one of these:
sex
religion
birth
war

DONALD HALL

To a Waterfowl

Women with hats like the rear ends of pink ducks
applauded you, my poems.
These are the women whose husbands I meet on airplanes,
who close their briefcases and ask, "What are *you* in?"
I look in their eyes, I tell them I am in poetry,

and their eyes fill with anxiety, and with little tears.
"Oh, yeah?" they say, developing an interest in clouds.
"My wife, she likes that sort of thing? Hah-hah?
I guess maybe I'd better watch my grammar, huh?"
I leave them in airports, watching their grammar,

and take a limousine to the Women's Goodness Club
where I drink Harvery's Bristol Cream with their wives,
and eat chicken salad with capers, with little tomato wedges,
and I read them "The Erotic Crocodile," and "Eating You."
Ah, when I have concluded the disbursement of sonorities,

crooning, "High on thy thigh I cry, Hi!"—and so forth—
they spank their wide hands, they smile like Jell-O,
and they say, "Hah-hah? My goodness, Mr. Hall,

but you certainly do have an imagination, huh?"
"Thank you, indeed," I say; "it brings in the bacon."

But now, my poems, now I have returned to the motel,
returned to *l'eternel retour* of the Holiday Inn,
naked, lying on the bed, watching *Godzilla Sucks Mt. Fuji*,
addressing my poems, feeling superior, and drinking bourbon
from a flask disguised to look like a transistor radio.

Ah, my poems, it is true,
that with the deepest gratitude and most serene pleasure,
and with hints that I am a sexual Thomas Alva Edison,
and not without collecting an exorbitant fee,
I have accepted the approbation of feathers.

And what about you? You, laughing? You, in the bluejeans,
laughing at your mother who wears hats, and at your father
who rides airplanes with a briefcase watching his grammar?
Will you ever be old and dumb, like your creepy parents?
Not you, not you, not you, not you, not you, not you.

TRY THIS 10.15
Write a poem as a satire: Pick a type you find boring, irritating, or worse, and give us a sharp picture in words. Extra points for comedy.

SHARON OLDS

The Language of the Brag

I have wanted excellence in the knife-throw,
I have wanted to use my exceptionally strong and accurate arms
and my straight posture and quick electric muscles
to achieve something at the center of a crowd,
the blade piercing the bark deep,
the haft slowly and heavily vibrating like the cock.

I have wanted some epic use for my excellent body,
some heroism, some American achievement
beyond the ordinary for my extraordinary self,
magnetic and tensile, I have stood by the sandlot
and watched the boys play.

I have wanted courage, I have thought about fire
and the crossing of waterfalls, I have dragged around

my belly big with cowardice and safety,
my stool black with iron pills,
my huge breasts oozing mucus,
my legs swelling, my hands swelling,
my face swelling and darkening, my hair
falling out, my inner sex
stabbed again and again with terrible pain like a knife.
I have lain down.

I have lain down and sweated and shaken
and passed blood and feces and water and
slowly alone in the center of a circle I have
passed the new person out
and they have lifted the new person free of the act
and wiped the new person free of that
language of blood like praise all over the body.

I have done what you wanted to do, Walt Whitman,
Allen Ginsberg, I have done this thing,
I and the other women this exceptional
act with the exceptional heroic body,
this giving birth, this glistening verb,
and I am putting my proud American boast
right here with the others.

TRY THIS 10.16

Write a brag. This will be a list poem. Find a refrain line (other than "I have wanted") to introduce each item on your list of excellences. Believe every boast.

JOHN BERRYMAN

Dream Song 14

Life, friends, is boring. We must not say so.
After all, the sky flashes, the great sea yearns,
we ourselves flash and yearn,
and moreover my mother told me as a boy

(repeatingly) "Ever to confess you're bored
means you have no

Inner Resources." I conclude now I have no
inner resources, because I am heavy bored.
Peoples bore me,
literature bores me, especially great literature,
Henry bores me, with his plight & gripes
as bad as achilles,

who loves people and valiant art, which bores me.
And the tranquil hills, & gin, look like a drag
and somehow a dog
has taken itself & its tail considerably away
into mountains or sea or sky, leaving
behind: me, wag.

TRY THIS 10.17
Write a poem that begins with an outrageous general pronouncement—try to make it more outrageous than "Life, friends, is boring." Develop a "proof" in imagery. Try using repetition, alliteration, assonance, and/or internal rhyme.

ACCOMPLISHING A DRAFT
Choose three rough drafts of poems that feel most promising. Spend a day with each, reading it aloud, tinkering with the sounds and syntax. Identify at least one place in each that makes you uneasy, dissatisfied. Concentrate on that place; play with it. Try loosening the rhythm, tightening the images, replacing the lines with something else altogether. Try cutting them entirely Try endings of radically different sorts.

Identify a line or lines you feel especially good about. Can you articulate what it is about them that satisfies you?

Is there action or a movement of meaning within the poem?

Put each poem away for as long as you can afford; then take it out again and read as if you had never seen it before. What will you do next?

Poetry Format

Whereas prose is always double-spaced in manuscript for ease of reading, poetry often is not. Because the look of the poem-as-object is important to its effect, most poets strive to produce a manuscript page that looks as much like the printed poem as possible. Single spacing usually achieves this better.

Poems do not require a title page. Center the title above the poem and put your name and address at the top of the page or at the end of the poem, toward the right side of the page. If your poem spills over onto a new page and the new page begins with a new stanza, make sure that the stanza break is clear.

Ben Jonson
123 Courtly Way
London W9 1NR
(020) 328-1563
bjonson@cavalier.edu

Still to Be Neat

Still to be neat, still to be dressed,
As you were going to a feast;
Still to be powdered, still perfumed:
Lady, it is to be presumed,
Though art's hid causes are not found,
All is not sweet, all is not sound.

Give me a look, give me a face
That makes simplicity a grace;
Robes loosely flowing, hair as free.
Such sweet neglect more taketh me
Than all the adulteries of art;
They strike my eye, but not my heart.

CHAPTER 11

Drama

- *The Difference Between Drama and Fiction*
- *Sight: Sets, Action, Costumes, Props*
- *Sound: Verbal and Nonverbal*
- *The Ten-Minute Play*
- *Some Notes on Screenwriting*
- *Drama Format*

On the stage it is always now.
Thornton Wilder

Pamela Hansen/Marek & Assoc/trunkarchive.com

WARM-UP

In preparation for writing a short dramatic scene between these two characters, do some mental or journal doodling. Who are these people? What is their relationship to each other? Perhaps it's not the obvious one. What town or city are they in, and how familiar are they with that locale? Why are they here? Whose room is this? What has happened in the preceding 24 hours? What does each of these characters want? What is the conflict between their deep desires? What is the specific conflict here, at this moment?

Write no more than five pages of dialogue in which the immediate conflict is brought to crisis and in some way or other resolved. (He leaves, she leaves, they both stay, they both go?) As with a short-short story, in order to accomplish this you'll have to dive straight into the conflict. Nevertheless, the answers to the above questions should all be stated or implied.

The Difference Between Drama and Fiction

Like fiction, a play

tells a story of human change,
in which a character goes on a psychic journey,
involving a power struggle between protagonist and antagonist,
through a process of discovery and decision,
connection and disconnection,
culminating in a crisis action,
to arrive at a situation different from that in which he or she began.

As with fiction, it's important to choose the plot you will make from this story, the particular portion that will be dramatized. Why does the action begin in this place, at this particular time? In reading this chapter, then, it might be helpful to review what you have learned in Chapters 6 and 9, on Story and Fiction.

But drama is different from fiction, in fundamental ways that mean you as a writer select and arrange differently if you choose to tell your story in the form of a play. Here, for a start, is a chart detailing the differences between the two forms:

Fiction	Drama
The writer writes what the reader reads.	The script is interpreted by the director and cast.
Takes place in the reader's imagination.	Takes place here, now, on the stage.
Takes place in private, in solitude.	Takes place in public, communally.
All images, sensory experiences, and ideas are in words, transcribed in the brain.	Actors, props, costumes can be seen; dialogue and music can be heard.
Can go into characters' thoughts.	All thoughts must be externalized.
Author may offer direct interpretations and analysis in the course of the story.	Only characters express opinions. The author's meaning emerges indirectly.
Can go into past action.	Past must be made part of present.
Can be any length; room to digress.	Length more or less prescribed; must be focused.
Can be taken up and put down at will.	Continuous performance.
After publisher's initial cost outlay, can be reproduced indefinitely.	Theater holds only a given number of seats; production remains expensive.

In stage drama, the process of story is condensed and intensified. Usually something has happened before the curtain opens, called the **inciting incident,** which creates the situation in which the protagonist finds himself/herself: *Hamlet's father has died and his mother has remarried.* The play will present this situation through **exposition**: *The watchmen reveal that the ghost of Hamlet's father has been walking near the castle at night.* Very soon, the action begins with a **point of attack**: *The ghost speaks to Hamlet, demanding revenge against Claudius.*

Now the play has set up its conflict, identified the protagonist and antagonist, and it is time for the complications to begin.

All of these traditions can also be identified in a story: The inciting incident of "Cinderella" would be that her mother has died and her father has remarried; the exposition tells us that the stepmother and stepsisters mistreat her; the point of attack arrives with the invitation to the ball.

But the core fact of theater is that it takes place right now! right here! before your very eyes! Fiction is usually written in past tense, and even when it is not, there is an implied perspective of "looking back" on an action completed. The constant effort of the fiction writer must therefore be to give the imaginative past the immediacy of the present. In drama, the effort is the opposite, to present the necessary information of the past as an integral part of the present drama.

A play is *short*. It takes much longer to say words aloud than to read them silently (test it by timing yourself reading a short story silently, and then reading it aloud). Whereas it might take five or fifteen hours to read a novel, it's unlikely you will get an audience to sit still for more than a couple of hours (and the current tendency is toward shorter plays)—yet the substance of a short story is unlikely to be rich enough for the effort of a full evening's staging.

This means that drama is an *intense* form; the dialogue must be economical and focused. Like a short-short story, a play asks that you throw the audience immediately into the action. Like a poem, it asks for several things to be going on at once.

Whereas poetry depends for its density largely on the interplay between sound and meaning, drama depends on the interplay between sight and sound. As poetry plays the rhythm of the line in tension with the rhythm of the sentence, so drama plays the revelation of the verbal in tension with the revelation of the visual.

When you write for the stage, you lose a great deal that you may indulge as a fiction writer—the freedom not only to leap from place to place and from past to future, but also to go inside your characters' minds to tell us directly what they are thinking; to interpret for us, telling us what to believe about them or the situation; and to digress on themes or topics that may be of interest but do not add to the action.

Moreover, the trade-off between fiction and drama requires an act of faith. The audience does not receive what you wrote in the form in which you wrote it, but in an interpretation of it filtered through the director, actors, and designers who may know less about it than you do. You are in effect handing them your baby to do with as they please. The theater is unforgiving, too, in terms of cost, so that practical constraints are always in the way of the imagination, demanding that you pare down the cast, presenting you with a meager version of your vision.

What you get in return is the live presence of sight and sound—movement, music, props, costumes, sound effects—to be used as inventively as you and your director can devise. You gain the immediacy and expressiveness of live actors. You gain the thrill of an organic collaboration in which a dozen or a few dozen people are bent on a single venture, their interest vested in the success of your script, their talents laid down in tracks along your own. Because all of these tracks must work together if the project is to succeed, theater succeeds less often than prose and poetry. You need stamina for such a strong chance of failure. But because the show is alive and has the depth of all that collaboration, when it does work, it works with exhilarating immediacy. As actor Kevin Spacey puts it, "Nothing comes close to it—this living experience between the actor and the audience, sharing the same space at the same time." And nothing in your experience as a fiction writer matches the thrill of sitting in an audience watching the live embodiment of your words, *feeling* the emotions of the audience around you as they laugh or cry with the work of your imagination.

TRY THIS 11.1

Take any passage of fiction or memoir in your journal and play with the idea of putting it onstage. Where would it take place? What would the characters say? How would they be dressed? How would they behave?

Sight: Sets, Action, Costumes, Props

I take it as my principle that words do not mean everything.

Antonin Artaud

The drama begins the moment the audience sees the stage, and this first sight sets the tone for everything that follows. The set may represent the extreme of **fourth-wall realism,** the convention that we are spying on what happens through the space where the fourth wall of the room has been removed; or the opposite extreme of **theatricalism,** the convention that acknowledges the stage is a stage, the actors are actors, and the audience is an audience. It may be anywhere between or a combination of the two. In Arthur Miller's *Death of a Salesman,* for example, two floors of a house are realistically represented, but when the characters move into memory or fantasy, they ignore the doors and walk through the walls.

The scenery will set the tone even if you decide on a bare stage, or no set at all, because the less there is on the stage, the more the audience will read into what is there. Human beings are meaning-making creatures; we love to interpret and conclude. So when scenery, clothing, and objects appear onstage, we will read significance at once. If the curtain opens on a maypole or a tribal mask or a backdrop of a bonfire, it's no use telling us that these are mere decoration. We will take them for clues.

This fact is full of rich possibilities for the playwright, and also for the actor. Choose clothes that characterize, objects that reveal. Remember that everything we wear and own bespeaks our desires, choices, background, gender, politics—and make your stage visually vivid with such hints.

If there are elements of familiar exterior or interior space on the stage, give them a distinct meaning. If the play takes place in a college dorm room (and you can probably make a more imaginative choice), then how do the wall hangings, clothes, objects, plants characterize the person who lives here? The playwright has no less an obligation than the poet or story writer to choose revealing specific details. How do you communicate with the readers of your play—and especially with the designer—in order to help them translate your vision either mentally or onto the stage? "A typical college dorm room" will *not* do it (in fact, avoid the words *normal, typical,* and *ordinary*—they are all cop-outs). A writer of stage directions is a writer and must paint the picture in the words.

It is even possible to introduce conflict before the actors enter, as in this opening stage direction from Simon Gray's *Butley*:

> *An office in a College of London University. About 10 in the morning. The office is badly decorated (white walls, graying, plaster boards) with strip lighting. There are two desks opposite each other, each with a swivel chair. BEN's desk, left, is a chaos of papers, books, detritus. JOEY's desk, right, is almost bare. Behind each desk is a bookcase. Again, BEN's is chaotic with old essays and mimeographed sheets scattered among the books, while JOEY's is neat, not many books on the shelves.*

Here, before a single character enters, we know a good deal about the characters of Ben and Joey, and that there will be conflict between them. When Ben enters, other props, his costume, and his way of relating to them further reveal his character, his current state of mind, the tone of the play we are going to see, and again the potential conflict:

> *As the curtain rises, BEN enters, in a plastic raincoat, which he takes off and throws into the chair. He has a lump of cotton wool on his chin, from a particularly nasty shaving cut. He goes to his chair, sits down, looks around as if searching for something, shifts uncomfortably, pulls the plastic mac out from under him, searches through its pockets, takes out half a banana, a bit squashed, then throws the raincoat over to JOEY's desk. He takes a bite from the banana. . . .*

One important thing to notice about stage directions is that they tell us *what we see* but do not give us any information that we must learn through dialogue. The stage direction above goes far enough to tell us that the cotton is on a bad shaving cut—which is a visual directive to the props and makeup department—but it does not say, "Ben has been quarreling with his wife." This is information that we will have to learn through dialogue, and it must wait for dialogue to be revealed. In general, the script reveals information in the order in which it is revealed onstage. What the audience learns through sight or nonverbal sound will appear in the stage directions. What it learns through dialogue will be revealed only when the characters say it.

Frequently, however, what the characters say is at odds with what they wear, handle, or, especially, do. They speak a text but reveal the subtext through these other means. The **stage lie** can be revealed by action, or by slips of the tongue, stumbling, exaggeration—all those verbal clues by which we learn in life that people are not telling the absolute truth. We never trust the frankness of anyone who begins, "To be frank with you..."

The sort of information that comes through a stage lie is a major source of understanding to the audience. The actor wears satin flounces and says, "I've always preferred the simple life." He clutches the wallet to his chest and says, "The money doesn't mean a thing to me, it's the principle." She says, "Oh, good, I was just coming to see you," and quickly slips the folder into the drawer. In all these instances, sight is at odds with sound, and we are likely to believe the evidence of our eyes. Here is Ben's first line of dialogue:

The telephone rings.

BEN: Butley, English. Hello, James, have a nice break? (*A pause—he mouths a curse.*) Sorry, James, I can't talk now—I'm right in the middle of a tutorial—'bye.

Because the truth is often revealed in the discrepancies between sight and sound, text and subtext, stage directions are important. But not *all* stage movement is worthy of a stage direction. Most movement is "blocking," that is, a decision on the director's part about where the actors should move and what they should do during a given passage. As playwright, you can make your stage directions count by specifying only the sights and movements that help tell a story—as "*he mouths a curse*" does above. It's fine if you see the play taking place in your mind, but "*She moves left from the chair to the couch and sits again*" is usually not going to help tell the story, and should be left up to the director.

In Chapter 5 on setting, I said that relationship to place is revealing of character, and that when there is discomfort or conflict in that relationship, a story has already begun. Playwrights productively exploit this phenomenon. The curtain opens on a huge room dominated by a mahogany desk and leather chair. One door opens. A young woman enters clutching her handbag in front of her. She cranes her head forward, peering at the ceiling, the walls. She reaches out gingerly and touches the desk with two fingers. She steps sideways, stops, then perches on the edge of a straight back chair. Another door opens. Another woman enters, shrugging off her coat and hooking it with one motion on the coat rack behind her. She juggles a clipboard through this process, crosses without looking at the first woman, slings herself into the leather chair, and swivels it around. How much do you know about the situation already? More important, how much do you know about the relationship between these people by their relationship to the room? Who belongs here? Who has the power? Who, so far, has your sympathy? (And remember that in literature the sympathy of the reader or the audience is very great power!)

TRY THIS 11.2

Choose a setting that seems to you both familiar and slightly dull: that dorm room, a kitchen, a restaurant, or something similar. Then write an opening stage direction of no more than a hundred words that makes it both interesting to look at and revealing of its owner.

Introduce into this setting one character who is familiar with it and comfortable with it, and one who is unfamiliar and uncomfortable. What does each want? Write a page or so of their dialogue (with stage directions as appropriate).

Sound: Verbal and Nonverbal

Dialogue is the most important element of most stage plays, but there are hundreds of nonverbal sounds that are ripe with emotional content. Make yourself aware of them and be alert to ways you can take advantage of them. A baby's cry, a scream, whistling, sobbing, laughing, a howl of pain, a sneeze, a cluck of irritation, fingers drumming, feet tapping—all of these are human sounds that are often clearer indications of mood than speech. But nonhuman sounds also often produce in us immediate reaction: a crash, splintering glass, a ringing telephone, squealing tires, a siren, a gun shot, horse's hooves...

TRY THIS 11.3

Make two lists, one of human nonverbal sounds, one of nonhuman sounds with emotional potential in our reaction to them. Make the lists long. Keep adding to the lists. Think about ways to use them.

Music, too, though its choice is often the province of the director, can be incorporated into the written text as an indicator of mood, period, or character, or can even be made a part of the action by representing a conflict between two characters: Daughter wants to practice her tryout cover for *American Idol* while Dad wants to listen to his Schubert CD. **Diegetic** sound and music, like this example, occurs realistically within the action: Someone practices the violin, or the sounds of traffic come through the open window. **Nondiegetic** sound is stylized, not arising from the action but as an accompaniment or background to it: The hero bursts into song at the office water cooler, or a jazz riff covers the blackout between scenes.

In this short excerpt from *Death of a Salesman,* dialogue, action, and diegetic sound come together to create a composition of meanings that is almost like the texture of music itself. The aging salesman and his wife are in the bedroom while their son Biff wanders through the house:

LINDA [*Timidly*]: Willy, dear, what has he got against you?

WILLY: I'm so tired. Don't talk any more.

Biff slowly returns to the kitchen. He stops, stares toward the heater.

LINDA: Will you ask Howard to let you work in New York?

WILLY: First thing in the morning. Everything'll be all right.

Biff reaches behind the heater and draws out a length of rubber tubing. He is horrified and turns his head toward Willy's room, still dimly lit, from which the strains of Linda's desperate but monotonous humming rise.

Here we have the husband and wife in "no dialogue" (*what has he got against you/Don't talk any more*); their son, in contrasting action, confirms his father's suicide attempt, while the mother hums (nonverbal) and, against Willy's reassurance—*Everything'll be all right*—the lighting symbolically fades. This very small scene, with its interlocking elements, represents **dramatic irony,** which occurs whenever the audience knows more than the characters know. In this instance, we have known for most of the act about the suicide attempt Biff has just learned about, and unlike Linda we already guess what Biff "has against" his father. We know with grim certainty that "everything" won't be all right.

TRY THIS 11.4

Rewrite the scene you did for Try This 11.2 on page 327, this time for radio. "Translate" your stage direction into sound alone, verbal, nonverbal, and musical, trying to reveal everything through the one sense.

Theatrical Dialogue

Unlike the other genres, all the dialogue in drama is direct. There is no place for indirect or summary dialogue. With the single exception of "ad lib"—which means that the actors fill in at their discretion with, for instance, greetings to each other or background mumble—you write the words any character speaks. You may not, for example, say in a stage direction, "*Joe calls in from the bathroom, still complaining.*" It's the playwright's obligation to provide the words.

The most difficult dialogue to write is often the exposition, in which you must give the audience the necessary information about what has gone on before curtain rise, and what the situation is now. A useful tradition, and probably the most frequently used device, is to have a character who knows explain to a character who doesn't know. But if you don't have a character who is handily ignorant, you can have two characters talk about the situation and make it sound natural as long as they concentrate on how they feel about it, or disagree about it, so that the information comes out incidentally, sideways. If a character says, "My sister's train is due at four o'clock into Union Station," we get the facts, but if he says, "I can't talk now! I've got to make it to Union Station by four—my sister goes bananas if I'm not there to meet her train," we know something about his attitude and the relationship as well as the situation—and it sounds like talk.

A third expository device, if your play is stylized, is to have a character come forward and speak directly to the audience. Ever since film began to prove itself the best medium for realism, this **theatricalist** technique (acknowledging that the play is a play and the audience an audience) has become more and more popular in the theater.

> **SALIERI:** I can almost see you in your ranks—waiting for your turn to live. Ghosts of the future! Be visible. I beg you. Come to this dusty old room... Will you not enter this place and stay with me till dawn?... There. It worked. I can see you!... And now, gracious ladies! Obliging gentlemen! I present to you—for one performance only—my last composition, entitled *The Death of Mozart; or Did I Do It?*... Dedicated to posterity on this, the last night of my life!
>
> Amadeus, *Peter Shaffer*

Good dialogue will carry most of its tone as an integral part of the lines, and when this is the case, there is no need to announce the tone of voice in a stage direction—and it can in fact be insulting to the actors. An example:

> **SHE** [*Slyly*]: By the way, did you get the rent money from the Smiths?
> **HE** [*Suspiciously*]: What makes you ask that?
> **SHE** [*Casually*]: Oh, nothing, I just wondered.
> **HE** [*Angrily*]: You've had all the money you're going to get this week!

Not a single one of these tonal directions is necessary; the tone is inherent in the lines. Contrast with this version:

> **SHE:** By the way, did you get the rent money from the Smiths?
> **HE:** What makes you ask that?
> **SHE** [*Slipping the catalogue behind the cushion*]: Oh, nothing, I just wondered.
> **HE** [*Laughing*]: You've had all the money you're going to get this week! (*He begins to tickle her.*)

Here, actions and tone reveal a contradiction or qualification of what the words suggest, so the stage directions are appropriate.

Here are a few further things to remember about play dialogue, to make it natural and intense:

- The sooner you introduce the conflict, the better. A certain amount of exposition will be necessary, but if you can reveal *at the same time* the point of attack, it's all to the good. *Hamlet* begins with two guards discussing the fact that the ghost has walked (the inciting incident). But they immediately anticipate the conflict: *Will it walk again?*

- Dialogue is action when it contains both conflict and the possibility of change. Keep alert to the possibility that characters discover and decide through the medium of talk. Debate between two firmly decided people is not dramatic, no matter how mad they are. Disagreement between people who must stay in proximity to each other, especially if they care about each other, is inherently more dramatic than if they can walk away.
- Use "no" dialogue, in which people deny, contradict, refuse, qualify, or otherwise say no to each other.
- Dialogue has to be said, so say it aloud and make sure it flows easily, allows for breath, sounds like talk.
- Remember that people are not always able or willing to say just what they mean, and that this breaks the flow of the talk. This is especially true when emotions are heating up. People break off, interrupt themselves and each other. Use sentence fragments. Don't always finish their...
- Silence can be white hot. The most intense emotions are the ones you can't express in words. When a character spews out an eloquent paragraph of anger, he is probably not as angry as if he stands, breathes hard, and turns away.
- Vary short exchanges with longer ones. A change of pace, from a sharp series of short lines to a longer speech and back again, keeps the rhythm interesting.
- Nearly everybody tries to be funny now and again. You can often reveal character, and also what a character may be hiding, by having her try to make light of it. A joke that falls flat with other characters is a great tension-raiser. Conversely, beware of having the characters too amused by each other's wit; the funnier they find the jokes, the less likely the audience is to be amused.
- Similarly, avoid having the characters comment on each other's dialogue; it's self-conscious. If He says, "That's a clever way to put it!" we'll hear the author in the praise.

TRY THIS 11.5

Choose one of the characters you have written about in your journal. Write a monologue in that character's voice beginning with one of the following trigger lines:

- I knew right away I'd said the wrong thing.
- You never let up, do you?
- I didn't hear the doorbell.
- What took you so long?
- What I remember best...
- It started out fine.

Now introduce stage directions into the monologue, describing anything we can see—what the character is wearing, doing, and so forth—so as to change, contradict, or qualify the meaning of the speech.

Revealing Thought

There are also several deliberate theatrical traditions for revealing thought. In the **soliloquy** the character simply talks to himself/herself (*To be or not to be...*), and the audience accepts that these words take place in the mind. In an **aside,** the character says one line to another character and another to the audience or to thin air. Traditionally, the aside is always the truth of that character's feeling. In a **voiceover,** the thoughts are recorded and play over the live scene. All of these techniques are stylized and can tend to be self-conscious. Use *very sparingly*—especially if your basic mode is realistic.

Crucial events of the past can be difficult to introduce naturally. One useful technique for doing this is the **emotional recall,** in which one character tells another about an incident from the past. But a narrated event is no more inherently dramatic than a debate, and you must not rely on the narration to hold the audience's interest. In order to keep the drama in the here! and now! the narration must hold the potential for change. The important emotion in an emotional recall is not the emotion of the teller but of the listener. Typically, a charged situation exists between one character and one or more others (it can be her mother or a mob). The first character tells a story. The listener(s) change attitude entirely. The dramatic situation is not the one in the story; it is the one on stage, where we see the change.

TRY THIS 11.6

Write a half-page monologue in which one character invites another to dinner. Now add asides to the audience telling us what the speaker *really* wants.

The Ten-Minute Play

Over the last couple of decades the ten-minute play, which used to be a rarity, has grown in popularity and frequency of production. This is largely due to the Humana Festival of the Actors Theatre of Louisville, which fostered the form in order to give more playwrights the chance to show their stuff. Because an abundance of good ten-minute plays demanding minimal staging resulted, theaters began to produce "evenings of"—five to eight plays at a time. Production begat more interest, which generated plays, which generated production, and so forth. Theatrical groups like Chicago Dramatists initiated challenge projects or "instant theater," in which playwrights are given a week to write a ten-minute play on a given theme ("the heat is on," "it's so hard to say goodbye"), with a particular stage problem (something onstage is alive; every third line is a cliché). It probably didn't hurt that a ten-minute play is all a student can be expected to bring forth in a multi-genre creative writing course. In any case, this form is now established, widely produced, and accepted as part of the American theatrical canon.

Like a short-short story (and the scope of a ten-minute play probably lies somewhere between a short-short and a short story), the form is excellent for practice in economy, originality, and punch. You have to, in the words of a writer friend, "hit it and get out." With fewer than a dozen pages to write, you must lead off with the conflict, develop it fast, and bring it to quick resolution. There will probably be only two or three characters and little in the way of set or stage décor. Therefore it is the language that must delineate character, and quickly. The form seems to ask for experimentation. Something offbeat in the way of plot or concept will stand out. And for the playwright, ten minutes is not much of a commitment. You have very little to lose, so you can take a risk.

TRY THIS 11.7

Write a ten-minute play in which two characters must somehow divide up a quantity of goods. Is it an inheritance? A divorce? A charity sale? Leftovers? What's the conflict? What particular thing or things represent the conflict? Who wins?

Or:

Write a ten-minute play in which two characters are unfailingly polite to each other. On the last page, one of the characters turns viciously on the other, and the audience is not surprised.

Or:

Write a ten-minute play on one of the following themes:

- Something left unsaid
- Excessive celebration
- Up the garden path
- The proof is in the pudding
- Follow the money
- Nothing but net

Some Notes on Screenwriting

Like theater, film is a visual and an audible medium in which human drama is presented directly to the senses, and in which sight can be played off against sound to heighten, reveal, and intensify.

The great difference is in the capacity of the camera to direct our attention and so create meaning. By changing angle or focus, by cutting from one sight to another, by exploiting the flexibility of technology, film can enhance both the range and the possible subtlety of the drama. Sound too can be manipulated to separate background noise from crucial dialogue, to effect a transition, or signal a crisis. And of course the possibilities for special effect are now limitless.

The stage being a more or less constant area, our attention must be *taken*, by dialogue, gesture, color, or sound, so the theater tends toward simplification and exaggeration. By contrast, film actors may mumble, barely glance, merely raise a finger, and the camera will make the meaning large and clear. It is a lucky historical accident that the "Stanislavski Method" of acting, which emphasizes emotional realism rather than stylized gesture, developed and spread from its origins in the Moscow Art Theatre to Europe and America at the same time as film was developing. The combination of internalized acting and technological advance has led to a film vocabulary that is ever more visual and less verbal—and, not incidentally, to the rise of the "auteur," the director as the real creator of the film. Curiously, the three-act structure, with its pattern of conflict, crisis, and resolution, has remained the standard for the Hollywood film.

In the early days of cinema, most directors and writers naturally considered film the sister-art of the stage, since it involved actors, sets, and so forth. (A great exception was D. W. Griffith, who declared that he had learned everything about film technique from Charles Dickens.) As the cinema developed, it became ever clearer that the camera uses many of the techniques of fiction—the ability to move instantly in space and time, the advantage of point of view, close-ups and slow motion for intensity, quick cuts and juxtaposition for revealing metaphor. At the same time, it became evident that film is a far better medium for realism than the stage, since the camera can go "on location" to depict actual city streets, aerial views, interiors, crowds, and so forth. Stage "realism," with painted flats for rooms and plywood cutouts for trees, was no match for film's ability to explore real homes and real forests. As a result, although realistic plays still abound, the general direction of the theater in the second half of the twentieth century was toward still greater stylization—theatricalism, the use of minimal stage elements and symbolic exaggeration, the incorporation of costume and set changes into the action. Since one thing the theater has over the movies is the living relationship of actor with audience, playwrights began to exploit this strength. Characters directly address or interact with the audience; the script is self-reflexive, calling attention to the fact that it's a play.

This movement toward stylization, which would appear severely limiting, has in fact been strangely freeing for the theater. Playwrights have been more inclined to borrow elements from other disciplines—dance, mime, puppetry, technology—to break the mold of "the well-made play" and display their psychological or social insights in the context of spectacle.

My advice to those who want to write for film is that, for the same reason a painter should begin with a still life, a screenwriter should begin with a stage play. It isn't easier, but it does reveal the necessary craft more clearly. Film does offer many of the freedoms of the novelist. But filmmakers who rely on these freedoms do not learn storytelling in images as well as those who grapple with the stricter discipline of the stage.

It may seem paradoxical to say that playwriting is the best first discipline toward film. But just as formal verse can teach you the possibilities of verbal music, so the limitations of this confined space can focus your efforts on the telling of a dramatic story. Many young screenwriters become so seduced by the marvels of what the *camera* can do, that they fail to learn what the writer must do. The delicious vocabulary—*cameo, rack focus, wipe, dolly shot, dissolve*—can mask the simple need that a film, like a story, like a memoir, like a play, must be about these people in this place with this problem. If you can put a man, a woman, a box, and a bottle, say, in a rectangular frame on a bare floor, and make us *care*—then you can *write*, and you can write a film. The imagination must come first. The machine will follow.

More to Read: On Playwriting

Sweet, Jeffrey. *The Dramatist's Toolkit: The Craft of the Working Playwright.* New York, Heinemann, 2000. Print.

Spencer, Stuart. *The Playwright's Guidebook: An Insightful Primer on the Art of Dramatic Writing.* New York: Faber and Faber, 2002. Print.

More to Read: On Screenwriting

Field, Syd. *Screenplay: The Foundations of Screenwriting.* 3rd ed. New York: Dell, 1984. Print.

Johnson, Claudia. *Crafting Short Screen Plays That Connect.* Boston: Focal Press, 2000. Print.

READINGS

ANTON CHEKHOV

The Proposal

Translated by Paul Schmidt

Characters

Stepán Stepánich Chubukóv, *a landowner*
Natália Stepánovna [Natásha], *his daughter*
Iván Vassílievich Lómov, *their neighbor*

The action takes place in CHUBUKÓV's *farmhouse.*
A room in CHUBUKÓV's *farmhouse. Enter* LÓMOV, *wearing a tailcoat and white gloves.* CHUBUKÓV *goes to meet him.*

CHUBUKÓV: By God, if it isn't my old friend Iván Vassílievich! Glad to see you, boy, glad to see you. [*Shakes his hand*] This is certainly a surprise, and that's a fact. How are you doing?

LÓMOV: Oh, thanks a lot. And how are you? Doing, I mean?

CHUBUKÓV: We get by, my boy, we get by. Glad to know you think of us occasionally and all the rest of it. Have a seat, boy, be my guest, glad you're here, and that's a fact. Don't want to forget your old friends and neighbors, you know. But why so formal, boy? What's the occasion? You're all dressed up and everything—you on your way to a party, or what?

LÓMOV: No, I only came to see you, Stepán Stepánich.

CHUBUKÓV: But why the fancy clothes, boy? You look like you're still celebrating New Year's Eve!

LÓMOV: Well, I'll tell you. [*Takes his arm*] You see, Stepán Stepánich, I hope I'm not disturbing you, but I came to ask you a little favor. This isn't the first time I've, uh, had occasion, as they say, to ask you for help, and I want you to know that I really admire you when I do it... Er, what I mean is... Look, you have to excuse me, Stepán Stepánich, this is making me very nervous. I'll just take a little drink of water, if it's all right with you. [*Takes a drink of water*]

CHUBUKÓV [*Aside*]: He wants me to lend him some money. I won't. [*To him*] So! What exactly are you here for, hm? A big strong boy like you.

LÓMOV: You see, I really have the greatest respect for you, Stepán Respéctovich—excuse me, I mean Stepán Excúsemevich. What I mean is—I'm really nervous, as you can plainly see... Well, what it all comes down to is this: you're the only person who can give me what I want and I know I don't deserve it of course that goes without saying and I haven't any real right to it either—

CHUBUKÓV: Now, my boy, you don't have to beat about the bush with me. Speak right up. What do you want?

LÓMOV: All right, I will. I will. Well, what I came for is, I came to ask for the hand of your daughter Natásha.

CHUBUKÓV [*Overjoyed*]: Oh, mama! Iván Vassílievich, say it again! I don't think I caught that last part!

LÓMOV: I came to ask—

CHUBUKÓV: Lover boy! Buddy boy! I can't tell you how happy I am and everything. And that's a fact. And all the rest of it. [*Gives him a bear hug*] I've always hoped this would happen. It's a longtime dream come true. [*Sheds a tear*] I have always loved you, boy, just like you were my own son, and you know it. God bless you both and all the rest of it. This is a dream come true. But why am I standing here like a big dummy? Happiness has got my tongue, that's what's happened, happiness has got my tongue. Oh, from the bottom of my heart... You wait right here, I'll go get Natásha and whatever.

LÓMOV [*Intense concern*]: What do you think, Stepán Stepánich? Do you think she'll say yes?

CHUBUKÓV: Big, good-looking fellow like you—how could she help herself? Of course she'll say yes, and that's a fact. She's like a cat in heat. And all the rest of it. Don't go away, I'll be right back. [*Exit*]

LÓMOV: It must be cold in here. I'm starting to shiver, just like I was going to take an exam. The main thing is, you have to make up your mind. You just keep thinking about it, you argue back and forth and talk a lot and wait for the ideal woman or for true love, you'll never get married. Brr...it's cold in here. Natásha is a very good housekeeper, she's kind of good-looking, she's been to school...What more do I need? I'm starting to get that hum in my ears again; it must be my nerves. [*Drinks some water*] And I can't just *not* get married. First of all, I'm already thirty-five, and that's about what they call the turning point. Second of all, I have to start leading a regular, normal life. There's something wrong with my heart—I've got a *murmur;* I'm always nervous as a tick, and the least little thing can drive me crazy. Like right now, for instance. My lips are starting to shudder, and this little whatsit keeps twitching in my right eyelid. But the worst thing about me is sleep. I mean, I don't. I go to bed, and as soon as I start falling asleep, all of a sudden something in my left side goes *drrrk!* and it pounds right up into my shoulder and my head...I jump out of bed like crazy and walk around for a while and then I lie down again and as soon as I start falling asleep all of a sudden something in my left side goes *drrrk!* And that happens twenty times a night—

[*Enter* NATÁSHA]

NATÁSHA: Oh, it's just you, and Papa said go take a look in the other room, somebody wants to sell you something. Oh, well. How are you anyway?

LÓMOV: How do you do, Natásha?

NATÁSHA: You'll have to excuse me, I'm still in my apron. We were shelling peas. How come you haven't been by to see us for so long? Sit down...

[*They both sit.*]

You feel like something to eat?

LÓMOV: No, thanks. I ate already.

NATÁSHA: You smoke? Go ahead if you want to; here's some matches. Beautiful day today, isn't it? And yesterday it was raining so hard the men in the hay-fields couldn't do a thing. How many stacks you people got cut so far? You know what happened to me? I got so carried away I had them cut the whole meadow, and now I'm sorry I did—the hay's going to rot. Oh, my! Look at you! What've you got on those fancy clothes for? Well, if you aren't something! You going to a party, or what? You know, you're looking kind of cute these days...Anyway, what are you all dressed up for?

LÓMOV [*A bit nervous*]: Well, you see, Natásha...well, the fact is I decided to come ask you to...to listen to what I have to say. Of course, you'll probably be sort of surprised and maybe get mad, but I ... [*Aside*] It's awful cold in here.

NATÁSHA: So...so what did you come for, huh? [*Pause*] Huh?

LÓMOV: I'll try to make this brief. Now, Natásha, you know, we've known each other for a long time, ever since we were children, and I've had the pleasure of knowing your entire family. My poor dead aunt and her husband—as you know, I inherited my land from them—they always had the greatest respect for your father and your poor dead mother. The Lómovs and the Chubukóvs have always been on very friendly terms, almost like we were related. And besides—well, you already know this—and besides, your land and mine are right next door to each other. Take my Meadowland, for instance. It lies right alongside of your birch grove.

NATÁSHA: Excuse me. I don't mean to interrupt you, but I think you said "my Meadowland." Are you saying that Meadowland belongs to you?

LÓMOV: Well, yes; as a matter of fact, I am.

NATÁSHA: Well, I never! Meadowland belongs to us, not you!

LÓMOV: No, Natásha. Meadowland is mine.

NATÁSHA: Well, that's news to me. Since when is it yours?

LÓMOV: What do you mean, since when? I'm talking about the little pasture they call Meadowland, the one that makes a wedge between your birch grove and Burnt Swamp.

NATÁSHA: Yes, I know the one you mean. But it's ours.

LÓMOV: Natásha, I think you're making a mistake. That field belongs to me.

NATÁSHA: Iván Vassílich, do you realize what you're saying? And just how long has it belonged to you?

LÓMOV: What do you mean, how long? As far as I know, it's always been mine.

NATÁSHA: Now wait just a minute. Excuse me, but—

LÓMOV: It's all very clearly marked on the deeds, Natásha. Now, it's true there was some argument about it back a ways, but nowadays everybody knows it belongs to me. So there's no use arguing about it. You see, what happened was, my aunt's grandmother let your grandfather's tenants have that field free of charge for an indefinite time in exchange for their making bricks for her. So your grandfather's people used that land for free for about forty years and they started to think it was theirs, but then, when it turned out what the real situation was—

NATÁSHA: My grandfather and my great-grandfather both always said that the land went as far as Burnt Swamp, which means Meadowland belongs to us. So what's the point of arguing about it? I think you're just being rude.

LÓMOV: I can show you the papers, Natálya Stepánovna!

NATÁSHA: Oh, you're just teasing! You're trying to pull my leg! This is all a big joke, isn't it? We've owned that land for going on three hundred years, and all of a sudden you say it doesn't belong to us. Excuse me, Iván Vassílich, excuse me, but I can't believe you said that. And believe me, I don't care one bit about that old meadow: it's only twenty acres, it's not worth three hundred rubles, even, but that's not the point. It's the injustice of it that hurts. And I don't care what anybody says—injustice is something I just can't put up with.

LÓMOV: But you didn't listen to what I was saying! Please! Your grandfather's tenants, as I was trying very politely to point out to you, made bricks for my aunt's grandmother. Now, my aunt's grandmother. Now, my aunt's grandmother just wanted to make things easier and—

NATÁSHA: Grandmother, grandfather, father—what difference does it all make? The field belongs to us, and that's that.

LÓMOV: That field belongs to me!

NATÁSHA: That field belongs to us! You can go on about your grandmother until you're blue in the face, you can wear fifteen fancy coats—it still belongs to us! It's ours, ours, ours! I don't want anything that belongs to you, but I do want to keep what's my own, thank you very much!

LÓMOV: Natálya Stepánovna, I don't care about that field either; I don't need that field; I'm talking about the principle of the thing. If you want the field, you can have it. I'll give it to you.

NATÁSHA: If there's any giving to be done, I'll do it! That field belongs to me! Iván Vassílich, I have never gone through anything this crazy in all my life! Up till now I've always thought of you as a good neighbor, a real friend—last year we even lent you our threshing machine, which meant that we were threshing *our* wheat in November—and now all of a sudden you start treating us like Gypsies. *You'll* give *me* my own field? Excuse me, but that is a pretty unneighborly thing to do. In fact, in my opinion, it's downright insulting!

LÓMOV: So in your opinion I'm some kind of claim jumper, you mean? Look, lady, I have never tried to take anybody else's land, and I'm not going to let anybody try to tell me I did, not even you. [*Runs to the table and takes a drink of water*] Meadowland is mine!

NATÁSHA: You lie! It's ours!

LÓMOV: It's mine!

NATÁSHA: You lie! I'll show you! I'll send my mowers out there today!

LÓMOV: You'll what!

NATÁSHA: I said I'll have my mowers out there today, and they'll hay that field flat!

LÓMOV: You do, and I'll break their necks!

NATÁSHA: You wouldn't dare!

LÓMOV [*Clutches his chest*]: Meadowland is mine! You understand? Mine!

NATÁSHA: Please don't shout. You can scream and carry on all you want in your own house, but as long as you're in mine, try to behave like a gentleman.

LÓMOV: I tell you, if I didn't have these murmurs, these awful pains, these veins throbbing in my temples, I wouldn't be talking like this. [*Shouts*] Meadowland is mine!

NATÁSHA: Ours!

LÓMOV: Mine!

NATÁSHA: Ours!

LÓMOV: Mine!

[*Enter* CHUBUKÓV.]

CHUBUKÓV: What's going on? What are you both yelling for?

NATÁSHA: Papa, will you please explain to this gentleman just who owns Meadowland, him or us?

CHUBUKÓV: Lover boy, Meadowland belongs to us.

LÓMOV: I beg your pardon, Stepán Stepánich, how can it belong to you? Think what you're saying! My aunt's grandmother let your grandfather's people have that land to use free of charge, temporarily, and they used that land for forty years and started thinking it was theirs, but it turned out what the problem was—

CHUBUKÓV: Allow me, sweetheart. You're forgetting that the reason those people didn't pay your granny and all the rest of it was because there was *already* a real problem about just who *did* own the meadow. And everything. But nowadays every dog in the village knows it belongs to us, and that's a fact. I don't think you've ever seen the survey map—

LÓMOV: Look, I can prove to you that Meadowland belongs to me!

CHUBUKÓV: No you can't, lover boy.

LÓMOV: I can too!

CHUBUKÓV: Oh, for crying out loud! What are you shouting for? You can't prove anything by shouting, and that's a fact. Look, I am not interested in taking any of your land, and neither am I interested in giving away any of my own. Why should I? And if it comes down to it, lover boy, if you want to make a case out of this, or anything like that, I'd just as soon give it to the peasants as give it to you. So there!

LÓMOV: You're not making any sense. What gives you the right to give away someone else's land?

CHUBUKÓV: I'll be the judge of whether I have the right or not! The fact is, boy, I am not used to being talked to in that tone of voice and all the rest of it. I am twice your age, boy, and I'll ask you to talk to me without getting so excited and whatever.

LÓMOV: No! You think I'm just stupid, and you're making fun of me! You stand there and tell me my own land belongs to you, and then you expect me to be calm about it and talk as if nothing had happened! That's not the way good neighbors behave, Stepán Stepánich! You are not a neighbor, You are a *usurper!*

CHUBUKÓV: I'm a *what?* What did you call me?

NATÁSHA: Papa, you send our mowers out to Meadowland right this very minute!

CHUBUKÓV: You, boy! What did you just call me?

NATÁSHA: Meadowland belongs to us, and I'll never give it up—never, never, never!

LÓMOV: We'll see about that! I'll take you to court, and then we'll see who it belongs to!

CHUBUKÓV: To court! Well, you just go right ahead, boy, you take us to court! I dare you! Oh, now I get it, you were just waiting for a chance to take us to court and all the rest of it! And whatever! It's inbred, isn't it? Your whole family was like that—they couldn't wait to start suing. They were always in court! And that's a fact!

LÓMOV: You leave my family out of this! The Lómovs were all decent, law-abiding citizens, every one of them, not like some people I could name, who were arrested for embezzlement—your uncle, for instance!

CHUBUKÓV: Every single one of the Lómovs was crazy! All of them!

NATÁSHA: All of them! Every single one!

CHUBUKÓV: Your uncle was a falling-down drunk, and that's a fact! And your aunt, the youngest one, she used to run around with an architect! An architect! And that's a fact!

LÓMOV: And your mother was a hunchback! [*Clutches his chest*] Oh, my God, I've got a pain in my side...my head's beginning to pound! Oh, my God, give me some water!

CHUBUKÓV: And your father was a gambler and a glutton!

NATÁSHA: And your aunt was a tattletale; she was the worst gossip in town!

LÓMOV: My left leg is paralyzed...And you're a sneak! Oh, my heart! And everybody knows that during the elections, you people...I've got spots in front of my eyes...Where's my hat?

NATÁSHA: You're low! And lousy! And cheap!

CHUBUKÓV: You are a lowdown two-faced snake in the grass, and that's a fact! An absolute fact!

LÓMOV: Here's my hat! My heart! How do I get out of here...where's the door? I think I'm dying...I can't move my leg. [*Heads for the door*]

CHUBUKÓV [*Following him*]: And don't you ever set foot in this house again!

NATÁSHA: And you just take us to court! Go ahead, see what happens!

[*Exit LÓMOV, staggering.*]

CHUBUKÓV [*Walks up and down in agitation*]: He can go to hell!

NATÁSHA: What a creep! See if I ever trust a neighbor again after this!

CHUBUKÓV: Crook!

NATÁSHA: Creep! He takes over somebody else's land and then has the nerve to threaten them!

CHUBUKÓV: And would you believe that wig-worm, that chicken-brain, had the nerve to come here and propose? Hah? He proposed!

NATÁSHA: He proposed what?

CHUBUKÓV: What? He came here to propose to you!

NATÁSHA: To propose? To me? Why didn't you tell me that before!

CHUBUKÓV: That's why he was all dressed up in that stupid coat! What a silly sausage!

NATÁSHA: Me? He came to propose to me? Oh, my God, my God! [*Collapses into a chair and wails*] Oh, make him come back! Make him come back! Oh, please, make him come back! [*She has hysterics*]

CHUBUKÓV: What's the matter? What's the matter with you? [*Smacks his head*] Oh, my God, what have I done! I ought to shoot myself! I ought to be hanged! I ought to be tortured to death!

NATÁSHA: I think I'm going to die! Make him come back!

CHUBUKÓV: All right! Just stop screaming! Please! [*Runs out*]

NATÁSHA [*Alone, wailing*]: What have we done? Oh, make him come back! Make him come back!

CHUBUKÓV [*Reenters*]: He's coming, back and everything, goddamn it! You talk to him yourself this time; I can't... And that's a fact!

NATÁSHA [*Wailing*]: Make him come back!

CHUBUKÓV: I just told you, he *is* coming back. Oh, God almighty, what an ungrateful assignment, being the father of a grown-up girl! I'll slit my throat, I swear I'll slit my throat! We yell at the man, we insult him, we chase him away... and it's all your fault. It's your fault!

NATÁSHA: No, it's your fault!

CHUBUKÓV: All right, I'm sorry, it's my fault. Or whatever.

[LÓMOV *appears in the doorway.*]

This time you do the talking yourself! [*Exit*]

LÓMOV [*Entering, exhausted*]: I'm having a heart murmur, it's awful, my leg is paralyzed... my left side is going *drrrk!*

NATÁSHA: You'll have to excuse us, Iván Vassílich—we got a little bit carried away.... Anyway, I just remembered, Meadowland belongs to you after all.

LÓMOV: There's something wrong with my heart—it's beating too loud... Meadowland is mine? These little whatsits are twitching in both my eyelids...

NATÁSHA: It's your—Meadowland is all yours. Here, sit down.

[*They both sit.*]

We made a mistake.

LÓMOV: It was always just the principle of the thing. I don't care about the land, but I do care about the principle of the thing.

NATÁSHA: I know, the principle of the thing... Why don't we talk about something else?

LÓMOV: And besides, I really can prove it. My aunt's grandmother let your grandfather's tenants have that field—

NATÁSHA: That's enough! I think we should change the subject. [*Aside*] I don't know where to start... [*To* LÓMOV] How's the hunting? Are you going hunting anytime soon?

LÓMOV: Oh, yes, geese and grouse hunting, Natásha, geese and grouse. I was thinking of going after the harvest is in. Oh, by the way, did I tell you? The worst thing happened to me! You know my old hound Guesser? Well, he went lame on me.

NATÁSHA: Oh, that's terrible! What happened?

LÓMOV: I don't know; he must have dislocated his hip, or may be he got into a fight with some other dogs and got bit. [*Sighs*] And he was the best hound dog, not to mention how much he cost. I got him from Mirónov, and I paid a hundred and twenty-five for him.

NATÁSHA [*Beat*]: Iván Vassílich, you paid too much.

LÓMOV [*Beat*]: I thought I got him pretty cheap. He's a real good dog.

NATÁSHA: Papa paid only eighty-five for his hound dog Messer, and Messer is a lot better than your old Guesser!

LÓMOV: Messer is better than Guesser? What do you mean? [*Laughs*] Messer is better than Guesser!

NATÁSHA: Of course he's better! I mean, he's not full grown yet, he's still a pup, but when it comes to a bark and a bite, nobody has a better dog.

LÓMOV: Excuse me, Natásha, but I think you're forgetting something. He's got an underslung jaw, and a dog with an underslung jaw can never be a good retriever.

NATÁSHA: An underslung jaw? That's the first I ever heard of it!

LÓMOV: I'm telling you, his lower jaw is shorter than his upper.

NATÁSHA: What did you do, measure it?

LÓMOV: Of course I measured it! I grant you he's not so bad on point, but you tell him to go fetch, and he can barely—

NATÁSHA: In the first place, our Messer is a purebred from a very good line—he's the son of Pusher and Pisser, so that limp-foot mutt of yours couldn't touch him for breeding. Besides which, your dog is old and ratty and full of fleas—

LÓMOV: He may be old, but I wouldn't take five of your Messers for him. How can you even say that? Guesser is a real hound, and that Messer is a joke, he's not even worth worrying about. Every old fart in the country's got a dog just like your Messer—there's a mess of them everywhere you look! You paid twenty rubles, you paid too much!

NATÁSHA: Iván Vassílich, for some reason you are being perverse on purpose. First you think Meadowlands belongs to you, now you think Guesser is better than Messer. I don't think much of a man who doesn't say what he knows to be a fact. You know perfectly well that Messer is a hundred times better than that...that dumb Guesser of yours. So why do you keep saying the opposite?

LÓMOV: You must think I'm either blind or stupid! Can't you understand that your Messer has an underslung jaw!

NATÁSHA: It's not true!

LÓMOV: He has an underslung jaw!

NATÁSHA [*Shouting*]: It's not true!

LÓMOV: What are you shouting for?

NATÁSHA: What are you lying for? I can't stand any more of this. You ought to be getting ready to put your old Guesser out of his misery, and here you are comparing him to our Messer!

LÓMOV: You'll have to excuse me, I can't go on with this conversation. I'm having a heart murmur.

NATÁSHA: This just goes to prove what I've always known: the hunters who talk the most are the ones who know the least.

LÓMOV: Will you please do me a favor and just shut up... My heart is starting to pound... [*Shouts*] Shut up!

NATÁSHA: I will not shut up until you admit that Messer is a hundred times better than Guesser!

LÓMOV: He's a hundred times worse! I hope he croaks, your Messer... My head... my eyes... my shoulders...

NATÁSHA: And your dumb old Guesser doesn't need to croak—he's dead already!

LÓMOV: Shut up! [*Starts to cry*] I'm having a heart attack!

NATÁSHA: I will not shut up!

[*Enter* CHUBUKÓV.]

CHUBUKÓV: Now what's the matter?

NATÁSHA: Papa, will you please tell us frankly, on your honor, who's a better dog: Guesser or Messer?

LÓMOV: Stepán Stepánich, I just want to know one thing: does your Messer have an underslung jaw or doesn't he? Yes or no?

CHUBUKÓV: Well? So what if he does? What difference does it make? Anyway, there isn't a better dog in the whole county, and that's a fact.

LÓMOV: But you don't think my Guesser is better? On your honor!

CHUBUKÓV: Now, loverboy, don't get all upset; just wait a minute. Please. Your Guesser has his good points and whatever. He's a thoroughbred, got a good stance, nice round hindquarters, all the rest of it. But that dog, if you really want to know, boy, has got two vital defects: he's old and he's got a short bite.

LÓMOV: You'll have to excuse me, I'm having another heart murmur. Let's just look at the facts, shall we? All I'd like you to do is just think back to that time at the field trials when my Guesser kept up with the count's dog Fresser. They were going ear to ear, and your Messer was a whole half mile behind.

CHUBUKÓV: He was behind because one of the count's men whopped him with his whip!

LÓMOV: That's not the point! All the other dogs were after the fox, and your Messer was chasing a sheep!

CHUBUKÓV: That's not true! Now listen, boy, I have a very quick temper, as you very well know, and that's a fact, so I think we should keep this discussion very short. He whopped him because none of the rest of you can stand watching other people's dogs perform! You're all rotten with envy! Even you, buddy boy, even you! The fact is, all somebody has to do is point out that somebody's dog is better than your Guesser, and right away you start in with this and that and all the rest of it. I happen to remember exactly what happened!

LÓMOV: And I remember too!

CHUBUKÓV [*Mimics him*]: "And I remember too!" What do you remember?

LÓMOV: My heart murmur... My leg is paralyzed... I can't move...

NATÁSHA [*Mimics him*]: "My heart murmur!" What kind of hunter are you? You'd do better in the kitchen catching cockroaches instead of out hunting foxes! A heart murmur!

CHUBUKÓV: She's right—what kind of hunter are you? You and your heart murmur should stay home instead of galloping cross-country, and that's a fact. You say you like to hunt; all you really want to do is ride around arguing and interfering with other people's dogs and whatever. You are *not*, and that's a fact, a hunter.

LÓMOV: And what makes you think you're a hunter? The only reason you go hunting is so you can get in good with the count! My heart! You're a sneak!

CHUBUKÓV: I'm a what? A sneak! [*Shouts*] Shut up!

LÓMOV: A sneak!

CHUBUKÓV: You young whippersnapper! You puppy!

LÓMOV: You rat! You rickety old rat!

CHUBUKÓV: You shut up, or I'll give you a tailful of buckshot! You snoop!

LÓMOV: Everybody knows your poor dead wife—oh, my heart!—used to beat you. My legs... my head... I see spots... I'm going to faint, I'm going to faint!

CHUBUKÓV: And everyone knows your housekeeper has you tied to her apron strings!

LÓMOV: Wait wait wait... here it comes! A heart attack! My shoulder just came undone—where's my shoulder? I'm going to die! [*Collapses into a chair*] Get a doctor! [*Faints*]

CHUBUKÓV: Whippersnapper! Milk sucker! Snoop! You make me sick! [*Drinks some water*] Sick!

NATÁSHA: What kind of a hunter are you? You can't even ride a horse! [*To* CHUBUKÓV] Papa! What's the matter with him? Papa! Look at him, Papa! [*Screeching*] Iván Vassílich! He's dead!

CHUBUKÓV: I'm sick! I can't breathe... give me some air!

NATÁSHA: He's dead! [*Shakes* LÓMOV's *shoulders*] Iván Vassiílich! Iván Vassílich! What have we done? He's dead! [*Collapses into the other chair*] Get a doctor! Get a doctor! [*She has hysterics*]

CHUBUKÓV: Oh, now what? What's the matter with you?

NATÁSHA [*Wailing*]: He's dead! He's dead!

CHUBUKÓV: Who's dead? [*Looks at* LÓMOV] Oh, my God, he *is* dead! Oh, my God! Get some water! Get a doctor! [*Puts glass to* LÓMOV's *mouth*] Here, drink this... He's not drinking it... That means he's really dead... and everything! Oh, what a mess! I'll kill myself! I'll kill myself! Why did I wait so long to kill myself? What am I waiting for right now? Give me a knife! Lend me a gun! [LÓMOV *stirs*] I think he's going to live! Here, drink some water. That's the way.

LÓMOV: Spots... everything is all spots... it's all cloudy... Where am I?

CHUBUKÓV: Just get married as soon as you can and then get out of here! She says yes! [*Joins* LÓMOV's *and* NATÁSHA's *hands*] She says yes and all the rest of it. I give you both my blessing and whatever. Only please just leave me in peace!

LÓMOV: Huh? Wha'? [*Starts to get up*] Who?

CHUBUKÓV: She says yes! All right? Go ahead and kiss her... And then get the hell out of here!

NATÁSHA [*Moaning*]: He's alive... Yes, yes, I say yes....

CHUBUKÓV: Go ahead, give him a kiss.

LÓMOV: Huh? Who?

[NATÁSHA *kisses him.*]

Oh, that's very nice... Excuse me, but what's happening? Oh, yes, I remember now.... My heart... those spots... I'm so happy, Natásha! [*Kisses her hand*] My leg is still paralyzed....

NATÁSHA: I'm... I'm very happy too.

CHUBUKÓV: And I'm getting a weight off my shoulders. Oof!

NATÁSHA: But all the same—you can admit it now, can't you?—Messer is better than Guesser.

LÓMOV: He's worse!

NATÁSHA: He's better!

CHUBUKÓV: And they lived happily ever after! Bring on the champagne!

LÓMOV: He's worse!

NATÁSHA: Better! Better! Better!

CHUBUKÓV [*Tries to make himself heard*]: Champagne! Bring on the champagne!

CURTAIN.

TRY THIS 11.8

Imagine for a few days what a contemporary version of "The Proposal" would look like. Who would intend to propose to whom? In what setting? Whose "permission" would be needed, or would that part of the story be left out? What would the couple quarrel about? Then set yourself just one hour (five minutes per page, max) to write a rough draft of a ten- to fifteen-page play on the theme.

JOSÉ RIVERA

Gas

For Juan Carlos Rivera

Cast

Cheo

Time: Start of the ground offensive of the Persian Gulf War.

Place: A gas station.

(A car at a gas station. CHEO stands next to the pump about to fill his car with gas. He is a working-class Latino. Before he pumps gas he speaks to the audience.)

CHEO: His letters were coming once a week. I could feel his fear. It was in his handwriting. He sat in a tank. In the middle of the Saudi Arabian desert. Wrote six, seven, eight hours a day. These brilliant letters of fear. This big Puerto Rican guy! What the fuck's he doing out there? What the fucking hell sense that make? He's out there, in the Saudi sand, writing letters to me about how he's gonna die from an Iraqi fucking missile. And he's got all this time on his hands to think about his own death. And there's nothing to do 'cause of these restrictions on him. No women, no magazines, 'cause the Saudis are afraid of the revolutionary effects of ads for women's lingerie on the population! Allah would have a cow! There's nothing he's allowed to eat even remotely reminds him of home. Nothing but the fucking time to sit and think about what it's gonna be like to have some fucking towelhead—as he calls them—run a bayonet clean through his guts. He's sitting in the tank playing target practice with the fucking camels. Shooting at the wind. The sand in all the food. Sand in his dreaming. He and his buddies got a camel one day. They shaved that motherfucker clean! Completely shaved its ass! Then they spray-painted the name of their company, in bright American spray-paint, on the side of the camel, and sent it on its way! Scorpion fights in the tents! All those scenes from fucking *Apocalypse Now* in his head. Fucking Marlon Brando decapitating that guy and Martin Sheen going fucking nuts. That's what fills my brother's daily dreams as he sits out there in the desert contemplating his own death. The Vietnam Syndrome those people are trying to eradicate. His early letters were all about that. A chronicle. His way of laying it all down, saying it all for me, so I would know what his last days, and months, and seconds were like. So when he got offed by an Iraqi missile, I would at least know what it was like to be in his soul, if just for a little while. He couldn't write to save his life at first. Spelled everything totally, unbelievably wrong. "Enough": e-n-u-f. "Thought": t-h-o-t. "Any": e-n-y. But with time, he started to write beautifully. This angel started to come out of the desert. This singing angel of words. Thoughts I honestly never knew he had. Confessions. Ideas. We started to make plans. We start to be in sync for the first time since I stopped telling him I loved him. I used to kick his fucking ass! It wasn't hard or nothing. That's not bragging, just me telling you a simple truth. He was always sick. Always the first to cry. He played drums in a parade back home. He couldn't even play the fucking instrument, he was so uncoordinated. Spastic. But they let him march in the parade anyway—without drumsticks. He was the last guy in the parade, out of step, banging make-believe drumsticks, phantom rhythms on this snare drum—playing air drum for thousands of confused spectators! Then he got into uniforms and the scouts. But I knew that bullshit was just a cover anyway. He didn't mean it. Though after he joined the army and was in boot camp, he took particular delight in coming home and demonstrating the fifty neat new ways he learned to kill a guy. One day he forgot he weighed twice my weight and nearly snapped my spine like a fucking cucumber! I thought, in agony, "where's my bro? Where's that peckerhead I used to kick around? The first one to cry when he saw something beautiful. The first one to say 'I love that' or 'I love Mom' or 'I love you.'" He never got embarrassed by that, even after I got too old to deal with my fucking little brother kissing me in front of other people. Even later, he always, always, always ended every conversation with, "I love you bro," and I couldn't say, "I love you" back, 'cause I was too hip to do that shit. But he got deeper in it. The war thing. He wrote to say I'd never understand. He's fighting for my right to say whatever I want. To disagree. And I just fucking love how they tell you on the news the fucking temperature in Riyadh, Saudi Arabia! Like I fucking care! And a couple of times the son-of-a-bitch called me collect from Saudi! *I said collect!* And I told him if Saddam Hussein didn't kill him, I would! He told me about troubles with his wife back home. He'd just gotten married a month before shipping out. He didn't really know her and was wondering if she still loved him. My brother always loved ugly women. It was a thing with him. Low self-esteem or something. Like he couldn't love himself and didn't understand a woman that would. So he sought out the absolute losers of the planet: trucker whores with prison records who liked to tie him up and whip him, stuff like that. I honestly have trouble contemplating my little brother being whipped by some trucker whore in leather. Love! He didn't know another way. Then he met a girl who on their first date confessed she hated spiks—so my brother married her! This racist looked him in the eye, disrespected his whole race to his face, and my brother says, "I do." Last night somebody got on TV to say we shouldn't come down on rich people 'cause rich people are a minority too, and coming down on them was a form of racism! And I thought, they're fucking afraid of class warfare, and they should be! And the news showed some little white punk putting up flags all over this dipshit town in California and this little twirp's story absorbed twenty minutes of the news—this little, blond Nazi kid with a smile full of teeth—and the protests got shit. And this billboard went up in my town showing Stalin, Hitler, and Hussein, saying we stopped him twice before we have to stop him again! This billboard was put up by a local newspaper! The music, the computer graphics, the generals coming out of retirement to become media stars, public hard ons. And we gotta fight NAKED AGGRESSION—like his asshole president should come *to my fucking neighborhood* if he wants to see naked aggression! I never thought the ideas in the head of some politician would mean the death of my brother and absolutely kill my mother. I'm telling you, that woman will not survive the death of my brother no matter how much she believes in God, no matter how much praying she does. But I keep that from him. I write back about how it's not going to be another Vietnam. It's not going to be a whole country that spits on you when you come back. That we don't forget the ones we love and fight for us. Then his letters stopped. I combed the newspapers trying to figure out what's going on over there, 'cause his letters said nothing about where he was. He wasn't allowed to talk about locations, or troop size, or movement, 'cause, like, I was going to personally transmit this information to the Iraqi fucking Ministry of Defense! I thought about technology. The new shit Iraq has that was made in the United States, shit that could penetrate a tank's armour and literally travel through the guts of a tank, immolating every living human soul inside, turning human Puerto Rican flesh into hot screaming soup, the molecules of my brother's soul mixing with the metal molecules of the iron coffin he loved so much. I couldn't sleep. My mother was suicidal. Why wasn't he writing? The air war's continuing. They're bombing the shit out of that motherfucking country! And I find myself ashamed. I think, "yeah, bomb it more. Level it. Send it back to the Stone Age. Make it so every last elite Republican Guard is dead. So my brother won't get killed." For the first time in my life, I want a lot of people I don't hate to die 'cause I know one of them could kill the man I love most in this fucked up world. If my brother is killed, I will personally take a gun and blow out the brains of George Herbert Walker Bush. And I'm sick. I'm sick of rooting for the bombs. Sick of loving every day the air war continues. Sick of every air strike, every sortie. And being happy another Iraqi tank got taken out and melted, another Iraqi bunker was bombed, another bridge can't bring ammunition, can't deliver that one magic bullet that will incapacitate my brother, bring him back a vegetable, bring him back dead in his soul, or blinded, or butchered in some Iraqi concentration camp. That the Iraqi motherfucker that would torture him won't live now 'cause our smart bombs have killed that towelhead motherfucker in his sleep! They actually got me wanting this war to be bloody!

(*Beat.*)

Last night the ground war started. It started. The tanks are rolling. I find my gut empty now. I don't have thoughts. I don't have dreams. My mother is a shell. She has deserted herself and left behind a blathering cadaver, this pathetic creature with rosary beads in her hands looking up to Christ, and CNN, saying words like "Scud," "strategic interests," "collateral damage," "target rich environment"—words this woman from a little town in Puerto Rico has no right to know. So I fight my demons. I think of the cause. Blood for oil. I NEED MY CAR, DON'T I? I NEED MY CAR TO GET TO WORK SO I CAN PAY THE RENT AND NOT END UP A HOMELESS PERSON! DON'T I HAVE A RIGHT TO MY CAR AND MY GAS? AND WHAT ABOUT FREEING DEMOCRATIC KUWAIT?!

(*Beat.*)

So I wait for a sign, anything, a prayer, any sign. I'll take it. Just tell me he's okay. Tell me my brother's gonna kill well and make it through this alive. He's gonna come home and he's gonna come home the same person he left; the spastic one who couldn't spell . . . the one who couldn't play the drums.

(*CHEO starts to pump gas. As he pumps the gas, he notices something horrifying. He pulls the nozzle out of the car. Blood comes out of the gas pump. CHEO stares and stares at the bloody trickle coming out of the gas pump.*)

BLACKOUT

TRY THIS 11.9
Write either a monologue or a ten-minute play for two, in which a physical object or action functions as a symbolic comment on the words.

ALICE O' NEILL

What I Came For

Characters

Amy
John

At rise: AMY sits at the bar, speaks to JOHN, the Irish bartender. Her eyes are on the door. She's tipsy.

AMY: I'm so glad *they're* gone. Soap people. I mean, did you pick up on that? Well, when you're in a room where half the guys are named Jeremy and there's more hair gel per capita than anywhere in Italy. That's how you know you're in a room full of soap people. What's so hard about memorizing that drivel? They're really good at furrowing their brows.

Not that I have anything against soap operas. Actually, I do have something against soap operas. They're just not what they used to be, know what I mean? It used to be like, "Oh, Godfrey, I'm in love with Chad, even though he's on trial for murder!" But now the soaps are all, "Oh, Clay, Monica's having a crack baby! Let's all turn out to show her how much we support her and love her for it!"

JOHN: Last call.

AMY: Already? Well. I'll have another *pint.* Another *pint,* please. This place is really authentic. Why do they call it The Great Eastern Rock?

JOHN: Don't know.

AMY: Where I live, all the Irish bars are called things like, Michael Patrick O'Shea McCleery's Place. They string a bunch of Irish-sounding names together and to them that spells *fun*. But this place is like the real thing. Not that I've ever been to Ireland, but if you're in Ireland, you don't have to go out of your way to let people know they're in an Irish Pub. Right? Where are your people from?

JOHN: My *people?*

AMY: Mine are from County Tyrone. That's in the North.

JOHN: I've heard of it.

AMY: Though I'm almost ashamed to say it, what with the "troubles" and all. You don't hold it against me, do you?

JOHN: Very much so.

AMY: I'm the one who knew about this place. I'm the one who suggested it to Kara. Then she was all, oh, there's this really gritty little Irish Pub over in Montauk! Let's go, everybody! As if it was her discovery. She was the one everybody was toasting; did you see her? As if you could miss her, in that tacky wedding dress. I'm surprised she even made it down the aisle in that antebellum hoop skirt she was wearing. And everybody's all, "Isn't Kara the most beautiful bride you've ever seen?" And I just want to say, number one, either you've been going to a lot of weddings in Appalachia or you're blind; and two, her name isn't really Kara; it's *Carol.* Not Kara, Carol! Sometimes I think, this is something *Soap Opera Digest* might like to know. She can just get over herself. I mean, so what if she bought her own fax machine? That doesn't make her half the mature person she thinks she is. And, not to mention that her father paid the rent the whole time we lived together. I had to hold down two jobs. She just sat at home doing I don't know what. Sending faxes. Okay and now she's on a soap and married to the perfect guy with the house in Amagansett. Another Daddy to pay the rent. I wouldn't be her for all the tea in China.

When she first moved in, Carol—I mean *Kara*—used to say we were a great team. Like Laverne and Shirley, she used to say. Like, TV's first *lesbians?* Whatever.

What's on the jukebox? (*AMY goes and checks out the jukebox.*) My Da used to play the Clancy brothers at home. Any Clancy Brothers?

JOHN: I don't think so.

AMY: Watch this. (*AMY does a few* Riverdance *steps for JOHN.*) I bought the videotape and taught myself. Not too bad, right? There's this guy works with me at Pottery Barn—he says he's not gay, whatever. But his sister-in-law is a Rockette and she can get free tickets to certain things at Radio City Music Hall so this guy is going to see if he can get me in to see the *Lord of the Dance* next time he comes. I'm not a real dancer, it's just something I like to do for myself, if you know what I mean. It's just mine; it's like just because I enjoy something doesn't mean I have to make money off of it, or try to make a *career* out of it. I'm pretty sure they're going to make me assistant manager after Christmas, so. (*JOHN puts chairs on tables.*) Oh, you're closing up. Okay. So I should pay, right?

JOHN: Three fifty for that last one.

AMY: So how long have you been here?

JOHN: Eleven and a half hours.

AMY: No! How long have you been in the *States*?

JOHN: Even longer.

AMY: And do you miss Ireland?

JOHN: No.

AMY: It's just something in the blood, isn't it? I've never been to Ireland and I'm pretty far removed, but there's something about the music and the language that calls me back.

JOHN: What language? English?

AMY: No, Gaelic. Do you speak it?

JOHN: Yup.

AMY: There' something really primal about it. And what's this about? (*She does some more* Riverdance *steps.*) Why do they keep the arms down? I have a theory. Do you want to hear it?

JOHN: More than anything.

AMY: To me it's like the ultimate in *controlled fire.* You know? It's like, my heart and my gut want to move with wild abandon, but I can't let anyone know, because that's the Irish way. Not like the Greeks with their arms flailing everywhere, kissing all the ladies. No, I can dance all day and night and no one will ever know the passion in my heart. Because that's the Irish way. My father is like that. I mean, he's mostly German, but. Anyway.

JOHN: That's three fifty for the last one.

AMY: Oh right. Oh, *ay.* So tell me about *where you're from.*

JOHN: Why?

AMY: Because I'd like to get to know you.

JOHN: Why?

(*Silence. AMY practices a few more steps.*)

You're not going to finish a whole pint. Here's some coffee.

AMY: Oh, don't give me coffee. Coffee makes me crazy.

JOHN: Will you have anything else then? Time to close up.

AMY: How about. Some. I don't know what I want. Wait! Yes I do. What's that? In that heart-shaped bottle there? On the back shelf?

JOHN: What, that? Tell you the truth, no one ever orders that. Probably been on the shelf for a decade.

AMY: Looks sticky. I'm Amy. (*She holds her hand out for him to shake. He does.*)

JOHN: John.

AMY: I do know what I'd like, John. (*Long silence.*)

JOHN: Well?

AMY: Could I stick around for a while? After you close up?

JOHN: Sure. But I don't know what you'd do by yourself all night, locked inside a bar.

AMY: John! No; is there somewhere you like to go? Some other pub where you hang out after this one closes? Maybe listen to some music? Have a few drinks?

JOHN: Nope.

AMY: Oh. (*Pause.*) What do you do?

JOHN: What d'you mean?

AMY: I mean. You tend bar. And what else?

JOHN: That's what I do. I tend bar.

AMY: You can't tell me you're not a writer or something.

JOHN: Nope. Just a bartender.

AMY: But you see, I love that! A guy who just is what he is! I bet you know a million jokes, too.

JOHN: I know one or two.

AMY: Tell me a joke.

JOHN (*Reluctantly.*)**:** Long or short?

AMY: I don't care.

JOHN: Okay. Eh. Why is a giraffe's neck so long?

AMY: I don't know. Why is a giraffe's neck so long?

JOHN: Because its head is so far away from its body. (*Pause.*)

AMY: I don't get it.

JOHN: Well, never mind.

AMY: Oh. Oh! I do get it. I get it. That's funny.

JOHN: Not really. It's just the first thing that came to mind.

AMY: Well. I got my joke. I didn't get what I came for, but I did get a laugh.

JOHN: Good night, then.

AMY: 'Night. Thanks. (*After a bit.*) Before I go. Will you kiss me? Just once. It can be anywhere. On my face. Or my shoulder, or. Doesn't matter. Just a little...peck.

JOHN: Ah, well. That's against the rules, now.

AMY: How about a caress?

JOHN: What about that guy standin' next to you at the bar? What was his name?

AMY: Jeremy.

JOHN: Why didn't you ask him for a kiss? He looked like he was good for it.

AMY: I guess I didn't notice him. I guess because I was looking so hard at you all night. (*Pause. AMY looks for her purse under the bar.*)

AMY: Where's my . . . ? I can't find my—

JOHN: Here.

(*He puts her purse up on the bar.*)

JOHN: Can't trust anyone in Montauk this time of year. Not with all those soap people running around.

AMY: Three fifty? (*AMY digs in her purse; she puts a bill down on the bar.*) Maybe I'll have another wedding to come to in Montauk sometime soon. Or maybe you'll have a reason to come to the city.

JOHN: I never do.

(*She pauses for a moment, then turns away from him and starts out. She turns around.*)

AMY: You know, the least you could do is, I don't know. Be *charming* when you throw me out. You're Irish! Couldn't you sing me a sad lullaby; or spin me a yarn? Couldn't you weave me a *little* Irish magic?

(*JOHN's brogue thins out now.*)

JOHN: You want me to spin you a yarn? Here's one. I had a wife. I had a job at the Bank of Ireland, made lots of money. Had a house; big, ugly house in Wicklow. I stayed with it for three years, then one day I woke up with a stunning hatred for all of it. Well, I told Jeanine that I was going to visit my cousin here in Montauk. I don't have a cousin here in Montauk. But I did come and I never went back.

I don't miss Ireland. My only regret is that I have to be so goddam Irish in this goddam job. But bartending suits me. I can move around. I spend my winters in Key Largo, and my summers here. Still an alien, legally, but I make enough money to get by; I learn enough jokes to keep people happy; and I meet enough women to keep me down.

Now, that's the truth of me, and probably thousands of others like me. Just a little tip for you. Better just to steer clear.

AMY: Well. I guess you've done the honorable thing. All I wanted was a little. I don't know. Contact. But this is better than nothing. (*She starts to leave.*)

JOHN: Amy. Show me that shoulder of yours. (*After a moments, she lifts up her sleeve and bears her shoulder. He approaches her. He kisses her shoulder, then her neck, and her forehead. She throws her arms around him. He gently pushes her away.*)

JOHN: Good night.

AMY: Thanks.

(She exits. JOHN goes behind the bar: puts on the Clancy Brothers. He whistles along as he puts chairs up on tables.)

END OF PLAY

TRY THIS 11.10

Write a ten-minute play in which the main character intensely wants something, but the audience only learns during the last two minutes what it is.

LANFORD WILSON

Eukiah

Characters

Butch

Eukiah

Time: *The present*

Setting: *An abandoned private airplane hangar*

A dark empty stage represents a long abandoned private airplane hangar. The space is vast and almost entirely dark. A streak of light from a crack in the roof stripes the floor.

Butch walks into the light. He is a young, powerful, charming man; everybody's best friend. He is also menacing. Nothing he says is introspective. Everything is for a purpose. During the indicated beats of silence he listens; for Eukiah to answer, for the sound of breathing, for the least indication of where Eukiah is. The play is a seduction. Voices have a slight echo in here.

BUTCH: Eukiah? (*Beat.*) Eukiah? (*Beat.*) Barry saw you run in here, so I know you're here. You're doin' it again, Eukiah, you're jumping to these weird conclusions you jump to just like some half-wit. You don't wanna be called a half-wit, you gotta stop actin' like a half-wit, don't ya? You're gettin' to where nobody can joke around you, ya know that? What kind of fun is a person like that to be around, huh? One you can't joke around? We talked about that before, remember? (*Beat.*) Eukiah? What are you thinkin'? You thinkin' you heard Barry say something, you thought he meant it, didn't you? What did you think you heard? Huh? What'd you think he meant? Eukiah? (*Beat.*) You're gonna have to talk to me, I can't talk to myself here. (*Beat.*) Have you ever known me to lie to you? Eukiah? Have you ever known that? (*Pause. He might walk around some.*) Okay. Boy, this old hangar sure seen better days, hasn't it? Just like everything else on this place, huh? Been pretty much a losing proposition since I've known it, though. Probably you too, hasn't it? Hell, I don't think they have the wherewithal anymore, give even one of those ol' barns a swab a paint. You think? Might paint 'em pink, whattaya think? Or candy stripes. Red and white. Peppermint. You'd like that. (*Beat.*) This'll remind you of old Mac's heyday, though, won't it? Private airplane hangar. Talk about echoes, this is an echo of the past, huh? Ol' Mac had some winners, I guess, about twenty years ago. That must have been the life, huh? Private planes, keep 'em in your private hangar. You got your luncheons with the dukes and duchesses. Winner's Circle damn near every race. If they wasn't raised by Ol' Mac or their sire or dam one wasn't raised by Ol' Mac, I don't imagine anybody'd bother to bet on 'em, do you? Boy that's all gone, huh? Planes and limos and all, dukes and duchesses—good lookin' horses, though. Damn shame we can't enter 'em in a beauty contest somewhere. I know, you're attached to 'em, but I'll tell you they make damn expensive pets. What was you? Out by the paddock when Barry was talkin' to me? You think you overheard something, is that it? What do you think you heard? You want to talk about it? I know you'd rather talk to me than talk to Barry, huh? Eukiah? (*Pause.*) Is this where you come? When you run off all temperamental and sulking? Pretty nasty old place to play in. Echoes good though. Gotta keep awful quiet if you're trying to be secret like you always do in a place like this. Why do you do that? You got any idea? I'm serious, now. Run off like that. They're waitin' supper on you, I guess you know. You know how happy they're gonna be about it, too. (*Beat.*) Eukiah? What was it you think you heard, honey? What? Was it about horses? 'Cause I thought I told you never trust anything anybody says if it's about horses.

EUKIAH: (*Still unseen.*) I heard what Barry said. You said you *would*, too.

BUTCH: (*Relaxes some, smiles.*) Where the dickens have you got to? There's so much echo in here I can't tell where you are. You back in those oil drums? You haven't crawled up in the rafters have you? Watch yourself. We don't want you gettin' hurt. I don't think those horses would eat their oats at all, anybody gave 'em to 'em 'cept you. I think they'd flat out go on strike. Don't you figure?

EUKIAH: They wouldn't drink, you couldn't get 'em to.

BUTCH: Don't I know it. Pot-A-Gold, for sure. You're the only one to get him to do anything. I think he'd just dehydrate. He'd blow away, you wasn't leadin' him. We could lead him to water but we couldn't make him to drink, isn't that right? (*Beat.*) What are you hiding about? Nobody's gonna hurt you. Don't I always take up for you? You get the weirdest ideas. What do you think you heard Barry say?

EUKIAH: He's gonna burn the horses.

BUTCH: What? Oh, man. You are just crazy sometimes, these things you dream up. Who is? Barry? What would he wanna do something crazy like that for?

EUKIAH: I heard you talkin'.

BUTCH: Can you answer me that? Why would he even dream of doin' something like that?

EUKIAH: For the insurance.

BUTCH: No, Eukiah. Just come on to supper, now, I got a date tonight, I can't mess around with you anymore. You really are a half-wit. I'm sorry, but if you think Barry'd do something like that, I'm sorry, that's just flat out half-witted thinkin'. It's not even funny. The way you talk, you yak all day to anybody around, no idea what you're saying half the time; anybody heard something like that there wouldn't be no work for me or you or anybody else around here, 'cause they just lock us all up.

EUKIAH: You said you would.

BUTCH: *I* would? I would what?

EUKIAH: You said it was about time somebody did somethin'.

BUTCH: Eukiah, come out here. I can see you over by that old buggy, my eyes got used to the dark. There ain't no sense in hiding anymore. (*Beat.*) Come on out, damn it, so we can go to supper. I'm not going to play with you anymore. Come on. Well, just answer me one thing. How's burnin' 'em up gonna be any better than maybe splittin' a hoof or somethin' like that? Come on, crazy. The least little thing happens to make a horse not run, it's the same as if he had to be destroyed, you ought to know that. (*Eukiah is just visible now. He is maybe sixteen years old. He is slow and soft; he has the mentality of an eight-year-old.*)

EUKIAH: Yeah, but they already took Pot-A-Gold and Flashy and that gray one, the speckled one, off. They already sold 'em.

BUTCH: Which one do you call Flashy, you mean Go Carmen? The filly? And Old Ironside? Why would they do that?

EUKIAH: 'Cause they're the best ones. Then they put three no good horses in their stalls, so nobody would know. And they're gonna burn 'em and nobody can tell they ain't the horses they're supposed to be, Butchy.

BUTCH: Nobody could run Pot-A-Gold somewhere else, Euky. You know those numbers they tattoo in his mouth? That's gonna identify him no matter where he goes, anybody'll know that's Pot-A-Gold.

EUKIAH: Some other country. They wouldn't care.

BUTCH: Anywhere on earth.

EUKIAH: They got some plan where it'll work, 'cause I heard 'em.

BUTCH: I don't know what you think you heard, but you're really acting half-witted here.

EUKIAH: Don't call me—

BUTCH: Well, I'm sorry, but what would you call it? A person can't burn down a barn full of horses, Euky. What a horrible thing to think. No wonder you get scared, you scare yourself thinking things like that. Those horses are valued, hell I don't even know, millions of dollars probably. Insurance inspectors come around, they take a place apart. You tell me, how would somebody get away with a trick like that?

EUKIAH: What was you talkin' about then?

BUTCH: I don't even know. Where it was you heard what you thought you heard. You're too fast for me. You'll have to go into supper and ask Mac what Barry was talking about, won't you? Would that make you feel better? Instead of jumpin' to your weird conclusions. Now, can you get that out of your head? Huh? So we can go eat and I can take a bath and go on my date? Is that all right with you? Then I'll come back and tell you all about it. Got a date with Mary, you'd like to hear about that, wouldn't you?

(*Eukiah begins to grin.*)

BUTCH: Yes? That's okay with you, is it?

EUKIAH: I guess. (*He moves into the light, closer to Butch.*)

BUTCH: You guess. You're just going to have to trust me, Eukiah, nobody needs money that bad. Not even on this place. I don't even think nobody could get away tryin' to pull something like that. (*He puts his arm around Eukiah's neck and they start to move off, but Butch has Eukiah in a head lock. He speaks with the strain of exertion.*) Not unless there was some half-wit on the place that got his neck broke being kicked in the head and got burned up in the fire. (*Eukiah goes to his knees. Butch bears down on his neck; it breaks with a dull snap. He lets Eukiah slump to the floor. Butch is breathing hard, standing over Eukiah's body.*) I thought I told you. Never trust anything anybody says if it's about horses.

END

TRY THIS 11.11

Villains are most effective when they are also charming, convincing, touching, or otherwise not being villainous. Write a speech for an unsympathetic character that makes us for the moment sympathetic.

ACCOMPLISHING A DRAFT

Stuart Spencer claims that, "A play is more wrought than written. A playwright constructs a play as a wheelwright once constructed a wheel: a general shape is laid out, and then hammered, bent, nailed, reshaped, hammered again and again. . . ." Take the most promising idea you have for a ten-minute play and submit it to the wheelwright's test:

- What is its general shape? Does it express a character's journey from one condition or state to another?
- Does the set help to convey the characters and their situation? Does costume reveal? Do props further the action?
- Does the protagonist deeply desire something? Is the antagonist a match in power for the protagonist? Are they both consistent and complex?
- Is the dialogue sayable? Does it further the conflict? Does it reveal more than one thing at a time?
- Does the action unfold as a series of discoveries and decisions?

Hammer, bend, reshape, and hammer again.

Drama Format

The formats for prose and poetry are relatively straightforward and easy to master. The format for plays, unfortunately, is not. It is nevertheless necessary either to learn or to achieve by software created especially for this purpose, because every peculiarity annoying to the writer is an aid to the actors, director, and designers who must interpret the script in living action. For instance, the names of characters (except when used as a form of address in dialogue), and the pronouns that refer to them, are always in capital letters and are centered before speeches because this visually helps actors spot what they say and do. Short stage directions are put in parentheses and long ones to the right of the page because that signals where the action is indicated. Pages are numbered not merely consecutively but also by act and scene because in rehearsal a director specifies "Take it from the top of scene two" rather than "Take it from page 38," which has less meaning in the structure of a play. And so forth.

The format thus designed for production is not necessarily the same one you will encounter in a printed "trade" or textbook edition of the play, where there's a higher priority on saving space than on convenience to the company. But as a playwright your goal is production and your allegiance to the theatrical troupe; your manuscript should reflect that.

Software that automatically produces a submission-ready play or screenplay is available, and is worth the investment for anyone who intends to pursue these fields. The software most often recommended by playwrights and screen writers is Final Draft.

Playwrights often feel that they *do* need to copyright their work because it may be circulated to many people, and could be produced without their knowledge; it's difficult to prove production after the fact. If you intend to send your work out to production companies and feel more comfortable with a copyright, you should write for "Form PA" to: U.S. Copyright Office, Library of Congress, Washington, DC 20559.

Plays should have a cover page with title, some sort of designation such as "A play in two scenes" or "A comedy in one act," and the author's name and address. Plays should be typed in 12-point (or "pica") "Broadway Courier" font, and should be (at least for submission—probably not for class) sent in a sturdy binder.

THE SCHOOL FOR SCANDAL
A Play in Five Acts
by
Richard Brinsley Sheridan

Eng. 4701, Drama Workshop
Prof. Joseph Surface
Drury Lane University
Feb. 28, 1777

Cast of Characters

Sir Peter Teazle
Sir Oliver Surface
Joseph Surface
Charles Surface
Crabtree
Sir Benjamin Backbite
Rowley
Trip
Moses
Snake
Careless (*and other* Companions to Charles Surface)
Servants, *etc.*
Lady Teazle
Maria
Lady Sneerwell
Mrs. Candor

SCENE
London

TIME
The present.

1-1-1

Act I

Scene 1

LADY SNEERWELL*'s house.* LADY SNEERWELL *at the dressing table*, SNAKE *drinking chocolate.*

LADY SNEERWELL

The paragraphs, you say, Mr. Snake, were all inserted?

SNAKE

They were, madam, and as I copied them myself in a feigned hand, there can be no suspicion whence they came.

LADY SNEERWELL

Did you circulate the reports of Lady Brittle's intrigue with Captain Boatstall?

SNAKE

(HE *kisses his handkerchief.*) That is in as fine a train as your ladyship could wish—in the common course of things, I think it must reach Mrs.

1 - 1 - 2

SNAKE (Continued)

Clakit's ears within four-and-twenty hours; and then, you know, the business is as good as done.

LADY SNEERWELL

Why, truly, Mrs. Clakit has a very pretty talent, and a great deal of industry.

SNAKE

True, madam, and has been tolerably successful in her day. To my knowledge, she has been the cause of six matches being broken off, and three sons being disinherited, of four forced elopements, as many close confinements, nine separate maintenances, and two divorces. Nay, I have more than once traced her causing a *tête-a-tête* in the *Town and Country Magazine*, when the parties had perhaps never seen each other's faces before in the course of their lives.

LADY SNEERWELL

She certainly has her talents, but her manner is gross.

(SHE *dons her wig.* SNAKE, *taken aback, spills chocolate on his waistcoat.* HE *wipes at it with the handkerchief.*)

SNAKE

'Tis very true. She generally designs well, has a free tongue, and a bold invention; but her

appendix a

A BASIC PROSODY

Prosody is the study of versification, the metrical and auditory structure of poetry. What follows here is a very basic prosody, outlining the major units of sound and meter, the basic principles of rhyme, and a few common stanza patterns.

To begin with, these are the building blocks of poems:

- A **phoneme** is the smallest unit of sound in a language that is capable of conveying meaning. For example, the *s* in *as* conveys a different meaning in conjunction with the *a* than the *t* in *at*. A different meaning still is conveyed by adding the *b* sound in *bat*, and a different meaning still by adding the *r* sound in *brat*. Phonemes are either **vowels,** produced by relatively free passage of air through the oral cavity—for example, *a, o, e;* or **consonants,** produced by a partial obstruction of the air stream: *t, p, g*. Vowels may be pronounced as **long** sounds (ā, ē, ō, as in *place, wheat, own*) or **short** sounds (ă, ŭ, ĕ, as in *cat, up, when*). Consonants are divided into categories according to which part of the mouth obstructs the air or the manner of its obstruction, as the *labials* by the lips, the *dentals* by the teeth, the *nasals* by the nose, the *plosives* in a sudden burst, and so forth.
- A **syllable** is a unit of sound uttered in a single expulsion of breath, typically containing one or more consonants and a vowel: *mup-, done, ba-*. A syllable may be either **stressed** or **unstressed (accented** or **unaccented)** according to the relative force with which it is pronounced: *be-GUN, PO-e-try*. In the **scansion** or measuring of poetry, the stress is marked (avoiding the cumbersome capitals) as follows: *bĕgún, pŏ̋ĕtrÿ̋*. The double accent mark indicates a **secondary stress** (lighter than a stressed, heavier than an unstressed syllable; some prosodists hear a secondary stress in most three-syllable words).
- A **poetic foot** is a measure of syllables usually containing one stressed and one or more unstressed syllables. The poetic feet are marked by slashes:

  Í hăve / bĕgún / tŏ wríte / ă vérse.

- A **poetic line** is a unit of verse ended by a typographical break. The line may be **syllabic,** in which case its length is determined by the number of syllables without regard to how many accents it has. Or it may be **accentual,** in which case it has a given number of stressed or accented syllables and any number of unaccented syllables. It may be **metered verse,** in which both accents and syllables are counted and the lines will have a predetermined number of poetic feet or repetitions of a pattern of stressed and unstressed syllables (see "Stress and Scansion," below). Or it may be **free verse,** its length determined by the poet according to the needs of the particular poem. A **caesura** is a pause that occurs within the line. In a line that is **end-stopped,** the line break coincides with a pause; if the sense continues from the end of one line to the next, it is called a **run-on** line, or **enjambment.**

- A **stanza** is a grouping of lines within a poem, often predetermined by the chosen form, with a space break between such groupings.

TRY THIS A.1
With no attempt to make sense, write a four-line verse in which the vowel sounds are all short. (For example: *Flat on his back / the summer shop cat runs / his love and supper pot./ What fickle chumps.*) Then a four-line verse in which all the vowel sounds are long.

Time

Three terms having to do with the time element of poetry are sometimes used interchangeably, though in fact they differ in meaning.

- **Tempo** refers to the speed or slowness of a line.
- **Meter** comes from the Greek "measure," and refers to the mechanical elements of its rhythm, the number of feet, stresses and unstressed syllables; it is a relatively objective measurement.
- **Rhythm** refers to the total quality of a line's motion, affected by tempo and meter but also by emotion and sound.

Meter is something that can be measured, whereas rhythm is a feeling, a sense. It would be appropriate to say of a line or poem that the tempo is *fast* or *slow*, the meter is *iambic pentameter* or *trochaic dimeter,* and that the rhythm is *lilting, urgent, effortful,* or *sluggish.*

Stress and Scansion; the Poetic Foot

English is a stress language, the pattern of speech determined by the emphasis given to some syllables over others. This fact is so ingrained in us that it's difficult to understand a language otherwise constituted, but Greek, for example, is a language measured in vowel length, and Chinese is patterned in pitch rather than stress.

Accentual verse employs a meter in which only the stresses are counted:

When the wátchman on the wáll, the Shíeldings' loókout
whose jób it wás to guárd the séa-cliffs,
sáw shíelds glíttering on the gángplank
and báttle-equípment béing unloáded
he hád to find óut whó and whát...

Seamus Heaney's translation of Beowulf

(Here, each line has four stresses, but they have 12, 9, 9, 11, and 8 syllables, respectively.)

Syllabic verse employs a meter in which only the syllables are counted, as in these lines by W. H. Auden, which keep to nine syllables each although the number of stresses diminishes from five to four to three:

Blúe the ský beyónd her húmming sáil
As I sít todáy by our shíp's ráil
Wátching exúberant pórpoises...

> **TRY THIS A.2**
>
> Write a "phone poem" as syllabic verse. Use as the title a phone number (of any length you choose) real or invented. The subject of the poem is a phone call to that number; it may be a narrative about the call, or in dialogue, or a monologue of one side of the conversation, or any combination. Each line has the number of syllables of each consecutive digit. So if the phone number is 587-9043, the first line has five syllables, the second eight syllables, the third seven, and so forth. A zero is silence.

Most formal English verse counts both stresses and syllables and is *scanned* by measuring the line into stressed (or accented) and unstressed (or unaccented) syllables.

A **poetic foot** is a unit of measurement with one stress and either one or two unstressed syllables, scanned in these basic patterns:

- An **iamb** has one unstressed syllable followed by one stressed: ăróund.

  Iambic is the most common meter in English, probably because we tend to begin sentences with the subject, and most nouns are preceded by an article, as in: thĕ gírl, thĕ ský, ăn ápplĕ.

  Hĭs hóuse / ĭs ín / thĕ víl/lăge thóugh.

  Note that when the scansion is marked, the feet are separated by slashes even if the foot ends between two syllables of a word.
- A **trochee** is the opposite of an iamb—a stressed syllable followed by an unstressed: heavy.

  Trochaic rhythms do tend to be heavy, hitting hard and forcefully on the stress.

  Dóublĕ, / dóublĕ / tóil ănd / tróublĕ;

- An **anapest** consists of two unstressed syllables followed by a stress: uňděfinéd.

  Notice that *anapest* is not an anapest, though it would be if I say: *You're a nuisance and a pest! Anapestic* rhythms tend to be rollicking frolic and light verse; it is the meter of Gilbert and Sullivan.

  Frŏm m̆y héad / tŏ m̆y tóes / I'm̆ all̆ cóv/erĕd iň rós/ĕs.

- A **dactyl** is a poetic foot that begins with a stress followed by two unstresses: cárpĕntĕr.

  Dactylic meters tend toward the mysterious or incantatory and are rare, though you are likely to have encountered a few in school:

  Thís ĭs thĕ / fórĕst prĭ/méväl, thĕ / múrmŭriňg / píňes aňd thĕ / hémlŏcks.

- A **spondee** is a foot with two stresses, which can be substituted for any other foot when special emphasis is wanted (you won't want to, and can't, write a whole poem in it):

  Óne, twó. / Búcklĕ / m̆y shóe.

- A **pyrrhic** foot is the opposite, a substitute foot with two unstressed syllables:

  Thŏu árt / iňdeéd / júst, Lórd, / ĭf Ĭ / cŏnteńd

  With thée...

  Sometimes, as here, a spondee is balanced with a pyrrhic, so the number of stresses remains the same as in a regular line.

Those are the feet, four basic and two substitute, that you need to begin with, although infinite variations are possible, many of which have names (*chiasmus, ionic, amphibrach, anacreusis*) if your interest inclines you to seek them out.

TRY THIS A.3

Practice scanning anything at all, marking the stresses of a sentence or a cereal box, exaggerating as you pronounce the words to hear the stresses. Although scansion is not a science—people pronounce words with different emphasis according to region and habit—the more you practice the more you will hear the pattern of stressed and unstressed syllables, and the more you will be able to direct the stresses of your own poetry.

A line of poetry in a regular **meter** will be scanned according to the number of feet in that line (the following examples are in iambs):

- *Monometer*—one foot: Ĭf Í
- *Dimeter*—two feet: Ĭf Í / dŏn't gó
- *Trimeter*—three feet: Ĭf Í / dŏn't gó / awăý
- *Tetrameter*—four feet: Ĭf Í / dŏn't gó / awăý / tŏdáy
- *Pentameter*—five feet: Ĭf Í / dŏn't gó / awăý /tŏdáy / Ĭ wón't

- *Hexameter*—six feet: Ĭf Í / dŏn't ǵo / awăý / tŏdáy / I'l̆l név/er̆ ǵo
- *Heptameter*—seven feet: Ĭf Í / dŏn't ǵo / awăý / tŏdáy / I'l̆l név/er̆ ǵo / ăt áll.

You're unlikely to run into (or write) a metered line longer than this.

TRY THIS A.4

Practice meter—remember not to worry about making sense—by setting yourself more or less arbitrary rules: write three lines of iambic tetrameter, six of trochaic trimeter, and so forth. Mark the scansion of your lines; read them aloud until you're confident you hear the stresses.

Pick a favorite nursery line or lyric (country, Irish, rock, Shakespeare, hip hop, opera); write it down and mark the scansion. Then substitute other words in the same pattern of scansion.

Rhyme

Rhyme is to sound as metaphor is to imagery—that is, two things are at once alike and unlike, and our pleasure is in the tension between that likeness and unlikeness. In the case of rhyme, there are patterns of consonants and vowels that correspond to each other, usually involving the accented syllable and whatever comes after it; there also is a diminishing order of correspondence.

- In **rich rhyme,** the whole accented syllable sounds alike—any consonants before the vowel, the vowel, and any consonants after. So *tend* would be a rich rhyme with *pretend* and *contend* and *intend*. Because so many sounds in these syllables correspond, they quickly tire the ear, so whole poems in rich rhyme are rare.
- In a **true rhyme**—the sound of nursery rhymes and the first word-play in which most of us indulge—the vowel sounds of the stressed syllable are alike, as are the consonants after the vowel, but not the consonants before it. So *tend* is a true rhyme for *mend* and *lend* and *offend*. Because true rhyme also requires that the unaccented syllables after the stressed syllable correspond, *tender* rhymes with *spender* and *tendency* with *dependency*. When the accented syllable ends a rhymed line, it is called a *masculine rhyme* (out of some outdated notion of strength): *tend, send*. When it is followed by an unaccented syllable, it is called a *feminine* or *weak rhyme: tender, blender;* and when followed by two unaccented syllables, *a triple or treble rhyme: tenderly, slenderly*. (Perhaps these are androgynous?)
- **Off-rhyme,** also called **slant rhyme, near rhyme,** or **half rhyme** is an imperfect or partial rhyme, usually some consonance or assonance. So *tend* is a slant rhyme for *bland*, or *tender* for *splendid*. The use of slant rhyme exponentially increases the number of available rhymes in English and can introduce unexpected effects, subtle aural surprises, and interesting variations in tone.
- **Assonance** occurs when the vowel corresponds but not the consonant. *Tend* assonates with *spell* and *weather* and *met*. As with slant rhyme, assonance teases the ear with subtle correspondences.

- **Consonance** is a correspondence or likeness of the consonants that end a syllable: *tend, breed, groaned.*
- In **alliteration,** consonants (usually at the beginning of the word or stressed syllable) correspond: *tender, tickle, take, entreat.* Alliteration is often used to try to reproduce the sound or emotion of the content:

  The mildest human sound can make them scatter
  With a sound like seed spilled...

- Rhymes may be **end rhymes,** coming at the ends of lines, or **internal rhymes,** within the lines. Often the end rhyme of one line will rhyme into the middle of another:

  Body my <u>house</u>
  my <u>horse</u> my hound
  what will I <u>do</u>
  when <u>you</u> are fallen

  "Question," May Swenson

In general, poetry tends toward **euphony,** the change of one quality of sound to another, from consonants to vowels and back again to facilitate pronunciation and so contribute to flow. But sometimes you will want to produce a sound that is not mellifluous or euphonic but effortful. One way of doing this is the **consonant cluster** demonstrated in the Pope line:

When Á/jăx strívés / somé róck's / vást weíght / tŏ thrów.

Here the consonants butt up against each other at the end of one word and the beginning of the next, so you have to stop between in order to pronounce both: *Ajax || strives; rock's || vast; weight || to.* At the same time, the two spondees give the line especially heavy stress: *sóme róck's vást weíght.* A different sort of **cacophony** is achieved when vowels end one word and begin the next:

Aňd óft / thĕ eár / thĕ ó/pěn vów/ěls tíre.

TRY THIS A.5

Go back to Try This 10.3 on page 301— the list of words related to your area of expertise. Are there any rich rhymes? True rhymes? Slant rhymes? Arrange a short list to form a line that alliterates: (my list of spices might yield *Cardamom, cayenne, curry, cloves*); and a line that assonates: (*Sage, bay, carraway, arrowroot*); and a line with rhymes true or slant: (*Dill weed, poppy seed, cumin seed, bay leaves, cloves*). Play around with combinations of rhyme, alliteration, and assonance: *Chili, cilantro, oregano, cinnamon, / Carraway, cardamom, gumbo, garlic, / Cinnamon, cumin, sesame, rosemary.* Can you find consonant clusters? *Nutmeg / gumbo; bay leaves / turmeric / cayenne.*

Verses with end-rhymes are said to have a rhyme scheme, and this is counted by giving the rhyme-words a single letter of the alphabet, so a rhyme in which the first and third lines rhyme, and the second and forth line rhyme, would be said to have an ABAB rhyme scheme.

Stanzas

The most common form of English poetry is **blank verse,** unrhymed iambic pentameter—iambic probably because of our habitual arrangement of articles and nouns, pentameter probably because that length represents a comfortable expulsion of breath, unrhymed probably because it is the most flexible of the formal patterns—the nearest to free verse. It is the form of Shakespeare's plays, of Milton's *Paradise Lost,* of Robert Frost's "Mending Wall," Wallace Stevens's "Sunday Morning," and innumerable modern poems. Blank verse runs to any length and is not broken into set blocks of lines. But most patterned verse is written in stanzas.

A **stanza** is a division of lines in a poem, usually linked by a pattern of meter or sound, and usually repeated more than once. It is beyond the scope of this book to enumerate the various, multifarious, loose and strict, simple and elaborate, Eastern and Western stanza forms. But here are a few that are basic to English verse, and a few from other cultures that have attracted a good deal of poetic play in the English of the past few decades.

- **Couplet.** A two-line stanza, usually consecutively rhymed, although unrhymed couplets are also common in modern verse. A **heroic couplet** is two lines of iambic pentameter, consecutively rhymed:

  The little hours: two lovers herd upstairs
  two children, one of whom is one of theirs.

  "Almost Aubade," Marilyn Hacker

- **Tercet,** or **triplet,** is a stanza of three lines (rhymed or unrhymed):

  While mopping she muses over work undone,
  Her daily chores. The blue floor tiles
  Reflect where she cleans and her thoughts run…

  "The Housekeeper," Wendy Bishop

- **Quatrain** is a stanza of four lines, of which the **ballad meter** is famous in English, usually four lines of iambic tetrameter, or alternating tetrameter and trimeter, rhymed only on the second and fourth lines (though there are many variations, of both meter and rhyme scheme). The ballad tells a story, often of betrayal and violence:

  Put your hand behind the wainscot,
  You have done your part;
  Find the penknife there and plunge it
  Into your cold heart.

  W. H. Auden

- The **song** or **lyric** is often in quatrains of iambic tetrameter with a rhyme scheme of ABAB or ABBA.
- And so forth. A **quintet** has five lines, a **sestet** six, a **septet** seven, and an **octave** eight.
- The **sonnet** is a poem of fourteen lines, usually printed without a stanza break although the lines are internally grouped. The sonnet gained its popularity as an import from Italy during the Renaissance, where it was densely rhymed and usually dealt with the subject of love, especially unrequited (something like country western music today.) Because of the paucity of English rhymes, the Italian or Petrarchan rhyme scheme (ABBA ABBA CDECDE) was adapted in English to the looser scheme ABAB CDCD EFEF GG. The sonnet is a good example of the way form influences meaning. Petrarchan sonnets have a strong tendency to develop an idea in the first eight lines (or **octet**) and then to elaborate or contradict or alter it at some length in the last six lines (**sestet**). But the English sonnet, including those of Shakespeare's, developed in such a way that the three quatrains develop an idea, which must then be capped, or contradicted, or changed in a punchy couplet at the end. Here is an example from Shakespeare that is likely to be familiar:

  Let me not to the marriage of true minds
  Admit impediments. Love is not love
  Which alters when it alteration finds,
  Or bends with the remover to remove:
  O no! it is an ever-fixed mark
  That looks on tempests and is never shaken;
  It is the star to every wandering bark,
  Whose worth's unknown, although his height be taken.
  Love's not Time's fool, though rosy lips and cheeks
  Within his bending sickle's compass come:
  Love alters not with his brief hours and weeks,
  But bears it out even to the edge of doom.
    If this be error and upon me proved,
    I never writ, nor no man ever loved.

Stanzas are arranged in many set, traditional—and many more invented and original—groups, to form the poems. Like the sonnet, most of the forms that we think of as typically English were actually adapted from other languages. Terza rima, rondeau, sestina, ghazal, pantoum, villanelle—any and all of these are worth seeking out (the books recommended in Chapter 10, page 310, will provide definitions and examples). Meanwhile, of the non-English forms that have become popular, none is more so than the shortest of them, the Japanese **haiku,** an unrhymed verse of seventeen syllables arranged in three lines of five, seven, and five syllables. And none of them provides better practice for encapsulating an emotion or idea in a sharply etched observation, whether *reflective:*

Escaped the nets,
escaped the ropes—
moon on the water

Buson

—*or cynical:*

a bath when you're born
a bath when you die,
how stupid.

Issa

—*or contemporary:*

These stamps are virgins—
not even licked yet. Date night
alone at my desk.

Devan Cook

TRY THIS A.6

Write a series of quatrains. Choose some meter and rhyme scheme in advance—iambic tetrameter in a pattern of ABBA rhymes, for example. This will be an "altar poem" to someone you want to honor. In the first line, name or describe a place that would be appropriate to honor this person. In subsequent lines, list or describe the objects you would bring and assemble in that place. Try slant rhymes to augment your possibilities. Play around to see if you can use and identify caesura, enjambment, alliteration, assonance.

Write a sonnet as a story: in quatrain one, introduce two characters in a setting; in quatrain two, they are in conflict; in quatrain three, a third character arrives and complicates things; in the couplet, all is resolved.

Write a haiku. Write another. One more.

appendix b

LINE EDITING

Editing Symbols

sp	Misspelling	dm	Dangling modifier
gram	Grammatical mistake	mm	Misplaced modifier
¶	Begin new paragraph	cs	Comma splice, run-on sentence
^	Insert a letter, word, or phrase	˅"	Quotation marks
^,	Insert comma	X l.c.	Use lower case
^, (crossed out)	No comma needed	≡	Capitalize
⊙	Period needed	ital	Italicize
^;	Semicolon needed	rom	No italics needed
^:	Colon needed	frag	Sentence fragment
˅'	Apostrophe needed	awk	Awkward construction
^ (dash)	Dash needed	cit	Missing source or citation
( )	Parentheses needed	dev	Needs development
[ ]	Brackets needed	rep	Unnecessary repetition
...	Ellipses needed	vb	Error in verb tense
/	Slash needed	trans	Transition needed
#	Insert space	w	Wordy
⌒	Close up space between words	ww	Wrong word
⊂⊃	Close up space within a word	??	Illegible or unclear
no ¶	No new paragraph needed	d	Diction, word choice
ℓ	Delete	//	Faulty parallel
∼	Transpose	∝	Cliché
agr	Error in noun-verb agreement	mx	Mixed metaphor
ant	Error in pronoun-antecedent agreement		

An Example of Line Editing

At the Dolphin Inn on the Sandbar Key, Dale and I are hosting a birthday party for his daughter Sam and her two friends Dolly and Grappa. I give all of us pseudonyms for reasons that will become clear. It's clear that these three eleven year olds are teetering on the edge of puberty. Now they are gigling and whispering over the angelfood skirt of the birthday-cake doll, now checking out the clevage in Self Magazine, now haggling over whether to watch Scooby Doo, now thrusting butt and belly into the line of vision of the red-headed boy in the Dolphin Inn pool. We have got a "suite," which means a bedroom a and living room with a pull-out couch. The theory being that the bed room is for Dale and I, three eleven-year-olds cannot remove so much as a sandy sock in the presence of an adult male, so so most of the time our bedroom is either locked against us or stroun with wadded up under wear, wet bathing suits, and dessiccated angel food. Every swim requires a shower before and a bath after, three girls showering, swimmming, bathing four times a day—you do the math while I sopp up the bathroom floor and hanga dozen towels over the deck railing.

TRY THIS B.1

Everyone bring in one or two typed pages of the worst piece you have written. Pass them to the right, or shuffle the pages and pass them out. Line-edit the piece you now have, correcting for typos, spelling, punctuation, grammar, and (careful now) style. Take some time to go over the page with the author. Are you in agreement? Have you as editor improved the professionalism of the piece?

glossary

Note: Technical terms concerning **prosody** (the study of meter and sound in poetry) are also found in Appendix A on page 365.

Accent, or stress Vocal emphasis given to a particular syllable, word, or phrase. The AC-cent or STRESS can be HEARD in the VOICE. See pp. 365 and 366.

Accentual verse Poetry in which only the accented syllables in each line are counted; there may be any number of unaccented syllables. See p. 367.

Alliteration Repeated consonants, particularly at the beginning of words or stressed syllables, as in "With a sound like seed spilled…" See pp. 299 and 370.

Anapest (n.), **anapestic** (adj.) A poetic foot consisting of two unaccented (unstressed) and one accented (stressed) syllables, as in: in the SKY. See **Poetic foot** and p. 368.

Antagonist In narrative, the character who provides the major impediment or obstacle to the main character's desire. See **Protagonist.**

Aside A theatrical convention whereby a character says something that the audience hears but the other characters do not. See p. 331.

Assonance Repeated vowel sounds, as in "The rain in Spain stays mainly in the plain." See pp. 300 and 370.

Atmosphere The tone and attitude, as well as the setting, period, weather, and time of day, of a story. The background to the characters' foreground. See p. 140.

Authorial interpretation; authorial intrusion The author speaks directly to the reader, rather than through the point of view of the character. By and large, the device is interpretive any time the author tells us what we should think or feel; it is intrusive if we mind this. See pp. 98 and 238.

Backstory Past events that are necessary to understand a narrative or its significance. See p. 271.

Ballad meter A stanza of four lines, usually of iambic tetrameter, usually rhymed ABCD. See p. 371.

Blank verse Unrhymed iambic pentameter. The most common line in English poetry. See p. 371.

Brainstorm A problem-solving technique that can also generate ideas for an imagined situation. The writer free-associates a list of ideas, connections, solutions, then uses these as prompts for writing. Often takes the form "*What if…?*" See p. 6.

Cacophony Jarring, discordant sound. See p. 370.

Caesura A pause within a line of poetry, often indicated by a comma or period. See p. 366.

Central Narrator See **Narrator.**

Character A fictional person. The basis of literary writing. See Chapter 4.

Characterization May be direct, through describing how the character looks, acts, etc. or indirect, through summary or interpretation. See Chapter 4.

Cliché A word, phrase, or metaphor that represents the predictable or overly familiar, and usually indicates lazy writing. See pp. 24 and 303.

Climax See **Crisis.**

Complications Aspects of the conflict that build the plot toward its climax. The "*nouement*" or "knotting up" of the action. See p. 171.

Conceit A metaphor in which the connection between the two things compared is not immediately clear. In Samuel Johnson's words, "yoked by violence together," as in John Donne's comparison of a flea to the holy trinity, or Nathanael West's "love is like a vending machine." The author must explain the similarity. See p. 303.

Concrete, significant details Specifics that address the senses in meaningful ways. The basic building blocks of imaginative writing, and what is meant by the advice: *Show, don't tell.*

- *Concrete* means that there is an image, something that can be seen, heard, smelled, tasted, or touched.
- *Detail* means that there is a degree of focus and specificity.
- *Significant* means that the specific image also suggests an abstraction, generalization, or judgment.

See p. 17.

Connotation The complex of meanings and ideas that come to be associated with a word, as "rose" suggests not only the flower but beauty, fragrance, womanhood, perhaps ephemerality, and/or the hidden threat of thorns. See p. 303.

Conflict The struggle between protagonist and antagonist, or between two opposing forces. Considered necessary to narrative, because it generates a desire in the reader to find out what is going to happen. See p. 169.

Consonant The sound produced by any obstruction of the air stream, brought about by a constriction of one or more of the organs of voice. In English, all the letters of the alphabet that are not vowels (a, e, i, o, u, sometimes y) are consonants. See p. 365.

Consonant cluster A poetic effect created by "back to back" consonants, so that the speaker has to stop between words in order the pronounce them, as in "The self forgets such strength." See p. 370.

Couplet Two lines of verse, usually rhymed, which can constitute an entire poem or stand as part of a longer stanzaic form. An example:

"Wales, which I have never seen,
Is gloomy, mountainous, and green..."

See p. 371.

Creative nonfiction The essay, enlivened through attention to stylistic and dramatic devices, personal voice, and a search for range and resonance. Also called **literary nonfiction.** See Chapter 8.

Crisis The point of highest tension in a story, at which a discovery or a decision is made that decides the outcome of the conflict. See pp. 169 and 171.

Dactyl (n.), **dactylic** (adj.) A poetic foot consisting of one accented (stressed) and two unaccented (unstressed) syllables, as in: FOR-ti-fy. See **Poetic foot** and p. 368.

Dead metaphor A metaphor so common that it has lost the original sense of comparison and acquired a further definition, as "sifting the evidence" no longer calls a sieve to mind. See p. 305.

Denotation The most direct or specific meaning of a word; how it is defined. See p. 303.

Denouement The resolution at the end of a story. The return to order after the conflict, its complications, and climax have passed. See p. 171.

Density In literature, the arrangement of words and images to pack maximum meaning into minimum space. See p. 306.

Dialogue The characters' talk. Dialogue may be:

- **Direct,** the spoken words quoted: "No, I can't stand the little monsters and I won't herd a bunch of them to the damn park unless I'm paid."
- **Indirect,** the words related in third person: She said she couldn't stand kids and wouldn't take them to the park unless she got paid.
- **Summarized,** reported at a distance: She claimed to hate children, and irritatedly demanded payment for taking them to the park.

See pp. 92.

Diction A combination of *vocabulary,* the words chosen, and *syntax,* the order in which they are used. Diction will convey not only the facts but also the tone and attitude of the person whose voice speaks to us from the page. See p. 48.

Diegetic Musical or other effects that occur naturally as part of the dramatic narrative (a character turns on the radio and a song comes out). **Nondiegetic** effects occur when there is no such natural or realistic link (a suspenseful scene is accompanied by music to enhance the tension). See p. 327.

Dimeter A line consisting of two poetic feet. See **Poetic foot** and p. 368.

Direct dialogue See **Dialogue.**

Distance The position, close or far, of the author in relation to the characters or narrator, often implying the degree to which we are intended to identify with or trust them. Distance will be affected first of all by diction and tone, and may involve a literal distance in time or space (the narrator, for example, is telling a story about himself as a child) or a psychic distance (the author is describing the exploits of a psychopath). See p. 59.

Dramatic irony The audience (or reader) knows something that the character doesn't know. See p. 328.

Emotional recall A theatrical convention in which one character tells another about an incident from the past, and the story changes the attitude of the second character in some dramatically significant way. See p. 331.

End rhyme The rhyming words or syllables occur at the end of the poetic line, as in:

"Ever let the fancy roam,
Pleasure never is at home."

See p. 370.

End-stopped The phrase, clause, or sentence punctuation occurs at the end of poetic line, as in the example just above. See p. 302.

Enjambment The opposite of end-stopped; the sentence and its meaning carry on from one line (or stanza) to the next:

"Notwithstanding you are in your grave
These fifteen months, you are invited to apply
For a fixed-rate zero-percent American Express..."

See p. 301.

Epistolary May describe an essay, poem, novel, or story consisting entirely or mainly of letters written to another character, a person, or an institution.

Essay From the French word meaning "a try," a prose piece with a basis in fact, on a single subject, presenting the view of the author. Kinds of essay include the expository, narrative, descriptive, persuasive, article, feature, profile, literary nonfiction, and creative nonfiction. See Chapter 8, p. 231.

Euphony Pleasant and smooth-flowing sound, the opposite of cacaphony. See p. 370.

Exposition In narrative and especially theatre, the laying out of the situation at the opening of the action. See pp. 171 and 322.

Falling action The portion of a plot that follows the climax and leads to the resolution. A "walking away from the fight." Also called **denouement.** See p. 171.

Figure of speech (or **trope,** or **figurative speech**) A nonliteral use of language, such as metaphor, simile, hyperbole, personification, and so forth, to enhance or intensify meaning. See pp. 21 and 303.

First person See **Person.**

Flashback In narrative, film, or drama, a leap into the past. The earlier scene is inserted into the normal chronological order. See p. 271.

Foot See **Poetic foot.**

Formal verse Verse written in a predetermined pattern of rhythm and rhyme. See Appendix A, "A Basic Prosody," p. 365.

Fourth-wall realism A theatrical convention in which the stage represents a room with the fourth wall removed. Both actors and audience pretend that what is happening onstage is "really" happening at the present time. See p. 324.

Free verse or **informal verse.** Verse that lacks a regular meter or rhyme scheme, and uses irregular line lengths according to the demands of the particular poem. See p. 295.

Freewrite A piece of writing undertaken without any plan or forethought whatever; writing whatever comes into your head at the moment. Gertrude Stein called this "automatic writing." A **focused freewrite** is a piece written with the same unplanned freedom, but on a chosen topic. See p. 6.

Genre A form of writing, such as poetry, drama, or fiction. The term is problematic because "genre fiction" and "genre writing" are terms used differently, to indicate writing in narrow, plot-driven conventions such as the western, romance, detective story, and so forth.

Haiku A form of poetry taken from the Japanese, representing a moment of perception, in three lines with a pattern of five, seven, and five syllables, for a total of seventeen syllables. See p. 372.

Heptameter A poetic line of seven feet. See **Poetic foot** and p. 369.

Heroic couplet Two lines of poetry consecutively rhymed, as in:

"Suspicious, dour, morosed, perplexed,
And just a little oversexed."

See p. 371.

Hexameter A poetic line of six feet. See **Poetic foot** and p. 369.

Hyperbole Extreme exaggeration, as in: "You are the sun, the moon, and the stars." See **Figure of speech.**

Iamb A poetic foot consisting of one unaccented (unstressed) and one accented (stressed) syllable: hoo-RAY. See **Poetic foot** and p. 367.

Idiom An expression that is grammatically peculiar to itself and can't be understood by understanding its separate elements. English abounds in idioms: *put 'er there, keeps tabs on, of his own accord,* and so forth. The line between idioms, clichés, dead metaphors, and figures of speech is often not distinct. See p. 305.

Inciting incident The event that has created the situation in which the protagonist finds him/herself at the beginning of a drama. For example, Hamlet's father has died and his mother has remarried. See p. 322.

Indirect dialogue See **Dialogue.**

Informal verse See **Free verse.**

Intensity In literature, the raising of tension or emotion through character conflict, language, rhythm, situation, irony, or other artistic device.

Internal rhyme A rhyme in which at least one of the rhyming words occurs within, rather than at the end of, a line, as:

Subdued, the mournful measures falling *under*
The *thunder* of this cascade ...

See pp. 300 and 370.

Irony Always involves a contradiction or a denial of expectation in some area. *Verbal irony* occurs where one thing is said and another or its opposite is meant, as in *Brutus is an honorable man. So are they all, all honorable men.* In *dramatic irony,* the audience knows something that the character does not, and so puts a different interpretation on events. Example: Oedipus thinks it great good news that King Polybus has died of old age, for this seems to disprove the oracle that he would kill his father. The audience knows that Polybus was not really his father. So-called *cosmic irony* is a contradiction inherent in human action or the human condition: *Using DDT to poison the insects and so grow healtheir crops, farmers poison the water in the aquifer from which people drink.*

Long vowel See **Vowels.**

Line A series of words after which there is a typographical break. In prose, the line ends because the type has arrived at a margin, and may vary from one edition or font to another. In poetry, the line implies a slight pause and is used in conjunction with or opposition to the sentence as a means of creating significance. Consequently the line is considered an integral feature of the poem, and will remain the same in each reprinting. See pp. 301 and 365.

Line editing Careful, often final, revision of a manuscript at the level of checking punctuation, spelling, and grammar as well as the nuance of final word choice. See p. 207.

Literary nonfiction See **Creative nonfiction.**

Lyric A type of poem expressing subjective thoughts or feelings, often in the form of a song. See p. 372.

Memoir A story retrieved from the writer's memory, with the writer as protagonist. See p. 232.

Metaphor The comparison of one term with another such that a tension is created between what is alike and what is unlike between the two terms.

- A *metaphor* assumes or states the comparison, without acknowledging that it is a comparison: *My electric muscles shock the crowd; Her hair is seaweed and she is the sea.* The metaphor may come in the form of an adjective: *They have a piggy and a fishy air.* Or it may come as a verb: *The bees shouldering the grass.*
- A *simile* is a type of metaphor that acknowledges the comparison by using the words *like* or *as: His teeth rattled like dice in a box; My head is light as a balloon; I will fall like an ocean on that court.*

See p. 22.

Meter From the Greek "measure," a relatively objective or mechanical way of measuring time in poetry, according to the number of feet and syllables in a line. See p. 366.

Metered verse Verse that can be so measured. See pp. 366–369.

Metonymy A figure of speech in which one word or phrase is used as substitute for another with which it is associated, as in *the pen is mightier than the sword,* or when *inside the beltway* is used to mean *the U.S. government in Washington.* See p. 21.

Mnemonic Helpful to or intended to help memory. See p. 296.

Monologue A speech of some length by a single character. See p. 52.

Monometer A line consisting of a single poetic foot. See **Poetic foot** and p. 368.

Mood See **Atmosphere.**

Narrative A story; the telling of a story.

Narrator The one who tells the story. We often speak of the author as narrator if the piece is told in the third person, although literally a story "has a narrator" only when it is told by a character. This character may be:

- The **central narrator,** the *I* writing *my* story as if it were memoir, or

- The **peripheral narrator,** someone on the edge of the action, who is nevertheless our eyes and ears in the story and therefore the person with whom we identify, and with whom we must be moved or changed.

See p. 56.

Nondiegetic See **Diegetic.**

Ode A lyric poem of some length, usually meditative or serious, with a formal structure and elevated diction.

Octave In poetry, a group of eight lines, especially the first eight lines of a Petrarchan sonnet. See p. 372.

Off rhyme, or **slant rhyme** An imperfect or partial rhyme, usually a consonance, as *stoned* is an off rhyme for *hand* and *blind.* See p. 369.

Omniscience The narrative convention by which the author knows everything—past, future, any character's thoughts, the significance of events, universal truths. It is the godlike authorial stance. See p. 57.

Onomatopoeia The use of words that sound like what they mean: *buzz, whine, murmur.* See p. 298.

Oral history An essay developed from an interview of a subject by the author, arranged and presented entirely in the words of the subject.

Outline A preliminary plan for a piece of writing, summarizing in list form its major parts or points. See p. 200.

Oxymoron A figure of speech that combines or juxtaposes two contradictory words: *burning ice, shouting whisper, plain decoration.* The term comes from the Greek meaning "sharply foolish," which is itself an oxymoron and expresses the potential of the figure to reveal although it appears not to make sense. See p. 22.

Paradox A seemingly contradictory statement of which both parts may nevertheless be true, as in, "A writer is someone for whom writing is more difficult than for other people." (Thomas Mann) See p. 307.

Pentameter A line of five poetic feet. See **Poetic foot** and p. 368.

Peripheral narrator See **Narrator.**

Person In grammar and narrative, any of three groups of pronouns identifying the subject. **First person:** *I look out the window.* **Second person:** *You look out the window.* **Third person:** *He looks out the window.* See p. 55.

Persona A mask adopted by the author, which may be a public manifestation of the author's self; or a distorted or partial version of that self; or a fictional, historical, or mythological character. See p. 50.

Personal essay An essay in which the author is overtly present, either in the events described or because of his/her "take" on the subject through reflection, research, or opinion.

Personification The technique of giving human attributes or emotions to animals, objects, or concepts, as in, "the water lapped eagerly at the shore." See p. 22.

Phoneme The smallest sound or phonetic unit that may convey a distinction of meaning, as cat *is distinguished from* hat. See p. 365.

Plot A series of events arranged so as to reveal their significance. See **Story.**

Poetic foot A unit of measurement with one accented or stressed syllable, and one or two unstressed syllables. See p. 366 and 367.

Poetic line A unit of verse recognizable by the typographic break at the end of it, but also by general consent the basic unit of poetry. The break represents a slight pause or very brief silence. In formal poetry, it may also provide a rhyme and/or signal that a certain number of feet has been reached; in free verse, these formal elements may be absent, but the line break may still convey emphasis, suggest connotation, or imply double or even contradictory meaning. See p. 301.

Point of attack In drama, the first event that sets the plot in motion: for example, the ghost speaks to Hamlet, demanding revenge against Claudius. See p. 322.

Point of view A complex technique of narrative involving who tells the story, to whom, in what form. Importantly, the **person** in which the story is told, and the vantage point from which the story is told, contribute to the ultimate meaning of events. See p. 55.

Prose poem A poem that is not written in lines but continues to the margins of the page like prose. See p. 185.

Prosody The study of meter and sound in poetry. See Appendix A on p. 365.

Protagonist The main character of a narrative; usually, one with whom we identify. See p. 170.

Pun A figure of speech that plays on different meanings of the same word, or the different sense or sound of two similar words. "Hair today and gone tomorrow." See p. 22.

Pyrrhic A substitute poetic foot with two unaccented (unstressed) syllables. See p. 368.

Quatrain A verse of four lines. See p. 371.

Quilting A (metaphor for a) method of drafting, especially a prose piece, by gathering paragraphs and physically moving them around to produce a rough structure. See p. 201.

Quintet A verse of five lines. See p. 372.

Realism A narrative or dramatic convention that aims at accuracy and verisimilitude in the presentation of period, place, speech, and behavior.

Replacement poem An exercise for reproducing the vigor of an admired poem: replace all of the verbs, nouns, adjectives, and adverbs with other words representing the same part of speech. See p. 311.

Resolution The end of conflict, usually involving the restoration of order, at the end of a plot. See pp. 169 and 171.

Rhyme A similarity or correspondence of sounds. In a true rhyme, the vowel sound of the accented syllable and everything thereafter correspond, as in *laugh* and *staff*, or *laughter* and *after*. In a rich rhyme, the consonant preceding the vowel also corresponds, (the *p* in) *pair* and *repair* and *despair*. In assonance, only the vowel sound corresponds: *why I might*; in consonance, only the final consonant corresponds: *greet the white cat*. See p. 369.

Rhythm The pattern or flow of sound created by stressed and unstressed syllables. Unlike meter, which is a mechanical measurement of such pattern, rhythm generally expresses a quality achieved by the pattern, so one may say that the rhythm is lighthearted or swaggering or effortful or numb. See p. 366.

Rich rhyme See p. 369.

Run-on line See **Enjambment.**

Scansion The measuring of verse into poetic feet, or a pattern of stressed and unstressed syllables. See Appendix A, p. 365.

Scene and **summary** Methods of treating time in fiction. A summary covers a relatively long period of time in relatively short compass; a scene deals at length with a relatively short period of time. See p. 268.

Secondary stress Many poets see a secondary stress—less emphasis than a stress, more than an unstress—in the scanning of English poetry. Most three- and four-syllable words offer such a secondary stress: "cáre-fŭl-lӳ" "in̆-sí-di-óus". The secondary stress is marked with a double accent mark. See p. 365.

Second person See **Person.**

Self-reflexivity Referring back to the self. Generally used to indicate that the work, rather than pretending to represent a true picture of real events, acknowledges in some way that it is a fiction, an artifact, a work of imagination. See p. 313.

Septet A group or verse of seven lines. See p. 372.

Sestet A group or verse of six lines, especially the last six lines of a Petrarchan sonnet. See p. 372.

Setting The place and period in which a story or drama takes place. See Chapter 5.

Short-short story A plotted fiction of no more than 500 words, usually fewer. Also sometimes called *flash fiction* or *microfiction* See p. 169.

Short vowels See **Vowel.**

Simile A comparison using the terms *like* or *as*. See **Metaphor.**

Slant rhyme See **Off rhyme.**

Soliloquy A theatrical convention in which a character alone onstage makes a speech that we understand to represent his or her thoughts. See p. 331.

Sonnet A poem of fourteen lines. See p. 372.

Song May refer to any poetry or verse, but most often to a lyric or a verse meant to be set to music.

Spondee A subsitute foot consisting of two accented (stressed) syllables. See p. 368.

Stage lie A theatrical convention in which the character says one thing but betrays the opposite through contradiction or visible behavior. See p. 326.

Stanza A group of lines within a poem, usually set off by white space on the page. In formal verse, the stanzas will typically all have the same number of lines with the same rhythm and rhyme pattern. In free verse, the stanzas indicate some deliberate grouping of images or thoughts. See p. 371.

Story A sequence of fictional or remembered events, usually involving a conflict, crisis, and resolution. Humphry House, in his commentaries on Aristotle, defines story as everything the reader needs to know to make coherent sense of the plot, and plot as the particular portion of the story the author chooses to present—the "present tense" of the narrative. See Chapters 6 and 9.

Stress See **Accent.** See pp. 296 and 365–369.

Summary See **Scene.**

Summarized dialogue See **Dialogue.**

Syllable A unit of spoken language that is a single uninterrupted sound. A syllable will always contain a vowel; it may contain one or more consonants. So *I* and *Oh* are each a single syllable, but so are *light* and *sow* and *soap*. The word LIGHT-ning thus contains two syllables, of which the first is accented or stressed and the second unaccented or unstressed. The syllable is crucial to English poetry because it is the pattern of accented and unaccented syllables that form the basis of the rhythm. See p. 365.

Syllabic verse Poetry in which line length is fixed by the number of syllables in the line; the number of accents is irrelevant. Some poetic forms are intrinsically syllabic, like the haiku, which consists of three lines in the pattern of five, seven, and five syllables. See p. 365.

Symbol Something, usually an object, that stands for something larger, often an interrelated complex of ideas, values, and beliefs. For example, the flag stands for love of country. In literature, this object is particular to the work. The golden bowl in Henry James's *The Golden Bowl* stands for a situation involving deception, self-deception, betrayal, and flawed marital love. See p. 140.

Synecdoche A figure of speech in which a part stands for the whole, as in *all hands on deck* or *I'm going to get some new wheels.* See p. 21.

Syntax The arrangement of words within a sentence. See p. 48.

Tempo The pace, speed, or slowness of a rhythm. See p. 366.

Tercet A three-line stanza. See p. 371.

Tetrameter A poetic line consisting of four feet. See **Poetic foot** and p. 368.

Theatricalism The dramatic convention by which the actors acknowledge that the stage is a stage, the play a play, and themselves players of parts. See p. 324.

Third person See **Person.**

Trimeter A poetic line consisting of three feet. See **Poetic foot** and p. 368.

Triplet A tercet (three-line stanza) of poetry in which all the end-words rhyme. See p. 371.

Trochee (n.), **trochaic** (adj.) Poetic foot consisting of one accented or stressed and one unaccented or unstressed syllable, as in TI-ger. See **Poetic foot** and p. 367.

Trope See **Figure of speech.**

True rhyme See pp. 300 and 369.

Unaccentedor **unstressed** A syllable that receives relatively little emphasis. See **Accent.**

Unstress See **Unaccented.**

Villanelle An intricate poem, in which the first and third lines are repeated at the end of alternating successive verses and as a couplet at the end. See pp. 213 and 312.

Vocabulary The sum total of words known and used by a writer (or a person or group of people); the choice of words in a particular work. See p. 48.

Voice The recognizable style of a particular writer or character, composed of syntax, vocabulary, attitude, and tone. See Chapter 3.

Voiceover In film and theatre, the voice of an unseen character providing narration, usually by mechanical means. See p. 331.

Vowel The speech sound created by a relatively free passage of breath through the larynx and oral cavity, in English represented by the sounds of *a, e, i, o, u* and sometimes *y*. Vowels may be either *long,* as pronounced in the words *main, feet, dine, rope,* and *cute;* or *short,* as in *cat, pet, in, hop,* and *up*. The designations *long* and *short* hark back to Greek and Latin verse, which was counted not in accented and unaccented syllables but by the length of time it took to pronounce a given syllable. See p. 365.

credits

Photos

Page 13 G. Baden/Corbis
Page 47 Queen of the Scottish Faeries Illustration by Rutu Modan 2007
Page 87 John Grant
Page 132 Gerth Roland/Prisma/age fotostock
Page 167 LARRY DOWNING/Reuters/Corbis
Page 196tl Macduff Everton/Corbis
Page 196bl William Karel/Sygma/Corbis
Page 196tr Chris Carroll/Corbis
Page 196br Ken Seet/Corbis
Page 230 Laurie Lipton
Page 264 Andrew Fox/Corbis/Corbis
Page 294 Jerry Uelsmann
Page 321 Pamela Hansen/Marek & Assoc/trunkarchive.com

Readings

Sherman Alexie, "At Navajo Monument Valley Tribal School." Reprinted from *The Business of Fancydancing* © 1992 by Sherman Alexie, by permission of Hanging Loose Press.

Quote from A. Alvarez, *The Writer's Voice*. New York: W. W. Norton & company, 2004.

From *Borderlands/La Frontera: The New Mestiza*. Copyright © 1987, 1999, 2007 by Gloria Anzaldúa. Reprinted by permission of Aunt Lute Books.

Philip Appleman, "Nobody Dies in the Spring." By permission of the author.

"The Female Body," from GOOD BONES AND SIMPLE MURDERS by Margaret Atwood, copyright © 1983, 1992, 1994, by O.W. Toad Ltd. A Nan A. Talese Book. Published in Canada by McClelland & Stewart Ltd. Used by permission of Doubleday, a division of Random House, Inc., and by permission of McClelland & Stewart Ltd.

Quote from Paul Auster, *Man in the Dark*. New York: Henry Holt, 2008.

"The School" from *Sixty Stories* by Donald Barthelme. Copyright © 1981, 1982 by Donald Barthelme, reprinted with permission of The Wylie Agency LLC.

Alan Bennett, "Bed Among the Lentils." From From TALKING HEADS / THE COMPLETE TALKING HEADS by Alan Bennett, published by BBC Books and Picador respectively, copyright © 1998 by Forlake Ltd. and reprinted by permission of Picador and The Random House Group Ltd.

Alan Bennett, a quotation from "A Cream Cracker Under the Settee." From TALKING HEADS / THE COMPLETE TALKING HEADS by Alan Bennett, published by BBC Books and Picador respectively, copyright © 1998 by Forlake Ltd. and reprinted by permission of Picador and The Random House Group Ltd.

Reprinted by permission of Farrar, Straus & Giroux, LLC: Dream Song #14 from THE DREAM SONGS by John Berryman. Copyright © 1969 by John Berryman. Copyright renewed 1997 by Kate Donahue Berryman.

Reprinted by permission of Farrar, Straus & Giroux, LLC: "One Art" from THE COMPLETE POEMS 1927–1979 by Elizabeth Bishop. Copyright © 1979, 1983 by Alice Helen Methfessel.

"The Story," from A BLIND MAN CAN SEE HOW MUCH I LOVE YOU by Amy Bloom, copyright © 2000 by Amy Bloom. Used by permission of Random House, Inc.

Roger Bonair-Agard, "American History looks for light—a prayer for the survival of Barack Obama." Used with permission.

Matt Bondurant, "The Pathos of Charles Schulz" from *Ninth Letter* vol. 4, no. 2 (Fall/Winter 2007). Used with permission.

"The Book of Sand," from *COLLECTED FICTIONS* by Jorge Luis Borges, translated by Andrew Hurley. Copyright © 1998 by Maria Kodama. Translation and notes copyright © 1998 by Penguin Putnam Inc. Reprinted by permission of Viking Penguin, a division of Penguin Group (USA) Inc., and by permission of Penguin Group (Canada), a Division of Pearson Canada Inc.

Warren J. Bowe, "Guns for Teachers." Used with permission.

"Bigfoot Stole My Wife," from A KIND OF FLYING: SELECTED STORIES by Ron Carlson. Copyright © 2003, 1997, 1992, 1987 by Ron Carlson. Used by permission of W. W. Norton & Company, Inc.

Angela Carter, "The Werewolf" from *Burning Your Boats*. Copyright © Angela Carter. Reproduced by permission of the author's Estate c/o Rogers, Coleridge & White Ltd., 20 Powis Mews, London W11 1JN.

Quote from Michael Chabon, *The Yiddish Policemen's Union*. New York: HarperCollins, 2007.

"The Proposal" from THE PLAYS OF ANTON CHECKHOV, A NEW TRANLSATION by PAUL SCHMIDT. Copyright © 1997 by Paul Schmidt. Reprinted by permission of HarperCollins Publishers.

Excerpt from the journal of Billy Collins, used with permission of the author.

"Snow Day," copyright © 2001 by Billy Collins, from SAILING ALONE AROUND THE ROOM by Billy Collins. Used by permission of Random House, Inc.

Reprinted by permission of the publishers and the Trustees of Amherst College from THE POEMS OF EMILY DICKINSON: READING EDITION, Ralph W. Franklin, ed., Cambridge, Mass.: The Belknap Press of Harvard University Press, Copyright © 1998, 1999 by the President and Fellows of Harvard College. Copyright © 1951, 1955, 1979, 1983 by the President and Fellows of Harvard College.

Reprinted by permission of Farrar, Straus & Giroux, LLC: "At the Dam" from THE WHITE ALBUM by Joan Didion. Copyright © 1979 by Joan Didion.

"Heaven and Earth in Jest" from PILGRIM AT TINKER CREEK by ANNIE DILLARD. Copyright © 1974 by Annie Dillard. Reprinted by permission of HarperCollins Publishers.

Stuart Dybek, "Thread," as it appeared in *Five Points*, Vol. 2, No. 3, 1998, and *Harper's Magazine*, September 1998. Used with permission of the author.

"This Is How I Remember It" by Elizabeth Kemper French from Micro Fiction, edited by Jerome Stern, W. W. Norton & Company, 1996. Used by permission of the author.

"Fire and Ice" from THE POETRY OF ROBERT FROST edited by Edward Connery Lathem. Copyright 1923, 1969 by Henry Holt and Company. Copyright 1951 by Robert Frost. Reprinted by arrangement with Henry Holt and Company, LLC.

2 lines from Reginald Gibbons, "We Say," *The Ruined Motel: Poems*. Houghton Mifflin, 1981. © Reginald Gibbons; reprinted by permission of the author.

All lines from "TO AUNT ROSE" FROM COLLECTED POEMS 1947–1980 by ALLEN GINSBERG. Copyright © 1958 by Allen Ginsberg. Reprinted by permission of HarperCollins Publishers.

Michael Golamco, "Heartbreaker" from *2007: The Best Ten Minute Plays: 2 Actors*. Smith and Kraus, Inc. Used with permission.

Albert Goldbarth, "Columbine High School / Littleon, CO" from *The Gods* by Albert Goldbarth (Ohio State University Press, 1993). Reprinted with permission of the author.

"The Diamond Mine" from LOOT AND OTHER STORIES by Nadine Gordimer. First published in Viking Canada hardcover by Penguin Group (Canada), a division of Pearson Penguin Canada Inc., 2003. Published simultaneously in the U.S.A. by Farrar, Straus & Giroux. Copyright © 2003 by Felix Licensing, B.V. Reprinted by permission of Farrar, Straus & Giroux, LLC and Penguin Group (Canada), a Division of Pearson Canada Inc.

Siân B. Griffiths, "Fistful" from *Ninth Letter* vol. 4, no. 2 (Fall/Winter 2007). Used with permission of the author.

"To a Waterfowl" from WHITE APPLES AND THE TASTE OF STONE: Selected Poems, 1946–2006 by Donald Hall. Copyright © 2006 by Donald Hall. Reprinted by permission of Houghton Mifflin Harcourt Publishing Company. All rights reserved.

"Ode to American English" from *Babel*, by Barbara Hamby, © 2004. Reprinted by permission of the University of Pittsburgh Press.

"Red Sky in the Morning" from *I Could Tell You Stories* by Patricia Hampl, W. W. Norton & Company, 1999. Used by permission of Mary Rusoff & Associates, Inc.

"A Story About the Body" from HUMAN WISHES by ROBERT HASS. Copyright © 1989 by Robert Hass. Reprinted by permission of HarperCollins Publishers.

Reprinted with the permission of Scribner, a Division of Simon & Schuster, Inc., from THE SHORT STORIES OF ERNEST HEMINGWAY. Copyright 1925 by Charles Scribner's Sons. Copyright renewed 1953 by Ernest Hemingway.

Reprinted with the permission of Scribner, a Division of Simon & Schuster, Inc., from THE SHORT STORIES OF ERNEST HEMINGWAY. Copyright 1927 by Charles Scribner's Sons. Copyright renewed 1955 by Ernest Hemingway.

"The Philadelphia" from ALL IN THE TIMING: FOURTEEN PLAYS by David Ives, copyright © 1989, 1990, 1992 by David Ives. Used by permission of Vintage Books, a division of Random House, Inc.

"One Flesh" from *New Collected Poems* by Elizabeth Jennings (Carcanet Press). Used by permission of David Higham Associates.

"Half a Day," translated by Denys Johnson-Davis, copyright © 1991 by American University in Cairo Press, from THE TIME AND THE PLACE & OTHER STORIES by Naguib Mahfouz. Used by permission of Doubleday, a division of Random House, Inc.

Quote from Mary Karr, *The Liar's Club*. New York: Viking, 1995.

Excerpt from "A Poem to Galway Kinnell" from *The Essential Etheridge Knight*, by Etheridge Knight, © 1986. Reprinted by permission of the University of Pittsburgh Press.

Yusef Komunyakaa, "Facing It" from *Dien Cai Dau* © 1988 by Yusef Komunyakaa and reprinted by permission of Wesleyan University Press. www.wesleyan.edu/wespress.

Yusef Komunyakaa, "Nude Interrogation" from *Thieves of Paradise* © 1988 by Yusef Komunyakaa and reprinted by permission of Wesleyan University Press. www.wesleyan.edu/wespress.

Ted Kooser, "Tattoo" from *Delights & Shadows*. Copyright © 2004 by Ted Kooser. Reprinted with permission of Copper Canyon Press, www.coppercanyonpress.org.

"The Grammar Lesson" by Steve Kowit is reprinted by permission of the author.

"Woodchucks." Copyright © 1972, 1997 by Maxine Kumin, from SELECTED POEMS 1960-1990 by Maxine Kumin. Used by permission of W. W. Norton & Company, Inc.

Reproduced by permission of Farrar, Straus & Giroux, LLC and Faber and Faber Ltd.: "Annus Mirabilis" from COLLECTED POEMS by Philip Larkin. Copyright © 1988, 2003 by the Estate of Philip Larkin.

The quotation from "Toads" by Philip Larkin is reprinted from *The Less Deceived* by permission of The Marvell Press, England and Australia.

Li-Young Lee, "The Hammock" from *Book of My Nights*. Copyright © 2001 by Li-Young Lee. Reprinted with the permission of BOA Editions, Ltd., www.BOAEditions.org.

All pages from "THE HANDSOMEST DROWNED MAN IN THE WORLD" FROM LEAF STORM AND OTHER STORIES by GABRIEL GARCIA MARQUEZ. Copyright © 1971 by Gabriel Garcia Marquez. Reprinted by permission of HarperCollins Publishers. Originally appeared in Playboy magazine.

Jane Martin, "French Fries" is reprinted by permission of the Actors Theatre of Louisville.

Excerpt from the journal of Cris Mazza, used with permission.

"Cowboy" from GALLATIN CANYON: STORIES by Thomas McGuane, copyright © 2006 by Thomas McGuane. Used by permission of Alfred A. Knopf, a division of Random House, Inc. Originally published in The New Yorker.

Heather McHugh "Earthmoving Maldediction" from *Shades* © 1988 by Heather McHugh and reprinted by permission of Wesleyan University Press. www.wesleyan.edu/wespress.

Quote from David Mitchell, *Black Swan Green*. New York: Random House, 2006.

"Prue" from THE MOONS OF JUPITER AND OTHER STORIES by Alice Munro, copyright © 1982 by Alice Munro. Used by permission of Alfred A. Knopf, a division of Random House, Inc., and by permission of William Morris Endeavor Entertainment, LLC on behalf of the Author.

COME INTO THE GARDEN MAUD by Don Nigro. Copyright © 2007 by Don Nigro. Used with permission. CAUTION: Professionals and amateurs are hereby warned that COME INTO THE GARDEN MAUD being fully protected under the copyright laws of the United States of America, the British Commonwealth countries, including Canada, and the other countries of the Copyright Union, is subject to a royalty. All rights, including professional, amateur, motion picture, recitation, public reading, radio, television and cable broadcasting, and the rights of translation into foreign languages, are strictly reserved. Any inquiry regarding the availability of performance rights, or the purchase of individual copies of the authorized acting edition, must be directed to Samuel French Inc., 45 West 25 Street, NY, NY 10010 with other locations in Hollywood and Toronto, Canada.

Excerpt from "Feared Drowned" from *Satan Says* by Sharon Olds, © 1980. Reprinted by permission of the University of Pittsburgh Press.

Excerpt from "The Language of the Brag" from *Satan Says* by Sharon Olds, © 1980. Reprinted by permission of the University of Pittsburgh Press.

"The One Girl at the Boys' Party" from THE DEAD AND THE LIVING by Sharon Olds, copyright © 1987 by Sharon Olds. Used by permission of Alfred A. Knopf, a division of Random House, Inc.

Carol Oles, "Stonecarver" from *Quarry*, 1983. Reprinted by permission of the author.

Quote from Mary Oliver, "Verse That Is Free," *A Poetry Handbook*. Houghton Mifflin Harcourt, 1994, p. 67.

Alice O'Neill, "What I Came For." Reprinted with permission of the author.

2 lines from Alicia Ostriker, "My Lecture to the Writing Students, *A Dream of Springtime*. The Smith: distributed by Horizon Press, 1979. This poem originally appeared in *US 1 Worksheets*.

"Fathers" by Grace Paley, from *The New Yorker*, February 17 & 24, 2003. Used by permission of Elaine Markson Literary Agency.

Quote from Ann Patchett, *Run*. New York: HarperCollins, 2007.

Gayle Pemberton, "Do He Have Your Number Mr. Jeffrey?" From *The Hottest Water in Chicago* © 1998 and reprinted by permission of Wesleyan University Press. www.wesleyan.edu/wespress.

Quote from Robert Pinsky, *The Sounds of Poetry: A Brief Guide*. New York: Farrar, Straus & Giroux, 1999.

Three lines from "Rhyme" ["I've got a stubborn goose…/ … won't lay one."] from THE COLLECTED POEMS OF SYLVIA PLATH, EDITED by TED HUGHES. Copyright © 1960, 1965, 1971, 1981 by The Estate of Sylvia Plath. Editorial material copyright © 1981 by Ted Hughes. Reprinted by permission of HarperCollins Publishers and Faber and Faber Ltd.

"Stillborn" from CROSSING THE WATER by SYLVIA PLATH. Copyright © 1971 by Ted Hughes. Reprinted by permission of HarperCollins Publishers and Faber and Faber Ltd.

Liam Rector, "Him, His Place," from *American Prodigal*. Story Line Press, 1994. Used with permission.

Henry Reed. "Naming of Parts" from *Collected Poems* by Henry Reed, edited by Jon Stallworthy. Oxford University Press, 1991. By permission of Oxford University Press.

Rita Mae Reese, "A History of 'A History of Glass,'" reprinted by permission of Rita Mae Reese.

Rita Mae Reese, "A History of Glass." Reprinted with permission from the May 30, 2005 issue of *The Nation*. For subscription information, call 1-800-333-8536. Portions of each week's Nation magazine can be accessed at http://www.thenation.com.

Gas by Jose Rivera. Reprinted with permission.

"I Knew a Woman," copyright 1954 by Theodore Roethke, from COLLECTED POEMS OF THEODORE ROETHKE by Theodore Roethke. Used by permission of Doubleday, a division of Random House, Inc.

From WHEN YOU ARE ENGULFED IN FLAMES by DAVID SEDARIS. Copyright © 2008 by David Sedaris. By permission of LITTLE, BROWN & COMPANY.

Excerpt from "Her Kind" from TO BEDLAM AND THE WAY BACK. Copyright © 1960 by Anne Sexton, renewed 1988 by Linda G. Sexton. Reprinted by permission of Houghton Mifflin Harcourt Publishing Company. All rights reserved.

"Young" from ALL MY PRETTY ONES by Anne Sexton. Copyright © 1962 by Anne Sexton, renewed 1990 by Linda G. Sexton. Reprinted by permission of Houghton Mifflin Harcourt Publishing Company. All rights reserved.

Poems reprinted with permission of Patty Seyburn. The poem "The Penitent" originally appeared in *Prairie Schooner*, Vol. 72, no. 1, Spring 1998 and then in Vinz's collection *Affinities*, Dacotah Territory Press, 1998. "Insomniac" is the unpublished draft of that poem.

Line from Peter Shaffer, *Amadeus*, Act I, Scene II. New York: Harper & Row, 1981.

"Columbia the Gem" by Gerald Stern from *Rejoicings: Poems 1966–1972*, copyright 1984 is reprinted by permission of the author.

2 lines from James Tate's poem "Nirvana." First appeared in The American Poetry Review, May/Jun 1999. Used with permission of the poet.

Copyright © 1995 Coming of Age: Growing Up in the Twentieth Century by Studs Terkel. Reprinted by permission of The New Press. www.thenewpress.com.

"The Slow Train to Kandy" from GHOST TRAIN TO THE EASTERN STAR by Paul Theroux. Copyright © 2008 by Paul Theroux. Reprinted by permission of Houghton Mifflin Harcourt Publishing Company. All rights reserved.

Quote from Steve Carl Tracy, Langston Hughes & the Blues. University of Illinois Press, 1988.

"Rock Threat Subsides" by Calvin Trillin. From *TOO SOON TO TELL*. Published by Farrar, Straus & Giroux. Copyright 1991, 1995 by Calvin Trillin. Granted by permission of Lescher & Lescher, Ltd. All rights reserved.

William Trowbridge, "Kong Looks Back on His Tryout With the Bears" from *Enter Dark Stranger*. Copyright © 1989 by William Trowbridge. Reprinted with the permission of the University of Arkansas Press, www.uapress.com.

"The Penitent" by Mark Vinz, from *Poem, Revised: 54 Poems, Revisions, Discussions*, edited by Robert Hartwell Fiske and Laura Cherry, copyright © 2008 Marion Street Press, a division of Acorn Guild Press, LLC.

"Short Story", from THE LOTUS FLOWERS by Ellen Bryant Voigt. Copyright © 1987 by Ellen Bryant Voigt. Used by permission of W. W. Norton & Company, Inc.

Excerpt from the journal of Ayelet Waldman used with permission.

David Foster Wallace, "Incarnations of Burned Children." From OBLIVION by David Wallace. Copyright © 2004 by David Foster Wallace. By permission of LITTLE, BROWN & COMPANY.

"Beauty: When the Other Dancer is the Self" from IN SEARCH OF OUR MOTHERS' GARDENS: WOMANIST PROSE, copyright © 1983 by Alice Walker, reprinted by permission of Houghton Mifflin Harcourt Publishing Company.

Quote from Eudora Welty, *One Writer's Beginnings*, p. 10. Harvard University Press, 1995.

Reprinted by permission of International Creative Management, Inc. Copyright © 2000 by Lanford Wilson for *Dramatics Magazine*.

S. L. Wisenberg "Margot's Diary" as found in *Holocaust Girls: History, Memory & Other Obsessions*, pp. 103–106. University of Nebraska Press, 2002. First appeared in Creative Nonfiction 10 (Summer 1998), pp. 23–26. Reprinted with permission of the author, S.L. Wisenberg.

"Powder" from NIGHT IN QUESTION by Tobias Wolff, copyright © 1996 by Tobias Wolff. Used by permission of Alfred A. Knopf, a division of Random House, Inc.

Lois-Ann Yamanaka, "JohnJohn's World." Copyright © 2003 by Lois-Ann Yamanaka. First published in *Dream Me Home Safely: Writers on Growing Up in America*, Houghton Mifflin, 2003. By permission of Susan Bergholz Literary Services, New York, NY and Lamy, NM. All rights reserved.

Reprinted with the permission of Scribner, a Division of Simon & Schuster, Inc. from THE COLLECTED WORKS OF W.B. YEATS, Volume I: THE POEMS, Revised Second Edition by Richard J. Finneran. Copyright 1928 The Macmillan Company; copyright renewed 1956 Georgie Yeats.

index

additional titles of interest

Note to Instructors: Any of these Penguin Group (U.S.A.) titles can be packaged with this book at a special discount. Contact your local Pearson Education Softside Sales Representative for details on how to create a Penguin Value Package. If you don't know who your sales representative is, please go to www.pearsonhighered.com/replocator.

Akhmatova, *Selected Poems*
Albee, *A Delicate Balance*
Albee, *Three Tall Women*
Albee, *Who's Afraid of Virginia Woolf?*
Allison, *Bastard Out of Carolina*
Alvarez, *How the Garcia Girls Lost Their Accents*
Alvarez, *Once Upon a Quinceañera*
Alvarez, *Something to Declare*
Ambrose, *Rise to Globalism*
Anand, *Untouchable*
Antin, *The Promised Land*
Azuela, *The Underdogs*
Baer, *Getting Control*
Baer, *The Imp of the Mind*
Baker, *Growing Up*
Basho, *On Love and Barley*
Bellamy, *Looking Backward*
Bellow, *The Adventures of Augie March*
Bellow, *Dangling Man*
Bellow, *Seize the Day*
Boyden, *Three Day Road*
Boyle, *The Tortilla Curtain*
Carles, *A Life of Her Own*
Carter, *Little Red Riding Hood, Cinderella, and Other Classic Fairy Tales of Charles Perrault*
Chopin, *The Awakening and Selected Stories*
Christie, *Death on the Nile*
Christie, *The Mousetrap and Other Plays*
Díaz, *The Brief Wondrous Life of Oscar Wao*
Díaz, *Drown*
Edwards, *The Memory Keeper's Daughter*
Fielding, *Bridget Jones' Diary*
Greenberg, *I Never Promised You a Rose Garden*
Hansberry, *A Raisin in the Sun*
Harris, *Chocolat*
Hosseini, *The Kite Runner*
Kerouac, *The Dharma Bums*
Kerouac, *On the Road*
Kesey, *One Flew Over the Cuckoo's Nest*
Kidd, *The Secret Life of Bees*
King, *Apt Pupil: Different Seasons*
King, *Misery*
Kingsley, *The Water-Babies*
Miller, *Death of a Salesman*
Miller, *The Crucible*
Mujica, *Frida: A Novel*
O'Brien, *The Things They Carried*
Orwell, *Animal Farm*
Ozeki, *All Over Creation*
Ozeki, *My Year of Meats*
Puzo, *The Godfather*
Rand, *Anthem*
Silko, *Ceremony*
Sinclair, *The Jungle*
Twain, *Adventures of Huckleberry Finn*
Williams, *A Streetcar Named Desire*
Williams, *Cat on a Hot Tin Roof*
Wilson, *Fences*
Woolf, *Jacob's Room*